SPORT AND THE SHAPING OF ITALIAN-AMERICAN IDENTITY

Sports and Entertainment
Steven A. Riess, *Series Editor*

Other titles in Sports and Entertainment

Abel Kiviat, National Champion
Twentieth-Century Track & Field and the Melting Pot
Alan S. Katchen

Beyond Home Plate
Jackie Robinson on Life after Baseball
Michael G. Long, ed.

Blacks at the Net
Black Achievement in the History of Tennis, Two Volumes
Sundiata Djata

Fair Dealing and Clean Playing
The Hilldale Club and the Development of Black Professional Baseball, 1910–1932
Neil Lanctot

Muscle and Manliness
The Rise of Sport in American Boarding Schools
Axel Bundgaard

My Los Angeles in Black and (Almost) White
Andrew Furman

The New Cathedrals
Politics and Media in the History of Stadium Construction
Robert C. Trumpbour

The Sport of Kings and the Kings of Crime
Horse Racing, Politics, and Organized Crime in New York, 1865–1913
Steven A. Riess

Tarnished Rings
The International Olympic Committee and the Salt Lake City Bid Scandal
Stephen Wenn, Robert Barney, and Scott Martyn

SPORT AND THE SHAPING OF
ITALIAN-AMERICAN
IDENTITY

GERALD R. GEMS

Syracuse University Press

Copyright © 2013 by Syracuse University Press
Syracuse, New York 13244-5290

All Rights Reserved

First Edition 2013

13 14 15 16 17 18   6 5 4 3 2 1

Segments of chapters 3 and 4 were used in a forthcoming article in *Sport and History*. Quotations from the following sources are reprinted here with permission: Chicago Oral History Collection, University of Illinois at Chicago Richard J. Daley Library; Theodore Roosevelt speech, Walter Chauncey Camp Papers (MS 125), Manuscripts and Archives, Yale University; *Beyond DiMaggio: Italian Americans in Baseball* by Lawrence Baldassaro by permission of the University of Nebraska Press. Copyright 2011 by Lawrence Baldassaro; "Savoldi's Keed," *The Notre Dame Alumnus*, December 1929, page 119, by permission of the Archives of the University of Notre Dame; Oral History Interviews, Ellis Island Museum.

∞ The paper used in this publication meets the minimum requirements of the American National Standard for Information Sciences—Permanence of Paper for Printed Library Materials, ANSI Z39.48-1992.

For a listing of books published and distributed by Syracuse University Press, visit our website at SyracuseUniversityPress.syr.edu.

ISBN: 978-0-8156-3341-9 (cloth)   978-0-8156-5254-0 (e-book)

Library of Congress Cataloging-in-Publication Data
Available from the publisher upon request.

Manufactured in the United States of America

To the entire Di Benedetto clan, especially my mother and her siblings who lived the experience.

GERALD R. GEMS is a full professor in the Health and Physical Education Department at North Central College in Naperville, Illinois. Gems earned his PhD from the University of Maryland, and he has authored or edited more than 160 publications, including eight books. Gems served as a Fulbright Senior Scholar to Denmark in 2011–12 and has been a visiting professor at the University of Copenhagen and Beijing Sports University. He is a past president of the North American Society for Sport History and currently serves as the book review editor of the Journal of Sport History and on the editorial boards of the International Journal of Sport Sciences and Physical Education and East Asian Sport Thoughts: The International Journal of the Sociology of Sport.

Contents

Acknowledgments • ix
Introduction • xi

1. The Lack of Identity • 1

2. Constructing an Italian Identity • 22

3. Winning Whiteness • 55

4. The Emergence of Sport as a Cultural Force • 102

5. Hyphenated Americans • 141

6. The Resurgence of Ethnicity • 179

Appendix A. Italian-American Boxers,
Ring Magazine Rankings, 1924–39 • 221
Appendix B. Average Annual Employment
Rates at CUNY by Race and Ethnicity • 223
Notes • 225
Bibliography • 275
Index • 303

Acknowledgments

I would like to thank those whose time and generosity helped bring this project to fruition. First and foremost, the deepest gratitude and love are extended to my mother and her siblings, in particular my uncle, Frank "Chico" Di Benedetto. It is largely their story, and my uncle's skills as a raconteur extraordinaire, that have regaled me for years, sparking an interest and an appreciation for all that they endured and overcame.

The librarians at North Central College have been most helpful in acquiring resources and acceding to my numerous requests. The archivists at the Baseball Hall of Fame proved diligent and quick to respond. Maria Del Giudici, librarian at the Center for Migration Studies on Staten Island, provided valuable assistance, as did Janet Levine at the Ellis Island Oral History Collection. Eric Seiferth at the Williams Research Center in New Orleans directed me to new materials, as did Professor John Fair of Georgia College and State University and Professors Jan and Terry Todd at the University of Texas. Professors and friends Gertrud Pfister and Linda Borish shared materials and contacts, as did David Chapman, and Sal Serio, director of the Italian American Sports Hall of Fame and librarian of the Italian American Renaissance Foundation in New Orleans, afforded me access to a wealth of sources. Casa Italia in Stone Park, Illinois, provided me with access to its helpful library. Scholars Joe Sciorra of the John D. Calandra Italian American Institute and Dominique Padurano patiently answered my questions and provided valuable insights. Their knowledge and expertise are greatly appreciated. Donna

Lopiano generously extended her valuable time to answer my questions and provide greater understanding of her own experiences.

Gertrud Pfister and Steve Riess painstakingly critiqued each chapter, while Murry Nelson and anonymous reviewers provided insightful suggestions. I thank the editors for patiently shepherding the manuscript through the publication process. Any factual errors or faulty analyses are entirely my own.

Introduction

A multitude of European ethnic groups migrated to the United States over the course of the nineteenth and twentieth centuries, and their stories have been well chronicled and copiously analyzed. Numerous books abound relative to the travails of the Irish, the Jews, and African Americans who migrated internally from the South to the North. Each group confronted obstacles to assimilation owing to different historical and cultural circumstances. Italians, however, despite being one of the largest groups of immigrants, are relatively underrepresented in such examinations.

Italian influences permeate the national culture, and Americans owe much to Italy. The Italian Renaissance ushered in the modern world. Christopher Columbus is credited as the European "discoverer" of the American continent, and another Italian explorer, Amerigo Vespucci, allegedly provided its name. Italians John Cabot (Giovanni Caboto) and Giovanni da Verrazano were among the earliest investigators of its coastlines. The latter is memorialized in the Verrazano Bridge, which connects Brooklyn to Staten Island in New York City.[1]

A Venetian, Pietro Caesar Alberto, settled in New York as early as 1635, but Italians represented a trickle of immigrants to America until the late nineteenth century. More than four million Italians traveled to the United States between 1880 and 1924, bringing their culture, their food, and their wineries to America. During that time, Italian inventor Guglielmo Marconi gave the radio to the world, and in 1904 A. P. Giannini founded the Bank of Italy (later merged with the Bank of America) in San Francisco. Italy is the ancestral home to many of America's greatest politicians, scientists, athletes, and entertainers.

Fiorello La Guardia led New York through the Depression and World War II, while Enrico Fermi led the scientific team that provided the nuclear energy that eventually ended the war and changed the world. Joe DiMaggio, Frank Sinatra, Madonna, Lady Gaga, and a host of others became idols of American popular culture.[2]

But early immigrants possessed no sense of being American, nor did they even have any sense of being Italian. Stuart Hall has claimed that "identification is constructed on the back of a recognition of some common origin or shared characteristics with another person or group, or with an ideal, and with the natural closure of solidarity and allegiance established upon this foundation."[3] Identity is a socially constructed sense of being, both personal and communal in nature. It is a fluid process in which one perceives of him- or herself as an individual and as a member of a larger social group, with whom a solidarity is shared as well as a sense of difference from other groups. Benedict Anderson termed such compositions "imagined communities."[4] Such perceptions are learned over time, contested and changeable as one encounters new ideas, new environments, new loyalties, and new allegiances, hence the importance of memory and history in the construction of one's self and group identity. Initial bonding with a group usually takes place at familial levels, as children learn adherence to a family unit with its norms, standards, and values. As they grow older, they accept, reject, and adopt or adapt to larger social groups with their own identities, such as peers, students, or gender groups, or join like-minded individuals in recreational, intellectual, musical, athletic pursuits, and so forth. Such identities can be gained or shed over time.[5]

In the case of Italians, particularly southern Italians and Sicilians who constituted the vast majority of immigrants, personal identities merged with family identities as children assumed roles within the family hierarchy that required absolute adherence to established norms and values. A lesser allegiance may or may not have developed toward communal members of one's village. Beyond one's immediate region, there was little affinity for suspicious "outsiders."

National identity for Italians, whose history had been mired in centuries of quarrels among city-states and foreign occupiers, proved an impossibility until the country was unified under one national government by 1870. Even then, a common identity was thwarted by geographical divisions between the North and the South, alienation between the state and the papacy, and the differences of political parties. That identity became more complicated as immigrants moved and settled, temporarily and then permanently, in the United States over the course of the next half century.[6] Those who chose to stay in America faced a long and difficult road to assimilation and acceptance.

In 1990 Michael Walzer titled an article "What Does It Mean to Be an American?" in the journal *Social Research*. He determined that an American is a member of an association of citizens who agree on a particular political system and otherwise have no single identity, which allows for an ethnic, racial, or religious consciousness.[7] Rudolph Vecoli added that assimilation involved the acceptance of the Protestant ethic that valued aspiration, education, and respect.[8] In this work, I invoke Pierre Bourdieu's concept of habitus, the predilection or predisposition to act based on one's social class, to contend that the cultural values of southern Italians and Sicilians were inconsistent with such prescriptions. Of largely peasant origin, the Italian immigrants valued their physicality more so than education. American individualism and aspiration often conflicted with the communal values of the Italian family structure, where one accepted fate and labored for the good of the family rather than oneself. Popular culture, however, allowed for the convergence of disparate values systems, and sport in particular afforded practitioners, their families, and their fans an entrée into the American mainstream, as well as a measure of self-esteem, acceptance, and respect. Sport provided a sense of national identity, and later an American identity, but the process of assimilation proved long, difficult, and not entirely complete.[9]

The role of sport, as a major component of popular culture, has been relatively neglected in assimilation research. "While historical studies have acknowledged the importance of numerous processes embedded in the texture of everyday life that instructed immigrants on how to conduct themselves in American urban society, the project of how and where Americanization transpired has only recently begun to move beyond the workplace."[10] My analysis differs from previous studies in that it pays particular attention to the role of sport in the process of cultural transition as it evolved from virtually no sporting practice among the peasants of Italy to Italian-American youth who become ardent practitioners and consumers of American sport forms. Sociologists have claimed that, through sport, "the individual learns to view his or her body as an instrument for sports performance: for running (track); for throwing punches (boxing); for catching passes (football); or for hitting a ball (baseball). This experience, in communities where sports are valued and confer social esteem, is likely to transform the individual's identity."[11] I ask why sports had a particular appeal for Italian-American youth and what role it played in the assimilation process.

Although professional athletes garnered the most media attention and celebrity status, I also focus on the nonelite, semipro, neighborhood, and female athletes to derive a more complete picture of the obstacles, prejudice, and triumphs Italians faced in their transition to an American identity. The study traces that evolution chronologically over four generations to analyze the extent of acculturation, its residual cultural values and practices, and the creation of a persistent hybrid lifestyle that accommodates the new with the old.[12]

The book should appeal to the general public, as it provides a rich descriptive narrative and personalized stories over the course of four generations with which many can relate. It situates sport within the larger popular culture that includes music, leisure, and entertainment. It should have particular relevance for scholars as well, owing to its interdisciplinary approach and the incorporation of assimilation theories. As the globalized economy continues to foster the migration of immigrant labor to more developed countries and urban localities, it can even be helpful to policy makers who are confronted with assimilation issues.

Cultural studies are necessarily interdisciplinary and transdisciplinary. This study invokes Gramscian hegemony, but crosses theoretical frameworks. It employs history, sociology, and anthropology as it attempts to examine the evolution of identity from the individual to the community, from the local to the national, from racial to ethnic. The historical context helps to explain the breakdown of a national identity. After the fall of the Roman Empire, Italians continually faced the invasions of foreign peoples, who settled and intermingled with them. They were ruled and dominated by outside forces from European nations, Africa, and the Middle East, and, in the case of southern Italians and Sicilians, even oppressed by a dominant native class of bureaucrats and landed gentry. Such a series of events requires several analytical factors involving cultural, political, ethnic, gender, and social class characteristics to investigate the complex notion of identity. In that sense, what did and does it mean to be an Italian, an Italian-American, or an American? This study chronologically considers the extent of assimilation, acculturation, and adaptation to American mainstream society and its norms, values, and practices across generations in various locations. Whereas acculturation involved the learning of the ways of the host society, assimilation required the acceptance and adoption of such procedures and customs. That transition was never a unilateral, linear progression for immigrants, and the Italian experience differed from those of other migrant groups (such as Irish, Germans, or Jews), by culture, social class, gender, and locality and across different historical contexts. The experiences of northern Italians proved significantly different from southerners and Sicilians. Although the Italian experience is often framed in the story of the largest contingent that settled in the Northeast, the urban ghettos of New York or Chicago differed markedly from the plantations of Louisiana and the farms or fisheries of California.[13]

The term *Italy* is used for practical purposes to define the region encompassed by the modern unified state and the term *Italians*, unless otherwise indicated, to refer to residents or immigrants of that country. That general designation clouds the distinct differences between northern Italians and those from the South and Sicily. Such differences extended well beyond geographical and residential patterns and included culture, language, food, fashion, and social class, as well as habitus, which has been defined as a deeply rooted, internalized disposition that guides one's expectations, aspirations, and behaviors.[14]

Regional contrasts in lifestyles, foods, and linguistic dialects set them apart by their differences rather than similarities. One scholar has characterized the regional relationship as one of "reciprocal ignorance and reciprocal fear."[15] Northern Italians and scientists of the nineteenth and early twentieth centuries considered southerners and Sicilians to be a separate race. Such differences were further reinforced by US government policies and agents who ascribed racial characteristics that categorized immigrants as different from the white Anglo-Saxon Protestant (WASP) culture of mainstream America. In this respect, northern Italians were counted separately from the southerners as more desirable.[16]

The complex nature of Italian assimilation proceeded through a process of exclusionary racialization, the gradual designation of ethnicity that allowed for greater social mobility, and an eventual measure of acceptance within the white mainstream society. Three general models of assimilation have emerged in the early twenty-first century: the classic model that posits gradual acculturation over time, the racial-ethnic disadvantaged model that recognized obstacles to assimilation and allows for pluralism within the society and reactionary responses by immigrants, and the segmented assimilation model that includes selective acculturation, often based upon class interests.[17] Italians, however, may remain a work in progress.

SPORT AND THE SHAPING OF ITALIAN-AMERICAN IDENTITY

1

The Lack of Identity

June 28, 1877, marked an inauspicious start to Italian athletic enterprises in the United States. On that date Cesare Orsini attempted to introduce pallone, billed as "the Italian national game," to New Yorkers. He had witnessed the Americans' excitement over baseball games as a resident in the city and intended to capitalize on such fervor by erecting an arena and bringing fourteen Italian professional players to the United States. Pallone, the most popular sport of the nineteenth century in Italy, was played throughout northern and central Italy and included professional players on teams of three to four competitors. The professionals earned fifty to sixty dollars per month. Like American athletes of the same era, they returned to their jobs as tradesmen and craftsmen when the season ended.

The objective of pallone was to hit a ball against a wall with the wooden gauntlet, known as the bracciale, and return it in like manner on the fly or after one bounce. The inability of an opponent to do so scored a point.

The Italians also demonstrated another Italian game similar to tennis, played on a court that is divided in the middle by a line. The introduction of a tambourine-like racket, known as a tamburello, produced more powerful strokes, with higher and longer ball flight. By the late nineteenth century, tamburello had gained popularity even among the peasant class in Italy.[1]

Orsini went to considerable expense and expected to profit handsomely from the commercialized venture, but few paying spectators showed up for the competitions. Despite the exotic nature of the sport, the *New York Times* declared that "it is seldom sufficiently exciting to arouse American enthusiasm."[2] After only eight exhibitions, the Italians, who had expected to play into October, were operating at a severe financial loss and could not cover their expenses. Most of the spectators were Italians already residing in New York and Brooklyn, and the enterprise proved a dismal failure. The Italian players, who had expected to make two hundred dollars per month and have all their expenses paid, were left destitute. Exhibition tamburello matches were then arranged with British and local American athletes as charity fund-raisers to alleviate the Italians' plight and allow them to return home.[3]

In the United States, the "space" for sport was already occupied. According to authors Markovits and Hellermann, sports compete for positions in the hierarchically structured field of sport. A certain sport achieves and sustains power and dominance because it is interwoven with political, social, and cultural practices as well as with the everyday lives of a specific period. The lack of interest in pallone and tamburello may have been caused by the already established interest in baseball. The American game of baseball had long gripped the New York area, and the Italian sport had little chance of displacing it or even gaining a niche during the summer season of 1877. The National League of professional baseball players had begun play in 1876, providing a distinct nationalistic identity to the game. The labeling of baseball as an American game set it apart from British and European influences as the United States developed its own cultural characteristics.[4]

The episode served as a prelude to the plight of the multitude of Italians who descended upon American shores after 1880. Neither the Italian game nor the Italian immigrants could gain ready recognition, much less respect and acceptance. Italians who wanted to be acknowledged in the world of baseball had to Anglicize their name and their behavior. Lewis Pessano Dickerson, born in Maryland in 1858, but better known as Buttercup Dickerson, joined the Cincinnati Reds as a nineteen-year-old outfielder in 1877 and led the league in triples the following year. He played for eight different teams until 1885. The Anglicization of Pessano's name, however, obscured and cast doubt upon any Italian ancestry, a dilemma that challenged later immigrants.[5] The attraction to the game of baseball proved a harbinger of turmoil between second-generation American-born children and their parents after the turn of the century. The pursuit of baseball as an occupation would presage even greater opportunities for Italian youth who relied upon their physical prowess as a means to gain greater socioeconomic status.

It would take at least two generations and a close association with American sports and popular culture for Italians to gain a sense of identity, affirmation, and appreciation in their adopted land. The reasons for the long road of Italian migrants to recognition in sport and society can be identified in the political and economic situation as well as culture and society in their home country.

Italy: A Country of Contrasts and Conflicts

Italians had little recognition of themselves as a nation, defined as "a stable, historically developed community of people with a territory, economic life, distinctive culture, and language in common."[6] Historian Annette Hofmann has further asserted that "collective memory is a recollection shared by the members of a group or society; it constitutes the medium which binds the individual to a community . . . [and] enables them to distinguish themselves from others."[7] Historian and sociologist Gertrud Pfister has further asserted that "social memory identifies a group, giving it a sense of the past and defining aspirations for the future."[8] The conflicting memories and allegiances of the Italians hindered any group action, and their aspirations became largely individual endeavors.

Although technically a united country after 1860 when Giuseppe Garibaldi won military victories over foreign powers and the Piedmont king Victor Emmanuel II consolidated a nominal national government, the economy, culture, and multitude of local linguistic dialects belied any sense of national unity or identity. The disparate regions of the new country remained fragmented by local and familial alliances that distrusted outsiders, including the new government, and a feudal class structure that separated the rich from the poor and exploited the latter. During the 1860s southern Italian bands waged a guerrilla war against the northern government that required the resources of 40 percent of the national army for the suppression of the uproar. "During the civil war, execution by firing squad became the emblematic method of dealing with the brigands: the thuggish General Pinelli announced that it was the penalty for insulting the House of Savoy, the king's picture or the Italian flag. Vast numbers of peasants seem to have met their end this way." Through force and negotiation, Piedmont secured a unified Italy by 1870, but annexation of the Papal States engendered the king's excommunication by Pope Pius IX.[9] The conflicts between the pope and the secular state would endure over the next two generations. The cultural divisions between northern and southern Italy remained beyond that time. The collective memories that produced a national identity could not develop under such circumstances and would have to be built over time.

An American report on Italian immigrants in 1881 indicated the degree of differences and lack of acceptance between regional groups. "Ligurians [northern Italians] repudiate indignantly all kinship with the Neapolitans and Calabrians [southern Italians], whom they refuse to recognize as Italians, thereby showing how little the sectional sentiment of Italy has been affected by the union of its parts under one ruler."[10]

The Lombards of the North referred to the Sicilians as "little black fellows," and even the US Immigration Bureau listed immigrants from the North and South as two different races.[11] In contrast, Americans had developed a much clearer sense of national identity, based upon the belief in American democracy, the promise of opportunity, and the assimilation of myriad ethnic groups under the leadership of a white Anglo-Saxon Protestant male authority.

Sporting Activities in Italy: A Matter of Class and Region

Italian migrants brought little interest in sport and, as a rule, few sporting experiences to their new country. In Italy sporting opportunities were limited by social class, facilities, and regional cultures. The upper classes increasingly distanced themselves from the peasants by prescribed forms of etiquette, speech, and ostentatious leisure activities, as detailed by Norbert Elias in his tome *The Civilizing Process*. Pierre Bourdieu, too, marked the establishment of certain fields or social strata characterized by habitus, or class-based tastes and predispositions. Sport and leisure practices clearly distinguished individuals and groups in the social hierarchy. Court life in northern Italy and in Naples exuded a wealth of leisure activities that included art, dance, music, theater, equestrian activities, tennis, and the thrill of the hunt among a host of pastimes. Fencing masters instructed gentlemen in urban academies, and hunting also proved popular among the gentry. Such pursuits, however, were open only to those of means and expendable amounts of time for leisure.[12]

In several of the Italian cities, exhibitions and contests were organized at certain festivals. Participants demonstrated their physical prowess in wrestling matches and the folk football games between villages or throngs of male combatants. In Venice the competing contingents had staged fights for control of the city's bridges, to the amusement of thousands of spectators. For centuries, Venetians also engaged in combative activities between city factions, sanctioned by the government because such battles prepared them for seafaring and military ventures.[13]

When villagers quarreled over the use of the bucket in the local well, the turmoil was somewhat quelled with the introduction of a ball thrown into the bucket. The contest evolved into a game that was incorporated into festivals until the practice lapsed, only to be revived in the twentieth century. Folk games similar to soccer attracted other villagers.[14]

Siena had staged the Palio, an annual horse race, for centuries. The celebration marked a local contest between rival neighborhoods and required the jockeys to complete three laps around the central plaza. An American spectator described the affair as "ten violent jockeys who are all determined to win by fair means or foul, and who rely quite as much upon soundness of blows as sureness of speed . . . [with] excitement over . . . the jockey who has successfully used his whip, not on his pony but on his rivals."[15] Beside the upper-class "sports," the majority of sporting activities were not an everyday occurrence but were restricted to certain events, such as religious festivals. The lower classes might pursue utilitarian needs through hunting and fishing.

Modern sport reached Italy at the end of the nineteenth century as a leisure pursuit among some of the middle and upper classes predominantly in the cities of the North. By the end of the century, a host of sport associations had been founded (1869, gymnastics; 1879, sailing; 1885, cycling; 1888, rowing; 1892, swimming; 1895, tennis; 1898, soccer; 1899, running), and competitions were organized, among them gymnastic and fencing contests for both men and women, which occurred in Naples in the 1880s.[16]

Casati's law of 1859, which reorganized the school system, required gymnastics in the schools but was rarely implemented. In any case, schooling for the children of the South and Sicily was an unknown luxury for many. There peasants spent much of their day walking to and from their fields, where they labored to produce a minimal sustenance. Still, young men found some time to establish their physical prowess through wrestling matches. In spite of the above-mentioned activities, an American commentator traveling in Italy claimed that the Italians were "indifferent" to the wave of athletic sport sweeping the United States in the late nineteenth century and that the American upper classes aped the British in effecting fox hunts and public displays of conspicuous consumption as a means to gain social capital.[17]

At that time sport began to flourish in the United States, as professional baseball, boxing, horse racing, cycling, track and field competitions, and college football, among a host of lesser activities, fascinated the populace. Newspapers glorified athletes, and fans traveled great distances to absorb the revelry of commercialized sporting events. Boxing matches, baseball games, and horse races crossed class, racial, and ethnic lines in the composition of audiences and participants.

In contrast, sport participation in Italy was, to a large degree, the pastime of the upper classes and a phenomenon of the cities. Peasants had little time and energy for "useless" activities.[18] Male peasants participated in passatella (a drinking game), card games, bocce (a bowling game without pins, in which balls are tossed or rolled at a marker, similar to horseshoes), morra (in which opponents try to guess the number of fingers displayed), and cheese-rolling contests. Older men languished in the town plaza on Sunday afternoons to swap stories and take casual evening strolls. Leisure choices for women were even more restricted, amounting to socializing while engaging in chores or family visits, or when religious festivals incorporated the whole village in a procession and festival. On festive occasions, the tarantella, the national dance of Sicily, provided an exuberant release of emotion. More affluent southerners might attend the puppet theaters, but the physical culture of the Mezzogiorno [the territory south of Rome] revolved largely around the labors of work as well as passive forms of leisure. An Italian book of 1870 identified particular cultural differences when it claimed that the "Italian works only to live, while the English live only to work. . . . [T]he English and Germans use their spare time while the Italians are satisfied to waste it."[19] Such cultural and class differences in southern Italy and Sicily meant that migrants from these regions to the United States brought little in the way of a sporting culture.

Life in the Mezzogiorno

The overpopulation, poor soil, long hours, and low wages at manual labor, combined with the high cost of living in poor and unhealthy conditions, especially the continual hunger, left little to no opportunity for a better life. Because of the exploitation of their labor by absentee landowners or their henchmen, peasants were mired in a distinct sense of despair and fatalism, known as *la miseria*. The corrupt local governments and an uninterested national government did nothing to alleviate the situation. Professors Frances Malpezzi and William Clements assert that, "to be a peasant, a contadini, in southern Italy was to be a stupid and despicable earthworm, an image accepted even by the peasant himself."[20] However, life also meant close relationships to an extended family that might provide support and consolation in difficult times.

Living Conditions

Everyday life for the peasantry in southern Italy meant terrible housing conditions, hard work, and little pay. The Italian census of 1880 showed that buildings in the Mezzogiorno housed four to six people per room, and in some cases as many as ten to fifteen, some with only one bed. The conditions had not changed by 1910 when an American journalist reported that "the house of the emigrant is of one room, scantily furnished, usually in confusion and almost always dirty. Often he shares this room with his one donkey or mule, his pig, and a few chickens. . . . [It] generally has no windows. . . . [T]here is no chimney." The maximum wage for a long day of hard labor in the fields amounted to sixty cents, and the typical peasant family spent 75–85 percent of its income on food. In 1900 the life expectancy of a field laborer in Cosenza Province amounted to only twenty-nine years.[21]

Women were usually sheltered in the home to avoid depredations of landlords during the absence of the male family members. They too had to work long and hard. Among their responsibilities were fetching water, washing clothes in nearby rivers or a borrowed washtub, weaving, sewing, child care, and cooking, while tending to the family livestock, exchanging food at the market, or bartering one's labor for sustenance with the gentry and picking crops in the harvest season.[22]

The drudgery and disparity of Sicilian life in particular did not go unnoticed by commentators. Karl Marx noted that "in all human history no country or no people have suffered such terrible slavery, conquest and foreign oppression and no country and no people have struggled so strenuously for their emancipation as Sicily and the Sicilians."[23] Booker T. Washington, the acknowledged leader of African Americans in the late nineteenth century, remarked upon a trip to Italy: "The Negro is not the man farthest down. The condition of the coloured farmer in the most backward part of the Southern States in America, even where he has the least education and the least encouragement, is incomparably better than the condition and opportunities of the agricultural population in Sicily."[24]

The Lack of Identity • 9

Family Relations and the Little Joys of Life

For those without hope for future change, food and family represented the primary joys of life. Meals were the highlight of the day and united the family members. Food and wine enhanced the senses, maintained life, and served as a means of hospitality when inviting or visiting family and friends. To let a family member go hungry would invite dishonor. To refuse food, which had been gained through hard labor and was lovingly prepared, might constitute an insult, and to waste food was seen as sinful.[25] For generations of migrants, Italian food and the meaning of meals provided a sense of cohesion and a way to identify with their ancestral home.[26]

Family life constituted the core of life in the Mezzogiorno, and migrants transferred family practices to their new country where rules about and loyalties to the family had a strong influence on the decisions and behavior of all family members. The family required an ultimate level of allegiance and unquestioned loyalty. When arrayed against myriad forms of oppression and exploitation, only the family provided a sure bulwark of support. The sense of family extended to distant cousins and even godparents. Within a patriarchal hierarchy, the father assumed virtually dictatorial power, making all major decisions, while the mother often had invisible influence as educator and caretaker and as the day-to-day controller of the family finances. A Sicilian mother "nurtured physically and psychologically. . . . [S]he sacrifices her whole life to her family, denying herself in the process and becoming a victim of her dedication to others." Sons contributed with their wages to the income of the entire family. Daughters, closely sheltered until marriage, awaited their arranged unions. There was little room for individuality in the family of the Italian South.[27]

A system of unwritten rules dictated familial relationships that extended to relatives to the third or fourth degree. Sicilians were taught to be wary of strangers, who were completely distrusted. Once an Italian immigrated to the United States, the extended family counted on such a reciprocal sense of duty to effect a chain migration in which a follower might be ensured of food, shelter, and employment assistance in the new country.[28] But the close family ties and the adherence to traditions also restricted the opportunities and choices of Italian migrants—with regard to education, professions, and leisure practices, including sports.

Migration to the United States

Italians came to America seeking opportunities unavailable in their homeland, and some were among the earliest explorers and colonial settlers. A considerable number of Italians came to California during the Gold Rush of 1848. Books about the "promised land" aroused interest in America, and Italians, mostly from northern Italy, answered the call, with twelve thousand traveling to the United States between 1860 and 1870, followed by another fifty-six thousand in the next decade.

American companies began importing Italians as strikebreakers by 1874, and Italian labor bosses already settled in the United States, known as padrones, made a lucrative business by supplying human cargo.[29] They even offered full passage, the early form of credit repaid in sweat and labor upon arrival. Emigration from the South greatly increased owing to the deteriorating living conditions and the political conflicts in the Mezzogiorno in the later nineteenth century. Cholera epidemics, a severe economic depression, strikes and revolts, and the consequent military interventions imposed by the central government in the 1880s were additional woes to the hardships and grinding poverty, which were exacerbated by population growth. In 1908 a massive earthquake and consequent tsunami with two hundred thousand casualties destroyed hopes for a better future. Italians, in increasing numbers, joined other European groups in the search for a better life in the United States.

From 1880 to 1924 the number of Italian migrants surpassed four million; the vast majority of the immigrants of this period came from southern Italy and Sicily. When Prime Minister Giuseppe Zanardelli, at the beginning of the twentieth century, traveled south to see conditions there for himself, he was shocked when the mayor of one town, Moliterno, greeted him "on behalf of the eight thousand people of this commune, three thousand of whom are in America and the other five thousand preparing to follow them."[30]

Most passengers were single, young men who had the best opportunity to secure employment. Their primary purpose was to work and earn money. They had little intentions to play. The first generation of immigrants viewed sports and games as useless and contrary to one's obligations to provide subsistence for the family, including members in the United States and also those left in Italy.

Italians, however, faced more severe disadvantages relative to some of the other immigrant groups. The earlier arrival of the Irish and Germans afforded them a head start on assimilation. The Irish, furthermore, spoke English, and the largely middle-class migrants and skilled tradesmen of the German diaspora were well suited to accommodation within the growing American economy. Although Jews faced harsh discrimination, they valued the educational opportunities that would allow them to advance and succeed within the American culture. The Italian peasants had no such abilities or qualifications. Despite these impediments, all Italians came in hopes of a better future, some to settle in a new land, but many more intended to earn enough to return to Italy in a more comfortable condition.[31]

Many of the entrants had no intention of settling permanently in the United States, while others made multiple trips before making a final decision. Known as "birds of passage," they amounted to seasonal workers who traveled back and forth until they obtained enough money to purchase land in Italy.

The currency sent or brought back to Italy had a great effect on the local and national economy, greatly buttressing Italian solvency. But their economic success in America also gave them a new identity as *Americani*, as men who made their money abroad. Their earnings enabled many returnees to purchase a new home or land in their homeland. Such factors spurred additional migration with the expectations of social mobility or at least a greater sense of security. However, the plans to return to Italy greatly influenced their everyday lives in the

States. They engaged primarily in making money and had no time, energy, or interest in adopting American lifestyles, including sports and games. Such transience did not lend itself to the development of a national identity, as sojourners lived temporarily in two cultures and had little allegiance to either beyond their own families.

Italian Settlers in America: Facing Resentment

Opportunities for Italian migrants in the "promised country" were influenced by their skills and aspirations, but also by the widespread stereotypes about Italians in ethnic communities, which helped them to survive but also restricted their way of thinking and their engagement in American society. This point refers to education, political orientation, and choice of professions, as well as their attitudes to and participation in sport.

Italians who intended to make a new life in America faced an uphill battle owing to prejudice, stereotypes, and the assumption that they were only transient seasonal workers. "Few argued on behalf of the assimilability of the Italians at the time of their arrival, for they entered as one of the most despised of European immigrant groups."[32] Woodrow Wilson, then a professor at Princeton University and later president of the United States, published a history of the United States in 1902, in which he bemoaned the "alteration of stock" caused by the "multitudes of men of the lowest class from the south of Italy."[33] Given such negative perceptions held by American leadership, Italians faced daily prejudice in their social encounters with mainstream America. They were called "dagoes," "wops," or "guineas"; not admitted to popular nickelodeon shows; and restricted to specific housing areas.[34]

The nativist white Anglo-Saxon Protestants supported their prejudices with data on cultural and presumably racial differences. Because of the high rate of illiteracy in Italy, many immigrants from the Mezzogiorno scored in the lowest category in mental tests administered at Ellis Island. WASP educational standards did not allow for cultural or economic differences. Social commentators judged illiterates to be "incapable of becoming good citizens by reason of intellectual deficiency, and they should be allowed no place in this country and no voice in its affairs."[35] Such diatribes eventually led to immigration quotas aimed largely at limiting the numbers of southern and eastern Europeans in 1924.

Little Italies within the Cities

Given the ethnocentric racializing of Italians and other European groups and the xenophobic fears of nativists, it is no wonder that they chose to congregate largely within urban subcommunities of their own, where they could rely on friends and relatives for material and psychological support.[36]

The Italians, like other ethnic groups, moved into the dilapidated but cheap housing previously occupied by earlier immigrants. One of the early sociologists of the Chicago School reported on the ethnic succession in that city. "Two generations ago this district was an Irish shantytown called Kilgubbin. A generation ago it was almost equally Irish and Swedish. Then the 'dark people' began to come. . . . The Irish and Swedish, more prosperous, moved out of the district and northward. And by 1910 Kilgubbin and Swede Town had become Little Sicily."[37]

The early Irish and German immigrants who also lived in ethnic communities tended to gain more rapid social mobility and gradually diffused throughout the mainstream population, whereas Italians, Poles, Russians, and African Americans continued to cluster in more segregated enclaves within the cities. Both sociologists and historians have engaged in numerous case studies of the ghetto phenomenon over the past century with a variety of conclusions relative to causes and effects.[38] Isolation in the ghettos hindered and prolonged acculturation and the attainment of citizenship. It can be assumed that the adherence to "Old World" customs and tastes (in the sense of Bourdieu) in ethnic enclaves contributed to the immigrant's lack of interest in American culture, lifestyle, and enthusiasm for sport.

Life within the enclave may have been poor and threatened by diseases, but it permitted the choice of retaining one's own culture or a gradual transition to the new one. Traditional hierarchies and gender roles survived the ethnic communities. However, as an adaptation to the necessities of the new life, many Italian women took on work outside the home. Still, Italian families maintained traditional patriarchy within the home, as female laborers did not question male authority. Moreover, Italian women never took jobs as domestic workers, not only to safeguard their virtue, but because such service to another man might dishonor their own.[39]

In their urban enclaves the Italians often grouped by the same regional and village associations that they had in Italy. By the 1890s the Bowery area of New York had been neatly divided. The Neapolitans resided on Mulberry Street, while the Genoese inhabited Baxter Street near the Five Points juncture, and Sicilians lived between Houston and Spring Streets.[40] In Boston's North End neighborhood, the immigrants from Campania, Sicily, Abruzzi, and Genoa all inhabited separate blocks.[41] In Philadelphia, too, residence was marked by separate streets and different dialects. There the "Abbruzzesi regarded the Sicilians as dishonest and revengeful."[42] Such division of urban neighborhoods into Italian "tribes" did not lend itself to any collective sense of an Italian or an American identity, as residents had no sense of belonging to any group or nation beyond their *paesani*.[43] Conflicts between the various ethnic groups were frequent. In New York's Greenwich Village neighborhood, a 1903 report determined that "the racial feeling is very strong. The Irish hate the Italians ('Dagoes') and the negroes ('niggers'); and the North Italians hate the Sicilians."[44]

However, the Little Italies differed significantly from the Italian villages in that they could not exclude other groups, which exposed them to new languages, foods, customs, and lifestyles. Many neighborhoods were or became multicultural. A good example is the Lower East Side of Manhattan which was inhabited by twenty-seven different nationalities. An 1885 Health Department Report in Chicago determined that "they [the tenement buildings] are inhabited by Italians, Poles, Bohemians, and others, who in their trans-Atlantic homes have been accustomed to live in crowded quarters, in close proximity to their domestic animals, which in this city are not allowed to be kept within the premises used for human habitation." Such regulations seemed absurd to European peasants who needed their animals for warmth in the cold winters. Within the overcrowded spaces, residents crammed into blocks of tenement buildings with limited light, heat, water, and toilet facilities. The New York Sanitary Commission conducted a survey in 1891 that found 1,225,411 people living in 37,358 tenements. In 1888 nearly one-third of the babies died in such an environment. The situation in other large cities was similar.[45]

Twenty percent of the renters shared their apartments with other families, while others took in boarders. In one Philadelphia tenement, inspectors counted 30 families, a total of 123 people, sharing 34 rooms. A 1904 survey found 102 people sharing one bathtub. Sickness proved an ever-present danger in such an environment. A 1904 study found that "Italian children reared in the Italian quarter of New York, Boston, Philadelphia or Chicago are prone to tubercular disease and rickets, and compare unfavorably with children brought up in Sicily or Italy. Consumption is frequent in tenement-house Italians, although extremely rare in recently arrived immigrants."[46] Even the best intentions of medical authorities lacked cultural awareness. When New York City launched a campaign against tuberculosis in 1909, it offered posters featuring an idyllic Venetian scene to Italian tenement dwellers, but few Venetians settled in that city. Many of those to whom the posters were addressed could not read the English slogans imprinted upon them, which urged residents to open their windows at night for fresh air. The prescribed practice ran contrary to Italian beliefs that night air resulted in disease owing to the proximity of marshlands in their homeland.[47]

Within the neighborhood vendors hawked their goods, and children roamed the streets, as *padrones* recruited labor gangs. Young men congregated in the numerous billiard halls and saloons or the sixteen banks that proliferated in the New York Italian community. Shoppers supported the peddlers, bakeries, and storekeepers of their *paesani*, villagers who spoke and understood their Italian dialect.[48]

Religious Life

The adherence to the Catholic religion permeated everyday lives and clearly marked and excluded Italians from the Protestant culture of mainstream America. Italians' religious life centered in the parish church, where Catholic rituals and ceremonies marked life, death, and the celebration of saints' feast days. Despite the Italians' traditional suspicions regarding the church, Catholic rituals and ceremonies that defined important stages of life, such as baptisms, marriages, and funerals, were important rituals in Italian families and communities. In addition, the celebration of saints' days was a key component of Italian culture. Southern Italians and Sicilians had a very personal relationship with their saints, to whom they prayed for favors, the curing of sickness, and deliverance from calamities and hardships. The statues of saints kept in homes faced retribution, even shattering, if they did not deliver on expectations. Italians also merged folk beliefs with religion, wearing amulets to ward off the evil eye (*malocchio*) and curses.[49]

Italians, like all Catholics, faced the wrath of the nativists and a resurgent Ku Klux Klan (KKK) in the early twentieth century, but they also battled with other ethnic Catholic groups. The American Catholic Church was ruled and administered by an Irish American hierarchy, but Germans, Poles, and Italians, in particular, refused to acknowledge leadership by the Irish. An Irish priest in Philadelphia barred Italians from his parish and refused to baptize Italian infants. In Boston some Italians even turned to Protestantism rather than submit to an Irish priest. The pope sent Mother Frances Cabrini, an Italian nun, to the United States in 1889, and she founded Catholic schools, orphanages, and hospitals in New York, Chicago, and New Orleans. The missionary Scalabrini priests, members of an Italian order independent of the Irish hierarchy, also traveled to the United States and served as priests for the Italian communities, which somewhat alleviated the problem, although some tensions and clannishness persisted. Alfredo Tasinari, a 103-year-old Bostonian at the time of his 1977 interview, remembered that "I would have gotten very upset if a member of my family went to church at St. Leonard's. It was just not our church. The only time this would be allowed would be if we had to attend a funeral or a wedding of a friend."[50]

The Italians' close relationship with their saints, their adherence to folk beliefs, and the annual very public festivals set them apart not only from the more staid Protestants but fellow Catholics as well.

Italian Communities Outside the Ghetto

Italian clannishness sometimes dissipated, especially in smaller communities where Italians were less segregated from the rest of the population.[51] Italians sometimes allied with other groups—for example, with Mexicans in Arizona or the local Indians in California—to the point of intermarriage, especially when Italians were ostracized or excluded from social events.[52] Unlike the Little Italies of the cities that provided a source of refuge, Italian immigrants in smaller towns sought allegiance with those individuals similarly oppressed, as a joint recognition of social class status superseded ethnic identity.

Conditions differed in Louisiana, where Sicilians and their offspring constituted 39 percent of the population by 1910 and the French Quarter of New Orleans assumed the new moniker of Little Palermo. Yet there were no tenements in that city. Sicilians thus assumed greater control of their future, and many enjoyed relatively rapid social mobility as commercial entrepreneurs.[53]

New Orleans proved an exception to the urban enclaves of the Northeast and Midwest, indicating that residential patterns were not consistent throughout the immigrant communities in the United States or in other countries in which the Italians settled. "The fact that Italian immigrants to Latin America did not form Little Italies suggests that it was primarily the effects of discrimination, not the instinct to replicate the southern Italian villages, which determined residential patterns in the United States."[54]

In California northern Italians intent on more permanent settlement began arriving in San Francisco by the 1850s, drawn by the mild climate and fertile soil. In addition to farming, these early Italians established wineries and restaurants and worked in the lumber and mining industries. They too were subjected to stereotyping and vilification. Despite such obstacles, the Italians living in smaller towns often gained easier and quicker assimilation in California.[55]

In urban centers, such as San Francisco and Monterey, Italians congregated in enclaves similar to ones in the eastern states. In both San Francisco and Monterey, Italians monopolized the fishing industry, but the regional and village rivalries of the homeland persisted in the New World. Sicilians from different villages clashed with each other, the Genoese, and nativists over fishing rights.[56] In Monterey the Sicilians pursued the traditional work that preserved their identity, something that was lacking in the industrial occupations of the East and Midwest. They also maintained and reinforced their specific identity by adhering to their Sicilian dialect and marrying within the group. Intermarriage with non-Sicilians invited ostracism. Such factors indicated considerable adherence to Old World traditions.[57]

Clubs

Italians' historical aversion to government, and the traditional reliance on family and friends, led them to eschew civic charity. Within the Italian communities, the residents established numerous self-help institutions. Rarely did they become wards of the state, for family pride and Italian honor dictated that they take care of their own. Because of the lack of governmental intervention in what were deemed to be personal matters, Italians formed fraternal organizations to aid compadres. In the process they began to perceive a recognition of common issues and problems, if not yet a common identity.

As early as 1858 the Societa Italiana di Mutua Beneficenza in San Francisco provided aid to the sick. Within a decade it numbered one thousand members. In 1867 the Societa di Unione Fratellanza Italiana attempted to provide assistance to all Italians in Philadelphia, regardless of their clan loyalties. In 1873 Italians made an early attempt to create a national federation, but despite many attempts a national consolidation of the mutual-aid societies did not come to fruition until the organization of the Order of the Sons of Italy after 1924. The Unione Siciliana renamed itself the Italo-American National Union in 1925 for "closer unity among those of our race into one homogeneous group, which would be a credit to ourselves, to America, and to Italy." Despite the intention, the stated purpose indicates a still fractured identity, somewhere between Italian-American, American, and Italian.[58]

In the cities Italians founded a number of social-athletic clubs, which served as subcommunities that replaced village life within the larger urban society. There adults socialized with compadres in their native dialect and found solace for rejection by the dominant Anglo society; for the aspiring middle-class members, they also provided an element of social status. In these clubs younger males learned to box and play baseball and American football in the transition to gradual Americanization.[59]

Settlement Houses

Like the early Irish immigrants and the Jews who followed them, the Italians were not welcomed into WASP society. Many reports and studies of the WASP social agencies blamed the condition of the urban ghettos on the residents, citing their lack of organization and failure to adhere to middle-class standards of propriety and hygiene. In response the WASP reformers established settlement houses, social agencies located within ethnic communities, to gain a greater understanding of immigrant cultures and began to fuse the Europeans' values with their Americanization efforts. Lillian Wald of the Henry Street Settlement in New York realized, "Great is our loss when a shallow Americanism is accepted by the newly arrived immigrant, and their national traditions and heroes are ruthlessly pushed aside." In Chicago Jane Addams reveled in the parades and festivals of the Italian community, and she included Italian arts and crafts in her Hull House Museum. Addams even incorporated athletic teams into the Hull House program. She stated that "I believe sports will be the only agency powerful enough to break into this unwholesome life. . . . [(O)n the playground] a rude sort of justice prevails; which may become the basis for a new citizenship and will overthrow the gang leader and the corrupt politician." The female basketball team offered a new sense of liberty, but the closely sheltered Italian girls risked conflict by upsetting traditional Italian norms.[60]

Italian writer Edmondo De Amicis explained, "We [Italians] cannot understand a lady who capers about, turns somersaults, lifts heavy weights, handles weapons or wrestles, or even performs any exercise that causes her clothing to fly about."[61] Given such attitudes, Italian girls faced an uphill battle if they wished to engage in the sporting opportunities offered in America.

Sociologists and other scholars, often working with the settlement houses, eventually identified poverty, rather than cultural deficiencies, as a root cause of many urban ills. Robert E. Park, one of the sociologists at the University of Chicago, explained the immigrants' plight as one of marginalization, caught between two cultures.[62] In New York presumably middle-class Italians founded their own settlement house with programs that retained the Italian language, but offered American sports such as football.[63] The social reformers soon turned their attentions to the education of immigrant children in order to foster their Americanization efforts.

Parks and Playgrounds

In 1885 Bostonians established a sandlot at the Parmenter Street Chapel in the North End neighborhood, which would become the center of its Little Italy. The area was intended as a safe play haven for young children, but the concept soon expanded as a space for older children as well. Shortly thereafter the playground concept was tied to the public school spaces, where children might congregate under the watchful eyes of adult supervisors. Other cities adopted the idea, and the Playground Association of America was formed in 1906. Chicago incorporated the concept of the field house in its larger parks, which included community meeting rooms, libraries, and gyms, while the outdoor areas included ball fields and swimming pools. The play spaces were staffed by adult supervisors who taught immigrant children American values through sports and games. The public spaces thus served as an alternative form of education for the vast numbers of immigrant children who did not attend schools, and sports became an important means of transforming identities in the second generation.[64]

Conclusion

Italian immigrants faced the quandary of multiple identities and allegiances. After the unification movement known as the Risorgimento, the Italian national government's consolidation plans theoretically established a nascent sense of an Italian identity, but in actuality the southerners and Sicilians had little sense of inclusion in the nation. Ostracized as backward, primitive, and racially inferior, they resorted to reliance on their families and neighbors. As conditions worsened in Italy, a chain migration ensued to the Americas, based on such communal ties. Life in the United States further confounded and perplexed the newcomers, such as differences in lifestyles between Italy and the United States and the expectations of immigrants versus the expectations of American citizens. Despite the promises and rhetoric of democracy and opportunity, the Italian immigrants did not find ready acceptance, and even less respect. Over the ensuing generations, discrepancies between the Old World and the New caused them to wrestle with issues of identity, allegiance, and loyalty. They would literally and figuratively have to fight for inclusion in the American polity.

2

Constructing an Italian Identity

In 1915 a New Jersey newspaper article acknowledged the success of Italian boxers by stating:

> The sons of sunny Italy have taken a prominent part in the boxing game. Although boxing has never been popular in Italy itself . . . the Italian expatriates . . . have long been among the most enthusiastic devotees of the game. . . . Little Casper Leon, the Sicilian, was a bear in the bantamweight division some twenty years ago. . . . Hugo Kelly, also a native of Italy, was a middleweight star . . . of all the Italian boxers since the beginning of the game the ring now has the best in the person of Joseph Carrora. . . . Joe and his people emigrated [*sic*] to New York and in the Italian quarter of the metropolis he developed into a little bundle of fighting energy. . . . [H]is destinies were taken charge of by Scotty Monteith. The first thing Scotty did was to pull off a christening party, and Joe emerged duly tagged as Johnny Dundee. Since then he has traveled under that monaker [*sic*], and is known from coast to coast as the Scotch Wop.[1]

The deconstruction of such a passage offers many clues to the early experience of Italian migrants in the United States and the distorted sense of identity. The designation of Casper Leon as Sicilian marks him as something other than Italian, while the reference to "his" people and the "Italian quarter" indicates the Italians as segregated "others" who did not qualify as Americans. The prescribed aliases denote the affectation of pseudoidentities to gain acceptance and the power relationships within the boxing hierarchy, while the denigrating nickname of Scotch Wop symbolizes the widespread disparagement of Italians in the mainstream media. For any young Italian boy capable of reading the story or hearing about the successes of Italian boxers, the message clearly suggested that one's physicality was a means to recognition and wealth.

Conflicting Cultures

The vast migration of about twenty-five million, mostly Europeans, to the United States between 1866 and 1915 produced a host of problems for the American society and the migrants.[2] Overcrowding in the teeming cities, poverty, exploitation, and the lack of social services confronted the multitudes who sought a better life. French sociologist Pierre Bourdieu proposed the concept of a field or a contested space in which groups or individuals competed for resources. Italians had to contend with the Anglos and upper classes that set policies and controlled most resources. They also vied with multiple other ethnic and working-class groups for income, space, jobs, and social acceptance. The lack of an Italian national identity meant that they also fought with other regional immigrants from Italy for limited opportunities to realize their dreams. The insults, frustrations, and stress generated hostility and aggression that gave way to physical combat within the Little Italies and across the ethnic borderlands of the cities. Fighting, and eventually the more regulated sport of boxing, became commonplace within the popular culture that afforded a means to achieve recognition, a measure of respect, and an income that did not require an unaffordable education.[3]

While Italian boys learned to fight in hostile urban environments, they also engaged in gambling and other activities deemed to be exercises in juvenile delinquency by the WASP authorities. Their fathers, meanwhile, had to seek more gainful employment. Italian newcomers often relied on family members or the services of a *padrone*, a labor boss and organizer, to secure jobs. Although some padrones extorted fees for their services and exploited their workers, they served a necessary function by finding employment and negotiating a labor process unfamiliar to newly arrived immigrants. They also provided services for their charges, such as writing letters for the illiterate, banking, and finding lodging. American mining companies were especially diligent in their European recruitment efforts, regaling the opportunities available in America to the unemployed or poorly paid. Workers, however, were often misled and charged excess fees for the services rendered. Disillusioned miners wrote back that we "are buried alive.... [W]e sit here crying, thinking of Italy," and in the "company town ... they owned all land and houses—a slave camp."[4]

Another immigrant complained that they were met at the New York dock by a *padrone*, who took them to his hotel, where they were fleeced of their money. Upon arrival at the mines in Missouri, they were lodged in flimsy shacks and required to walk two to three miles to the mines. By the 1890s Italian men supplanted the Irish as the construction workers on municipal projects in many of the large cities.[5]

Laborers earned only $1 per day in the years following the economic depression of 1893. That figure had reached $3 a day by 1904 but required additional working hours, and a 12 percent inflation rate wiped out any economic gain. From 1895 to 1910 laborers averaged $1.98 per day for twelve hours of work. More than 50 percent of the Italians in New York worked as laborers by 1916. Discrimination proliferated throughout the country. In the Arizona copper mines of 1903, only 6 percent of Italians working in the mine were paid $3 per day, but 11 percent of Hispanics and 43 percent of whites earned that figure for the same job.[6]

In the Louisiana sugar-cane fields, "Italians performed tasks which native whites considered as suitable only for Negroes.... Native whites generally classed them with Negroes, because they did what the whites looked upon as Negroes' work."[7] Italian men, women, and children worked the plantations. Men might earn $1.50 a day by working three six-hour shifts, while women got $1 and children (as young as five) received only 10 cents.[8]

Italian women entered the workforce in increasing numbers in the United States, a distinct departure from their domestic roles in Italy. In Buffalo, New York, and Monterey, California, they took to the canneries; others worked in factories or served as midwives. By 1925

Italian women made up 96 percent of the female workers at the factories in Endicott, New York, and 64 percent of the employees in the New York fashion industries, mostly in the needle trades. Contrary to the Italian family-centered lifestyle, many Italian women adapted by taking in boarders. The 1905 Milwaukee census indicated that 42 percent of Italian families did so in that city. Some Italian women even became entrepreneurs by running small bakeries, groceries, or flower shops. "Their business enterprises helped establish an economic base in the ethnic enclave, while preserving cultural traditions important to sustaining an Italian way of life."[9]

Other Italian women emerged as labor leaders. As early as 1897 women went on strike against the oppressive conditions in the Paterson, New Jersey, silk mills. They participated in numerous strikes over the next decade in New York City. Anna Valenti incited one such protest, proclaiming, "I was a fighter." Carrie Golzio, a child worker in a Paterson mill, admitted that the supervisors "were tough. But I was tough too. My father always said 'no matter where you work, don't let them step on you.' That was instilled in me when I was a kid and I always fought. . . . I used to fight like hell. . . . If there was a strike I was the first on the line." During the 1913 Paterson strike, Mary Gasperano not only bit a policeman, but slapped another strikebreaker who faltered in the campaign. The Bambace sisters, Angela and Maria, gained their start as radical organizers in the early Paterson strikes. Angela was known to use her fists if needed, while their mother, Giuseppina, accompanied her daughters with a rolling pin that could be employed as a weapon on their unionizing crusade. Such women carried the toughness of the Italian boxers into the workplace as they assumed more actively political roles in America.[10]

Welfare Capitalism

Throughout the latter nineteenth century, the American working class began to adopt European perspectives relative to the nature of capitalism, the exploitation of workers, and the growing division of wealth. As a reaction to the increasing politicization of the workers, employers devised means to distract their employees from radical sympathies and unionization known as welfare capitalism. One way to pacify workers was to offer them benefits or at least opportunities that they "sold" as benefits to their workers, such as housing, insurance, health care, and recreation. As early as 1882 George Pullman built a company town near Chicago to manufacture railroad sleeping cars. He supplied the community with lavish athletic facilities, but denied blue-collar workers access to the saloon, which might affect their productivity. Pullman stated that "the disturbing conditions of strikes and other troubles that periodically convulse the world of labor would not be found here." His program intended to control workers' leisure time by offering them a wide array of activities, including track and field, rowing, soccer, baseball, football, tennis, cricket, ice skating, billiards, bowling, and shooting as wholesome alternatives to drinking. In addition, he expected that their engagement in physical activities and sports would prevent their engagement in the labor unions. The company teams, which competed in local, regional, and national competitions, also provided widespread advertising for the company products. Many other companies copied Pullman's model throughout the United States over the next half century, among them the Endicott shoe factories in New York, whose workforce consisted of many Italians.[11]

The workers, however, learned to utilize such ventures to their own benefit. Athletes on company teams spent "work" time in practices and games rather than laboring over a machine. Forrest "Red" De Bernardi used his basketball skills to obtain positions at companies that competed in the Amateur Athletic Union. De Bernardi's teams won five national championships during the 1920s, and he was elected to the AAU All-American team seven times. He was further honored as an inductee into the Basketball Hall of Fame. Women, too, parlayed their athletic abilities into greater social and economic capital. Agnes Iori attracted attention as the star of her Kansas high school basketball team. The Employers Casualty Insurance Company of Dallas recruited her to play on its squad. Six times she won election to the AAU All-American team and garnered the 1931 AAU national championship as a teammate of Mildred "Babe" Didrikson, perhaps the greatest all-around athlete in American history.[12] Such teams provided more than just individual benefits in ways unanticipated by the employers, as nonathletes bet considerable sums on their colleagues in attempts to increase their income. Laborers and factory employees worked long and hard, but sport allowed workers to adapt employers' efforts at social control to their own benefit and fostered a broader inclusion in the mainstream American culture.

Leisure Pastimes

Protests, strikes, and the unionization of workers gradually forced a reduction in the hours spent on the job, and bouts of unemployment caused enforced periods of leisure for many. By the mid-1920s an average workweek consisted of fifty hours, and some industries moved to a five-day workweek. Some Italians engaged in informal leisure activities in their ethnic communities, such as visiting relatives or sitting in front of the houses and talking with neighbors, and some men went to the pub, while others played bocce, an Italian bowling game. In the communal Italian societies of upstate New York, they found their leisure within the ethnic clubs. Parades, dances, picnics, and bocce-ball games entertained the Italian residents of Utica, Canastota, Oneida, and Rome, New York, while Rochester offered a fencing academy and both boxing and wrestling matches occurred in Utica. Youth began to turn to American sport forms as well. As early as 1902 the Italian Columbia Club in Utica defeated an Irish team in a baseball game, and the Italian Athletic Club of Barre, Vermont, won the state championship in 1909. Another Italian team garnered the San Francisco city championship by 1912.[13]

In the early twentieth century a broad variety of places and forms of popular culture emerged, particularly in the big cities. Amusement parks, dance halls, nickelodeons, theaters, concert halls, movie houses, and increasingly sports arenas were the places where women and men of different social, racial, and ethnic origin spent their leisure time.[14] In the amusement parks, such as Coney Island in New York, Chicago's

White City, or Pittsburgh's Luna Park, young Italians were exposed to a new world, one unavailable even in their dreams in Italy.[15]

Leisure, and the places in which it was enacted, became contested spaces, in which a host of alternative groups vied with each other and the dominant WASP society for the control and direction of American pastimes. Politicians established laws regulating gambling, liquor consumption, and morality, while a multitude of consumers, establishment owners, and ethnic politicians worked to circumvent such impositions. In an ongoing battle over propriety and wholesome forms of leisure, racial, ethnic, and gendered performances continually challenged WASP authority.[16]

Leisure provided, to some extent, a measure of freedom, and ethnic groups could reject the dominant forms of entertainment, adopt them, or adapt them to their own cultural and social needs. In the course of assimilation processes and the growing acceptance of groups of migrants in the WASP society, some sorts of "ethnic" entertainments and entertainers even fascinated the US mainstream population.

When such luminaries as Eugen Sandow and Bernarr Macfadden traveled the vaudeville circuit exhibiting their muscularity as the masculine ideal, Italians offered their own stars. Romolo or Romulus (Cosimo Molino), known as the Sicilian Hercules, and his partner, Remus (Giacomo Zaffarana), were both born in Catania but embarked on the international vaudeville circuit, thrilling audiences with their feats of strength and offering an alternative to Anglo versions of the masculine ideal. The diminutive Romulus stood only five feet tall and weighed 167 pounds, but he lifted 119-pound dumbbells with each arm and pressed a 168-pound weight twenty times in succession. In the United States he even took to wrestling bulls. A host of other Italian strongmen, including Giovanni Belzoni, Felice Napoli, Jerome Ronco, Luigi Borra, and Nino, proliferated on the vaudeville and circus circuits, validating the quality of the Italian body. These and other "strongmen" served their countrymen as objects of admiration, identification, and emulation.[17]

Whereas opera star Enrico Caruso appealed to people of all social levels, including the white upper classes, Sicilian puppet shows and

Italian comedies touched only the Italian masses. An excellent example is the enactments of Eduardo Migliaccio, known as Farfariello (Little Butterfly), who achieved star status among the immigrants by assuming a clownish persona, effecting character sketches that poked fun at the confusing transitional process, especially the language difficulties of Italians living in multiple worlds that forced them to sort out the vagaries of English and their own dialects, resulting in a distinct Italian-American idiom. For example, the term *baccauso*, the Sicilian term for a toilet, represented a corruption of the English *back house*. Farfariello's career would last into the 1940s, making its own transition to radio, as the assimilation process continued throughout the war years. Italian theater enabled immigrants to carve out their own social space and interpret their experiences in America on their own terms. Women assumed the roles of playwrights and performers emblematic of the transition in gender roles in America.[18]

Music spawned both the reinforcement of traditional culture and an adaptation to American tastes. Workers purchased phonographs to hear the opera recordings of Enrico Caruso, while their offspring were attracted to American ragtime, jazz, and dancing by the 1920s. Rosa Ponselle (Ponzillo) gained initial popularity as a ragtime singer with her sister, but her evolution to opera star required the Anglicization of her name to gain acceptance. With the achievement of social status, Ponselle's leisure pursuits also grew to include the upper-class pastimes of cycling, mountain climbing, and flying airplanes.[19]

Radio, too, offered both ethnic programming and popular English programs. Singers, such as Louis Prima, employed Italian-American lyrics to ease the linguistic transition for older Italians. The commercialization of radio, funded by advertising and marketing spots on the broadcast schedules, further moved the ethnic populations toward the dominant capitalist culture as consumers of the advertised goods, which represented mainstream tastes.[20]

In the 1920s movies played an increasing role in popular culture. They reflected and shaped the taste of mainstream society and contributed to the assimilation of immigrant groups. Rudolph Valentino, born Rodolfo Guglielmi in Castellanetta in the Apulia region in 1895, achieved fame as a movie star in the United States, but remained an enigma to Italians. Valentino renounced his Italian citizenship to become an American, but never completed the required paperwork. His multiple identities mirrored the circumstances of many Italians in the United States. "In America he will be an Italian to all members of other nationalities, a Sicilian to all Italians. In Sicily, he will be a Milocchese. In Miloccha, he tends to remain a Piddizunna [clan] who has moved."[21] Despite, or perhaps because of, his confused identity, Valentino served as a new hero for young Italians and non-Italians, regardless of his birthplace. In the dawn of the hedonistic 1920s, he represented the individualism inherent in the American culture and its emphasis on achievement and mobility, evident by his grandiose mansion and ostentatious lifestyle. A young woman admitted, "When I saw Rudolph Valentino in 'The Sheik,' I could do nothing but think of him for days to follow. Several of my girl friends and I sent to Hollywood for the star's picture." For many of the older generation of Italians he retained identity with his ancestral roots, whose values he had betrayed, and his early death represented retribution for his disloyalty.[22]

The Role of Sport in Popular Culture

Throughout the Progressive Era, the urbanization, industrialization, and feminization of American society had cast doubt on the masculinity of American males. As middle-class men's jobs became more sedentary and boys spent more time under the care of their mothers and female schoolteachers, American leaders, most noticeably Theodore Roosevelt, expressed concerns over the lack of male physicality. He asserted:

> I emphatically disbelieve in seeing Harvard or any other college turn out molly coddles instead of vigorous men. . . . I do not in the least object to sport because it is rough. . . . In any republic, courage is a prime necessity for the average citizen if he is to be a good citizen; and he needs physical courage no less than moral courage. . . .

Athletics are good, especially in their rougher forms, because they tend to develop such courage. They are good also because they encourage a true democratic spirit, for in the athletic field, the man must be judged not with reference to outside and accidental attributes but by that combination of bodily vigor and moral quality which go to make up prowess.[23]

G. Stanley Hall, the first president of the American Psychological Association, lamented that "too much association with girls diverts the youth from developing his full manhood."[24] Doctors diagnosed a host of middle- and upper-class men and women with a malady known as neurasthenia, a debilitating psychosomatic disorder characterized by depression and fatigue. Roosevelt and others advocated a more strenuous life of outdoor activity and sports, and J. A. F. Adams called for physical training in the schools to "save our race from physical degeneracy."[25]

The social Darwinian beliefs of the era, grounded in the ideology of the "survival of the fittest," rationalized superiority or inferiority and engaged sport as a means to determine the physical qualities of different races. Scientists of the era divided the multitude of peoples into various races, as the concept of ethnicity had not yet gained currency.

The southern Italian immigrants possessed physicality in abundance, and Italian boys were easily attracted to the sports and games being offered in the settlements, parks, playgrounds, and schools. Although working-class southern Italians had different motives for immigration and different values from the more educated northerners, both wanted respect. "It was not for want of bread alone that the contadini left their villages. Rispetto [respect] is what they also sought, but in their native land they got precious little of it."[26] For the working-class Italians who had been reduced to purely physical beings by their labors in the homeland and for most in America, the body served as the primary mechanism of expression. Sport offered a natural attraction for such outlets, and the practice of American sport forms marked youth with a transitional identity in the process of becoming less Italian and more American. Whereas lifestyles, language, and religion often conflicted with the mainstream values, young Italian males found compatible cultural standards with American society in the expression of physicality and the demonstration of physical prowess inherent in sport.

By the end of the nineteenth century, sport played an increasing role in popular culture, and sports events became an important part of the entertainment industry. Sport consumption spread to all groups of the male population, however, the various Europeans favored and identified particularly with athletes of their own ethnic group. Within the leisure culture sport allowed Italians to compete with and compare themselves with other ethnic and racial groups, particularly those immigrants assumed to be their superiors. Italian successes not only developed an ethnic pride and a greater national identity, but head-to-head competition offered the opportunity to dispel notions of physical inferiority and gain a measure of retribution for the ethnic slurs and insults that accompanied the stereotypes of Italians. Even Anglo sportswriters had to acknowledge the skills of Italian champions such as Casper Leon (Gaspare Leoni), Hugo Kelly (Ugo Micheli), and Pete Herman (Pete Gulotta) in the pre–World War I era.[27]

Sport as a Marker of Identity

Boxing proved the perfect arena for the social Darwinian racial comparisons so popular at the time. Paul Kelly (Paolo Vaccarelli) migrated from Sicily to New York, where he took up boxing and performed well enough to turn professional as a bantamweight. Boxers often assumed Irish names at the time because the Irish were perceived to be inherently suited to the sport and Irish agents controlled much of the matchmaking. Kelly graduated from boxing to leadership of the Five Points gang, which often worked for the politicians of Tammany Hall. Kelly used his boxing earnings to buy bordellos, and he soon expanded his vice operations to gambling dens and nightclubs. Kelly's gang allegedly numbered as many as fifteen hundred members, organized into "athletic clubs," that fought with the rival Eastman gang. The Tammany politicians decided that the two rivals should settle their differences in a boxing match, in which Kelly fought the much larger Monk Eastman to a draw. Kelly's organization included gangsters Johnny Torrio, Al Capone, and Lucky Luciano, who would earn their own notoriety. Kelly later turned to labor union organization on the New York docks.[28] His athletic skills had provided him with a measure of notoriety, celebrity, and social mobility, although of a dubious nature, but no one questioned his toughness.

By the 1890s American commercial interests promoted a culture of consumption to alleviate the overproduction of its industries. Advertisers stressed the "good life" and commensurate products to achieve a state of wealth and happiness. Conspicuous consumption and display marked one's status in society. When some members of immigrant groups, such as the Irish, Jews, and Italians, were faced with limited opportunities to achieve social capital in legitimate commercial enterprises, they found their niche in criminal activities. Boxing had a long association with criminal figures and the underside of society, and the transition from one to the other seemed natural and logical for some who aspired to quick, if tainted, riches. Kelly had adapted to his new home by using his wits, his physicality, and an ethnic alias to overcome perceived obstacles in his rise to power.[29]

A host of other Italian pioneer fighters gained fame under ethnic aliases: Pal Moran (Paul Miorana), Frankie Conley (Conte), Benny Yanger (Frank Angone), Pete Herman (Pete Gulotta), Lou Ambers (Louis D'Ambrosio), Sammy Angott (Samuel Engotti), Young Corbett III (Ralph Giordano), Young Zulu Kid (Giuseppe Dimelfi), Fireman Jim Flynn (Andrew Chiariglione), Jack Sharkey (Giovanni Cervati), Packey O'Gatty (Pasquale Agati), Johnny Dundee (Giuseppe Carrora) Sammy Mandell (Samuel Mandella), and Midget Wolgast (Joseph Loscalzo) represent only a small sample of the most successful who reached the professional ranks.[30] The adoption of Irish aliases indicates the nature of the power relations within boxing at the time; nevertheless, their true identities were not unknown to Italian fans. Irish agents, promoters, and managers controlled the business and intended to maintain their position by marketing the top fighters as Irish, but Italians would eventually supersede the Irish in such roles.[31]

Countless other boxers fought in neighborhood and local arenas for lesser wages, where an Italian encounter with rival Irish or Jewish boxers would guarantee a sizable crowd as fans cherished the matchups that tested the social Darwinian stereotypes assigned to various groups. The ethnic rivalries of the city streets also transferred readily to the boxing ring and helped to focus increasing attention on one's national identity. Sicilians, Neapolitans, Apulians, and Tuscans might all be drawn to an event that featured an "Italian" athlete, such as Casper Leon (Gaspare Leoni), born in Palermo in 1872, who boxed throughout the United States from 1891 to 1904 as "the Sicilian Swordfish." Fighting in Italian areas throughout the states of New York and Connecticut, as well as in Philadelphia, Chicago, and St. Louis, he provided the residents with a greater sense of a national identity.

Although Leon was often acknowledged as the bantamweight champion before official rankings were established, the *Washington Post* denigrated Italian fighters in racial terms in a 1915 article. "In three decades the Italian race has been represented by only a select few star performers, and only one or two can truly be said to have had a chance for a title. . . . [I]t would seem that the sons of Italy are not of a boxing race; that they are ill fitted for the sport. . . . [T]he sport never has recognized even in a small way by the European nation. . . . [E]very Italian pugilist gained practically all his knowledge of the game after coming to the United States."[32]

The *Post* article was accurate in its claim that the Italians had gained their expertise in America, and its designation of a substantial list of boxers as Italians, despite their Irish aliases, helped to fix Italian fans with a particular national rather than a regional immigrant identity. Over the remainder of the decade, a growing list of Italian champions indicated that Italians could compete with and gain the respect they so desperately sought from others. By the 1920s Italian fighters would assume their own names, generating a great sense of pride in the Little Italies of America.[33]

While second-generation Italian-Americans began to adopt American sport forms by the latter nineteenth century, the appearance of athletes from Italy stirred a greater recognition among the immigrants of their Italian heritage. Italian cyclists and the famed runner Dorando Pietri drew crowds of Italian supporters in their competitions versus other ethnics.[34]

Marathon racing provided one of the greatest tests of human endurance and a means to test racial comparisons. Pietri had first gained international fame as the near winner of the 1908 Olympic marathon in London. Pietri collapsed just short of the finish line, and British officials assisted him to the tape. American protests regarding the British assistance resulted in the award of the victory to Johnny Hayes, the American who finished a close second. Later that same year Pietri traveled to New York to challenge Hayes to an indoor marathon at Madison Square Garden. Upon arrival Pietri was feted by the Italians in New York. "The Italians were received by deputations from the numerous societies in this city representing their native land and frantically embraced. On behalf of the Italian newspaper *Il Progresso*, it was stated that Dorando would get a silver cup and a purse containing $200 if he succeeded in defeating Hayes at Madison Square Garden next week."[35] Such notice by both American and Italian newspapers identified Pietri as a national rather than a regional symbol, one in which all Italians could claim a measure of glory.

Pietri provided greater recognition for Italians by not only defeating the Irish American Hayes but also setting a new world record by nearly twelve minutes before ten thousand spectators. Such a feat, combined with the efforts of the opera stars, indicated that Italians were capable of providing high culture and matching their physical prowess with the American nation that aspired to world leadership. "The Italian supporters cheered for five minutes and fairly swamped their champion, who was carried off on the shoulders of his countrymen." Despite his triumph Pietri received only two thousand dollars, plus his expenses, while Hayes got a guaranteed four thousand dollars, or 30 percent of the gate. The race got front-page coverage in the *New York Times*, which reported that "attendance . . . included every class, from the gallery gods to the patrons of first nights and grand opera . . . with . . . rival brass bands, one of Italian musicians for Pietri, whom the crowd insistently called by his first name . . . and another band, that of the Sixty-ninth Regiment, for the Irish-American athlete. . . . [T] housands packed from the roof down to the ground were in a state approaching hysteria." A riot erupted when patrons rushed the track with two laps left to go, necessitating police intervention. "Blows were struck and fights sprang up on every side" until order was restored. "There was intense excitement over the result of the race, as well as over the disturbance on the track, and it was nearly half an hour after the race was finished before the police could clear the building, the Italians remaining to the last and literally mobbing Dorando." Pietri had vindicated Italian honor, but was soon besieged with additional challenges and commercial offers for a vaudeville tour.[36]

Italians in Stamford, Connecticut, presented Pietri with a gold medal and a flower bouquet, and by the end of the year other Italian-American runners appeared in a New York marathon. Pietri, however, suffered setbacks in two encounters against Tom Longboat, a Canadian Indian, in New York and Buffalo, causing his brother to come to his defense. Ulpiano Pietri, unlike Dorando, spoke English, and he explained that his brother's defeats were owing not to improper training, but the fact that he suffered from a sprained ankle and cramps and had run six races, including three marathons, in a period of seven weeks in the United States. His training included daily jogs of ten to fifteen miles.[37] Such a schedule seemed superhuman, even to the ardent supporters of American superiority.

Pietri reclaimed his honor with victories in St. Louis and Chicago, and in a return to New York he won another match against Hayes. He drew great crowds of Italians wherever he went. In New York some Italian students had already been introduced to running in the Public Schools Athletic League, which was established in 1903. Two years later historian Camillo Cianfarra stated, "In our public elementary school competitions, our children are not inferior to the children of other nationalities, in the list of gymnastic [track and field] winners the Italian names appear quite frequently as they appear in the rosters of teams involved in inter-high school competition."[38]

Whereas his backers in New York consisted of Carlo Barsotti, editor of *Il Progresso*, and other middle-class supporters, his Chicago fans included a variety of patrons who transcended social classes and occupations. Pietri worked in Italy as a pastry chef and credited his family with much of his success and the strength of his 130-pound frame. He presented the image of the Italian values of hard work, focus on the family, and physicality, which endeared him to those Italians in America who sought vindication for their alleged inferiority and disrespect. Sport offered the merger of such values in Pietri, and his fans bet heavily on him against a French runner in Chicago.[39]

Pietri lost another race in Buffalo to the English standout Alfred Shrubb over fifteen miles, but returned to New York to beat Hayes in yet another marathon event in March 1909. The widespread interest in distance racing led sport promoters to organize an international field for a marathon, a veritable battle of the nations, to be run on the grass at the Polo Grounds, a baseball park in New York, in April of that year. "The six most famous runners in the world, each a champion in his own country, will be set on the long journey. . . . [T]wo bands, Bayne's Sixty-ninth Regiment and Viola's Italian Band, will alternate in a concert, which will last until the finish of the race. . . . [T]housands of dollars will change hands upon the result."[40]

Henri St. Yves, a Frenchman, claimed the victory, with Pietri second, but the race only heightened interest, and a second international marathon for ten thousand dollars in prize money with thirteen competitors from Canada, France, the United States, England, Ireland, Cuba, and Sweden, as well as an American Indian, entered. Fans, including many Italians, who could not witness the Polo Grounds event crowded into Times Square, where the newspaper issued bulletins of the proceedings. Pietri finished a disappointing sixth but still earned three hundred dollars, a bonanza to working-class Italians. In August he returned to Italy to marry Teresa Dondi, his Italian sweetheart.[41]

Pietri was not the first nor was he the only Italian athlete to generate a sense of identity among the immigrants, but his exploits in the media capital of New York spawned greater publicity. Perhaps spurred by the diminutive Pietri, Gaston Strobino (five foot three, 110 pounds) also took up the sport of running, where size was not a hindrance. He migrated from Europe as a young boy, but unlike Pietri he became a naturalized citizen. As a nineteen-year-old machinist's apprentice, he began running in distance events for the South Paterson, New Jersey, Athletic Club in 1911. The following year he qualified for the US Olympic team in a race of approximately twelve miles in New York. At the Stockholm Olympics he finished third in the marathon, earning a bronze medal for his adopted country. A large contingent from Paterson met him at the pier in New York upon his return, where his parents and sister "smothered him with hugs and kisses" and fans "cheered him wildly." The Paterson mayor and city administration awarded him "the freedom of the city" in recognition of his feat. It proved to be the only marathon of his career, as he moved to the Little Italy neighborhood of Chicago, where he became a toolmaker and eventually retired to a Chicago suburb.[42]

During and after such running feats captivated Italian-Americans, a number of Italian cyclists also joined similar international fields for competition. Newspaper reports continually emphasized the ethnicity (at that time ethnicity was conflated with race) of the athletes, with each contest assuming a Darwinian struggle.[43]

Fostering a Sense of Italian Pride

As their work and leisure lives drew immigrants into the larger society, other factors contributed to the development of a sense of cohesion among Italian communities and strengthened the identification with their ethnic group. Regular correspondence with family and friends, travel to Italy, and subsidies sent to family members maintained the relationships to their country of origin. The Italian newspaper editors in the United States made early and continued attempts to construct an Italian identity that might merge with American ideals of citizenship. The Italian newspapers reported upon affairs in Italy, highlighting stories about the Italian wars in Africa, and creating a bond to and retaining interest in the homeland.

Over the past three decades scholars have analyzed the development of "imagined communities," "invented traditions," and "sites of memory or places of remembrance" as ways to construct and maintain emotional alliances among groups, ethnicities, and societies. Proponents of an Italian national identity invoked each of these applications to build the perception of inclusion in an Italian national state.[44] For the vast numbers who remained citizens of Italy, the "birds of passage," and even those individuals who had permanently settled in the United States but maintained familial ties in their homeland, the growing sense of an Italian identity had yet to achieve cohesion. The development of pride in Italy and the achievements of Italian heroes provided a means to this end.

For many Italian immigrants of the first and second generations, pride in Italy was a matter of self-respect and social recognition. They propagated information of the Italian nation in order to gain attention and acceptance from other ethnic groups and the mainstream population. For some Italians economic reasons also may have played a role in their efforts to support identification with Italy and with the various Italian groups. Businessmen may have hoped that a united Italian populace in the United States would provide greater commercial opportunities and additional patrons beyond their own *paesani*. In particular the early northern Italian middle-class immigrants spearheaded the efforts to unite Italians in the United States by creating an "imagined community" among them through the establishment of clubs, fraternal organizations, and commercial associations.

Constructing Identities and Memories

Many editors promoted Italian nationalism through their newspapers, linking the New World with the Old. Italian-language newspapers appeared in any community in the United States with a sizable Italian population. At least twenty found a readership in Chicago between 1880 and 1921.[45] Editors of the Italian newspapers contributed to the promotion of an Italian national identity by campaigning for the recognition of Italian heroes. Christopher Columbus served as a universal symbol for all Italians, and Columbus provided obvious ties to America. Since the middle of the nineteenth century, statues of

Columbus, and later those of Giuseppe Mazzini, Garibaldi, Dante Alighieri, and other famous Italians, were erected in numerous American cities. In addition, festivals and celebrations dedicated to Italian heroes took place throughout the United States. The 1893 World's Fair in Chicago, also known as the Columbian Exposition, provided an excellent stage for the celebration of an Italian Day, as well as separate commemorations of Columbus, Amerigo Vespucci, Mazzini, and the Italian king's birthday. All such "places of remembrance" tied Italians to their homeland and created an imagined community of compatriots in the United States.[46]

Historians have charged that "public monuments reflect and shape the communities that erect and preserve them, making them keys to understanding both the past and how it is used in the present."[47] In that sense the attempts to create a sense of Italian identity depicted the aspirations of more affluent Italians to achieve a measure of acceptance within American society, as most of the celebrated Italian heroes were men, explorers, statesmen, poets, and artists, which represented the claimed heritage of northern Italian males of the upper classes. Southern Italians, however, had mixed feelings about such heroes. Garibaldi, for example, was both liberator and a collaborator with the northern government, offering various interpretations of what it meant to be an Italian. He had freed southern Italy and Sicily, only to deliver them to the king to form a new country, an undesirable turn of events for most southerners.

In such manner did the more educated Italians who edited newspapers and operated commercial enterprises celebrate Italian heroes with invented traditions held regularly and eventually annually in the case of Columbus. They erected public places of remembrance, dedicated to northern Italian figures, to construct and perpetuate an imagined community of pan-Italians residing in the United States.[48]

American nativists and educators who espoused full acculturation had little room for Italian heroes, however. In a 1904 public school lecture, an Italian student was told to forget Garibaldi because he was not an American, thus limiting his choice of role models. By 1920 a celebration of Garibaldi's birth had been merged with the commemoration of American independence, transferring his heroic deeds in Italy to an American context. In such fashion did the Anglos usurp the ideology of liberty and freedom as their own, to the confusion of young Italians. Columbus retained relevance for American history, but Garibaldi did not. Italian children grew up with a conflicted sense of identity.[49]

Columbus held symbolic significance for both Americans and Italians and can be interpreted as a transcendent figure who merged the cultures, with Columbus Day becoming a legal holiday in 1909 (and a national holiday in 1968). The multifaceted image of Columbus is mirrored by the diverse groups of his adherents who included Marxists, Italian nationalists, and union members. By 1911 an estimated twelve thousand Italians representing forty-one groups ranging from fraternal clubs to political organizations and labor unions marched in the New York Columbus Day Parade, while another ten thousand members of seventy-five Italian societies strutted in Brooklyn. William Randolph Hearst, New York publisher and former congressman, addressed the latter group, lauding the "Italian race as civilizers as well as discoverers."[50] Such rituals gradually incorporated Italians within the civic community by making a public show of acceptance and inclusion. In the following decades Italians found a greater sense of unity in competition with the myriad other ethnic groups competing for their piece of the American pie.

Americanization Efforts

At the turn of the twentieth century, education and child labor became ardently contested issues throughout the United States, as social reformers attempted to assimilate the various immigrant groups. Many Italians resisted government efforts to educate their children, while Progressive WASP reformers believed education to be a necessary prerequisite to participation in a democracy. Social reformers objected to child labor, which they considered to be a humanitarian issue, in a clear difference of opinion with the immigrant families, who depended on the additional income of their children.

In the latter nineteenth century, social reformers began to enact a concerted process to assimilate members of ethnic minorities via education. Settlement houses within the immigrant communities initially aimed at acculturating adults, but many already had fixed beliefs unamenable to change or mistrusted authorities. Accordingly, social reformers concentrated their efforts on the children and devised a three-step process to accomplish their goal of assimilation and acculturation. They passed child labor laws to limit their working hours or remove children from the factories and other places of employment. The reformers then required education intended to teach American values in the schools. By 1900, except for the South, most states had enacted compulsory education legislation. They enforced the edict with juvenile courts after Chicago established the prototype in 1900. Truancy officers ensured that the teachers would have a captive audience. As a result, Chicago's public high schools overflowed with more than 10,000 students by 1900.[51] Public school enrollment, which reached 308,000 in New York City in 1890, more than tripled to 942,000 by 1920. Chicago's schools increased from 136,000 to 394,000 during that period, and Detroit's student population more than doubled from 111,000 in 1920 to 232,000 a decade later.[52]

As many of the teachers' new charges did not speak English, physical education, sports, and games conducted under the auspices of trained teachers, coaches, and supervisors in the schools, parks, playgrounds, and settlement houses would instill the desired values. Chicago became the first city to adopt a formal physical education program into its curriculum in 1885. A national conference, held in Boston in 1889, failed to determine the best form of gymnastics to employ in the schools, and students soon tired of formal calisthenics and exercises. Sports and games proved more attractive, and schools began hiring coaches as faculty members in the 1890s. Sports inculcated competition, the ideological basis for the capitalist American economic system. Team sports, in particular, were believed to teach both self-sacrifice for the good of the whole as well as social and leadership skills, all elements of a functional democracy. The national game of baseball, in particular, seemed to mirror American principles, in particular the interplay of communalism and individualism. The American emphasis on individualism seemed antithetical to Italians and others who valued equality and community.

In baseball children learned that a team requires a communal approach on defense, as all players must contribute for success. However, on offense each player and the team are rewarded for individual achievement. Employers especially liked the alleged cultivation of a deference to authority via sport. Athletes learned to respect umpires and referees, and bosses hoped that such respect would be transferred to employer-worker relationships, a point often lost on contentious members of the growing labor unions.[53]

The prohibition of child labor and the engagement of Italian youth in both school and sport, however, presented new challenges for the Italian family. In Italy "sporting games were seen as divisive since they pitted one Italian against another," and Italians had long held schooling to be a means of proselytism by their homeland government and viewed it with suspicion.[54] They saw little value and no opportunity in education without influential benefactors. Moreover, Italians came to America to work and make money. Like the Slavs, Italians perceived the family as a "collective economic unit" in which all contributed to the family's welfare. With the meager wages paid to laborers, it was essential that as many family members as possible shoulder the family burden. Once boys reached puberty they assumed the responsibilities of a man. An Italian parent complained, "Why these boys and girls—particularly the boys—do nothing but play ball, morning, noon, and night. . . . [T]he school encourages play."[55] A perplexed Italian mother stated that "I always thought of the school as a place where one has to study. But play? Questo gioco e la rovina della famiglia [This play is the ruination of the family]."[56] Physical energy might be better spent in work that produced income for poor families. Italian immigrants also saw no need to educate girls, for a learned woman who knew more than her husband would upset traditional family roles and be a poor candidate for marriage. Such residual cultural values and economic considerations consistently conflicted with the aims of educators to educate and Americanize immigrant children.[57]

Despite the best efforts of the authorities, Italian families resisted attempts to curtail employment of their children. Immigrant families learned to falsify birth certificates with a notarization for twenty-five cents or simply lied about children's ages. In the 1890s Italian girls as young as nine found work in New York sweatshops, laboring daily from 7:00 a.m. to 8:00 p.m. for a meager dollar per week. Boys found jobs on the streets, shining shoes and hawking newspapers. In 1899 the city supervisor for compulsory education in Chicago complained: "We should rightfully have the power to arrest all these little beggars, loafers, and vagabonds that infest our city, take them from the streets and place them in schools where they are compelled to receive education be taken any too soon . . . which will make the control of this class easier of solution. The city had established a reformatory and 1,300 soon became inmates, one quarter of them for truancy violations."[58]

In 1911 more than 50 percent of Italian children between the ages of ten and fifteen remained employed. Within the southern Italian culture it was considered dishonorable for the sons to surpass a father's vocation, a mark of poor breeding and a lack of family etiquette, a clear conflict with the American values of aspiration, achievement, and social mobility. The disdain for education, an indication of the retention of Old World values, persisted over generations. An education survey as late as 1969 found that only 5.9 percent of Italian-American adults (older than thirty-five) had completed college, a figure lower than the number of college graduates in all other ethnic groups except Hispanics. Of those aged twenty-five to thirty-four, only 11 percent had a college education, still the second lowest among ethnic groups, although 50.4 percent of the members of the Italian community had gone to high school.[59]

Integration of American Culture

Children's involvement in the Americanization processes meant new activities, the appropriation of new public spaces, and interaction with other ethnic groups. Some ethnic relations proved more harmonious than others. After 1900, as the public schools saw a surge in working-class students, ethnic rivalries and animosities found new avenues of release. In the small Wisconsin town of Cumberland, George St. Angelo entered high school in 1908, but he stayed only six weeks. "I could not accept the ridicule and the harsh physical hazing that I was subjected to by the big town boys who delighted in taking care of the 'country dago kid.'"[60] The establishment of Catholic schools, taught by nuns, provided an alternative for many immigrants, but few Italians could afford the tuition payments. In Chicago only 10 percent of the Italian parishes had schools in 1910.[61] Thus, most children of Italian origin attended the public institutions.

In Chicago Jewish settlement-house workers at the Eli Bates Settlement effected a measure of rapport with their Jewish and Italian constituents. Cordial relations existed between Jews, Italians, and blacks in some areas as well. But in New Orleans the Mardi Gras associations excluded all three groups from their membership. All three suffered from the same stigma of a lack of perceived whiteness in a WASP culture.[62]

Dominion over less regulated public spaces, such as parks and playgrounds, proved more contentious. A Swedish pastor in Chicago voiced his concerns over the transition taking place as Sicilians took up residence. "This is *our* neighborhood, a Swedish neighborhood. . . . The dark people have come in farther south in the ward. If a playground is put in our neighborhood we fear these people will come with their children to live in our neighborhood." When two Sicilian girls, led by a black friend, did enter the playground, Swedish girls yelled, "Get out! Dagoes! Dagoes! You can't play here!" Despite a physical confrontation that followed, the three minority children defiantly appropriated the playground swings anyway.[63] Frank Di Liberto, born in Chicago to Sicilian parents, also related how, when his family moved to an Irish neighborhood, he first had to fight all the Irish kids to win acceptance into their club. Ruth Riha, of Dutch parentage, grew up in a mixed neighborhood on Chicago's West Side and recalled, "We always fought with Italians."[64]

The Promise and Potential of Sport

Italian fathers initially perceived sport as a waste of time when energy might be spent to make money. Professional sport was almost unknown in Italy; therefore, it took some time to understand that sport may offer remuneration that far surpassed that of laborers, and at the turn of the century parents began to embrace the earnings of professional athletes. Most young athletes who aimed at a sporting career would never attain professional status, but for those who did the compensation proved remarkable.

Ed Abbaticchio, the son of Italian immigrants and one of the first pro football players, performed for the Latrobe, Pennsylvania, team as a fullback and punter from 1895 to 1900, earning as much as fifty dollars per game. He has been credited with popularizing the spiral punt. In the summers he played baseball, including stints in Major League Baseball (MLB) from 1898 until 1910, where he earned as much as five thousand dollars for a season. During that time Abbaticchio played for teams in Philadelphia, Boston, Minneapolis, Milwaukee, Nashville, and Pittsburgh. An excellent base stealer, he also led the National League in putouts twice (1903, 1905) and in fielding percentage (1908) as an infielder. As a member of the Pittsburgh Pirates in 1909, Abbaticchio garnered a World Series championship. Abbaticchio's athletic success, the length of his baseball career, and his unmistakably Italian surname gave prominence to his nationality throughout the Northeast, Midwest, and the upper South at the turn of the century and provided a role model and greater aspirations for Italian youth with a growing interest in the American national game.[65]

Willie Garoni, the son of European immigrants, reached the Major League level as a pitcher for the New York Giants in 1899. Garoni gained recognition playing for clubs in Fort Lee, New Jersey, and New York. His brief career with the Giants lasted only three games at the end of the season. He expected to double his initial contract of six hundred dollars, but when the Giants did not accede to his expectations, he left the team to play with several New Jersey clubs before entering the sewer construction business. Lou Schiappacassa appeared in only two games as an outfielder with the Detroit Tigers in 1902, but Frank La Porte enjoyed a decadelong (1905–15) baseball career as an infielder with the New York, St. Louis, and Washington teams of the American League and Kansas City in the American Association, before joining Indianapolis of the short-lived Federal League in 1914, where he batted .311 and led the league in runs batted in.[66]

Toughness and physicality coincided with the habitus of the southern Italian, and athletes became role models for Italian youth, as evidenced by the large number of professional baseball players and boxers of Italian origin over the next decade. Although immigrant parents initially perceived sport as a waste of time and energy, they learned the value of athletic prowess in American society. Sport provided a measure of celebrity, a means for men to display their masculinity and gain a degree of respect, none of which was accorded to Italian peasants in their parents' homeland. Even for short-lived careers, sport broadened participants' social worlds, where they might make new contacts, generate business opportunities, and merge with the mainstream American culture. As the national pastime, baseball symbolized true Americanism, but the handful of early participants garnered largely local notice.

Public recognition and acceptance proved most noticeable in the national game of baseball. The new interests of Italian-American youth also sparked dissension within the family, as exemplified by the first Italian star in Major League Baseball. Francesco Pizzolo, born to Italian immigrants in San Francisco in 1887, left high school and pursued a baseball career under the pseudonym of Ping Bodie, an unforgivable offense for which his father disowned him. Although the father might abide the sizable income derived from a physical, if perceptively trivial, pursuit such as baseball, he could not suffer the abandonment of his proud Italian heritage by the corrupt Anglicization of his name. Playing for the San Francisco Seals of the Pacific Coast League in 1910, Bodie hit a record 30 home runs. The Major League best that year was ten. The Chicago White Sox quickly signed him to a contract. A slugger at five foot eight and 195 pounds, he was sometimes likened to an ape by sportswriters, but he proved a fan favorite as a jokester.

In his first home game of 1911, he delivered the winning hit. "It was the name of Ping Bodie that was on the lips of the happy fans as the wended their way out of the grounds. His feat had been impressed upon the minds of all, and the daring and spirited work of the other eight players was for the time forgotten." He led the team in runs batted in with 112 that year (fourth best in the American League).[67]

Two weeks later his stellar play led a sportswriter to gush that "it has made Ping Bodie first among men of the south side."[68] Only three days later, when his mighty bat produced another timely victory, he enjoyed a hero's reception after the game. "Some one yelled 'There's Bodie,' and instantly there was a riot. Sane men almost trampled over each other to get by his side and give him a joyful slap on the back. Women pushed and fought their way through the mob to get a glimpse of the hero, and it was necessary for the police to take a hand in the affair so the mighty batter could get out of the grounds."[69] By 1914, his last season in Chicago, he had begun writing baseball tips for a *Chicago Tribune* column and signed a vaudeville contract. The emulation of young children became evident when a lost child reported his name to the police as Ping Bodie.[70]

Bodie's career took him to Philadelphia and New York, where he became Babe Ruth's roommate. The Yankees signed Bodie with the hopes of attracting new fans, and the *New York Times* carefully noted that he was Italian and that "the Yanks have never had a player of such individuality."[71] He endeared himself to fans through his clowning as early as spring training that year when "the fence-busting Italian persisted in running the bases the wrong way, starting out by way of third, and cake-walked about the plate. After making a thrilling catch of Wegmann's Texas leaguer in the second Ping kept right on running and slid into third amid cheers and a cloud of dust."[72] In 1920 fans showed their appreciation with a Ping Bodie Day at the Polo Grounds. Although he would soon be overshadowed in New York by Babe Ruth, Bodie led the parade of professional baseball players who emanated from San Francisco, and he continued to play for many years in the Minor Leagues (batting .347 at the age of forty). Bodie was the first Italian to gain stardom and celebrity as a Major League ballplayer.

Bodie's public displays of physical prowess gained social capital in the masculine world of sport and beyond. The media coverage of Bodie provided recognition of an Italian athlete and even allowed for an Italian heroism within the American sporting culture, but his renown did not bring universal or even general acceptance to Italians.[73]

Immigrants not only shaped American society, but also had an impact on their home country. Mario Ottino, born in Turin, moved to the United States, where he became Max Ott and developed a love for the American game of baseball. Upon his return to Italy in 1919, and in association with Professor Guido Graziani, who had also learned baseball in America, the pair initiated games in their native country, an early example of reverse cultural flow.[74] Whereas baseball signaled the adoption of American habits and tastes, bocce and soccer were imported from Italy. First-generation immigrants, when they played at all, tended to adhere to games of the homeland. In Utica, New York, teams from several nearby towns competed for the bocce championship that offered a box of cigars to the champions in 1903. That same year Italians and Mexicans allied to form a soccer club for children in a mining town. Paul Moschella, a Sicilian immigrant, claimed that, as children, they used a lemon to play both bocce and soccer because they were too poor to afford the proper equipment.[75] Although sport and popular culture offered new possibilities for the children of Italians in America, others clung to the traditional and more familiar lifestyle. Italian immigrants continued to promote soccer over the next generation, and the game maintained its interest in Italian urban neighborhoods well into the twentieth century.[76]

Mainstream and Migrant Populations: A Clash of Cultures

Because of their cultural background, many Italians had difficulty discerning the American value system, which seemed at odds with their principles. Even "educated Italians . . . pictured the United States as a cultural desert, describing Americans as being so immersed in the making of money that they ignored the esthetic side of life."[77] American lifestyles and beliefs were an enigma in particular for the first generation of immigrant peasants who continued to enjoy Italian food and to live according to their traditional habits. Like in Italy, many laws seemed nonsensical, oppressive, or intended as a means of social control, and Italians willfully transgressed the ones that seemed to be so. In spite of the temperance advocates, they drank wine, which they considered an essential food rather than an alcoholic beverage. They dispensed their own justice rather than call on the police, whom they viewed as instruments of an exploitative state.

Italian isolation within the Little Italies of the cities and the perception of Catholicism as an alien religion had served to exclude them from the mainstream. Work offered both opportunities and obstacles. Faith in the family and tradition maintained a sense of cohesion, but such values seemed to be oppositional to the individualism espoused in their adopted land.

The southern Italians' neglect of education also placed them at a greater disadvantage than other immigrants. Germans and Jews progressed relatively rapidly into middle-class status, whereas most southern Italians came as unskilled workers, were relegated to hard labor, and rarely moved beyond their ascribed social standing. Eastern European Jews toiled in the sweatshops, but they had the benefit of advocates in the German Jews who had preceded them and had gained a comfortable assimilation. In contrast, the early northern Italian immigrants distanced themselves from the southern peasants, with whom they had little in common and whose image reflected poorly on Italians in general. Northern Italians inhabited or aspired to a middle-class world, whereas the southern peasants too often accepted their proletarian fate.

World War I and Issues of Identity

Events in Europe continued to hold Italians in the United States in a liminal state, no longer completely one (Italian) and not yet the other (American). The Italian entry into World War I in May 1915 raised Italian consciousness, which was magnified by the Italian government's policy of drafting American émigrés, whom it considered to be Italian citizens. Italian citizens were required to serve two years in the military at age twenty and were susceptible to reserve status until age forty-five. The number of returnees was estimated as high as ninety thousand in 1915 alone. A journalist who accompanied a contingent to Italy in 1916 declared that "they were the gayest lot I have ever seen, playing and singing all the way. . . . They came from every point of our country; miners from the West, some wearing caps with the inscription of some flour company or the name of an express company; others decked out in American overalls, suspenders, and sweaters; there was even one Italian from Kansas in a baseball suit! Many of them had the Italian tricolor and a button of the Madonna del Carmine on one lapel and an American flag pinned on the other."[78]

Southern Italians, however, still did not feel great allegiance to the Italian government, and they judged the war to be for the benefit of northerners. Still, Italian newspapers in America raised funds for those individuals who joined the Italian army and their families. Both Italian immigrants and Italians with American citizenship entered the US military in large numbers, indicating the burgeoning transition in identity and a continued concern for the security of the ancestral homeland. One Italian-American scholar claimed that three hundred thousand Italians fought in the US Army and that twenty thousand died as a result.[79]

American citizenship provided one incentive for those immigrants who chose to serve in the US military. Joe Rizzi, a twenty-year-old bricklayer who was born in Italy, and his brother were aroused by a recruitment parade and patriotic speeches, and both joined the army in 1917. A water boy who barely spoke English told a recruiter, "Ma name Tony Monaco. In dees countra seex months. Gimme da gun."[80] Boxer Pete Herman joined the navy and became a boxing instructor, while Piero Marchegiano, father of future heavyweight champ Rocky Marciano, fared less well. Although born in Italy, Marchegiano fought for the United States and was gassed and wounded at the Battle of Chateau-Thierry, injuries that would affect his health for the remainder of his life. Harry Costello and Jerry (Nero) Da Prato were both star football players in college, at the University of Detroit and Michigan Agricultural College (now Michigan State University), respectively. Da Prato led the nation in scoring during the 1915 season, and famed coach Glenn "Pop" Warner claimed that Costello "for his (size) was one of the greatest players that ever lived." Costello won the British Military Cross for his bravery in Russia, and both went on to play in the early professional football league. Other Italians were awarded the Medal of Honor, and one hundred earned Distinguished Service Crosses.[81]

Despite their bravery and the well-known abilities of Costello and Da Prato, the Italians who enlisted in the American military faced continued discrimination. The administration of puzzle-solving tests to determine the literacy of military recruits did not account for cultural or linguistic differences. Whereas only 8.7 percent of English speakers scored in the D category, equivalent to a nine- to eleven-year-old, 63.4 percent of Italians scored at that level. Only the Poles scored lower. "Men of the D class are physically well developed" but suffered from "emotional instability" and were assigned, like many African American troops, to "pioneer battalions for work that required muscular rather than mental strength."[82]

After the war the duality of Italians' identity faced further threat, as nativists lobbied for immigration restrictions and a "whiter" America. When the Rochester, New York, American Legion Post with more than 260 Italian-American members marched in the Memorial Day Parade, it was denied permission to carry the Italian flag alongside the American banner, as nativists deemed such a consideration to be unpatriotic.[83] The request by the Italians indicated an ongoing dilemma in their own loyalty and allegiance.

Identity and citizenship for many Italians remained problematic until World War II. An Italian immigrant testified to such confusion, torn between nostalgia and hope:

> When I went to night school, I had a good impression to me [*sic*]. . . . I learn little English, and about the American government, and how the people can make change and progress by legislation without the force of revolution, and I like very much this idea. The

teacher told me why not to become an American? . . . But I do not become American because I think always of the grandeur of the Italy civilization of the past! . . . Maybe I have a son, it is the future for him. America is to be his country. . . . Now comes the great day for America . . . and my son will be a man . . . and my son perhaps the greatest of any great man?[84]

With victory Italy's international prestige heightened after the war, and Italians in America had to decide if their children had the best chance of success, even greatness, in the United States or in their homeland. Gaining respect in American society was still an ongoing process. Sociologist Emory Bogardus conducted studies of racial attitudes after World War I that showed minimal change over the past decade. Thirty-four percent of respondents had a more favorable opinion of Italians, while 33 percent were less approving than they had previously been, a net gain of only 1 percent. Of the respondents, 71.3 percent allowed for Italian citizenship, but only 25.7 percent would consider an Italian as a friend, and only 15.4 percent would consider such a marriage. One, who patronized an Italian shoemaker, admitted that he "is courteous, hard working . . . but still I see blood and fire and pent-up anger in every Italian's eye and feel like keeping my distance and not getting too well acquainted."[85]

The rise of Mussolini to power in Italy after the war further complicated issues of identity for Italians living in the United States. Mussolini promoted a national language, essential to a common culture, in order to spawn a greater sense of unity among all Italians. But the Italians in America, still immersed in regional dialects and struggling with English, were caught in a liminal state, no longer one and not yet the other. Still, Mussolini fostered a pan-Italianism that included those living in America. His successes drew many to greater pride in their Italian identity.[86]

The cultural flow that had sustained Italian culture, dialects, and lifestyles in the United States since the nineteenth century came to a near halt when the US Congress established a quota system for immigrants in 1921 and lowered that figure again in 1924. By 1929 only about six thousand Italians were allowed to enter the country.[87] The American officials had sent a clear message regarding the desirability of Italians, and an Italian identity could no longer be sustained beyond the immigrant cohort. Tensions remained over the next generation, however, between the first generation of Italian immigrants, whose memories, family members, and allegiance remained in Italy, while their offspring adapted and adopted the new culture of America.

For at least a generation thereafter, forced to assimilate, Italians lived on the margins of both societies. Popular culture, and sport in particular, had promoted a greater sense of an identity and pointed the way to a compromise in cultural values. The attainment of a greater measure of acceptance as Americans, however, would require adherence to whiteness, which was more than a skin color and included the adoption and practice of particular values, norms, and standards of WASP culture.

3

Winning Whiteness

In June 1899 *Outing*, one of the most popular sporting magazines of the era, reported that Lawrence Brignoli (Brignolia), had won the Boston Marathon on April 19 in a spirited finish despite a heavy gale that forced six of the seventeen starters to give up. Richard Grant, a Harvard man and a member of the Knickerbocker Athletic Club, finished second, a half mile behind Brignoli, who had failed to win in two previous attempts. The son of immigrants, and whose father was a peddler, Brignoli(a) was apprenticed to a blacksmith at age fifteen. Unable to train properly due to his work hours, he showed enough promise that John Bowler, a professional trainer, took him under his wing and produced a champion. Brignoli(a)'s victory countered perceptions of Italian inferiority and provided an early recognition of an Italian identity. As a member of two middle-class athletic clubs, and a champion oarsmen, a sport that required some measure of leisure time and economic capital, Brignoli(a) symbolized the promise of America.[1]

The *Boston Globe* praised Brignoli's "wonderful endurance . . . indomitable courage . . . bull dog tenacity . . . wonderful physique and confidence," and his athletic club rewarded him with a gold watch.[2] Yet in the rematch with Dick Grant, the Harvard blue blood, in 1900, John Bowler claimed that Grant's chances depended on his scientific knowledge, while Brignoli had the advantage in endurance. The brain-versus-brawn characterization would often haunt Italian athletes over the next century.[3]

Brignolia spent much of that century engaged in sporting enterprises. After his marathon victory he continued to compete as an oarsmen and a baseball player before taking up harness racing. He owned his own stable of trotting horses and also promoted boxing matches.[4] Larry Brignolia Jr. attempted to emulate his father as a distance runner before baseball attracted his attention. He proved good enough to earn a tryout with the Chicago Cubs, but when that quest failed he turned to professional boxing, where rewards were more immediate. Despite his father's attainment of social capital, physical prowess apparently remained central to the identity of the son. Early Italian athletic stars continued to provide role models for the aspiring youth of the second and third generations, but the emphasis on physicality marked the self-perceptions of most immigrants and their children.[5]

Likewise, Ralph De Palma, born in Italy, arrived in New York with his family in 1892, and his rapid rise to stardom in the upper-class sport of road racing further accentuated the perception of sport as a meritocracy and a means to social mobility. He graduated from racing bicycles to motorcycles to autos by 1909. De Palma, driving for Fiat, and then Mercedes, captured the national championship in 1912 and 1914. In 1915 he won the Indianapolis 500 and set a world record in excess of 149 miles per hour in 1919. De Palma enjoyed a long career of twenty-seven years in auto racing, winning more than two thousand races. His brother John and nephew Pete De Paolo followed in his footsteps, with De Paolo winning the 1925 Indy 500.[6] Auto racing had a particular interest for Italians owing to the number of automobile manufacturers established in Italy at the turn of the twentieth century. The focus of auto racers on improving performance and challenging human and technological limits created new heroes for a modernizing world, symbolic of Italian advancement.

Both Brignoli and De Palma had achieved what scholars have termed *whiteness*, an adoption of WASP standards, norms, and values that signaled their conversion to modernity and won them acceptance within the mainstream society. They, however, represented the exceptions. In contrast, the vast majority of Italians residing in the United States adhered to traditional lifestyles and folkways deemed to be backward, primitive, and inferior by the dominant host culture.

Much of the animosity encountered by Italians emanated from faulty but nonetheless accepted scientific theories of the era that were rooted in social Darwinian beliefs about races that rationalized superior and inferior species. Such notions had emanated from comparative studies of Anglos and Native American tribes that emphasized differences rather than similarities. Scholars debated the genesis of humankind, suggesting the separate development of a variety of racial groups. By the twentieth century such views had become entrenched, augmented by evolutionary theory and the "scientific" research disseminated by scholars and published in the burgeoning academic journals and popular magazines. Overcoming such notions of inferiority proved a major obstacle for the immigrants from southern and eastern Europe, who were assumed to be less advanced in their development. Sport offered one means to confront the issue, as it allowed for direct comparisons of individual human performances under relatively equal conditions, such as boxing, rowing, or track and field events. The Progressives' belief in their ability to perfect society extended to the view that the human body, like a machine, could be improved through proper nutrition, training, and willpower.[7]

The Social Construction of Race

By the late nineteenth century the Darwinian theory of evolution adhered to human beings as well as animals, prompting the "survival of the fittest" doctrine that rationalized inequalities and racial superiority. The racialization of Italians reached prominence by the mid-nineteenth century with the rise of anthropology. Southern Italians and Sicilians, poor, largely uneducated, and illiterate, were labeled with derogatory stereotypes even before they embarked for America. Cesare Lambroso, a Jewish Italian scientist, believed that criminality was hereditary and could be shown by physical features such as large jaws, high cheekbones, dark skin, small heads, low brows, and an undeveloped, childlike mentality. Sociologist Enrico Ferri agreed and thought that he could deduce criminals by the size and shape of their skulls. Northern Italians, who considered themselves to be part of the presumably more civil Nordic race, stereotyped the southern Italians and Sicilians as biologically destined to commit evil deeds.

Such beliefs preceded the Italians' mass migration to America. By the latter nineteenth century social Darwinism rationalized the Italians as "beaten men from beaten races, the worst failures in the struggle for existence."[8] White Anglo-Saxon Protestants in English-speaking countries socially constructed racial pyramids in which they assumed their own superiority. The concept of ethnicities based on cultural or language groups did not gain precedence until after World War I.[9]

During the interwar years pioneering researchers at the University of Chicago, such as Robert E. Park, Ernest Burgess, Louis Wirth, and others, established the Chicago School of Sociology, emphasizing a systematic analysis of urban conditions, race, and immigrant groups that succeeded in separating the concepts of race and ethnicity from biological factors. The assimilation theory proposed by the Chicago School offered the concept of a "melting pot" in which the vast array of immigrant groups would eventually fuse with the mainstream WASP culture, adopting its language, values, and standards.[10]

By the 1960s anthropologist Victor Turner followed the sociologists in establishing that the assimilation process involved three phases: a separation from one's former group; a liminal period in which immigrants might exist in a marginal state, caught between two cultures, no longer one but not yet fully accepted in the other; and finally, the reaggregation phase of reincorporation in a more stable status within the mainstream. Italian philosopher Antonio Gramsci stated that cultural adoption was not a linear process but a continual power struggle between the dominant group (WASPs in the United States) and subordinate groups (Italians, among other immigrants), in which the subordinates might accept, reject, adopt, or adapt the norms, values, and standards of the mainstream. During that process of assimilation, sport provided an opportunity for subordinate groups, such as the Italians, to temporarily assert their physical dominance over supposedly superior WASP groups and eventually gain a measure of acceptance, or at least self-respect.[11]

"Whiteness studies" have accrued within the scholarly literature since the 1990s, and Italians have drawn their share of attention but without consensus. Among scholars whiteness refers not only to one's skin color, but also to the norms, values, standards, and practices of a dominant social group, what Pierre Bourdieu refers to as habitus, a lifestyle and taste that are deeply embedded, though not entirely fixed. The standards of whiteness in American society derived from the beliefs, principles, and decorum of white Anglo-Saxon middle-class Protestant culture.

Cheryl Harris acknowledged that "the law's construction of whiteness defined and affirmed critical aspects of identity [who is white]; of privilege [what benefits accrue to that status]; and of property [what legal entitlements arise from that status]." Ian Lopez claimed that the standard for whiteness rested upon common knowledge or scientific evidence before 1909.[12] But in 1907 a US attorney admitted that "there is considerable uncertainty as to just what nationalities come within the term 'white person.'"[13]

Such a broadly fluctuating and fluid definition of the "white person" has differed over time and place, allowing for permutations in the social construction of race. The federal Naturalization Act of 1790 stipulated the restriction of citizenship to "free white persons."[14] Some free blacks, over time, might gain a measure of whiteness by adhering to white middle-class standards, but a slave could never achieve that status. Even wealthy free blacks generally faced social and residential exclusion from elite white society. Southern and eastern European peasants, too, faced an uphill battle in pursuit of social acceptance. Scholars continue to disagree as to when Italians gained whiteness.[15] At the turn of the twentieth century the US Immigration Bureau characterized the northern Italians as "cool, deliberate, patient, practical . . . capable of great progress in the political and social organization of modern civilization," whereas southern Italians were seen as "excitable, impulsive, highly imaginative, impracticable . . . [with] little adaptability to highly organized society."[16]

The early negative impressions of Italians became entrenched throughout the nineteenth century. As early as 1830 a New Yorker remarked that "a dirty Irishman is bad enough, but he's nothing comparable to a nasty . . . Italian loafer." By midcentury another common comparison viewed the Italians unfavorably. "The lowest Irish are far above the level of these creatures [Italians]." By 1876 even the *New York Times* promoted the image of Italian criminality by stating that "the knife with which he cuts his bread he also uses to lop off another dago's finger or ear. . . . He is quite as familiar with the sight of human blood as with the sight of the food he eats."[17]

Criminal Stereotypes

Italians became immediate suspects in the event of any criminal activity. In 1860 at least twenty Sicilians were killed in New Orleans in retaliation for the death of a criminal court clerk. Over the next two decades Italians in New York were charged with engaging in a white slave trade, as young children were sold to *padrones* to become beggars, shoe-shine boys, and street musicians. In 1891 Sicilians in New Orleans endured the horrors of a mass lynching, the largest in American history, when nineteen were indicted for the murder of a police commissioner. Despite the fact that none was found guilty in the subsequent trial, a mob of thousands stormed the jail and took their own vengeance by shooting nine and lynching two others. None of the vigilantes was ever charged with a crime. The mayor wrote to a friend that Italians were the "most idle, vicious, and worthless people . . . [who] monopolize the fruit, oyster, and fish trades and are nearly all peddlers, tinkers, or cobblers . . . filthy in their persons and homes . . . without courage, honor, truth, pride, religion or any quality that goes to make a good citizen." Italy broke off diplomatic relations with the United States for a year over the affair; nevertheless, 50 percent of US newspapers supported the vigilante action. The mayor's words belied the truth of the matter and hinted at ulterior motives. More than sixty years later it was revealed that the lynch-mob leader and his associates had conspired to eliminate the Sicilians from the lucrative food-distribution business. One of the accused, Joseph Macheca, the wealthiest of the Italians whose industriousness had allowed them to corner the food markets, had raised the envy of the whites, who formed an Anglo corporation to take over the Italian businesses in the aftermath of the lynching. Lynchings of Italians in Louisiana continued throughout the decade and spread to other states as well. Only blacks were lynched in greater numbers than Italians from 1870 to 1940.[18]

The negative perceptions of southern Italians proved widespread and enduring. An editorial by an "American Citizen" to the *New York Times* in 1909 complained that "Calabria and Sicily breed a vile assortment of thugs and murderers and a race that deems it honorable to shield its crimes. Their presence here is a continual menace.... There is no question that The United States does not want them and they should be harried out to a man."[19]

Shortly thereafter, Chicago newspapers seized upon the blackmailing and extortion practices taking place in the Little Sicily neighborhood to socially construct a mythological Black Hand Society of organized criminals that continues to plague law-abiding Italians to this day. Robert Lombardo has convincingly shown that many of the perpetrators were delinquent youths and that much of the criminal activity was conducted by non-Italians. By the 1920s University of Chicago sociologists had determined that such crimes emanated from the urban social conditions in the United States rather than the influx of alleged criminals from Italy. The framing of crime as a particularly Italian activity by the media sensationalized such events and boosted newspaper sales, but it also labeled and stigmatized the immigrants and their offspring.[20]

The Quest for Whiteness

In 1895 Italian miners, in conjunction with other ethnic workers, made an early attempt to characterize themselves as white, in opposition to the African American residents of Spring Valley, Illinois. When black miners agreed to work for smaller wages than the unionized Italians during an 1894 labor strike, it resulted in a race riot the following year that pitted a number of European ethnic groups, led by the Italians, against the blacks, who had presumably attacked and shot an Italian as they stole his watch and paycheck. A large mob beat, shot, and chased the sizable black community from the town. The African Americans, supported by other blacks in the region and in Chicago, retaliated not with force, but in the court, where they invoked their rights as citizens against the ethnic foreigners. Nativist white newspapers sided with the blacks, characterizing the mob as "dago rioters, anarchists, rebellionists and assassins" and "a band of lousy, dirty, despicable, low bred, treacherous dago miners." Eight men were convicted, and seven went to prison, as the Italians' bid for whiteness proved premature.[21]

In the law, newspapers, and popular culture, vaudeville and theater Italians were characterized as less than white in slang and jokes and, especially in the South, treated similarly to blacks. The term *guinea*, previously used for African slaves, ascribed an equally low status to Italians by the 1890s. Many Sicilians disembarked at New Orleans, and they took work on the sugar-cane plantations of Louisiana, where hard, physical labor became known as "nigger work" and "dago work." On the plantations the Sicilians worked a seven-day week, twelve to sixteen hours per day (eighteen during harvest season) for seventy-five cents to one dollar per day. At the 1898 Louisiana state constitutional convention, representatives acknowledged a measure of whiteness in the skin color of Italians, but "according to the spirit of our meaning when we speak of white man's government [the Italians] are as black as the blackest negro in existence." Neither blacks nor Italians were allowed to serve on the New Orleans police force, and the 1898 convention succeeded in disenfranchising Italians by poll taxes, literacy tests, and residency requirements.[22]

The Louisiana lumber companies enforced segregated housing for both blacks and Italians. In Tallulah, Louisiana, Italian children were not allowed to attend the white schools. In 1904 Mississippi whites destroyed an Italian restaurant and chased the owner out of town because he had served a black customer. Bias was not limited to the South. Italians were paid less than other construction workers in New York, and a Minneapolis fraternal lodge excluded both blacks and Italians in 1902. Both Italians and Greeks were ascribed nonwhite status in Minnesota mining towns until the World War I era. The California lumber industry considered Italians to be nonwhite as well. In 1907 Sumrall, Mississippi, residents protested against Italian children in the public schools, and Frank Scaglioni, a crippled shoemaker and leader of the Italian community, was beaten and dragged for a mile with a rope. In the Arizona mines Italians got the lowest wages, and in the Alabama steel mills an immigration commission report of 1911 claimed that it was "practically universal opinion among employers that South Italians are . . . the most inefficient of all races, whether immigrant or native."[23] Such treatment forced Italians to confront their ascribed difference from other groups, a step in reaching a collective identity.

Prejudice and discrimination against Italians proved widespread during the period, and when Italians were employed they were often treated as beasts of burden. An Italian medical student employed on a railroad work gang in the Midwest during the summer detailed the living and working conditions. The Italian laborers slept in windowless boxcars on boards, boxes, and straw bags, their blankets covered in vermin, roaches, and bedbugs. They ate with rusty utensils. They awoke at 3:00 a.m. and started work at 5:00 a.m. The foremen explained that "if we let them go to work at seven, they will become lazy, and will not do enough work." They began the workday with a six-mile trip by handcar to repair heavy iron rails. The labor boss motivated them by continuous cursing and swearing for the next seven hours. He claimed that "the beasts must not be given a rest. Otherwise they will step over me." At noon they got a one-hour lunch break, which consisted of often stale bread, sausages for some, and water. They returned to work from 1:00 to 4:00 p.m. They complained that "not a farmer would give us water or sell us milk. . . . We were forced to fetch our water from a filthy trough—water that was covered with algae, greenish and stale, and the taste was an indescribable compound of the prevailing odors." At 7:30 p.m. they went to sleep. The monotony and abuse continued seven days a week.[24]

Scientific Racism

Edward Alsworth Ross, a sociologist and influential professor, consistently denigrated southern Italians and Sicilians under the guise of scientific expertise. In his book *The Old World in the New* (1914), he wrote:

> It is the backward and benighted provinces from Naples to Sicily that send us the flood of "gross little aliens." . . . Steerage passengers from a Naples boat show a distressing frequency of low foreheads, open mouths, weak chins, poor features, skew faces, small or knobby crania, and backless heads. Such people lack the power to take rational care of themselves; hence their death-rate in New York is twice the general death-rate and thrice that of the Germans. . . . In our cities the head of the [southern Italian] household earns on an average $390 a year, as against $449 for the Northern Italian, $552 for the Bohemian, and $630 for the German.[25]

Ross admitted that Italians "excelled the negro at every point" as cotton growers in the South, but southerners had little enthusiasm for Italians who wished to become landowners. "Then, too, a fear has sprung up lest the Italians, being without the southern white man's strong race feeling, should mix with the negroes and create a hybrid."[26] Such miscegenational attitudes made it increasingly clear to Italians that they would have to forsake racial harmony and distinguish themselves from blacks in order to achieve whiteness and its concordant privileges.

It would not be easy, however, to overcome Ross's charges, which exhibited his own racial biases rather than scientific evidence. He claimed the "inaptness of the South Italians for good team work. Individualistic to the marrow, they lack the gift of pulling together, and have never achieved an efficient co-operating unit larger than the family."[27] His own anecdotes countered such assertions, as in the case of railroad workers uniting against their boss. "In railroad work other nationalities shun camps with many Italians. Contractors are afraid of them because the whole force will impulsively quit work, perhaps flare into riot, if they imagine one of their number has suffered a wrong."[28] Had Ross bothered to investigate, he would have found that Italians across the country had already organized more than a thousand mutual-aid societies for their collective benefit by that time.[29]

Throughout the book Ross expounded upon his negative opinions without scientific supporting evidence. Relative to Italian students, he stated that "it *appears* that these children, with the dusk of Saracenic or Berber ancestors showing in their cheeks, are twice as apt to drop behind other pupils of their age as are the non-English speaking immigrants from northern Europe. . . . The South Italian is volatile, unstable, soon hot, soon cool. . . . [S]uch people are unreliable."[30] Though a distinguished sociologist, Ross exhibited little to no knowledge of southern Italian culture and paid no heed to the social and economic conditions that forced Italian children into the workforce for mere sustenance.

Ross deduced that "the Mediterranean peoples are morally below the races of northern Europe is as certain as any social fact."[31] He based his opinion on the contention that the immigrants' inability to answer the questions of immigration officers constituted lying. A more cogent analysis might have revealed their lack of familiarity with the English language and immigrants' natural inclination not to reveal any information that might prohibit their entry to the United States.

Ross's condemnations were not a solitary voice, but represented mainstream thought. Professor Ellwood Cubberley had already stated that "these southern and eastern Europeans are a very different type from the north European who preceded them, illiterate, docile, lacking in self-reliance and initiative and not possessing Anglo-Teutonic conceptions of law, order and government, their coming has served to dilute tremendously our national stock, and to corrupt our civic life."[32] The concerns of many WASPs over dilution of the racial stock intensified over the first three decades of the twentieth century, as public discourses show.

Shortly after the publication of Ross's *Old World in the New*, Madison Grant, a historian and anthropologist, championed the eugenics movement with his book *The Passing of the Great Race or the Racial Basis of European History* in 1916. For many Americans, Grant provided a rationale for racism by constructing an evolutionary history of racial hierarchy. He posited three racial types: the Nordic, the Mediterranean, and the Alpine races, based on geographical locations. He claimed that "the Nordic race is nearly everywhere distinguished by great stature."[33] To them he attributed the magnificence of the Roman civilization, the great soldiers, sailors, and maritime explorers and adventurers, as well as the rulers, organizers, aristocrats, and the spawning of the Renaissance. He allowed that the Mediterranean races were superior in intellect to the Alpines and capable of producing artists, but their small, light-boned, long-skulled physiques, with feeble muscular development and swarthy complexions, resulted in a lack of stamina. The Alpine races he judged to be of round face and round skull, stocky and moderately short. They "have played an unimportant part in European culture," and had always been agricultural peasants.[34] Grant maintained that the Nordics were the only pure race and that race mixing led to physical and societal decline. He asserted that the southern Italians were descended from southern and eastern Mediterranean slaves and that they were volatile, lacked cohesion, had a political incapacity, and were treasonous. (Prescott Hall, a founder of the Immigration Restriction League and a writer for the *North American Review*, had already claimed that southern Italians were partly Negroid in 1912.) Grant further cautioned that "moral, intellectual, and spiritual attributes are as persistent as physical characters, and are transmitted unchanged from generation to generation."[35]

Kenneth Roberts, writing in the *Saturday Evening Post*, a popular periodical, called for the restriction of southern and eastern European immigrants, or white Americans would face "a hybrid race of good for nothing MONGRELS."[36] Such reasoning held dire consequences for those persons deemed to be undesirable and unworthy of American citizenship. Buttressed by such racialization, the US government and health agencies embarked upon a eugenics program intended to sterilize African Americans, southern and eastern European women, and any others deemed intellectually, physically, or morally deficient in the early twentieth century. The eugenics movement would take on even more dire results under Hitler in Germany.[37]

Ethnic Animosity

The Irish, who had achieved whiteness due to their ability to speak English and their early inclusion in the educational and political processes, further distinguished themselves from blacks and those groups still in a liminal state. The Irish often referred to Italians as "niggers." During the 1920s Irish and Italian communities in Buffalo and Mamaroneck, New York, engaged in what were characterized as "racial" battles that carried over into community social life. In Hoboken, New Jersey, Frank Sinatra's father became a professional boxer, using the alias Marty O'Brien. Sinatra's biographer noted that "Marty, like his son in later years, hated to be called 'a wop.'" Both father and son engaged in street battles over such ethnic slurs.[38]

In Catholic parishes headed by Irish or German clergy, blacks and Italians were assigned seats in the rear of the church. Presbyterians disagreed with all Catholics, claiming that "American ideals derived from the Protestant faith," but they were particularly harsh on Italians and Slavs whom, they believed, favored "Sunday as a day of pleasure, the idea of a socialist government, community property, and paganism in religion."[39]

In 1916 the authors of an article in the *American Journal of Sociology* rated a variety of ethnic and racial groups in such categories as physical vigor, intellectual ability, self-control, moral integrity, sympathy, cooperation, leadership, perseverance, efficiency, and aspiration. Ratings were based on popular opinions in which Italians and blacks scored the lowest. The study revealed that there had been little intermingling between those minorities who had presumably achieved whiteness with either Italians or blacks.[40]

Minorities who aspired to a level of acceptance and social capital faced daunting prohibitions. Suburban housing developers increasingly enacted restrictions aimed at anyone that the white middle-class residents deemed to be inferior. "One even excluded foreigners of the Dago class." In Erie County, Pennsylvania, the Lake Shore Club District "barred 'any person of Hungarian, Mexican, Greek, Armenian, Austrian, Italian, Russian . . . Polish, Slavish [*sic*] or Roumanian [*sic*] birth.'"[41] Other racial covenants specifically rejected anyone other than the "white or Caucasian race."[42] The definition of "white" differed by one's social class as well as by one's country of origin, and the vast majority of Italians remained mired in the working class. Sociologists' interviews with an Italian woman revealed the extent of such discrimination. Signora de Blasio of the Italian Industrial School stated that "the best workers at Tiffany's are Italians. The best designers among garment workers are Italians. I do not understand why Italians have been treated in this country as they have been. I go to a store and they say to me, 'Are you French?' I say 'No.' They say 'Spanish?' 'No, I am Italian.' And then there is immediate coldness and contempt."[43]

Labor Conflict

Like other ethnic and working-class Americans, wages and work issues roused the ire of Italians. Although the Irish, Germans, and Jews are generally accorded to be the leaders of the late-nineteenth- and early-twentieth-century labor movement, Italians, too, reacted to the harsh working conditions as union organizers and strike leaders opposed to exploitation. They took pride in their physical toil and took offense at slights to their honor.[44] Italians in the United States exhibited a growing class consciousness that crossed ethnic lines and became active and public participants in opposition to their perceived exploiters. Both men and women became leaders in the labor movement, and some lost their lives in the workers' cause.[45]

Even when Italian workers did not resort to the strike, they devised other more subtle means of exacting revenge. When a Boston employer cut wages by 10 percent, Italian laborers cut one inch off their shovels to give him his money's worth. In the Alabama steel mills a government study found "practically universal opinion among employers that South Italians are . . . the most inefficient of all races, whether immigrant or native." The employers evidently did not recognize the slow pace as a reactionary resentment to low wages.[46]

Albeit a great departure from southern Italian culture, Italians prevailed in the unions despite initial attempts to ostracize them from membership. In Boston and New York the longshoremen refused to work with Italians. Excluded by the xenophobic American Federation of Labor, some Italians turned to the more radical but inclusive Industrial Workers of the World, known as the Wobblies. Italians, in conjunction with the IWW, held leadership roles in the successful strikes against the Lawrence, Massachusetts, mills in 1912 that united approximately twenty-five thousand workers in a class struggle against their employers. In Chicago the Italians were able to dominate the laborers' union, but in the steel mills south of the city they allied with the Serbs to share power. Although Italians still held others as suspicious, the work conditions in the United States that led them to unite with other ethnic workers increasingly brought them in contact with the multicultural workforce in a common cause.[47]

Italian and Jewish women composed the majority of the needle-trades workers in New York, Philadelphia, Baltimore, and Chicago, and they held a prominent role in the International Ladies' Garment Workers' Union by 1910. They eventually accounted for 51 percent of the ILGWU membership. In the Endicott, New York, shoe factories Italian women composed 96 percent of the female workforce by 1925. The Endicott Company thwarted unionization by offering a corporate welfare program that coincided with traditional Italian family values by educating the women about maternal responsibilities, providing supervised playgrounds for the children of working mothers, and the option to buy company-built homes at cost. Home ownership, a primary goal of Italian families, provided one more step in the journey toward whiteness.[48]

Many employers and nativists perceived union actions as ingratitude on the part of workers and designed to destroy the fabric of the capitalist economic structure by radial revolutionaries. Given such exclusionary sentiments and practices, the persecution continued after World War I. Despite Italians' service in the American military during the conflict, they were still perceived as foreigners, criminals, and radicals. A nativist mob in West Frankfort, Illinois, estimated to number three to four thousand, attacked Sicilian miners on August 5, 1920. They accused the Sicilians of murdering two youths and vowed to drive "all foreigners" from the town. Over the next three days the Italians were dragged from their homes, beaten, stoned, and killed, and their houses were burned. It took fifteen infantry companies to restore order.[49]

The Red Scare that polarized America in the aftermath of the Russian Revolution further haunted Italians. Some Italians brought socialist, communist, and anarchist sympathies with them owing to the long-standing persecutions and exploitation in their homeland, and Italians in the United States were quick to unionize in the 1890s.[50]

As some Italians slowly moved toward a limited accommodation with the mainstream white culture, labor strife forestalled any wholesale acceptance. As Italians unionized and joined forces with other ethnic workers, a growing sense of a collective working-class identity transcended the parochial narrow-mindedness of family and village allegiances that had limited their worldview.[51] Italians learned to cooperate and coordinate with non-Italians to achieve their goals. That did not mean, however, that Italians forsook their familial pride, as evidenced by the case of Anthony Marchese. The Marchese family had migrated from Sicily to New Orleans, where someone had apparently Anglicized the family name to Mike. Anthony Mike joined the US Army during World War I and rose to the rank of sergeant. After the war he joined the local American Legion post, worked on the New Orleans transit system, and earned a commendation for heroism when he saved a young girl about to be run over by a streetcar. He paid his poll tax and voted consistently. He might have claimed the privileges of whiteness and melded into the mainstream society, but in 1922 he paid the considerable sum of ten dollars to a civil court in order to have his name changed back to Marchese. Family correspondence continued to be conducted in Italian over the next two decades.[52] Marchese had successfully integrated with the mainstream culture, but did so on his own terms.

The settler mentality of Marchese and like-minded immigrants who chose to stay in the United States marked a bifurcation within the Italian communities. Settlers stood in opposition to the sojourners (*caffoni*) who intended to make money quickly and return to Italy.

Settlers felt that the *caffoni* represented a poor image that reflected upon all Italians.[53]

Setbacks to Acceptance

By 1915 a second generation of Italians outnumbered their immigrant parents. Brought up in the United States, subjected to American schooling, and less exposed to the Old World, they began to assimilate or adapt the mainstream values. These Italian-Americans skirted two cultures, integrating with the mainstream culture at school and in public spaces, but retaining traditional practices at home. Assimilationist progress faced a major hurdle soon after World War I, as the contentious and controversial case of Sacco and Vanzetti continued to question Italian loyalty to their new home country throughout the 1920s. In 1920 a shoe company paymaster and security guard were murdered and the payroll stolen in Massachusetts. Two Italian anarchists, Nicola Sacco, a shoemaker, and Bartolomeo Vanzetti, a fish peddler, were accused of the crime. In a clearly biased trial in 1921, with largely circumstantial evidence, (especially in the case of Vanzetti), both men were convicted and sentenced to death. The verdict resulted in widespread hostile reaction within the working-class labor movement. In the United States and abroad, the defendants were widely viewed as pawns, tried as much for their political views as any crime during the Red Scare. American government offices were bombed in Paris, Lisbon, Rio de Janeiro, Zurich, and Marseilles. During the six years that followed, both men were confined to prison, while an international protest and clemency movement united both radical and conservative Italians in the United States and abroad. In Italy "support for the two men was strong . . . , where supporters appealed to the men's status as 'fellow countrymen' and argued that their conviction was due to widespread prejudice against Italians in the United States." The trial and long incarceration galvanized a greater Italian identity as Italians in the United States raised funds for their defense, albeit in vain. When both men were electrocuted in 1927, hordes of supporters protested not only in the United States, but in Germany, France, England, Mexico, Argentina, Uruguay, and Australia. Wherever sizable numbers of Italians resided, Sacco and Vanzetti became martyrs.[54]

The image of Italians as anarchists combined with their characterization as gangsters to cast a continual negative light throughout the decade. Although Irish, Jewish, and even Chinese gangs proliferated in the inner cities, the Italian secret societies, known as the "Black Hand," the Camorra, and the Mafia, gained the greatest notoriety. The American media had portrayed the Italians as criminals since the 1891 lynching in New Orleans. The US Congress authorized a commission to study the causes and effects of immigration in 1907. After years of study the resultant Dillingham Report of 1911 amounted to forty-one volumes of data and statistics, much of it unfavorable to southern and eastern European groups. It contended that "certain kinds of criminality are inherent in the Italian race."[55] In Chicago police routinely raided the Little Italy neighborhood to round up suspects when a crime was committed, only to release their prisoners when they could not substantiate any charges.[56] Cultural differences added to the Italians' confusion. Police who did not understand the Sicilian concept of family honor wondered why the brother of a slain Italian nursed the wounded murderer back to health in his own home, only to kill him in revenge. Likewise, the father of a New Jersey girl felt equally dismayed after police arrested him for killing the sixteen-year-old boy who had seduced her. The father considered his reactions a just reprisal rather than a crime. Such calamities seemingly tainted all Italians with the violent gangster stereotype.[57] Gangsters, and the concept of the Mafia, held a particular familiarity for Italians despite the negative connotations. In Italy the Mafia served as a clandestine form of government. "The Mafia performed those functions that corrupt legitimate authorities were unwilling or powerless to carry out, and thus, bandits policed bandits, dished out justice, and kept a semblance of order. In time, these 'protectors' would themselves become instruments of injustice and they, too, would exploit the contadini."[58]

For some Italians, oppressed by a white Anglo-Saxon hierarchy that largely excluded them from its wealth and power structure, Al Capone represented a hero. Like the outlaws of the Old West or John Dillinger, the elusive bank robber of the Depression era, the gangster invoked his own code of honor and protected his territory. He made his money through brains and brawn, among the values that the Italians understood well. For some Italian youths, gangs such as Capone's substituted for the family bond. By 1925 the sociologists at the University of Chicago admitted that "gangs have exercised considerably greater influence in forming the character of the boys . . . than has the church, the school, or any other communal agency."[59] Gangs from the Little Sicily neighborhood of that city engaged in auto theft, assault, stealing from the wealthy residents of the nearby Gold Coast district, and gambling.[60]

Fred Gardaphe, scholar and author, claimed that "the Italian-American gangster makes a perfect 'other' by virtue of his connection with a tribal culture that does not play the game of capitalism according to the rule of law or the Protestant work ethic."[61] For the exploited worker, "The gangster became the symbol of the transformation of the Italian-American male from worker to power broker."[62] Elliott Gorn, historian and biographer of Dillinger, draws a clear distinction, however, between the gangster and the outlaw. The former is dark and ethnic, engaged in illegal activities, whereas the latter is native born and "assaults legitimate institutions."[63] Outlaws practiced elusion, whereas gangsters mingled with and employed friends and neighbors. Gangsters even shared their largesse with the community at times. In New York they sponsored community baseball teams and staked their bets on Italian teams against those of the Irish, Germans, and Poles. In Chicago they provided neighborhood recreation in a basement pool hall where youth bet on dice games and horse races. They backed ethnic boxers and might make or break careers. For the gangsters and gamblers, sport coincided with their illicit activities. Some Italians considered countrymen who became policemen to be traitors up until the advent of World War II.[64]

Nativism

The stereotypes of Italians as gangsters and anarchists, unwilling or unable to assimilate, made them easy targets for nativists, who acted upon the admonitions and recriminations of cultural doomsayers. In the rural areas the rise of the Ku Klux Klan during the World War I era posed a threat. The KKK opposed Italian immigrants and Catholics in general, burning crosses in the largely Italian village of Canastota, New York. In the South the White Farmers Association refused membership to Italians, blacks, and Asians, and yet another Sicilian lynching occurred in Johnstown, Illinois, in 1915. Six Italians were hung in Louisiana in 1924 after a trial run by a judge who was a KKK member. More than twenty neighborhood chapters of the KKK, with more than forty thousand members, operated in Chicago. In the cities Italians also faced the wrath of white Protestants as well as other ethnics, particularly the Irish, who meant to solidify their own claim to whiteness. In 1925 the Italian American National Union complained of an "Italophobia," pointing to widespread discrimination and imagining that the prohibition on alcohol was aimed at Italians. Others described "intense conflict" between Catholics and Protestants, fighting among youths, as well as the exclusion of Italians from social clubs. In response, Italian youths formed gangs for their own protection.[65]

A 1928 survey of the racial attitudes of native-born middle-class Americans showed widespread discrimination against Italians. The results indicated that only 15 percent would accept Italians as marriage partners, about 25 percent would allow them as club members, less than 35 percent considered them as neighbors, and less than 55 percent wanted them as coworkers.[66] A proliferation of gangster movies in the late 1920s and early 1930s only reinforced the negative stereotypes of Italians.[67]

Some scholars have contended that Italians gained whiteness by virtue of naturalization, but citizenship in itself did not include acceptance within the American mainstream society. African Americans had gained civil rights by 1868 with the ratification of the Fourteenth

Amendment to the Constitution, but an overwhelming abundance of evidence, such as Jim Crow laws and social ostracism, points to their social exclusion. Italians faced similar, if not as pervasive, prohibitions.[68] In 1922 an Alabama judge acquitted Jim Rollins, a black man, of miscegenation charges when he determined that the Sicilian women with whom he cohabited was as dark as Rollins, and therefore inconclusively white.[69] In 1924 even W. E. B. Du Bois, one of the founders of the National Association for the Advancement of Colored People (NAACP), stipulated that "now everybody knows that a black man is inferior to a white man (except, of course, Jews, Italians, and Slavs)."[70] Even in the working-class neighborhoods of South Chicago's steelworkers, "community life was filled with gang fights, sporting events that broke into ethnic conflict, and Irish churches that kept out Italians. It was not surprising to hear a native-born East Side man complain 'It is bad enough to work with Dagoes. I wouldn't think of living next to them.'"[71] Racism, nativism, and the Red Scare combined to elicit generalized opinions that particular groups, Italians among them, were not welcome in America.

In 1916 John Burnett, chairman of the US House of Representatives Committee on Immigration, rationalized the intent to limit the Italian peasants by stating that "the north Italian is white, the south Italian is not white. . . . [T]he people in the south of Italy have mixed their blood with the people across the Mediterranean and they are not entirely white." The quota system, devised by a congressional committee chaired by Madison Grant, also included Congressman Albert Johnson, president of the Eugenic Research Association.[72] Psychologist Arthur Sweeney testified that Latins [Italians] were "'imbeciles' who possessed primitive brain structures 'scarcely superior' to that of the ox. . . . who think with their spinal cord rather than their brain," and he urged Congress to employ intelligence tests "to protect ourselves against the degenerate horde." The resultant computations limited Italian entries to 5,802 by 1929, a precipitous decline from earlier years.[73] Although athletes such as Brignolia, De Palma, Abbaticchio, and Bodie had won social acceptance, it was clear that such privileges did not yet extend to Italians as a whole.

Italian-American Culture

The reduction in the numbers of immigrants effectively impaired the flow that had sustained the European immigrant cultures in the United States. Ethnic communities gradually eroded as second-generation youth, educated in the American schools, turned to English outside the home and adopted new lifestyles and interests, particularly the popular culture of music, movies, and sport. Such transitions were already evident in the Italian-American youth who turned to sport in the nineteenth century. In the taverns even older Italians began to eschew their favored wine for beer and hard liquor. Others operated on the fringes of popular culture in roles that eased the transition to the dominant WASP culture.[74]

By the 1920s the nickelodeons of the early twentieth century had been transformed into palatial movie palaces and had become the favorite form of recreation for youths. Programs featured American cowboys, heroes overcoming villains, and sports vignettes on newsreels, educating Italian men about the aggressive, martial masculinity of American culture. A young Italian remarked that "the older Italians used to go to these movies and when the good guys were chasing the bad guys in Italian—they'd say—'getem'—'catchem'—out loud in the theater."[75] The lure of the cinema and its adventurous portrayals transcended racial, ethnic, generational, and class lines, as moviegoers sought vicarious experiences in the new medium.

Jimmy Durante, born in Brooklyn to Italian-American parents in 1893, exemplified the continued transition of the Italian to an Italian-American via popular culture. He emerged as a piano player of ragtime music around 1911 in New York and evolved into a jazz musician by 1920. He interspersed his music with comedy routines that eventually gained him roles in Hollywood movies by the 1930s. His self-deprecating humor, which mocked his physical appearance and incorporated elements of the Italian-American vernacular, continued to play well into the television era.[76]

Durante's introduction to jazz emanated from the migration of New Orleans musicians, led by Italian Nick Oliva, to Chicago and

New York in 1917. In the multicultural context of New Orleans, blacks and Italians, neither possessing much social capital, combined their talents, often performing on the street corners, and in the bars and brothels, to produce a new musical genre. Nick La Rocca, a member of the Original Dixieland Jazz Band, produced some of the earliest jazz recordings and led a succession of Italian jazz artists from New Orleans such as Tony Sbarbaro, Freddie and Frank Assunto, Joseph Davilla, Irving Fazola, Louis and Leon Prima, Joseph "Sharkey" Bonana, Frank Federico, Tony Almerico, Sam Butera, Joseph "Wingy" Mannone, and Phil Zito. In Chicago Jimmy Petrillo led the Chicago Federation of Musicians by 1929. Like African Americans, Italians found in both sport and music a means by which they might entertain whites and be paid handsomely for their efforts in enterprises that did not upset the prevailing power structure.[77]

By the 1920s it had become fashionable for upper-class Anglos to go "slumming" for exotic interracial adventures in the black and tan cabarets of New York and Chicago, many of them run by Italian proprietors. Sport and music often mixed, as basketball games served as preludes or intermissions for dance bands. In Harlem Rocky Alvalony, an Italian immigrant owner of the Kosy Korner Club, sponsored a black baseball team. For young Italian males the music halls presented opportunities for social interactions unavailable within the confines of their own circumscribed ethnic culture. Whereas neighborhood Italian girls were well guarded by their families, one Italian youth reported that "he can date a Polish girl and have a 'red hot' time." Young Italian women, too, began to distance themselves from their parents' lifestyles and overbearing supervision by frequenting public dance halls, where they encountered young men from other ethnic groups and extended their activities beyond the home.[78]

Lou Costello (Cristillo), born in 1906, first earned notice as a star baseball and basketball player in New Jersey, which earned him an athletic scholarship to an elite military school in New York. Costello's interests and skills, however, were expressed in his physicality. He dropped out of school to pursue a career as a boxer and then turned to Hollywood, where he assumed the role of a stuntman. He gained greater fame as a vaudevillian and media star on the radio and in movies as part of the (Bud) Abbott and Costello comedy team. His basketball skills were prominently displayed in the 1945 movie *Here Come the Co-eds*. Thereafter, Italian musicians, singers, and actors proliferated in urban nightclubs and dance halls, reaching a prolonged crescendo with the appearances of Frank Sinatra, Dean Martin (Dino Crocetti), Perry Como, Tony Bennett (Benedetto), Vic Damone, Ann Bancroft (Anna Italiano), and Liza Minelli. By that time second- and third-generation Italians had long overcome their difficulties with the English language.[79] The popularity of English usage among the entertainers of the second generation signaled greater inclusion and integration and served as a badge of Americanization.

The Anglicization of Italian names, however, pointed to the continued denigration of Italian culture and a less than wholesale acceptance. Even in the latter decades of the twentieth century, boxer-turned-actor Rocky Graziano complained that "there's one thing that bugs Dean [Martin] and Frank [Sinatra] and me, and all my Italian buddies in and out of show business, and that's putting Italians down, or making cracks about us being part of the Mafia because we got some money and a [*sic*] Italian name."[80]

Sport as an Assimilative Factor

Some ethnic groups, such as the Germans, brought a well-developed sporting culture, such as the Turnvereine movement, when they migrated to America. Like the German turners, the Czech sokols and Polish falcons practiced a nationalistic form of gymnastics that reinforced their European languages, literature, and identities. Italian peasants, in contrast, brought little in the way of established sporting practices, but sport came more easily than some other aspects of WASP culture to Italian youth familiar with physical labor and the use of their bodies. Increasingly exposed to American sports in the public schools, parks, and playgrounds, boys and girls readily adopted activities that allowed for greater integration without violating the norms of their residual Italian culture. By the 1920s the Italo-American

Union sponsored baseball, basketball, and football teams, and Catholic parishes fielded a variety of athletic teams that brought greater inclusion in the American mainstream. That process accelerated with the establishment of the Catholic Youth Organization in Chicago in 1930, which soon reached national and international proportions in its athletic endeavors. Three of the eight members of the 1936 Olympic boxing team, including Andy Scrivani, had been CYO boxers, and Louis Laurie (Lauria) brought home a bronze medal. Such public displays of whiteness countered the perceptions of Italians as gangsters and greatly aided their gradual inclusion, acceptance, and identity as Americans.[81]

Within the field of sport Italians competed not only with native-born Americans, but also with other ethnics in pursuit of recognition, status, and a measure of power. Pierre Bourdieu's concept of a field envisioned a competitive social arena in which groups had both vertical and horizontal dimensions. On the vertical plane Italians contended with the Anglos and upper classes that held power and influence. On the horizontal plane they vied with multiple other ethnic and working-class groups for jobs, resources, and social acceptance. Unlike the Jews who placed an emphasis on education, and the Irish, who spoke English and gained access to political power, for the Italians sport and popular culture afforded a means other than crime to achieve recognition. The media attention given to athletes in the 1920s created a transformative space and a celebrity culture. American newspapers identified athletes as "Italians" rather than the regional identities preferred by their parents. As participants in American sport forms, the athletes became more acceptable to the mainstream society.[82]

Many second-generation Italian youth still adhered to their parents' disdain for education, which was rooted in the historical past, as the underclass traditionally perceived educated administrators or clerics as tools of the oppressive government in Italy. Only 5 percent of southern Italian children in Chicago attended public schools beyond the sixth grade in 1910, and only 1 percent went on to high school. By 1930 only 11 percent of Italians finished high school. Christopher "Battling" Battalino (Battaglia), featherweight boxing champion from

1929 to 1932, left school after the fifth grade, claiming that "I never cared to go to school. . . . I loved to fight, that's all."[83] Baseball great Yogi Berra quit after the eighth grade, noting that "I had never been able to see any sense in my going to school."[84] A resident of the Monte Carmelo neighborhood in the Bronx explained that "as far as schools were concerned, they were glorified jails. . . . [T]he principal [remonstrated] as though we had no possibility of being anything other than carpenters, street diggers, working in factories. . . . They never played up doctors or lawyers or encouraged aspirations to be one of those. No, we were always projected to be nothing more than laborers."[85] Without the benefit of education, southern Italians and Sicilians had developed a particular doxa over the centuries that revolved around their physicality, which regulated social practices. Humor, for example, might revolve around bodily functions or slapstick forms of comedy. Physical labor earned their sustenance, whereas physical power might generate a level of respect, honor, and self-esteem, that is, a means to gaining social capital.[86]

Within the contested field of sports, young Italian women even challenged their prescribed gender roles. In a clear departure from Italian lifestyles, Maud Nelson (Clementine Brida) also learned and loved to play baseball. By 1897, at the age of sixteen, she began pitching for the Boston Bloomer Girls. She pitched and played third base for a number of barnstorming teams for twenty-five years, playing with and against male teams from coast to coast. In 1911 she became manager and co-owner of her own Chicago-based team. Upon her death her second husband returned to Italy, but the attraction of American sports had turned a young Italian girl into an athletic entrepreneur, which would have been an impossibility in Italy.[87]

Nelson's entrepreneurial ventures proved to be more than the efforts of an isolated iconoclast, for she spawned social change over the next generation of young women. In 1929 sports promoter Dick Jess formed a semipro team centered around Josephine Parodi, who assumed the moniker of Josie Caruso, possibly to capitalize on the fame of Enrico Caruso, the famed opera star. The team drew large crowds to its games, and Parodi enjoyed some celebrity in newsreels until her marriage in 1931, when she returned to a more traditional domestic life. Other women stretched the gender boundaries thereafter. Margaret Gisolo learned to play baseball with her brother, a semipro and Minor League player. She starred at second base for the Blanford, Indiana, town team in the 1928 American Legion baseball tournament. Her winning hit in a state championship series prompted a protest by males, but a tribunal that included Kenesaw Mountain Landis, the commissioner of baseball, supported Gisolo's team. The case drew national attention, made Gisolo a celebrity, and spurred other girls to take up the game. When the American Legion banned girls from its competitions the next year, Maud Nelson hired Gisolo for her barnstorming teams during the 1930s. After Gisolo used her ball-playing salary to gain a college education, she then became a lieutenant commander in the Navy WAVES during World War II. Gisolo later became a college coach, inspiring women's teams through the Title IX era. Italian women had been among the pioneers of women's sport in America, challenging the hegemonic perceptions of gender roles and female physical abilities, while the Federazione Medici Sportivi (official sport medicine federation) in Italy warned in 1930 that "Italian women were first and foremost Italians and should, therefore, avoid any 'Americanization'" regarding their sport participation.[88]

The early professional players who encroached upon the enclaves of power in the sports world had to endure the animosity of more established groups. Babe Pinelli (Rinaldo Paolinelli) broke into the National League with Cincinnati in 1922 and later became a Major League umpire, but he bemoaned "a lot of strife in both the minor and major leagues."[89] The *New York Times* verified that "the fans behind third base took much delight in riding Pinelli before the game, but the little Italian had them cheering him before the game ended. He did some fancy fielding."[90] He enjoyed greater support from *La Falce*, the Italian newspaper in Cincinnati, and an Italian fan club known as the Pinelli Rooters, but Pinelli stated that "from 1922 to 1925 I was the only Italian in the National League. I'd taken a riding from the bench jockeys and I'd had to keep my fist cocked."[91] Such taunting led to a fight with Bob Smith of the Boston Braves. Pinelli insisted that "the riding he had to take because of it [being Italian] equals or surpasses anything dished out to the first Negro players." Such reactions illustrate the Italian reliance on physicality, but Pinelli learned to be more judicious as an umpire. In both roles as a player and an umpire he confronted the established Irish and Germans who had long dominated the playing fields. Nativist fans and players presented a more troublesome obstacle for Italians. In that era some players held membership in the Ku Klux Klan.[92] Prejudice still remained years later. When Don Mossi, an Italian-American, took the field for the Minor League team in Tulsa in 1953, a fan turned to his wife and exclaimed, "Good God, Maude, they got three niggers now."[93]

The growing number of Italians in professional baseball provided greater visibility of the assimilation process and greater social mobility for gifted athletes. Tony Lazzeri became a star second baseman with the New York Yankees in the 1920s, the golden age of sport. The New York media provided ready recognition to such symbols of ethnic pride during the era. Frank Graham, a New York sportswriter, admitted that "[Lazzeri] was almost as big a drawing card as Ruth. Italian societies in New York, Boston, Detroit, almost everywhere the Yankees played, held banquets in his honor and showered him with gifts." September 8, 1927, was designated as Lazzeri Day at Yankee Stadium, and more than a thousand attended a banquet in his honor, sponsored by Italian-Americans. By 1933 *Who's Who in Major League Baseball* asserted that Tony Cuccinello had become the "hero of the Brooklyn fans."[94]

References to Italian stars, although sometimes derogatorily reinforcing stereotypes, fostered a greater awareness of Italian presence and success in the American national game. Oscar Melillo got his start on the International Harvester Company team in Chicago, but as a second baseman for the St. Louis Browns he set a new record for fielding average in 1933. Gus Mancuso, a catcher for the New York Giants, along with Frank Crosetti, the Yankees' shortstop, and the inimitable Joe DiMaggio further established Italian credibility among baseball fans. By the 1930s so many Italians appeared in Major League Baseball that Italian-American newspapers started naming all-Italian all-star teams. A sports reporter for the *Corriere d'America* proudly informed his readers that "all in all the Italian boys have certainly made the grade in baseball and their prowess on the diamond is known to all sports lovers."[95] Meanwhile, the typical Italian construction laborer earned $294 in 1935 (about 60 percent of the proposed minimum wage that year) working for a private contractor and $768 working for the federal government. Joe DiMaggio made $6,500 the year before playing baseball. Italian boys increasingly aspired to such wealth and recognition.[96]

Even for the multitudes who did not earn a paycheck as professional baseball players, the game represented a badge of Americanism. Oral histories attest to the love of the game. As the Depression set in, an Italian mother of a fourteen-year-old lamented, "Nick no wanta work. He big man, fourteen and wanta play ball all the day. Father say, 'You go today and work in restaurant with your uncle.' . . . He make faces, cusses, laughs, and runs out to play ball. . . . He very bad boy. . . . He no wants work. . . . He like nothing but ball."[97] In New York Angelo Rucci endured the insults and fights at school because of his ethnicity, yet he endured to play baseball, football, and run track on the school teams to become "American." As a youth Angelo Vacca learned to play baseball when his father bought equipment for that purpose, as baseball presented a clear sign of integration in the mainstream culture. In Chicago Anthony Sorrentino faced similar issues with antagonistic Anglos at school. Baseball provided some respite, but he lamented that the injurious treatment affected both him and his sister long afterward.[98] The adoption of American sport forms brought a greater measure of integration and inclusion, but did not guarantee acceptance for the working classes, who still had to contend with ethnic rivalries.

As with baseball, Italian boys were introduced to football early in the assimilation process. Throughout the late nineteenth and early twentieth centuries, football had a particular social cachet, as it was associated with colleges and high schools, symbols of the educated upper classes. A sport club in the Italian colony in New York City offered American football as early as 1906, and Italian high school stars appeared on the New Orleans gridirons that same year. Paul Gallico, the son of immigrants and educated at Columbia University, became one of the famed sportswriters who spawned the golden age. He played football as a youth, but extolled the values of sport for much of his career. Good athletes soon learned that they could make more money on a multitude of professional and semipro teams than in industrial labor long before the advent of the American Professional Football Association (now the National Football League, or NFL) in 1920. Carl "Squash" Cardarelli, a center for the Akron, Ohio, high school football team, soon joined the local pro contingent. Murray Battaglia and Art Pascolini were among other pioneers of the early pro circuit with the Evanston North Ends, a Chicago suburban team in the World War I era. Performance on the football field sometimes garnered notice and advantage elsewhere. Historian Keith McClellan claimed that "Battaglia went from being a peddler's son to foreman for the Bowman Milk Company, at least in part because of the leadership skills he developed on the football field."[99] Another early pro player, Lou Little (Luigi Piccolo), a World War I veteran, assumed the head coaching duties at Georgetown University in 1924 before moving to Columbia University in 1930, where he produced the 1934 Rose Bowl winner en route to a Hall of Fame career.[100] Little was among the first Italian-Americans to use his sports acumen to achieve a leadership role with administrative and management responsibilities.

While the semipro players enjoyed local celebrity, the Italian college stars became nationally recognized, courtesy of the English-and Italian-language newspapers, as well as the burgeoning radio networks that broadcast the games. Radio, and later television, increased and enhanced the burgeoning attachment to the "imagined communities" of fans who developed loyalties to individual players, teams, or communities that led to further inclusion in the mainstream culture and its particular sport forms.[101]

In 1922 Elmer Mitchell, a University of Michigan professor, wrote an article, "Racial Traits in Athletics," in which he claimed that "the Italian was better fitted for games of quickness, dexterity, and skill, rather than of rugged strength. He lacked self-discipline and was too fiery and impulsive of feeling for contact sports. . . . Italians' tendency to the extreme of elation, or to the opposite extreme of despondency, made them fearless, daring, and reckless but also more easily stampeded into a rout if beaten."[102] By the end of the decade, Italian players had largely dispelled such notions.

In 1930 John Billi, a reporter for *Il Progresso Italo-American*, stated that "experts claim that Notre Dame University has the greatest backfield of the American gridiron. . . . Two Italians are the pivots of that backfield, the formidable fullback [Joe Savoldi], and Frank Carideo, the famous quarterback." Even famed coach Knute Rockne conceded that the Carideo-Savoldi backfield was the best that he ever had. Carideo won All-American honors in 1929 and 1930, leading Notre Dame to two undefeated seasons and two national championships. Billi went on to list a host of Italians starring on other college teams throughout the country. By 1932 he counted 56 Italian players and named an Italian all-star team. Within a few years Billi could pick his all stars from at least 115 Italian players on college teams.[103]

In contrast to the elitism of early college teams, by the 1920s football coaches recruited talent rather than ethnicity or social class in their quest to win. In the northern schools, even African American stars were awarded athletic scholarships. Many of the Italians played for Catholic colleges, and contests with secular rivals gradually dismantled religious barriers, as Catholic teams, most conspicuously Notre Dame, scheduled secular institutions in the quest for national glory. Sport, in that sense, proved more inclusionary in its incorporation of Italians and Catholics than other spheres of American life, and sport provided one means for Italian athletes to gain a college education.

Angelo Enrico "Hank" Luisetti, the son of Italian immigrants, won a scholarship to the elite Stanford University, after his high school basketball team won the San Francisco city championship. At Stanford Luisetti won All-American and Player of the Year honors during the 1930s, as he became the first collegian to ever score fifty points in a single game. In an era when the two-handed set shot was the norm, Luisetti revolutionized the game with his running, jumping one-handed attempts. His innovative approach fostered a transition from a more static game to one played off the floor and in the air with an emphasis on greater individualism. Youthful emulators soon adopted his style, modernizing and changing the nature of the game. Sam Trombatore followed Luisetti with innovative ball handling at Loyola University of New Orleans, where he was the second-highest scorer in the country in 1943 before joining the US infantry.[104]

In the inner cities impoverished youth who had little hope and perhaps little interest in attending college formed neighborhood teams, often sponsored by local businessmen or politicians, who sought their support. In Chicago one study found that twenty-two chartered athletic clubs were all involved in politics. The clubs numbered fifteen to three hundred members, and they worked for "the politician who promises the most."[105] Such involvement further incorporated the second generation within the mainstream political culture.

Italian teams often battled ethnic rivals, transferring school and workplace rivalries to the athletic fields in some cases. Such altercations transferred animosities to regulated contests within the sphere of organized sporting practices rather than the gang fights of the streets. The Italo-American National Union sponsored baseball, football, and basketball teams by the 1920s and its own boxing and softball tournaments in the 1930s. It made its intentions clear. "Our youth movement will give the boys and girls of Italian descent the opportunity to become known in the competitive sports field, which is rich with fame and fortune."[106] In such contexts athletic stars might replace gangsters as community heroes. In the Bloomfield area of Pittsburgh, Martin "Hooks" Donatucci's athletic fame spanned generations. "In a neighborhood that reveres athletes, Hooks is known as one of the greatest athletes that Bloomfield ever produced." The son of immigrants from Abruzzi brought pride to the community with his athletic prowess, and historians concluded that "Bloomfield's proud athletic past looms large in the community's consciousness, making the athletic field nearly as much of a unifying symbol as Immaculate Conception Church."[107]

Sports teams even united disparate ethnic and religious groups previously at odds. In Chicago the Wizard Arrows club emanated from a multicultural neighborhood that spanned the Lincoln Park and Lakeview districts, a transitional area that brought Italians together with a variety of other ethnics as the former residents of Little Sicily spilled into a previously German area. Its teams resembled the American melting pot envisioned by earlier sociologists and included Germans, Italians, Poles, Irish, Jews, and Greeks. Like many of the more than one thousand Chicago gangs studied by University of Chicago sociologist Frederic Thrasher, it was sponsored by a local politician and merchants, who equipped the men's baseball, football, and women's softball team in uniforms in return for expected patronage. The club united a disparate group of second-generation ethnics in a common pursuit that elicited local community pride. Two of its members became city billiards champions, while the football team had been unscored upon in thirty-four straight games as of 1936. Some members earned cash as boxers in club fights during the Depression, whereas several community residents won national boxing honors.[108]

Similar clubs in Italian neighborhoods implemented sport as a means to endure the Depression, earning money through dances as fund-raisers, softball leagues sponsored by local bookmakers or tavern owners, and gambling operations. Nick Zaranti stated that every precinct in the largely Italian suburb of Chicago Heights sponsored a softball team, and they played every night. Typical stakes on athletic contests amounted to twenty-five dollars, but larger bets reached three thousand dollars on occasion. Mario Bruno claimed that he once won sixteen hundred dollars on one game when the local bank would not give him a one-hundred-dollar mortgage on a paid-up home. Bruno parlayed his athletic skills and organizational abilities into political office in a Chicago suburb.[109]

Such community athletic clubs distanced their members from their parents' generation psychologically and ideologically. "When Chicago's working class youth were not socializing in movie houses, they could be found at their neighborhood clubs. . . . [Y]oung people built their social lives around clubs . . . away from parental eyes and ears, club members played cards, held 'socials,' and planned sports contests and annual dances."[110] Extensive betting on ball games and horse races provided expendable income for winners. One Chicago club reported winning more than a hundred dollars on a football game, while another in an Italian neighborhood claimed that "we played ball for money only" against black teams and other area gangs.[111]

Unlike their parents, second-generation Italians, bereft of European memories, adopted new means of coping with their liminal identities. For many unemployed people, sport more so than work allowed for greater, if temporary, socioeconomic gain and greater self-esteem. Aspirations to bourgeois status seemed irrelevant and out of reach during the Depression. Life proved hard and too often short, and many sought immediate gratification, a lifestyle popularized by the hedonism of the 1920s and the gangsters of the interwar era. The emphasis on the body as a source of pleasure and the means to social as well as economic capital continued to reinforce the class differences with the middle-class Anglo culture for most Italians.[112]

A few Italians managed to bridge the gulf between the proletarian and the elite sports, particularly in the sport of golf. In a sport completely alien to working-class Italians, youths offered their labor as caddies for the wealthier patrons of the golf links. Bruno Muzzacavallo of Chicago earned one dollar, which he dutifully turned over to his mother. Caddies not only learned the game, but were generally allowed to play during slack periods. Fred Ebetino grew up in Connecticut across from a golf course, where he became a caddy and a professional by the age of nineteen. Anthony Corica reached the professional ranks in a similar fashion. Johnny Revolta won the 1935 Professional Golfers' Association championship as well as the Western Open. Tony Manero had won the PGA Tournament in 1936. Both represented the United States on the Ryder Cup team (an international match versus British golfers) in 1937. Vic Ghezzi, the son of Italian immigrants, twice won the New Jersey caddy championship and played on the 1939 and 1941 Ryder Cup teams. Ghezzi enjoyed eighteen years on the pro golf tour, but the most successful was Gene Sarazen (Eugenio Saraceni), a dominant figure in the game for a half century as a player and promoter. Sarazen, too, learned the game as a working-class caddy, but proved good enough despite his diminutive size (five foot five, 145 pounds) to win both the US Open and the PGA Tournament in 1922 at the age of twenty. His fame reached such proportions that he was invited to play golf with President Warren Harding. Sarazen competed on six Ryder Cup teams and was the first player to achieve the modern Grand Slam (winner of all four major tournaments). As a member of the US national team in the international Ryder Cup play, Sarazen earned even greater recognition for Italians and symbolic capital as an American.[113]

Despite such excursions into the upper class, Italians won their greatest recognition in the sport of boxing. A parade of Italians followed the Irish and then the Jews as boxing champions after the turn of the twentieth century. John Sugden explained the symbiotic relationship between boxing and poverty, in which the latter feeds the former. Only the poor are willing to put their bodies on the line for the meager rewards of such punishment. Other ethnic groups (with perhaps the exception of the Irish) eschewed boxing as they gained greater socioeconomic status. Italians, however, persisted throughout the remainder of the century, contesting with blacks and Hispanics for the spoils of the ring. Despite a litany of Italian fighters (many fighting under Irish aliases) throughout the 1920s, the first Italian of magnitude among the heavyweight ranks hailed from South America. Luis Angel Firpo, the son of Italian immigrants to Argentina, burst upon the American boxing scene in spectacular fashion. His heavyweight world championship bout with Jack Dempsey in 1923 is still considered among the most thrilling boxing matches of all time and featured eleven knockdowns in only two rounds. In an era of open nativism, sportswriters characterized Firpo in racialist terms. A supposed psychological study claimed "the man is a combination of a Patagonian giant and a Genoese wild man. Like his progenitors, who were some of the most famous of Italian vendettists, he has the ability to curb his strength and his passions and disguise his feelings until the proper moment for action is arrived. . . . He is absolutely cold blooded."[114]

When Firpo fell in defeat, a journalist stated: "If Luis Angel Firpo had the brain power in proportion to his tremendous strength, there is no denying that he and not Jack Dempsey would be world's heavyweight champion this morning. Endowed with the mentality which would enable him to think and think quickly in emergencies, Firpo could afford to be slow moving and cumbersome. But Firpo with all his great strength to give and take punishment, lacked that one essential—a fighting brain."[115]

Firpo gradually faded from the public eye, and although a host of Italian champions thereafter had greater success, Italians remained grounded in the pursuit of physical excellence. That perception was reinforced with the rise of Primo Carnera, a six-foot-seven, 270-pound mesomorphic Italian strongman–turned–boxer, who made two tours to the United States starting in 1930 and fought before packed houses. Italians in America flocked to greet the phenomenon. Upon his arrival in New York, police had to restore order when more than two thousand fans showed up outside Stillman's Gym, and young mothers brought their babies to watch him train. Hundreds more met him at the train station in Memphis, and Italians even provided him with a twelve-foot bed for his large frame at his Memphis hotel.[116] During the second tour in 1932, Carnera killed Ernie Schaaf in a Madison Square Garden bout, and when he beat Jack Sharkey for the championship in 1933, the Italians of Brockport, Massachusetts celebrated with bonfires. In Italy Carnera assumed the symbolic stature of Mussolini's fascist superman. "He returned to Rome to a hero's welcome and, on the eve of Italy's invasion of Abyssinia, was feted by the Italian dictator as an icon of Italian prowess."[117] Boxing champion Carmen Basilio remembered that "I used to hear my father and all of his old Italian buddies talking about Primo Carnera all the time."[118] To Paul Gallico, a more fully assimilated Italian-American and one of New York's premier sportswriters, "His skin was brown and glistening and he invariably smelled of garlic." For Gallico, perhaps reinforcing his own sense of acquired whiteness, Carnera represented a "big, stupid Wop," whose victories were too often arranged by gangsters.[119] Carnera presented a more sinister image, however, when he toured an Italian orphanage in Pittsburgh, where he hailed young boys with the fascist salute and engaged in fascist songs.[120]

Media images of Carnera subjected him to the "gaze" of American viewers and can be read as cultural texts. Photos objectified and presented him as the gargantuan, deviant "other," one with criminal ties to gangsters and a fascist hero unworthy of Americanization.[121]

Mussolini and the Resurgence of Italian Culture

Carnera's reign and influence proved short-lived, but Mussolini proved a dilemma for Italian-Americans. For many he resurrected Italian pride, fostered a nationalistic Italian identity, and enhanced Italians' self-esteem. In 1933 Mussolini sent famed aviator Italo Balbo with twenty-four seaplanes in a spectacular show to the Chicago World's Fair to demonstrate Italian technological excellence and counteract the gangster image in America. There Balbo urged Italians to be proud Americans, but not to forget that they were also Italians, thus reinforcing the dilemma of cultural identity. An Italian-American girl, an antifascist, expressed her guarded admiration of Mussolini. "You have got to admit one thing, he enabled four million Italians in America to hold up their heads, and that is something. If you had been branded as undesirable by a quota law you would understand how much that means."[122] Paul Pisicano was more adulatory in his pronouncement that "Mussolini was a hero, a superhero. He made us feel special, especially the southerners, Sicilians, Calabrian. . . . We had the equivalent of your pep rallies for football teams." Thousands of Italian-Americans donated their gold wedding bands (one hundred thousand from New York, New Jersey, and New England) in a fundraising effort for the Italian conquest of Ethiopia in 1936 in the quest for a new Italian empire and a measure of global power. The extent of continuing ties to Italy and the pride fostered by Mussolini can be ascertained by Italian-Americans' support for the Ethiopian War: seven hundred thousand dollars from New York City, sixty-five thousand from Philadelphia, about forty thousand from San Francisco, and more than thirty-seven thousand from Providence, Rhode Island.[123]

Sport enabled Mussolini to demonstrate a newfound Italian masculinity in an era when the idea of national races still held prominence.

The United States, as well as European powers, such as Germany, and Asian ones, like Japan, utilized sport and the Olympic Games to demonstrate national and racial prowess and progress. Mussolini built sports facilities, established athletic and physical education programs, and promoted an aesthetic vision of Italian physical beauty that drew upon the splendor of ancient Rome. After Italy suffered setbacks in its African colonization efforts in the late nineteenth century, diminishing its bid for greater power and recognition in Europe, Mussolini resurrected the quest and invoked historical memories of the dominant Italian culture of past eras. He relished public displays of his own body and images of his athletic prowess. Italians gloried in their renaissance, and Carnera provided only the commencement of the resurgence.

Mussolini sent forty physical education instructors to the United States to learn Macfadden's system of physical training, diet, and hygiene in 1931. They would implement the methods upon their return to Italy as well as promote the American game of baseball. The dictator's grandiose plans for athletic supremacy included a 130,000-seat stadium and plans to host the 1940 Olympic Games. Italian-American newspapers recounted the successes of the ancestral homeland in athletic competitions, promoting popular Italian sports such as cycling, soccer, and auto racing. After Carnera's debut, numerous other Italian boxers appeared in New York to challenge the Americans, and in 1936 a combined Italian-Hungarian amateur boxing team won eight of the ten bouts in an international tournament. Italy placed second after the American delegation at the 1932 Olympics, as Italian men won in the fencing, cycling, and gymnastics events as well as the 1,500-meter run. *La Notizia* proclaimed Italy as the most dangerous rival to the United States in the Games of 1936 (Italy eventually finished third). In 1934 and again in 1938 Italy won the soccer World Cup. Italy hosted the tournament in 1934, easily defeating the American team 7–1. An American headline in Rome exclaimed that "Italy's Prestige Soared in '36 with [the] Ethiopian Conquest" and "Year 1 of the Empire Made Possible by Courage and Determination of Premier Benito Mussolini." In the largely illiterate oral culture of the southern Italians, public displays, including Mussolini's bombastic speeches, impressed the multitudes in Italy as well as in the United States. But as Mussolini's ideology departed from American democracy and his allegiance turned to Hitler's Germany, Italian-Americans were forced to make difficult choices.[124]

Body Culture

Since the late nineteenth century scientists, physicians, and educators had used anatomical measurements as a means to buttress their claims about physical superiority and racial differences. Eugen Sandow, the German strongman, represented the ideal mesomorphic male body, featured in vaudeville, public exhibitions, and postcards. At the 1893 World's Fair in Chicago, patrons viewed statues that displayed body symmetry and could have their own bodies measured against established norms.[125]

In the United States Italians also presented their bodies as a conduit to recognition and social mobility. By the 1920s "the ideal of a man changed to the physically fit, muscular body, so that dancers and athletes became favourite models."[126] Angelo Siciliano represented such an American success story as a contemporary parallel to Mussolini. Born in Calabria in 1893, he immigrated to New York with his mother after the turn of the century. Supposedly humiliated by a bully, he embarked on a mission to develop his body, later appearing as a Coney Island circus strongman. In 1921 he won Bernarr Macfadden's contest to find the "World's Most Beautiful Man." The following year he was judged to be "America's Most Perfectly Developed Man," which launched a mail-order body-building business based on exercises that did not require equipment. Siciliano changed his name to Charles Atlas and marketed his story through ads in comic books and the popular culture to sell more than four hundred thousand exercise programs by 1942. In the ads Atlas related how, as a "97 pound weakling," he had lost his girlfriend when a bully kicked sand in his face at the beach. After his physical self-improvement program, based on discipline and hard work, he avenged himself on the bully and won the girl back. The story combined elements of morality with physicality, as well as the values of diligence and work ethic portrayed on the road to success in America. Atlas's own feelings of inadequacy mirrored the plight of Italian-Americans. To them and to others so afflicted he sold the American dream of regeneration and a new form of robust masculinity, as he privately adhered to a traditional Italian lifestyle of domesticity, family life (a forty-seven-year marriage to Margaret Cassano), and frugality.[127]

Atlas served a particular symbolic function for Americans during the Depression. "The symbolism of the developed body can . . . be appropriated by a society or its government to reflect the prevailing national self-concept."[128] The public presentation of his body served as a performance of masculinity, an adherence to traditional Italian culture within a new American context. As Mussolini and Hitler presented images of their fascist supermen, Atlas served as an American counterpart, projecting strength in a period of economic depression.

Tony Sansone, born to Sicilian immigrants in New York City in 1905, followed a similar path to recognition and success based on Atlas's model. A sickly child, he used sport as a means to develop his body before adopting the exercise programs of Macfadden and Atlas. In 1923 he won a physique contest sponsored by Atlas and engaged on a modeling career for sculptors and photographers, known as the American Adonis. His body was presented as a work of art, and he progressed into brief careers as a ballet dancer and an actor, before settling on an entrepreneurial venture as the owner of three gyms.[129] For such men the body became a form of social capital, which provided access to the mainstream economic community. More important for Italians in general, in an era when scientific racialism emphasized the superiority of social Darwinian bodies, Siciliano and Sansone were acknowledged as the most fit and most aesthetic of American men. They legitimated Italian bodies as ideal physical specimens. Both men were depicted not only as strong and powerful, but also as graceful and elegant, the healthy ideal transformed by the modern American culture and an antidote to the fascist supermen of Hitler and Mussolini.[130]

The international competitions for superiority were played out in the Olympics, and numerous Italian-Americans represented the United States at the 1936 Games. They represented an American identity, less burdened by the dilemmas faced by their parents. In addition to the boxers, Connie Carrucio scored the most points for the women's gymnastics team and returned to win a bronze team medal in 1948. Archie San Romani nearly won a medal as a miler for the track team, and Tony Terlazzo captured the gold medal as a weight lifter in the featherweight class. Italians would form the core of the York Barbell Club that represented the United States in international competition for decades thereafter. Owner-coach Bob Hoffman paid his employees–club members ten dollars per week during the Depression to work in his oil-burner plant, with bonuses for setting American or world weight-lifting records. "Anthony Terlazzo, Joe Fiorito, Anthony Fiorito, Gus Modica, Angelo Taormine, Harry Thomasillo, and others are the Sicilian members. These Sicilians are small but mighty and have accounted for nine national championships in meteoric careers." In 1948 Joe De Pietro won the Olympic bantamweight division, and Chuck Vinci did the same in 1960 at Rome, a fitting location for the Italian-American saga. Such public demonstrations of physicality indicated that Italians measured up to the masculine ideals, as the prowess of the lower classes came to represent a traditional dimension of masculinity in an industrialized world.[131]

Whereas the appeal inherent in the physical manifestations of Siciliano and Sansone crossed ethnic, class, and gender lines, the attraction of boxer Tony Galento maintained ties to a strictly working-class constituency. Due to his portly five-foot-eight, 235-pound frame, sportswriters dubbed him "Two Ton Tony," the antithesis of Atlas or Sansone. Yet he rose from an ice delivery man in the 1920s to the top heavyweight contender by the end of the following decade. He bought a tavern in West Orange, New Jersey, with his winnings, where his training habits stood in opposition to the workouts of the abstemious Atlas. When his boxing career came to an end he turned to professional wrestling, using his physical abilities to overcome any inherent disadvantages incurred by his ethnicity or physical appearance. "To a sizable segment of the population, he was an idol and the embodiment of the American dream of equal opportunity for success regardless of education or life style. . . . He built up a following of supporters whose passion an [sic] enthusiasm for their amiable 'Falstaff of the Ring' bordered on fanaticism." For working-class American men, he represented the myth of the self-made man, who did so on his own terms.[132]

Transition from Race to Ethnicity

While Mussolini transformed the Italian image abroad, Italians in the United States experienced the transition from a racial to an ethnic group in their evolution toward whiteness. Anthropologists, such as Franz Boas at Columbia University, and sociologists like Robert E. Park and Ernest Burgess at the University of Chicago, argued for a greater recognition of cultural differences rather than the biologically determined categorization of races. Ethnicity became more precisely recognized as a common ancestry, belief system, language, place of origin, religion, or a shared historical past. "Ethnicity is understood not as a fixed ontological category but as a social construction that often represents a search for meaning in response to external socioeconomic circumstances." Such ideological changes, which took hold by the 1930s, had great repercussions for Italians and other groups on the margins of the mainstream culture. If they were categorized by ethnicity rather than race, they might aspire to and gain whiteness, and for second-generation Italian children, born and raised in the United States under different historical, social, economic, and political circumstances than their parents, they might become Americans rather than Italians.[133]

The Italian population of the United States was anything, however, but a coherent and unified group. In 1934 the Sons of Italy, a fraternal organization, called for greater unity and political involvement. "We of the older generation had to contend with economic conditions upon our arrival on these shores. . . . We could not afford either time nor [sic] money for political struggle. It is the duty of our boys and girls to prove to the other racial elements that our race is second to none in intelligence and ability in the administration of public affairs."[134] Italians appreciated the opportunities for suffrage and economic mobility afforded them in the United States, and their frugality merged with elements of the Protestant work ethic in America. Home ownership was readily attainable. The effects of *la miseria* in southern Italy and Sicily could be assuaged in their adopted land. But continued Italian insularity posed considerable obstacles to assimilation. Few Italians intermarried outside of their own clan, non-Italian social contacts were limited, and English remained a puzzle for many.[135]

The continued use of Italian dialects tied immigrants and their children to their ancestral past, and unlike the unifying effect of Yiddish for eastern European Jews, it impeded a cohesive identity. As late as 1937 one study of Italians in Chicago determined that only 22 percent of adults spoke only English in their homes, while 23 percent of Italian women spoke no English, and 87 percent of the children spoke both Italian and English. In Boston in 1929 more than 88 percent of Italian marriages occurred within one's own group (that is, the same province in Italy). In Rockford, Illinois, in 1935, however, all Italians did unite in opposition to a Polish priest assigned to an Italian parish. Despite the efforts of the Americanization campaigns, fewer than half of the Italian registrants completed citizenship classes. New York City introduced standard Italian, based on the Tuscan dialect, into the public school system with the intention of having students act as intermediaries to aid in their parents' assimilation. For southern Italians and Sicilians who retained their regional dialects, it was as unintelligible as English. It was a language favored by northern Italians and one deemed effeminate by southerners, who maintained the usage of their dialects into the twenty-first century. The intermediary role foisted upon children also demeaned parents as dependents in the family hierarchy, upsetting power relations and producing intergenerational conflict.[136]

Religion, too, continued to mark the Italians as different, despite the general Americanization of the Catholic Church during the interwar years. Italians practiced their religion differently than other ethnic groups, as they continued to rely on their personal relationships with the saints. Italian *festas* continued to tie communities to their ancestral roots in annual rituals enacted by public performances. In the Little Sicily section of Chicago, weekly festivals provided a historical continuity to the past during the 1920s. Such enactments provided psychological comfort and a sense of security for immigrants. For women, in particular, as those immigrants most excluded from the mainstream culture, festivals had particular prominence. Women initiated the St. Rosalia (patron of Sicilian fishermen) fest in Monterey in 1935. Women assumed a significant role in the organization and presentation of the feast, which served as a reaffirmation of their Sicilian identity and their role in the local economy.[137]

Similar festivals persisted in Italian communities throughout the United States. In Chicago the Santa Maria Incoronata festival promoted the Italian community more so than the Italian parish, headed by the priests. Clergy felt that the worship shown to the saintly statues bordered on idolatry and paganism. But festivals drew Italians from near and far, even ones who had left the old neighborhood for a better environment, in a mutual celebration of *Italianita*.[138]

In New York the *festa* dedicated to Our Lady of Mount Carmel in East Harlem drew pilgrims from Brooklyn, the Bronx, West Harlem, and New Jersey to participate in an elaborate ceremony that lasted for days. Italians housed and fed *paesani* in their homes, and a street fair of vendors sold religious mementos and a variety of culinary delights. Penitents crawled up the stairs of the church, while supplicants and beneficiaries carried devotional candles of various sizes according to the magnitude of one's request for divine assistance. A procession with the statue of the saint wound its way throughout the community, as a host of Jewish, German, and other assorted ethnic and Anglo onlookers witnessed the grandiose annual affair that continued to mark Italian difference. Joseph Sciorra, in his study of Italian *festas*, determined that "these annually staged public events are also territorial markers that map out geographic boundaries vis-à-vis the larger multi-ethnic neighborhood. . . . For Italian Americans, the symbolic control of the streets through religious festive display contributes to the ongoing endeavor to define what constitutes the 'neighborhood' and its inhabitants."[139] Such practices continued to define southern Italians and Sicilians as different and distinct from WASPs and other ethnics, even as they moved toward greater integration with the mainstream culture in other spheres of life.

In the Italian odyssey toward whiteness, the previously amicable relationships with African Americans began to erode. Italians had gradually learned that to gain the rights, privileges, and advantages of being white in America, it required a separation from blacks. In the great Chicago race riot of 1919, Italians reportedly lynched an African American, which prompted the response that "they [Italians] are becoming Americanized."[140] The black man was assaulted for allegedly speaking with an Italian girl, and the retribution more likely reflected the Italian concept of honor rather than one of racism. Jane Addams remarked that "before the riot Italians had no particular animosity toward Negroes," and the newspaper *L'Italia* even expressed sympathy for the African American victim. As blacks encroached on Chicago's Little Sicily, playground fights erupted between blacks and Italians during the 1920s, and some Italian mothers did not allow their offspring to play with black children. Thomas Guglielmo, however, argues that such confrontations also occurred between Italians and other ethnics, suggesting a growing sense of an Italian rather than a white identity. By the 1930s the *Corriere D'America* began running stories and photos of nonwhite groups in Africa and elsewhere, which emphasized an Italian sense of whiteness. The growing racial consciousness of African Americans during the 1920s fostered sentiments for Africa as their ancestral homeland. Relations further deteriorated between the blacks and Italians in 1935 when Joe Louis defeated Primo Carnera in a heavyweight bout. Both NBC and CBS refused to broadcast the fight for fear of reprisals between blacks and Italians. Harlem erupted in celebration without the expected interracial clash, but with Italy's imminent invasion of Ethiopia the two sides clashed in Jersey City in August, and again in Harlem and Brooklyn in October. Black leaders called for a boycott of Italian vendors. After Mussolini's troops invaded Ethiopia on October 3, 1935, more than a thousand Italian-American youths offered their services to the Italian consulate in New York, and more than one hundred actually embarked for Italy to join the military. Some Italians gloried in the conquest the following year. In Chicago four thousand Italian couples remarried in a celebration ceremony, which blacks resented. In Minneapolis Italian-American gangs began to threaten blacks as well.[141] Although Italian-Americans divided over the imperialist efforts, with many opposed to Mussolini's fascism, the focus on European events continued to mark many Italians in the United States as "others" whose allegiance remained with their ancestral homeland.

Housing and labor issues added to the ongoing tensions. In the Detroit race riots of 1943, both Italians and Poles led protests against black public housing in "white" areas. The economic depression of the 1930s had increased competition for jobs, and in the post–World War II era race exacerbated the problem. "Italians, who had been limited to poorer jobs, were annoyed when Negroes were hired to work alongside them, not because they disliked Negroes particularly but on the ground that—since they knew what people thought of Negroes—the hiring was additional evidence that management had a low opinion of Italians."[142] Italians thus learned to adopt racial and racist attitudes in order to become white.

The growing athletic successes of black athletes in the Olympic Games, boxing, and baseball may have pushed the dominant Anglo mainstream toward greater acceptance of Italians. A bevy of black track and field stars, led by Jesse Owens, dominated the 1936 Olympic Games, while Joe Louis held dominion over the heavyweight ranks after 1938. Negro League baseball teams often beat white professionals in exhibition matches, and the New York Rens won the first professional basketball tournament in 1939. As Italians gained similar lofty status in the athletic world, any continued designation of them as nonwhites would only reinforce the perception of WASP degeneration. The gradual endowment of whiteness to Italians served to counter the ascendance of African Americans and balance racial comparisons. Still, a 1945 sociology text continued to differentiate people based on skin color, listing southern Irish and English Jews as "light"

Caucasians and Sicilians as "dark" Caucasians. Such a gradual and contested process left the second generation wrestling with multiple identities of race, ethnicity, and nationality.[143]

The racialization that had transpired over the previous century proved to be poor science and even worse sociology, as current biological research and genetic mapping indicate that all human beings derive from one source. The different cultural practices that developed over historical periods, however, gave rise to territoriality, nationalism, and an assigned racial and then ethnic identity. Instead of focusing on common similarities, scientists and policy makers emphasized contrast, with social, psychological, and emotional repercussions for subordinate groups. For Italians that meant a transitional period of acculturation and assimilation in which they experienced a gradual transformation in identity, language, and even the perceptions of their physical bodies. Aspirations, goals, and identities differed between the immigrants and their offspring, as the former tried to retain a semblance of their traditional lifestyles, while the latter sought greater accommodation with the established American culture. That accommodation required the acceptance of particular norms, values, and standards of the dominant white middle-class Protestant society. Sport played a powerful role in the evolution of Italian ethnicity, identity, and the eventual claim of whiteness, as second-generation youth adopted the American sport forms that drew them closer to the mainstream WASP culture.

4

The Emergence of Sport as a Cultural Force

On September 14, 1923, Jack Dempsey engaged Luis Angel Firpo in the "most savagely fought heavyweight championship contest of all time."

> Luis sat in his corner as watchful as a beast of the jungle. . . . From the first the fighters flew at one another like savages. Dempsey hurled himself across the ring . . . a right to the body, a left to the jaw. . . . Firpo's mouth gushed blood. . . . In a frenzy of anger and desperation . . . Firpo pounded Dempsey on the jaw with a sledgehammer right. . . . [H]e was groggy, stunned . . . [but] under short left and right hooks to the jaw and right hands that threatened to tear the heart out of his side, Firpo went down seven times in that first round. He came up each time, not covered in defense, but lashing like a wild beast in a jungle fury.[1]

Firpo knocked Dempsey completely out of the ring in retaliation, only to have him recover and end the fight by knocking out Firpo in the second round. The characterizations of Firpo, the Argentine Italian, as a savage, beastly "other" have been discussed in chapter 3. Despite his loss, the media frenzy made Firpo a temporary celebrity in a decade that spawned a particular culture of renown centered on movie stars, athletes, criminals, and politicians that continues to captivate the multitudes. Dempsey and baseball star Babe Ruth led the coterie of athletes who gained such prestige, but Italian athletes who graced the media spotlight pushed the transition from an Italian to an

Italian-American identity as they gained fame within the framework of an American sporting culture.

Crossing Boundaries

The transition from Italian folkways to an American lifestyle based on Anglo-Saxon norms and practices became more evident in the second generation of Italians, those individuals born in the United States. As children of immigrants, they necessarily maintained traditional languages, customs, and habits of their parents in the home, but adopted English and some of the mainstream social values and practices in public. In 1937 sociologist Robert E. Park labeled such existence as marginalized. "The marginal man . . . is one whom fate has condemned to live in two societies and in two, not merely different but antagonistic cultures. . . . [H]is mind is the crucible in which two different and refractory cultures may be said to melt and, either wholly or in part, fuse."[2] Historian David Roediger has termed such adaptation "inbetweenness," living within two cultures, not unlike W. E. B. Du Bois's contention that blacks lived with a "double consciousness."[3]

Whereas African Americans and some ethnic groups sought integration and assimilation with the mainstream WASP culture, first-generation Italian immigrants, much like the Germans who arrived earlier, sought to retain their ancestral cultures. Germans did so due to a conviction that Americans might prosper by greater association with German values. Germans settled in like-minded religious or atheistic communities, retaining their language and rituals in singing societies, libraries, and the turner gymnastic societies. Turners introduced physical education to public schools throughout the Midwest. German breweries promoted beer drinking rather than hard liquor, and German saloons catered to family leisure and music. Germans provided the leadership of the American Bowling Congress in 1895, and American educators adopted the German university system in the late nineteenth century, as well as the kindergarten model of early-childhood education.[4]

Italians, however, sought to maintain their clan relationships owing to historic fears of government and outsiders. Margavio and Salomone contend that Italian immigrants came to America with several yearnings, among them freedom from hunger and want, security in the form of opportunities for work and property, and respect. Conditions in Italy prohibited any form of socioeconomic mobility, and home ownership was an impossibility. Such goals did not necessarily include citizenship or assimilation. The clannishness of the immigrant generation placed their American-educated offspring in the difficult position of having to negotiate their own existence and identity between often conflicting values and practices. The immigrant offspring sought not only citizenship and assimilation, but also acceptance and recognition as Americans.[5]

Such conditions are not unlike anthropologist Gregory Bateson's double-bind theory of schizophrenia, in which the mind receives contradictory messages, leading to skewed cognition and aberrant behavior. In the case of Italians, who were removed from their usual context in their homeland, they reacted to conditions in the United States based on what they knew from Italy and tried to retain their traditional lifestyles. Many of them, as peasants in Italy, earned their sustenance via physical labor, and in the United States they accepted similar, often menial, roles as laborers in the building trades, in railroad construction, in factory work, and as produce vendors. Adaptation to American culture involved a long process of learning via trial and error.[6]

Language, as well as religion, set the Italians apart from the mainstream white Protestant culture. Although many Italian males practiced a nominal Catholicism and maintained their Old World suspicions of the clergy, they continued to celebrate their saints' days in festivals and large communal meals for holy days. Some children still wore amulets to guard against the belief in *malocchio* (the evil eye), and folk remedies and midwives addressed health concerns and births. Such premodern artifacts and practices marked the southern Italians and Sicilians as backward and primitive. Italian women gradually chose hospital births in lieu of midwives and adopted birth-control practices, with such practices becoming more common by 1940, as social networks expanded and women learned from friends and Anglo and Jewish coworkers. The increased use of birth control by second-generation Italian women and lower birthrates indicated a clear departure from their mothers' practices. Many wakes for the dead, however, were still conducted at home. Italians ate traditional foods with vegetables grown in their own gardens. "Behind each six-family tenement house was a handkerchief of fenced-in land on which every Sicilian planted a fig tree. In the winter-time he covered it with rugs and linoleum so that the cold of North America would not kill the exemplar of his homeland, the symbol of Sicily."[7] Such sentiments lingered among the second generation. Long after he had gained the middleweight championship as a boxer and turned to acting, Rocky Graziano continued to grow tomatoes and basil in his swank New York penthouse to remind him of the Little Italy of his youth.[8]

Italian activism in the labor movement spawned greater engagement in the political process after World War I, as workers realized that collective action could produce change in a democracy. In Philadelphia the number of Italian voters doubled between 1926 and 1940. In New York Fiorello La Guardia made his initial bid for mayor in 1921, but he was soundly defeated in all five boroughs. La Guardia, the son of an Italian father and a Jewish mother, spoke seven languages, a distinct advantage in building an alliance among diverse ethnic groups. He proved successful the following year in a congressional bid and held that seat until 1933, when he became the mayor of New York City. La Guardia fostered the political career of Vito Marcantonio, the radical congressional champion of his Italian constituency in East Harlem throughout the 1930s and 1940s. La Guardia also aided Leonard Covello, who became principal of the Italian high school in East Harlem and a devoted advocate of assimilation. Italians increasingly sent their children to school. By 1930 more than 90 percent of second-generation children attended schools up to age fifteen, and more than half of the sixteen- to seventeen-year-olds did so.[9]

By the 1930s some Italian families turned to hospitals and funeral parlors, purchased homes and automobiles, and selectively adopted or adapted to American ways. Butter began to replace olive oil for cooking. They consumed white bread instead of whole wheat and ate more beef and less seafood. As Italian-American women joined the workforce, they had less time for cooking, and cheaper, mass-produced products took a lesser toll on the family budget. Still, the first generation adhered to their established patterns. Pasta remained a daily staple for some.[10]

The reminiscences of an Italian-American writer, Jerre Mangione, are instructive in this regard. Mangione related how he felt like an "outsider" leading a double life. At home he was forbidden to speak English. At school he came in contact with non-Italians, Anglicized his name, and developed a love for reading, something his parents perceived as harmful and productive of insanity if overindulged in. At school teachers preached Americanization and denigrated his Old World culture. He became ashamed of his parents' backwardness. The Sicilian disregard for education was reflected by his relatives' disapproval when he decided to pursue a university degree.[11]

His experiences were not an isolated occurrence, as numerous oral histories recount similar problems of identification and psychological trauma. Leonard Covello, who eventually became a New York high school principal, was struck by a teacher for his lack of English skills and had his name Anglicized. He asserted, "We soon got the idea that 'Italian' meant inferior, and a barrier was erected between children of Italian origin and their parents. . . . We were becoming Americans by learning how to be ashamed of our parents." Author Patrick Gallo also had his name changed (from Pasquale) by Catholic nuns. In a Chicago public school Frank Di Benedetto had to adhere to middle-class standards by donning a necktie each day, supplied by the teacher, and returning it before departing for home.[12] Name changes and the adoption of acceptable middle-class clothing masked ethnicity to some degree and enabled practitioners to meld, at least temporarily, with their peers and win a measure of acceptance from their teachers.

Writer Gay Talese expressed the sense of frustration and pain in the assimilation process. "I felt different from my young friends in almost every way, different in the cut of my clothes, the food in my lunch box, the music I heard at home on the record player, the ideas and inner thoughts I revealed on those rare occasions when I was open and honest. I was olive-skinned in a freckle-faced town, and I felt unrelated even to my parents, especially to my father who was indeed a foreigner."[13] Antonio Gramsci, Italian philosopher, explained such anomie among the immigrants and their children by stating that the working class felt the pain of such dislocation, but they did not understand it. Without full comprehension of the economic, social, and cultural forces that impacted their lives, they sometimes lashed out against perceived culprits, sometimes in labor strikes, confrontations with ethnic or racial rivals, and gang violence.[14]

Despite such hardships and lack of comprehension, the Italians experienced some economic progress. Still largely relegated to manual labor and reliance on kin networks for employment, Italians began to surpass Poles and blacks in the Pittsburgh mills after 1930. They got better jobs. Across the country in the Monterey, California, canneries, Sicilian women assumed the supervisory roles over Mexican workers by the 1940s. By 1951 a third of the homes and small businesses in the Monterey area were owned by Sicilians, but the lack of intermarriage and the exclusion of non-Sicilians from social clubs continued to reinforce their ethnic solidarity. Nor was progress universal among Italians. In St. Louis only six Italians from the Hill neighborhood worked in white-collar jobs, and only eleven men over the age of twenty-five had graduated from high school by 1940.[15]

The Americanization processes also proved contentious in Italian homes. Italian youth adopted the popular culture, especially sport, which their parents did not understand or appreciate. Jazz, like rock and roll of the next generation, seemed rebellious and senseless to immigrants of the first generation in comparison with the beauty of opera. Whereas older Italian males adhered to bocce for their recreation, their sons turned to baseball, basketball, boxing, football, and the pool hall. To immigrant parents, such sports seemed a waste of time, especially when the young men could be using their physical labor to contribute to family coffers.[16]

The attractions of the popular culture for young Italian women and girls seemed even more incongruous for the older generation, who objected to the lifestyles and appearances promoted by the media. "Sport celebrities, slender film stars, and the slim flappers of the 1920s provided visual images of ideal bodies. Attaining these ideals was particularly difficult for girls, for immigrants believed that slenderness in nubile young women denoted their frailty and feebleness, thus dwindling their marriage prospects." The independent and liberated lifestyle of the flappers of the 1920s contradicted Italian notions of patriarchy and protection regarding the female members of the family. More closely guarded than their male siblings, Italian women found it more difficult to engage in the popular culture. Many left school after the eighth grade, and those who progressed to high school had to cope with peer pressure to conform to American fashions and lifestyles that met with disapproval by their parents.[17]

The Respite of Sport

For young men of the second generation, sport provided entrée to American culture where they might be judged and accepted for their abilities, unlike some of the negative experiences in the classroom or the workplace. The unregulated pastimes of the neighborhoods allowed greater freedom for Italian youth who played without the watchful eyes of teachers or parents. The supervised games and sports taught in schools, parks, and playgrounds by physical educators and coaches promoted Americanization and allowed southern Italians and Sicilians to summon their physical talents. Joseph Cavalieri, born in Sicily, learned to play stickball at school and began identifying himself as an American. Angelo Rucci arrived in New York in 1923 and joined the school baseball, track, and football teams, which, he felt, made him an American. James Pavan immigrated in 1932 and soon picked up the American games as well, stating that "I used to love to play ball."[18] Anthony Catalano, born in Italy in 1916, came to the United States in 1920 and settled in Columbus, Ohio. He took an extensive interest in sports as captain of his high school football and track teams, and he also played golf. He felt that "sports helped me to stay away from getting in trouble. . . . I loved sports so much that I even liked sports better than I liked girls."[19]

The 1920s, considered to be the golden age of sport, promoted a commercialized culture of consumption in which sport played a major part. Progressive reformers of the previous era had introduced sport to the school systems as a means to assimilate and modernize immigrants through the values of competition, teamwork, and discipline.

By the 1920s sport became a psychological escape from the drudgery of the modern industrialized world. As spectators among the massive audiences in huge spectacles that filled large stadiums, fans could thrill to the exploits of athletic heroes. Media extolled the virtues of sports stars such as Babe Ruth, Jack Dempsey, and Red Grange as iconic symbols of working-class success. Boxing title fights produced million-dollar gates, and the 1924 World Series between the Washington Senators and the New York Giants garnered more notice than the presidential election. Italian youth aspired to a share of the riches and recognition. Unlike the schools that required verbal ability, sport provided the means to acclaim via physical prowess.[20] At the professional levels, such sports as boxing and football were relatively unregulated and operated outside the governing bodies of amateur sport. In 1908 an African American boxer, Jack Johnson, even gained the heavyweight championship, which he held for another seven years against a series of "white hopes" who tried to reclaim the crown. (Among the challengers were Italians Tony Ross [Antonio Rossilano] in 1909 and Fireman Jim Flynn [Andrew Chiariglione] in 1912.) In the nascent pro football league, numerous small-town teams proliferated for more than a decade, hiring the best players regardless of race or ethnicity to enhance their chances against opponents. The more closely governed professional baseball leagues had banned black players in the late nineteenth century, but light-skinned Cubans and American Indians gained inclusion. Within that evolving racial landscape, Italians' racial ambiguity won acceptance and opportunity.[21]

The Allure of Boxing

Boxing, the first sport in which Italians gained prominence, was learned not in school, but on the streets. The brutal nature of the activity relegated it to the lower rungs of the social order, allowing people of color, including blacks and Italians, to participate. Its fortuitous emergence as a sport spectacle in the 1920s greatly aided the recognition of an Italian identity. Despite its widespread attraction, particularly among the bachelor subculture, during the nineteenth century, progressive reformers sought to ban the activity. Boxing had been outlawed in many states as a barbarous, immoral affair that encouraged gambling until New York temporarily sanctioned, regulated, and also taxed the sport in 1911. By 1917 twenty-three other states followed that decision, and New York issued permanent approval with the Walker Act of 1920. The rapid expansion of radio during the following decade made many Italian fighters household names. Boxing fitted the Italian habitus, a disposition relative to physicality, and the ability to fight against real or suspected transgressors in the ethnic neighborhoods proved to be a necessity as rivals contested for the city streets, parks, and playgrounds. More formal instruction took place in the park districts, gyms, and Catholic parishes, where street fighters could be regulated, refined, and co-opted into the middle-class sport structure.

The Italians of Louisiana produced some of the early champions, as Pete Herman (Gulotta) claimed the bantamweight championship in 1917 at age twenty before entering military service in World War I. Pal Moran (Paul Miorana), a New Orleans lightweight from 1912 to 1929, fought seven world champions in his career, and Jimmy Perrin (La Cava), a New Orleans featherweight fought on the 1932 Olympic team and claimed the world featherweight championship in 1940. Tony Canzoneri, born in Slidell, Louisiana, in 1908, turned pro at the age of sixteen and won the featherweight championship in 1927 and both the lightweight and junior welterweight titles in 1930. By that time he was widely considered the top fighter in the world.[22]

Because of dire economic circumstances, many Italian boys turned to boxing at an early age, and their success even assuaged some parental misgivings when they contributed their winning purses to the family finances. Canzoneri fought for mere coins as a shoe-shine boy in New Orleans before moving to Brooklyn and turning pro. Boxing historians have rightfully claimed the sport to be "the refuge of those with no other alternatives, [and] a whole generation of Italian-American fighters was forced to adopt other names, other identities, in order to subvert racism and appeal to the ticket-buying audience."[23] In addition to Pete Herman, Giuseppe Carrora, the son of a Sicilian fish peddler, fought as Johnny Dundee. The media dubbed him "the Scotch Wop." An Italian sportswriter claimed that Italian boxers of that era "were fighting not only their rivals in the ring but also the cold hostility of the crowds of that period who could not bring themselves to believing that a 'wop' could fight with gloved fists."[24] Born in 1893 he turned pro by 1910. In the course of at least 330 bouts he eventually won the junior lightweight title (1921) and the featherweight championship (1922). Raffaele Capabianca Giordano assumed the moniker of Young Corbett III. Born in Italy in 1905, his family migrated to California, where he became a boxer at age fourteen, eventually claiming the welterweight crown in 1933. Billy Petrolle, born to Italian immigrants in 1905, had to fight his way through Irish and Polish neighborhoods in Schenectady just to get to his job with a fruit peddler as a teenager. By the time he was seventeen he turned his pugilistic skills into a professional career that saw him challenge for the lightweight championship. Christopher Battaglia became Battling Battalino, winning the national Amateur Athletic Union featherweight championship in 1927 en route to the world championship at that weight class in 1930. Sammy Mandell (Mandella) turned pro as a fifteen-year-old in 1919 and captured the lightweight championship in 1926. Midget Wolgast, born Joseph Loscalzo in Philadelphia in 1910, became a professional in 1925 and world flyweight champion in 1930. Frankie Genaro (Di Gennaro) won a gold medal in the 1920 Olympics as a flyweight before winning the American professional crown at that weight class in 1923. He lost that title to another Italian, Fidel LaBarba, who had been the 1924 Olympic champion. LaBarba learned to fight as a Los Angeles newsboy who had to protect his turf from interlopers. As a boxer he not only achieved a measure of economic capital, but also used that advantage to retire from boxing to study journalism at Stanford University, enhancing his social capital as well.[25]

Willie Pep (Papaleo) started boxing at the age of fifteen in 1937. He Anglicized his name as a marketing device, which garnered a protest from his immigrant father. As an employee of the Works Progress Administration (WPA), a Depression-era government program that put the unemployed to work, the elder Papaleo earned fifteen dollars per week. The son earned fifty dollars by fighting two bouts in one night and presented his father with forty dollars from his winnings. The father responded with his approval by stating, "If you fought tonight and you got forty dollars see if you can fight twice a week from now on."[26] By 1942 Willie Pep had become the featherweight champion of the world. The successes of such fighters only reinforced the perception of sport as a meritocracy and physical prowess as a means to social mobility.

The strides afforded by boxing eventually enabled some Italians to assume white-collar administrative roles within the sport as promoters and agents, while others served as managers and trainers. Al Rogers (Angelo Christiano), a Buffalo boxer, retired in 1921 to become a trainer and manager. Chris Dundee (Cristofo Mirena), Frank Loscalzo, Pete Carro, and Joe Tedesco also assumed managerial roles by the end of the decade. Lenny Marello managed featherweight champion Battling Battalino (Christopher Battaglia). As early as 1924 the Italian-American Good Fellowship Club began promoting amateur bouts in Chicago, where Benny Yanger (Frank Angone) was hired as a boxing instructor by the Chicago Athletic Association in 1926. By the 1930s Italian gangsters, such as Phil Buccola in Boston, started to gain control of boxers' careers, although amateurs found more freedom in local organizations. By 1937 the Italo-American National Union's youth organization in Chicago sponsored sixty-eight boxers, and the boxing tournament of the Order of the Sons of Italy drew eight thousand fans to its Chicago tournament that year.[27] For most, however, boxing was rooted in the battles of the streets, and sociologists, government officials, and reformers sought ways to address the ethnic conflicts, as park districts, settlement houses, churches, and gyms offered lessons.[28]

Stillman's Gym, founded by socialites in New York City in 1919, was intended to control and rehabilitate juvenile delinquents with disciplined training. In 1927 Paul Gallico, the Italian-American sports editor of the *New York Daily News*, initiated an amateur boxing tournament, known as the Golden Gloves, between the champions of New York and Chicago. *The Chicago Recreation Survey* rationalized the activity as follows: "Boxing has long been regarded as a means of self-defense; therefore, it is entirely consistent that the greatest number and also the highest ratio of competitors to the population should be in those areas and among those groups where survival of the fittest was long dependent upon one's ability to defend his rights with fists rather than words." The popularity of the event soon encompassed national competition, thereby elevating the status and glory of the competitors. The enterprise was greatly aided by the establishment of the Catholic Youth Organization in Chicago in 1930. The CYO and the Golden Gloves shared many of the same boxers and sent them on to the Olympic team and international competition. The Olympic Games in particular transferred Italian boxers' and their fans' loyalties from an ethnic group to a larger national identity as Americans. Others pursued professional careers in the ring.[29]

The CYO, founded by Bishop Bernard J. Sheil in Chicago, sought to utilize sport, boxing in particular, as a means to address criminality and provide alternatives for wayward youth. Sheil proclaimed, "We'll knock the hoodlum off his pedestal and we'll put another neighborhood boy in his place. He'll be dressed in C.Y.O. boxing shorts and a pair of leather mitts, and he'll make a new hero. Those kids love to fight. We'll let them fight. We'll find champions right in the neighborhood."[30] Sheil's enterprise proved wildly successful. The 1931 boxing tournament drew eighteen thousand fans to the Chicago Stadium. Winners earned a free trip to California, and the CYO soon formed an international boxing team that competed on a global level. All CYO tournament applicants got free medical care, and the members of the national team received a full suit of clothes, paid travel expenses, college scholarships, and managerial assistance and invested earnings if they turned professional. Unaccustomed to the privileges of a middle-class lifestyle, working-class youth began to accept the bourgeois tenets of discipline, sacrifice, and a strong work ethic. Sheil accepted all races and creeds in his program, providing they swore allegiance to God and country. Ernie "Blackie" Giovangelo, director of the CYO center in Chicago's Little Italy, admitted that "sport is not the answer, just the bait.... [U]se sport to get interest and respect."[31] Thousands of young men responded each year (more than twenty-two hundred in 1935). Frederic Thrasher's study of Chicago gangs found that gang members "had a special admiration for the . . . pugs" and that "boxing represents the nearest approach to fighting that has social sanction. . . . [A] flattened nose, cauliflower ear, or an otherwise battered 'phizz' . . . are marks of distinction." The CYO brought wayward youths from myriad ethnic and racial groups into a unified whole with a common purpose and an American identity.[32]

Lou Ambers (Luigi D'Ambrosio) learned to box under the tutelage of an Italian priest in Herkimer, New York. He claimed that "I was an amateur and I got paid. . . . For my first fight I brought home a bundle of money—I think it was $6."[33] Ambers turned professional in 1932 and eventually beat his idol, Tony Canzoneri, for the lightweight championship in 1936. The Depression of the 1930s hit working-class Italians especially hard, and boxing offered an alternative to the unemployment lines. Even less talented fighters earned a few dollars in local club fights to augment slim earnings. Ambers stated that "I never made up my mind to get married until I had my mother comfortably fixed. I bought her a nice house, and completely furnished it, in the swank section of Herkimer. . . . [M]y [immigrant] father . . . lost both his [saloon] business and his savings and was obliged to move us to a poorer section of the town. My parents had seven sons and three daughters."[34] Similarly, Canzoneri honored his family ties by spending more than half his ring earnings to buy a large New York farm for his parents. Petey Hayes (Anthony Ferranda) a New York lightweight, paid twelve thousand dollars for his parents' farm during the Depression, and his brother, one of eight siblings, soon entered the Golden Gloves competition.[35]

In the tough times of the Depression, Italian youth idolized boxers. Boxing allowed for the unmitigated expression of one's physical power, without any advantages of birth, wealth, education, or culture. Loic Wacquant, a French sociologist who conducted an ethnographic study of boxing in Chicago, explained that "sparring is a redoubtable and perpetually renewed test of strength, cunning, and courage, if only because of the possibility of serious injury can never be completely eliminated, in spite of the precautions. . . . [E]very time a boxer steps into the ring . . . he puts a fraction of his symbolic capital at stake." In the ethnically charged era, every bout between an Italian fighter and another ethnic boxer drew comparisons and presumably tested the mettle of all Italians. Boxing allowed the best Italian boxers to assume residency alongside the Irish and other ethnics who had gained a place in the pantheon of sporting heroes.[36] By 1933 the *Corriere d'America* bragged that "right now they [Italian boxers] come close to dominating the sport."[37] Such success spurred continued participation. (See Appendix 1.)

Fred Apostoli spent six years in an orphanage after his mother died. He preferred boxing to his job as a San Francisco bellhop. The Golden Gloves tournament provided him the opportunity he sought, winning the middleweight championship as well as the Amateur Athletic Union title in 1934. By 1937 he had captured the professional crown. Still, he endured ethnic slurs, particularly in a fight against Billy Conn in 1939 in which both boxers traded insults. Similarly, Gay Talese recounted the story of his uncle, a Golden Gloves boxer, banned from his high school when he hit a teacher who had called him a dago. The uncle turned to professional boxing, where insults might be avenged or the measure of one's manhood was not subject to middle-class sensibilities and levels of decorum. Boxing allowed the working class to accommodate traditional values and practices, as well as the Italian regard for honor and physicality, as athletes and their followers integrated with the dominant culture.[38]

In the decades following World War I, a host of ethnic groups contended for their piece of the American pie, and boxing allowed the toughest Italians to assert their own claims alongside the Irish, Jews, and others, as all traveled the road toward whiteness. Individually and collectively, Italians amassed physical and social, if not economic, capital in the process.

Sport as a Contested Field

Pierre Bourdieu described a social field as one in which people or groups compete with each other for significant rewards, such as money, status, or respect, that is, economic and social capital. Such contentions may occur horizontally with those competitors of superior rank or those of lower designations who aspire to a greater position. They can also be conducted horizontally with others within the same position, such as the struggle among various ethnic and working-class groups for social mobility. Sports other than boxing provided similar characteristics and even greater opportunities, but had to be enacted within more regulated confines. Football demanded the rugged physicality of boxing, but the teamwork and school settings in which it flourished demanded accommodations. Teamwork and eligibility rules required a level of cohesion, cooperation, and cognitive ability that surpassed the qualifications for boxers. For those persons willing to sacrifice a measure of the boxer's individualism on the team-oriented football field, the rewards could be substantial, including a free college education.[39]

Both Italians and Catholics in general continued to struggle for acceptance in the aftermath of World War I, as a renewed and vibrant form of nativism took hold. Albert "Luby" DiMelio helped lead the resurgence of the Pitt football program during the 1920s. Despite the urging of Coach Jock Sutherland, he refused to Anglicize his surname. When the players wanted to elect DiMelio, the team captain,

Sutherland, thwarted their choice in favor of a fraternity boy that he deemed to be more "proper."[40]

The ascendance of Notre Dame as a football power and a symbolic icon of Catholicism against the resurgence of the Ku Klux Klan in the 1920s had some resonance for Italians as well. The stinging defeat of Catholic Al Smith in the 1928 presidential election left no doubt that religion still posed an obstacle to full acceptance in American society. Football helped to salve such wounds, at least psychologically. Coached by a Norwegian immigrant, Knute Rockne, and featuring multiethnic players, the Notre Dame team represented a more inclusive, democratic America (although blacks remained noticeably absent). By the end of the decade Notre Dame featured an All-American (1929 and 1930) quarterback, Frank Carideo, and fullback Joe Savoldi. Carideo led the team to two national championships as a triple threat who could run, pass, and kick. Savoldi, a crushing runner, scored the touchdowns in big games, yet sportswriters demeaned him as a "Wandering Italian." An alumnus sent the following poem to Rockne in mock Italian dialect as a tribute to Savoldi:

> I nota know he's olda' man,
> But papers say he's Italian,
> I bat he's glad, I ama too,
> Maybe he sends some fruits ta you.
>
> Deesa Swartz is good, dees' Elder too,
> So's all de' resta "Micka" crew,
> So-I t'ink you should, for deesa fall,
> Just geev' Savoldi's keed de ball.[41]

The poem drew attention to the Irish, Jewish, and Italian composition of the football team, but only Italians were stereotyped as peddlers and mocked with pidgin English. At a time when intercollegiate and high school football greatly superseded professional football in popularity, the multitude of Italian players on such teams offered opportunities to overcome such depictions.

Catholic high schools around the country adopted the Notre Dame system and challenged the public, and presumably Protestant, school teams for state honors, providing greater inclusion in the mainstream sporting culture and recognition of Italian athletes at the local levels, as the popularity of high school football soared during the 1930s. In 1931 Jesuit High School in New Orleans, with Italian players, became the first private school to reach the state championship game. More than 120,000 spectators showed up at Soldier Field for the Chicago high school city championship football game between the Catholic and public league in 1937. In addition to the annual football spectacle in Chicago, the vast athletic enterprises of the CYO drew Italians further into the church and its assimilating influences.[42]

That assimilation process was hardly one of linear progression, however. Another Italian player related how he endured ethnic slurs during the 1933 season. "It was at a high school football game. One of the cheerleaders yelled to me "Get off the field, you dirty guinea wop!' I went right after him and the whole four hundred of us Italians there pitched in."[43] Such incidents occurred throughout the United States, and even in cosmopolitan New York Vince Lombardi, later to become an American icon as a coach, endured ethnic slurs as a high school player. On at least one occasion he retaliated by pummeling an antagonist who had called him a "guinea."[44]

On ethnically mixed neighborhood, industrial, and semipro teams, Italians found greater acceptance. The Mystery Athletic Club, Austin Blues, Roseland Mustangs, and Wizard Arrow football teams in Chicago fielded a variety of ethnic players, including Italians. Mario Bruno explained that there was much money riding on the outcome of games, and "you couldn't afford to come out here and throw your money away, so you went out and got a good team together." Such teams proliferated throughout urban areas, and the quest for the best players regardless of ethnicity eventually broke down social barriers. Bruno's sports contacts greatly enlarged his social network and provided other opportunities. He served as the city clerk, but refused the mayoralty and salary increases. He maintained a lifelong disdain for the trappings of wealth and prestige, claiming, "It makes me sick . . . almost makes me a socialist at heart."[45]

Others Italians, like Frank Di Benedetto, enjoyed the freedom of independent clubs unregulated by middle-class standards of decorum or regulation. Such "prairie league" teams arranged their own schedules, officials, sites, and funding to retain a level of autonomy rather than submitting to administrators in the middle-class bureaucracy. Sociologists Norbert Elias and Eric Dunning have addressed the development over time of state control and the inculcation of particular principles, rules, and standards of acceptable and disciplined behavior. Such expectations evolved in America over the course of the nineteenth and early twentieth centuries as sport governing bodies initiated guidelines for fair play based on British concepts of the gentleman amateur. Individual players and the independent teams, however, might reject such regulations and adapt their own styles of play more fitting to the working-class habitus.[46] As a lineman for the Wizard Arrows football team, Di Benedetto spit on the opposing center's hands before the snap and tossed dirt in opponents' eyes to gain an advantage. Such tactics were not welcome in organized leagues governed by middle-class administrators, who sought a more wholesome image. The Wizard Arrows scheduled their own games and split the gate revenues with opponents, including other Italians, when they could rent a local stadium. If no stadium was available, they played in the public parks and trained younger siblings to work the crowd of spectators, begging for donations. Working-class sensibilities of material gain thus superseded earlier ethnic attitudes of solidarity, as Italian-Americans learned to cope with the assimilation process on their own terms. The reliance on physicality and a disdain for outside regulation continued to be apparent in sporting enterprises.[47]

Adherence to European Sport

Assimilation occurred in uneven stages rather than a concerted progression. Despite the growing involvement in American sport forms, some Italian athletes preferred the European sport of soccer. Italian youth learned the game in America, however, as Mussolini's promotion of the game and Italy's ascendance occurred after their families had immigrated to the United States. Soccer proved especially popular among Italians in St. Louis, where more than one million spectators viewed the ethnic games in the 1927–28 competitions. The following year previous Italian factions united in a combined team that won the Foundry League championship in the Industrial League. Thereafter, Italians in St. Louis cooperated in a more uniform national identity versus German, Irish, and Spanish teams. A former Italian gang member in the community indicated that "it finally got to the point where Uncle Joe [social worker Joe Causino] got us working together. One of the things that welded us together was sports."[48] Thereafter, the Italian community became more cohesive. The St. Ambrose parish team in St. Louis, coached by the local priest, won perennial league championships from 1934 to 1945 and the state championship in 1940. Seventeen St. Louis players made the 1950 US World Cup team, with four of the starters coming from the Italian Hill District.[49]

In Chicago Umberto Mugnaini gained employment because of his soccer skills when he was recruited to play for a company team. Louis Baruffi also played for the Gonnella Bakery team against Jewish, German, Swiss, Luxembourgers, and other Italians in Chicago. In 1929 Mugnaini became one of the founders of a fully Italian club to compete against other ethnic teams. The new Italian team drew Italian players from other teams and continued to recruit players from Italy into the 1950s. Club newsletters were published in both English and Italian into the 1980s, long after other ethnic clubs had forsaken their ancestral language. Similar interethnic leagues continued throughout the country for decades. The Monte Carmelo community in the Bronx fielded three Italian soccer teams as late as the 1980s. Whereas ethnic teams reinforced the insularity of Italians, mixed teams dissipated ethnic ties.[50] Sport thus served contrasting functions, both integrating as well as insulating, by incorporating teams within the middle-class athletic bureaucracy, but maintaining some exclusively Italian teams that reinforced ethnic rivalries.

Merging Italian and American Identities

Some sport events might precipitate the merger or ascendance of one identity over another. Aldo "Buff" Donelli began his soccer career in 1925, playing for various teams until 1938. He represented the United States in the 1934 World Cup competition and proved to be the top scorer on the team, winning election to the Soccer Hall of Fame in 1954. As a student at Duquesne University he took up the American sport of football and founded a national Italian fraternity at the school in honor of his ancestral culture. Thereafter, he coached the Duquesne football team from 1939 to 1943. In 1941 he simultaneously coached the college team and the professional Pittsburgh Steelers in the NFL. His professional coaching career was interrupted by naval service during World War II, but Donelli resumed his football coaching duties for both NFL and college teams until his retirement in 1967, when he assumed a public relations role for the Professional Golfers' Association. His life personified the role of sport in the transition of identity.[51]

Ray Barbuti, a football star at Syracuse University, became more famous as a standout on the 1928 Olympic track team. At Amsterdam he was the only American to win an individual track event, the 400-meter run, and he helped the 1,600-meter relay team set a new world record, adding both luster and stature to Italians in America. As the sole American winner in the individual track events, he was portrayed as a hero by the American media, the savior of American pride in a dismal team performance. At the Amsterdam Games he was also cheered by spectators from Italy, and upon his welcome back to New York he asserted that "I am an American of Italian origin, and I am proud of it." The *Il Progresso* Italian-American newspaper awarded him a medal for his feats. He joined the US Army Air Corps in World War II, rising from the rank of private to major, and spent more than thirty years as a football official. Late in his life his allegiance and identity had intensified, as he claimed, "I am pro-American. I believe in this great country. It has given me my opportunity. It is the greatest country in the world."[52]

Other Italians on the national teams had similar experiences. Andy Scrivani and Louis Laurie fulfilled the Americanization hopes of the Catholic Youth Organization as members of the 1936 Olympic boxing team. Tony Terlazzo won a gold medal as a weight lifter on the same team, the only American to garner a medal in that sport. Two Italians also played for the 1934 US World Cup team in Italy, furthering the merger of an Italian-American identity, indicative of the fluid and parallel processes of changing and residual identities.[53]

Some sports offered opportunities for women as well, a great departure from the lives of their mothers. Eleanor Garatti-Saville swam on the 1928 and 1932 US Olympic swim teams. She had been the national champion from 1925 to 1929, set a world record in the 100-meter freestyle, and won two gold medals on the relay teams. Three Italian-American women competed for the US gymnastic team at the 1936 Olympics. Consetta "Connie" Caruccio had been the national all-around champion in 1933 and 1934, whereas Jennie Caputo won the 1936 US championship. Both joined Ada Lunardoni Cumiskey on the Olympic team. Caruccio returned in 1948 to join Helen Schifano and win a bronze medal. Such feats not only celebrated Italian-American achievement, but also served as an announcement of the changes taking place among Italian-American youth in the United States. Garatti-Saville and Lunardoni Cumiskey had married before their last Olympic competitions, a situation that would have relegated them to domestic duties and signaled the end of their athletic careers had they lived in Italy. Their athletic involvement indicated a departure from the norms and expectations of the first generation of Italian immigrants and gave evidence of the changing roles and lifestyles of Italian-American women in America. Their choice of activities and exposure to middle-class sports also indicated that some Italians had achieved a level of social mobility.[54]

Sport and the Working Class

Billiards had been a preferred sport of the gentry and the great plantation owners in the colonial period. Many of the latter imported billiard tables for their homes. By the mid-nineteenth century John Brunswick, a Swiss craftsman, began building billiard tables for public use in taverns and pool halls. Billiards soon became one of the first sports to professionalize by offering cash prizes in tournaments. Pool hustlers held particular esteem among the bachelor subculture that spent much of its time in the pool halls and saloons. Hustlers, as tricksters, used their skill and their guile to invert the middle-class standards of fair play for their own advantage.[55]

Italians developed a particular affinity for the cue stick, producing notable champions in billiards throughout the middle decades of the twentieth century. Pool halls offered regular tournaments with money prizes during the Depression and drew a diverse crowd of spectators even for exhibition matches. "One of the latent functions of the American poolroom, like the racetrack in many of its phases, was a place where the 'sporting' fringe of the upper class—the hedonists, and hell-raisers given to heavy drinking, and gambling and whoring—could get together with the 'sporting element' of the lower class and lower middle-class to the exclusion of those who subscribed to 'middle-class morality.'"[56] For many Italian men the pool hall proved a more inclusive and welcoming venue than other sporting enterprises.

Most notable among the Italian champions, Willie Mosconi began playing as a young boy in South Philadelphia. His father, a former professional boxer, ran a gym that included some pool tables. Willie proved so adept at the game that he began giving exhibitions at age six in 1919. With the onset of the Depression, with sick parents and seven siblings, Mosconi was forced to go to work, but he lost his job when he chose to go to a 1931 World Series game between the St. Louis Cardinals and his hometown Philadelphia Athletics. He turned to pool to make a living, earning seventy-five dollars in a local tournament, which he presented to his father. His father told him, "Now go out and find yourself another tournament."[57] By 1933 he was winning hundreds of dollars in local, regional, and national tournaments. The next year he began competing on the national tournament circuit, and his earnings bought his father a tavern. Mosconi went on to garner fifteen world championships, often competing against other Italian stars, such as three-time world champion Andy Ponzi (D'Allesandro), Onofrio Lauri, and the Oliva brothers (Nick, Frank, and Charlie, members of the Wizard Arrow club in Chicago). Charles Cacciapaglia, a midwestern champion, also competed on the national level as an amateur.[58]

Pocket billiards, also known simply as pool, lent itself to ascribed characteristics often attributed to the Italian psyche, such as honor, flair, style, and the public performance of masculinity. Mosconi and others enacted flair and style in their fashionable, often formal, dress and played the game with élan. In a 1940 Chicago tournament Nick Oliva maintained his honor in a show of sportsmanship. Although neither his opponent nor the match referee had noticed the infraction, he had brushed the ball when lining up his shot. He declared a foul on himself and forfeited the shot in a tournament that he had been winning.[59]

Mosconi considered a loss to be a transgression upon his honor and sought a rematch on such rare occasions. For him a loss meant a personal vendetta. He especially delighted in beating pool hustlers, deceitful tricksters whom he felt defeated their unwary opponents through fraud. In his autobiography he claimed that "the pool hustler is a part of America's informal mythology. He is a quixotic figure, a man who stirs the imagination and inspires a magical mix of fear and respect. He is, in a sense, the urban counterpart of the Old West gunfighter." Such imagery tied the pool player to a historic American past and an American identity.[60] As a matter of style Mosconi dressed elegantly for his matches and performed with grace and flourish. Ralph Greenleaf, himself a world champion, remarked, "It was a beautiful thing to watch; it was like watching a virtuoso playing the violin, just beautiful." During the 1930s Mosconi drew fifteen hundred spectators to his Chicago exhibitions, sometimes more than the Chicago Bears of the NFL.[61]

Like the pool hall, bowling alleys proved hospitable to Italians as well. During the Depression, tournaments sponsored by local newspapers offered cash prizes, and Italians distinguished themselves as champions. In the big cities newspapers promoted their own tournaments to increase reader interest and sales by offering cash prizes and jewelry for women. Many Italian boys had knowledge of bocce, an Italian bowling game imported from Italy with their immigrant neighbors, while others learned the game by working as pin spotters in the bowling alleys, or in the local saloons. Italians produced some of the top bowlers. Joe Falcaro and Hank Marino became world champions, and Carmen Salvino, Buzz Fazio, and Johnny Petraglia would later become members of the Bowling Hall of Fame. Falcaro claimed the world championship in 1929 and greatly popularized the game and himself with a blustery showmanship. He provided lessons for women bowlers and was even shot by an irate husband in 1933. One of Falcaro's biggest challengers was another Italian, Andy Varipappa, who came from Calabria at age eleven. Varipappa started his athletic career as a semipro baseball player and then turned to boxing and billiards before settling on bowling after losing his machinist job at the Brooklyn Navy Yard in 1921. He became renowned for his trick shots, but also set a world record for a ten-game series in a long Hall of Fame career. Marino dominated bowling in the 1930s, winning the national singles title from 1934 to 1938. He captured the world championship at the 1936 international tournament in Berlin. *Bowlers Journal* named him the top bowler of the first half of the twentieth century, while Carmen Salvino emerged as one of the best in the latter half of the century. Salvino, a bowling-alley pinsetter, honed his skills with relentless practice after his working day. Salvino rolled as many as fifty games in three- to four-hour sessions and turned pro while still in high school. He became a founding member of the Professional Bowling Association in 1958.[62]

By the 1930s it became clear that youthful Italians emulated such athletic heroes. A Chicago sociologist reported that gang members engaged in weekly bowling matches for prize money, where they gauged their prowess by their performance. Challenge matches ensued with other gangs, for which the gangs recruited better bowlers. They even competed with the bowling team of the middle-class Italian Community Club, composed of college men. The gang's victory over the middle-class aspirants reinforced their sense of self-esteem and masculinity in comparison with those individuals perceived to be their social superiors. Similar events transpired in St. Louis, where nearly fifty neighborhood clubs counted a thousand members by 1941. For such youth sport served as a leavening agent with which they generated social capital, selectively participating in the local settlement-house activities such as baseball and bowling based on their ability to gain remuneration and respect.[63]

Gambling on games not only added the element of risk, but also affected one's honor. As William Foote Whyte noted, "The corner boys consider playing for money the real test of skill, and, unless a man performs well when money is at stake, he is not considered a good competitor. This helps to fix the position of individuals and groups in relation to one another."[64]

The extent of working-class interest can be gleaned by the number of participants in such sports during the economic depression of the 1930s. In Chicago alone, the city recorded 580 licensed billiard halls and more than 300 commercial bowling alleys in 1936, nearly a half-million bowlers on nine thousand teams, and more than nine hundred bowling leagues by the end of the decade. Such figures did not include the informal matches of the gangs. The gambling opportunities inherent in pool halls and bowling alleys attracted the working class, and such "a black market economy upheld the faith in capitalism, negating the efforts of the radical workers' sports movements in the United States, which, unlike Europe, dissipated after the Depression." Blue-collar workers, many Italians among them, continued to adhere to the belief in "sport as a meritocracy where one might gain social mobility based on physical prowess rather than on wealth, social status, or education."[65]

The Social Promise of Baseball

Baseball, the national pastime, continually reinforced perceptions of the American meritocracy and had a great attraction for the second generation of Italians. Angelo Rucci, born in Italy in 1915, came to the United States in 1923. At school taunts of "dago" and "greaseball" resulted in fights, but by virtue of his athletic skills displayed on the school football, track, and baseball teams, he became an "American."[66] Michael Materia, born in Italy in 1923, arrived in the United States in 1931 and soon grasped the ideology of democracy, opportunity, and social mobility. "I observed this strange game called baseball.... I took it up and I like it." He earned a two-thousand-dollars bonus when he signed with the New York Giants, "and my father couldn't believe that they pay people for playing; but when I brought home the check he believed it and we helped buy a house with it."[67]

Len Merullo, one of a dozen children of immigrant parents who opposed his interest in baseball, had a similar experience. He was signed to a professional contract by the Chicago Cubs for fifteen hundred dollars. "When I got home, I just threw the check on the table. They didn't know what it was, they couldn't read or write. My older brother picked it up and read it to them. From that day on, my mother kicked the others out of the house, saying, 'Get out and play ball!'"[68]

In San Francisco Dario Lodigiani endured the verbal rebukes of his immigrant father, who deemed him a "bum" for playing baseball. When the son brought home more money than his hardworking parent, the older Lodigiani admitted, "Boy, you've got a good job." When he joined the Philadelphia Athletics in 1938, Lodigiani refused to let sportswriters Anglicize and abbreviate his name to Lodi, and he endured the ethnic slurs of fans. His Italian pride was better sustained when the Italians of South Philadelphia adopted him and invited him to community events, where he played bocce.[69] Mario Bruno turned down a Minor League contract in order to stay at home and help his widowed mother and four siblings, but managed to contribute with his semipro earnings in Chicagoland leagues throughout the 1920s and 1930s. In Chicago softball leagues paralleled the New York semipro baseball organizations, and Rocco "Lewa" Yacilla, a legendary Italian figure in the Chicago softball leagues, managed to pitch for more than fifty years.[70] In New York City a multitude of Italian players participated on semipro contingents. Both Marius Russo and Al Cuccinello played for the Bushwicks team. During the 1936 season Russo, a pitcher, got $15 per game as a substitute and $25 on days when he pitched. Cuccinello, who had a brief Major League career, got $350 per month for the six-month season, a salary that surpassed the $1,500 per year that he earned as a city sanitation worker. Players like Cuccinello made more money on the semipro teams than even the top Minor Leaguers during the Depression. One need not have been a player to benefit. Mike Iannarella made a living during the lean years by printing posters, tickets, and fliers for the semipro games that flourished in the area, often matching interstate teams, traveling Major League all-stars, or top African American squads against the local favorites.[71] Lew Menchetti played for the International Harvester Company team in Chicago. He practiced in the mornings and got release time for afternoon games. Team managers cared for his needs. A network of local sponsors, gamblers, and neighborhood followers provided additional support, as ballplayers enjoyed a measure of celebrity within the community.[72]

In Illinois Alphonse Leone found it difficult to gain the acceptance of his coworkers. That changed when he became manager of the company team.[73] In Pittsburgh another player on a company team quarreled with his brothers, who disdained baseball as they adhered to their ancestral notions of the proper role of work and play. "I made more money on a Wednesday and Friday night than my brothers did swinging a hammer, using a pick and shovel all week." He expressed his identity issues with his brothers, who were born in Italy, stating, "Immigrants were immigrants, Americans were Americans, and the gulf that existed between them was deep and wide. I was born here, and I wanted to be an American, and my bridge from her to there was baseball."[74] His success on the baseball diamond was eventually tempered by a growing class consciousness, and he quit the team at age twenty-eight to become a labor union organizer. He became a fan of the Brooklyn Dodgers because "they were a workingman's team. . . . Rooting for the Yankees was like rooting for AT&T. They were some god of capitalism."[75]

Sport fitted not only economic but social and psychological needs as well. Italian athletes moved beyond their closed social circles and won greater self-esteem as they contributed to community pride.

Professional athletes gleaned the greatest economic rewards, but semipro contingents and independent neighborhood teams provided plenty of opportunities for the less talented. Oscar Melillo, Johnny Lucadello, Phil Cavarretta, and assorted others graduated from Chicago sandlots to the professional ranks in baseball, while others like Bruno and Yacilla prospered in the neighborhood.[76]

The growing number of Italians who did make it to the professional leagues became national heroes for youthful admirers. At least twenty-one appeared at the Major League level in the 1920s, and Italians composed 8 percent of the rosters by 1941, but the pioneers paid a heavy price.[77] Tony Lazzeri, the biggest Italian baseball star of the 1920s, indicated that the journey had not been an easy one. He grew up fighting on the San Francisco streets and aspired to become a boxer. "It was always fight or get licked, and I never got licked."[78] He admitted that baseball was much easier than his previous occupation as a boilermaker, although he had to endure frequent misspellings of his name in the media and designations as "the walloping Wop."[79] The media referred to Lazzeri and other Italian athletes in unflattering terms as "wops" or "dagos" throughout the interwar period.[80]

Frank Crosetti quit school to play pro baseball at the age of seventeen in 1927. A star player for the Yankees, he earned renown as a coach, spending four decades in the game in a Hall of Fame career. Despite such renown, Crosetti eschewed celebrity and retained a strong work ethic and a sense of working-class habitus. He refused speaking engagements by stating, "We're just doing as job, like the butcher, the baker, or the plumber. Doctors, scientists and people who really do important work aren't bothered this way. I can't see it at all."[81] He later joined two other Italians, Al Gionfriddo and Dolph Camilli, in suing Major League Baseball over the use of his image for marketing purposes.[82] Ernie Orsatti of the St. Louis Cardinals was disparaged as "the colorful wop."[83] Ernie Lombardi, a Hall of Fame catcher, won two batting titles, but never felt appreciated. He traded his accordion for a baseball glove at age eight. He quit the family grocery business at age thirteen to play on an amateur team and bypassed high school to play with a semipro contingent. He dedicated his life to baseball, but the media depicted him in a cartoonish fashion, with caricatures that drew attention to the size of his nose, oversized hands, baggy pants, and slowness of foot rather than his generosity to all. An introvert who took the caricatures personally, he slit his own throat at age forty-five in an unsuccessful suicide attempt and lived a reclusive, depressed existence thereafter.[84]

Phil Cavarretta had better luck as a local sensation in Chicago. He grew up in an Italian neighborhood that a sportswriter described as follows: "The sawed-off shotgun, the flashing stiletto, and the staccato chatter of the tommy gun made that corner [Hell's Corner] a gang locale. . . . That atmosphere was an evil thing for kids. Each vicious hoodlum who flourished for a time as judge, jury and executioner was an idol to neighborhood punks."[85] Cavarretta sneaked into Cubs' games at Wrigley Field and cleaned the park to earn tickets for other games. He played at nearby Seward Park, the same site that produced Olympic swimmer Johnny Weissmuller, and claimed that baseball "kept me out of trouble." Despite parental disapproval of his ball playing, he led his high school team to multiple city championships as a pitcher, then starred on state and national championship teams in 1932 and 1933, earning him a professional tryout. Cavarretta left high school for the Minor Leagues, sending his money back to poor parents so that they might purchase their home. He also used some money to join the Italo-American National Union. He soon returned to Chicago as a member of the Cubs, where he enjoyed a long career as a player and manager, winning the National League batting title and Most Valuable Player award in 1945.[86]

Cavarretta became a local celebrity, as did Henry "Zeke" Bonura, who played for the White Sox on the south side of the city. The son of Sicilian parents from New Orleans, Bonura joined the White Sox in 1934 and led the team in home runs and runs batted in. Two years later he raised his batting average to .330 and knocked in 138 runs. In 1938 sportswriter Shirley Povich declared that "they have voted him [Bonura] the most popular player on the club, have presented him with two automobiles, four radio sets and several wardrobes of clothes."[87]

Both Cavarretta and Bonura were part of the growing phenomenon that emerged in the 1920s, as media created interest in personalities, making them news items to drive sales of the daily papers. The large number of city newspapers (New York had eighteen in 1920, Chicago nearly a dozen in 1925) engaged in circulation wars, and editors developed novel ideas to draw readers. Actors' and actresses' lives and Hollywood scandals became fodder for public review. Sports events became spectacles, hyped in ever-larger terms. Many editors initiated and then reported on their own sponsored sports events, such as the boxing tournaments, swimming marathons, or speed-skating races. They followed the daily exploits of sport stars such as Babe Ruth or Jack Dempsey. Ordinary people became fascinated by extraordinary lives, living vicariously through their heroes and heroines, dreaming of their own great exploits. Cavarretta and Bonura provided such dreams for Italian boys in Chicago. In New York, the media capital of the United States, a new hero replaced the aging Babe Ruth and the dying Lou Gehrig.[88]

The Phenomenon of Joe DiMaggio

The most valuable player in a symbolic sense proved to be Joe DiMaggio, one of three sons of a Sicilian fisherman who made it to the Major Leagues. Their father initially opposed ball playing as a wasteful activity and threw Vince's glove and spikes into a trash can, but each time their mother retrieved them. But when Vince, the eldest son, and then Joe got pro contracts, the father asked Dominic, "And when are you going to start playing baseball?"[89] Vince had a ten-year career (1937–46) in the National League with various teams, while Dom had an all-star career with the Boston Red Sox from 1940 to 1953, with three prime years spent in the navy during World War II. Both were overshadowed by their sibling Joe DiMaggio, who became an iconic figure. The family spoke only the Sicilian dialect at home and all nine siblings were expected to contribute to the family's needs. Despite the admonitions of his father, who expected him to follow the life of a fisherman, Joe DiMaggio pursued baseball. His younger brother, Dominic, explained that "baseball violated Dad's code of life which emphasized the work ethic. But Mom would stick up for us and calm him down eventually."[90] An early scouting report described Joe as "a gawky, awkward kid, all arms and legs like a colt, and inclined to be surly."[91] Writers often mistook his inherent shyness as being aloof or did not recognize that "the same distrust of outsiders that his father had brought to the United States from Sicily, Joe carried into his old age."[92]

DiMaggio joined the New York Yankees in 1936 as a reticent and humble high school dropout. Mired in the Great Depression, America needed a hero. Starting in left field, he made an immediate impact upon Italians, who bought seats in the nearby bleachers, waved Italian flags, and sent loads of fan mail. One such letter stated, "Dear Joe, I want to stop here and congratulate you for the great name you have made for yourself. You hold a very important place in the heart of every true Italian."[93] He soon moved to center field, and the Yankees won four World Series titles in a row, while DiMaggio got the Most Valuable Player award in 1939.

As a faithful son he sent most of his salary to his parents, for whom he bought a house in 1937. Adhering to tradition and family loyalty, he also bought a fishing boat for one of his brothers. Despite his immense success, a 1939 article by Noel Busch in the popular magazine *Life* continued to stereotype his abilities as owing to natural talent and genetic advantages rather than assiduous devotion to his craft. The author not only referred to him as a freak, but stated that "Joe was lazy, rebellious and endowed with a weak stomach. . . . Joe refused to go fishing because it made him seasick . . . refused to clean the boat, saying that it smelled bad."[94] Busch claimed that "Joe DiMaggio's rise in baseball is a testimonial to the value of general shiftlessness. . . . [T]he very indolence which later helped him to succeed almost ruined his career," and that "like heavyweight champion Joe Louis, DiMaggio is lazy, shy, and inarticulate."[95] The writer further denigrated his limited education by stating, "It cannot be said, however, that he has ever worried his employers by an unbecoming interest in literature or the arts, nor does he wear himself down by unreasonable asceticism.

In laziness, DiMaggio is still a paragon." Busch described DiMaggio's apparent Americanization by asserting that "instead of olive oil or smelly bear grease he keeps his hair slick with water. He never reeks of garlic and prefers chicken chow mein to spaghetti." The article could hardly have been less flattering by minimizing DiMaggio's greatness and reinforcing negative and stereotypical perceptions of Italians.[96]

DiMaggio's stellar play, all-around ability, and the grace with which he played the game matched with his proud yet dignified and humble demeanor eventually won over the American media and a multitude of baseball fans as he confronted the Italian stereotype. In the thirteen years that he played for the Yankees, they won ten American League pennants and nine World Series. DiMaggio was awarded the Most Valuable Player trophy three times, and he set perhaps the most enduring record in all of sports with his 56-game hitting streak in 1941. He became the new role model for countless American boys, Italians and otherwise. Schoolchildren in Cincinnati even voted him "the greatest American of all time" after the eventful season. Whereas Italians had aspired only to a good job, a good marriage, their own home, and a wealth of children, DiMaggio gave hope for equal acceptance in the American polity. The Sons of Italy organization declared, "We are proud of the fact that DiMaggio is of Italian extraction and a credit to our race. He would be a credit to any race. We wish politicians of Italian extraction could boast of as high attainments in politics as DiMaggio and the others have gained in sports. Rather than the politicians, our inspiration has been the sport [sic], the type represented by Joe DiMaggio, ball player and gentleman."[97]

Teammate Lefty Gomez stated, "All the Italians in America adopted him. Just about every day at home and on the road there would be an invitation from some Italian-American club." Actor Ben Gazzara offered "He was our god, the god of all Italian Americans."[98]

The De Simone family resided in Massachusetts, but they became Yankees fans because of DiMaggio, typical of Italians throughout the United States. Bonnie De Simone explained that "to Italian-Americans, he was someone just like us. . . . My father said 'If Joe DiMaggio can make it, why can't Vince De Simone make it?'" They perceived DiMaggio as "the epitome of class for a boy looking to improve his lot." Vince De Simone became a corporate executive.[99] Mario Cuomo, who became governor of New York, stated that "his [DiMaggio's] life demonstrated to all the strivers and seekers—like me—that America would make a place for true excellence whatever its color or accent or origin."[100] Tommy Lasorda, who would achieve his own baseball fame as manager of the Los Angeles Dodgers, asserted that "Joe DiMaggio was my hero. . . . Sinatra and Joe DiMaggio made me proud to be an Italian."[101]

DiMaggio transcended ethnic heroism and established himself as an American icon in the 1941 season when he hit safely in 56 straight games, a feat unmatched before or since in baseball history. (DiMaggio had a 61-game hitting streak with the Minor League San Francisco Seals team.) He rejected a suggestion to change his uniform number to 56, because "it would be like bragging."[102] One biographer claimed that he "embodied the ideal manhood for an era characterized by privation and sacrifice; he'd beat your brains in on the baseball field, but he wouldn't gloat over it or boast about it afterward."[103] DiMaggio's triumph overshadowed the success of another Italian, the Brooklyn Dodgers' Dolph Camilli, who won the National League's Most Valuable Player Award in 1941 when he led the league in both home runs (34) and runs batted in (120). The daily chronicle of DiMaggio's exploits in newspapers and on radio turned American males and some females into baseball addicts, and the astounding feat was even popularized in song ("Joltin' Joe DiMaggio," recorded by the Les Brown Orchestra and the Teddy Powell Orchestra in 1941). In Utica, New York, the Italian colony set up loudspeakers on the city streets so that residents could follow the daily drama of the hitting streak. DiMaggio's performance surpassed the feats of such American heroes as Ty Cobb, Babe Ruth, and Lou Gehrig. America had a new idol. George Pataki, later to become governor of New York, remembered that "he was every American boy's hero, including mine."[104] Ernest Hemingway solidified DiMaggio's status as a hero who transcended cultures in his Nobel Prize–winning novel, *The Old Man and the Sea*, in which the main character, a fisherman, looks to the great DiMaggio for hope, courage, and resilience. "But I must have confidence and I must be worthy of the great DiMaggio who does all things perfectly."[105] The reverence for Joe DiMaggio transcended American shores and Hemingway's fiction to include the real Cuban populace. In 1998 DiMaggio agreed to send an autographed ball to Fidel Castro in an attempt by the US government to better relations with communist Cuba.[106]

Historians, sociologists, and anthropologists have all addressed the need for cultural heroes. "Historians have asserted that heroes are a necessity in societies undergoing change, as they represent stability in uncertain times."[107] DiMaggio's hitting streak in 1941 occurred in a period of great historic change in the United States. Industrialization began to surpass agriculture in the late nineteenth century. The 1920 census indicated that urban residents outnumbered residents in rural areas for the first time. Millions of ethnic immigrants were still trying to find their way in the American society. The Great Depression had devastated the American economy, and world events were about to push the United States into a global conflict.

When Mussolini sided with Hitler in 1939, the loyalty of Italian residents in the United States came into question. After the attack of the Japanese on Pearl Harbor and the American entry into the war, the federal government acted upon the public suspicions of disloyalty and possible sabotage. Japanese Americans were apprehended and detained in prison camps, but the incarceration of Germans and Italians proved impractical because of their sheer numbers. Still, the government labeled more than 600,000 Italians and 264,000 Germans who had not yet attained citizenship as enemy aliens and required them to register and to relinquish their guns, maps, cameras, and radios. In New York City, despite its Italian-American mayor, Fiorello La Guardia, Italian nationals were fingerprinted, photographed, and registered with the Federal Bureau of Investigation as if they were criminals. Italians were given passbooks for limited travel and had to adhere to a nightly curfew. Italian homes were raided and goods seized, and more than 2,100 individuals were taken into custody. Between 1941 and 1945 the FBI arrested 3,596 as enemy aliens. In

California more than 10,000 Italians were forced to leave coastal areas to preclude possible spying and sabotage.[108]

DiMaggio's parents were labeled as enemy aliens and subjected to removal from their California coastal home, and even precluded from operating the family restaurant in San Francisco. Despite the maltreatment of his parents and the pall cast over Italians in general, DiMaggio only enhanced his status as a true-blue American when he enlisted, albeit reluctantly, in the US Army Air Corps in 1943. Although he spent most of his military service playing baseball in California and Hawaii, it marked him as a patriot willing to sacrifice his life for his country. A 1945 survey found DiMaggio to be more popular than Mussolini among Italian-Americans. In that respect, he negated the negative impressions of fascism and Italians as disloyal, and he also counteracted the stereotypical images of Italians as gangsters that prevailed throughout the period. During the "war for democracy," he represented the continued belief in American meritocracy. "They [the Italian-Americans] would tell you that his spectacular debut just nine years after the execution of Sacco and Vanzetti was for many of them the first emotional dividend of their American dreams."[109]

In that particular era of tension and transition, "DiMaggio was a hero happily unassociated with the unpleasant question of bigotry in American society, someone who was free of the stench of politics, and unencumbered by the grim realities of foreign policy. . . . To a country shadowed by bloodshed, tears, and turmoil, DiMaggio represented an oasis of simplicity, grace, and beauty, where weary minds could come to rest."[110]

For Italians, DiMaggio led the way to Americanization and acceptance. His marriage, though brief, to Hollywood goddess Marilyn Monroe in 1954 assured Italians that they had indeed achieved whiteness. Despite the couple's divorce DiMaggio's legacy remained intact. David Halberstam, an acclaimed American author, writing in 2008, remarked nostalgically that "when I think of DiMaggio, I see him, not so much at bat, though the stance was classic, but of him going back on a fly ball, or of running the bases, particularly going around second on his way to third; I had never seen a tall man run with more grace. He was the first of my heroes; my true (and pure) loyalty to the Yankees ends with his retirement."[111] DiMaggio's ability to win over non-Italians proved the tipping point in acceptability and solidified Italian presence in the pantheon of American heroes.

Historian Dick Crepeau has accurately assessed DiMaggio's importance as a cultural icon. "Heroes, whether they be from sport or from some other area of life, are essentially people who embody in some way the stated ideals rather than the realities of a society or culture." For Italians, DiMaggio "played out a mythic ideal for them about American dreams and American promise. . . . He was a hero to later generations because some came to believe that he embodied some lost ideal. . . . He was a successful non-WASP in the WASP world."[112] Joe DiMaggio's loyalty to Marilyn Monroe remained a lifelong devotion. He regularly delivered flowers to her grave, a deed admired by a later generation of Americans brought up on the importance of declining family values. His brother Dominic attributed his actions to the Sicilian code of respect and loyalty, however. At the end of the twentieth century the new athletic icon, Michael Jordan, was referred to as "the new DiMaggio," signifying the enormous influence of both athletes on subordinate, disadvantaged, and aspiring groups.[113]

DiMaggio's success opened doors for more Italian ballplayers, and a multitude followed in the 1940s and thereafter. Nearly five dozen Italian-Americans appeared on Major League teams from 1940 to 1950. None would reach the stature of DiMaggio, but many gained administrative and managerial roles, a clear sign of Italian progress and mobility. Several Italians figured among the best team managers in baseball by the latter twentieth century.[114]

Leadership roles, greater acceptance of Italian athletic stars, and the requisite demonstration of loyalty during World War II all contributed to greater trust in the American democracy. The mistrust of all government displayed by the first generation of Italian immigrants that caused them to shun citizenship gave way to greater involvement in the political process in their children. The success of Italians, most notably Joe DiMaggio, in America's national game, gave promise of a better future for succeeding generations.[115]

Italian Female Ballplayers

Italian women had less sporting opportunities relative to Italian men and other ethnic women, largely because of cultural constraints and parental prohibitions. Sports participation increased significantly for women after 1920 in local parks and industrial leagues. Although female physical educators frowned upon intercollegiate competition, the Amateur Athletic Union and newspaper-sponsored competitions increasingly sanctioned women's sports.

In a clear departure from traditional Italian gender roles, women, too, began to pursue sporting lives despite any parental misgivings. The early pioneers of the 1920s were followed by Freda "Toni" Savona and her sister, Olympia, who starred on the Ajax softball team from New Orleans that claimed numerous world championships during the 1940s. In the 1940s and 1950s several Italian women played professionally in the All American Girls Professional Baseball League (AAGPBBL). Betty Trezza, from a large Brooklyn family, played for seven years as an infielder after she was discovered in a New York City softball tournament. Lillian Faralla, from Southern California, threw two no-hitters as a pitcher. Jean Cione, from Rockford, Illinois, played for five different teams in a long tenure (1946–54) and garnered three no-hit games. As a child Cione played on boys' teams, requiring her to challenge the physical and psychological perceptions of gender inferiority. Both Trezza and Cione started play in the AAGPBBL as seventeen-year-olds, where they earned a salary for their physical skills. Like the Italian men, women utilized sports to better their lives. Cione used her off-season to gain a both a college diploma and then a master's degree, enabling her to become a high school teacher and a college professor. She served as the women's athletic director at Eastern Michigan University before her retirement. After her mother died Josephine D'Angelo joined the AAGPBBL as an outfielder at the age of nineteen to supplement the family income. She had previously played for company teams in Chicago and saw Joe DiMaggio as a hero. Her AAGPBBL earnings allowed her to pay for a college education and led to a career as a teacher. Lenora Mandella, from McKeesport, Pennsylvania, was also a fan of Joe DiMaggio. After three years in the league she became a top bowler and golfer and managed a girls' softball team for thirty years. Lucille Colacito spent two years in the league as a catcher after spending her childhood in an orphanage.[116] The influence of DiMaggio, the widespread interest in baseball among Italian girls across several regions of the United States, and their willingness to push beyond the boundaries that constrained previous generations of Italian women demonstrated the changes that had taken place among the immigrants' offspring. Each of these women had joined the American mainstream. They no longer represented an Italian village, but an American team, both figuratively and literally.

Such predecessors set the stage for Donna Lopiano a decade later. Lopiano followed the exploits of such pioneers to become the most powerful woman in American sports by the end of the century. A star athlete in several sports, she played for the famous Raybestos Brakettes softball team during the 1960s and 1970s along with several other Italian-American women, winning six national championships. She earned a PhD and coached men and women at Brooklyn College before becoming the women's athletic director at the University of Texas. As a strong proponent of Title IX, part of the Educational Amendments Act of 1972 that provided for equal opportunities for all, Lopiano became a champion for women's athletic rights. She served as president of the Association for Intercollegiate Athletics for Women, a female parallel to the male-dominated National Collegiate Athletic Association (NCAA). From 1992 to 2007 Lopiano served as the chief executive officer of the Women's Sports Foundation.[117]

Aftermath of the Interwar Era

The interwar period proved to be a transitional one for Italian men and women. The curtailment of immigration halted the flow of Italians coming to the States that had sustained Italian culture in America, forcing adaptations to the mainstream WASP culture by those immigrants who chose to remain in the United States. Whereas the immigrant generation struggled to maintain elements of their past, especially language, their children adopted and adapted to the new life. The physicality of boxing bridged the Italian working-class habitus with some traditional values, while baseball transferred physical prowess to an American setting. Sport became a very visible sign of that transition, as a host of athletes negated some stereotypes (though the specter of criminality persisted) that enabled Italians to stake a claim to whiteness and inclusion within the American society. World War II, however, endangered that sense of progress, as loyalty remained an issue to be resolved.

5

Hyphenated Americans

In the thirteenth round, "the Rock shot his right, and it landed flush on Walcott's jaw. . . . From the instant of its sickening impact there was never a doubt of what had happened. Jersey Joe, an admirable old fighter in his final defense, went down as though he had been pole-axed. He was insensible as his head struck the floor, and there was never a chance he would get up again." Rocky Marciano had won the heavyweight championship in a fight televised in thirty-one cities across the United States, marking a Golden Age for Italian-Americans.[1] The new medium of television enabled viewers to participate in a variety of imagined communities that united sports fans, Italians, and other Americans in a common interest.[2]

Americanization

The first generation of immigrants remained largely Italian in their language, lifestyle, and identity. The children of the immigrants lacked the memories of their parents' homeland, but still shared its languages, foods, and values. Glazer and Moynihan, in their influential sociological study, *Beyond the Melting Pot*, wrote, "As the old culture fell away . . . a new one, shaped by the distinctive experience of life in America, was formed and a new identity was created, Italian-Americans."[3] The hyphenated identity recognized their existence within two cultures, as they adhered to their ancestral culture at home, yet sought acceptance as Americans in the mainstream Anglo culture. Despite years of residence in the United States, numerous obstacles to integration persisted. The immigrants had few rights as citizens in Italy, and hence little interest in government. In the United States citizenship was not only a right, but an expected duty. The lack of proficiency in English hindered such participation, especially for Italian women who had little exposure to life outside their ethnic enclaves. The rise of Italian fascism further questioned their loyalty, and it remained for their offspring to demonstrate their allegiance by voting with their bodies in World War II. Military service and sport provided public displays of Americanization. The physicality of sport matched the working-class habitus of many Italian-Americans and allowed them to assimilate, to some degree, on their own terms. Still, Italian lifestyles did not merge easily with the mainstream culture. The Italian-American children of the immigrants had to learn and adopt new racial attitudes to demonstrate their own whiteness and overcome the stereotypes assigned to them. By the 1950s they had found the means to greater acceptance and influence in the mainstream society through the popular culture of entertainment and sport.

Obstacles to Integration

For many Italian-Americans integration was desirable, yet difficult. Italians immigrants wanted respect and Italian-Americans wanted acceptance, but they had to comply with the tenets of whiteness and conform to the prescribed language, attire, and behaviors to achieve their goals. Italian-American poet Diana Di Prima explained the dilemma. "This pseudo 'white' identity . . . was not something that just fell on us out of the blue, but something that many Italian Americans grabbed at with both hands. Many felt that their culture, language, food, songs, music, identity, was a small price to pay for entering the American mainstream. Or they thought, as my parents probably did, that they could keep these good Italian things in private and become 'white' in public."[4]

The transition to the English language proved especially difficult, and even insurmountable, for many of the first-generation immigrants. A study of ten different ethnic groups in Chicago found that Italians had the lowest number of English speakers between 1930 and 1950.[5] Although the children of the immigrants had to learn the English language in school and adopted it for usage in public, they continued to speak their Italian dialects at home with their parents, thus maintaining the most important aspect of the ancestral culture. Italian organizations exhibited a gradual transition to English. St. Anthony of Padua parish in Chicago presented a typical example. Its Holy Name Society was founded in 1925, with all meetings conducted in Italian. Bilingual meetings transpired over the next decade until the full usage of English in 1935.[6] In St. Louis the Italian language remained predominant in the Hill District, and Yogi Berra (a Hall of Fame baseball player) admitted that his mother never learned to speak English.[7] By 1938 more than sixteen thousand students in fifty New York schools studied the Italian language. Parish schools provided instruction for many more, and more than seventeen thousand in New York, New Jersey, and Connecticut attended Italian-language classes sponsored by Mussolini's fascist government in 1940.[8]

The advent of World War II presented additional obstacles to the maintenance of the Italian-language newspapers, some of which had begun to publish bilingual editions by the 1930s and made a switch to English during the war. Italian radio stations were monitored and censored by the federal government, causing some stations to discontinue Italian newscasts. Between 1942 and 1948 foreign-language broadcasts decreased by 40 percent.[9]

Media images of Italians had consistently portrayed them in a negative light, often as criminals. Newspapers sensationalized gangsters, and most movies, starting with *The Black Hand* in 1906, consistently capitalized on that theme. Italians were typecast as racially different foreigners, emotional, melodramatic, sexual, and dangerous. Even the more alluring and romantic Rudolph Valentino gained popularity as an erotic, passionate, and exotic character. Throughout the 1930s gangster movies reinforced and entrenched the popular images and stereotypes of Italians. Athletes and soldiers helped to assuage such characterizations, but they had a long and steep road to climb.[10]

War and Its Impact

After the successful Italian invasion of Ethiopia in 1935, Mussolini's aggression only increased. His alliance with Germany in 1939 placed Italy in the role of a potential American enemy and cast doubt on the allegiance of all Italian-Americans. In 1940 Italy embarked on a war with Greece and invaded France as the Axis powers (Germany, Italy, Japan) soon expanded the conflagration in Europe and Asia. The turmoil carried over into American cities, where Greek and Italian children fought each other and Italian students were attacked in schools. An opinion poll in 1940 found Italians to be the most undesirable immigrants in the United States. The following year a survey determined that 42.5 percent had not yet become citizens.[11] Despite his incomparable 1941 season and the consequent acclaim, even the great Joe DiMaggio was not immune to nativist attacks. Letters chided him to "go back to Italy with the rest of the coward wops."[12]

In San Francisco two parents of Italian-American servicemen killed at Pearl Harbor were forced to evacuate their home because of the government regulations regarding aliens. "In Santa Cruz, Steve Ghio came home on leave from the Navy to find houses in his neighborhood boarded up. He could not find his parents or relatives."[13] Many others similarly affected had sons already serving in American military units. Rocco Buccellato complained, "Here I am fighting for my country, and they kick my mother out of her home."[14] The Italians responded to the apprehension in various ways.

The Sicilian fishermen in California donated their boats to the US Navy and pledged fifty thousand dollars in defense bonds. Upon getting his draft notice from the Italian government on his eighteenth birthday, Ugo Giantini chose American citizenship. Another Italian was denied American citizenship owing to his inability to pass the oral exam, even though his son had been killed in the Pacific. Choosing sides between Italy and the United States was not easy for Italians. Should the Axis powers win the war, they would be considered traitors by the Italian government. Some returned to Italy rather than risk fighting against their Italian relatives. Others experienced consternation, such as the father of future boxing champ Jake La Motta. Born in Sicily, but drafted into the US Army at age forty-five, the senior La Motta remarked, "Imagine me, I gotta go and fighta my owna people. What a stupida [sic] country."[15] In St. Louis Roland De Gregorio resolved such an issue by joining the US Marine Corps because it was fighting in the Pacific. He told his father, "I won't fight against your brother and cousins in Italy." Italians who were incarcerated were, like the Japanese, sent to internment camps in Montana, North Dakota, or Nevada. Ironically, there they played baseball and horseshoes to pass the time. Saverio Di Tomaso, detained at Ellis Island upon his arrival in the United States in 1941, learned to play baseball in an empty yard at that facility. On Columbus Day of 1942 the government finally rescinded the prohibitions against Italian-Americans. By that time their Americanized sons had flocked to the US military services.[16]

An estimated half-million Italian-Americans answered the call, including seventy thousand sons of the "enemy aliens." As a measure of their achieved social status, all were assigned to white units in a still-segregated military. The Italian Hill neighborhood of St. Louis numbered sixty-three hundred residents, and eleven hundred joined the armed forces, including six sons from one family. Yogi Berra, future baseball star, left the Hill to join the navy and served with the D-day invasion forces. Joe Garagiola joined the military service and served in the Philippines. Twenty-four of their neighbors gave their life for the American cause. Pete Santoro, a Golden Gloves boxing champion in New England, told the recruiter for the Marine Corps, "I didn't want to go in the army because my father and mother came from Italy, and Italy was fighting against us, and I had relatives in Mussolini's army. I'd said I'd be fighting my own relatives and I'd feel bad shooting at them." Others did fight with the army in Italy, and some died there.[17]

Domenick Tutalo also joined the Marines, as did his cousins. One of them, Jimmy Zarrilla, was killed in the Pacific, while another won the Navy Cross, the second-highest award for bravery. Tutalo stated that "I did believe in serving my country. We were all very patriotic."[18] Angelo Bertelli, star quarterback at Notre Dame and winner of the Heisman Trophy in 1943, was born in Italy, but joined the Marines and earned a Purple Heart and the Bronze Star in the Pacific. Ten Italian-Americans won the Navy Cross, while a dozen were awarded the Medal of Honor. John Basilone, an Italian-American from New Jersey, had previously served three years in the army when he joined the Marines in 1940. Basilone caddied at a golf course before joining the military, where he became a boxing champion in the Philippines, emulating his Italian hero, Primo Carnera. Still, he endured the anti-Italian taunts of southerners upon enlisting in the Marines until he beat the transgressors into submission. He won the Medal of Honor at Guadalcanal and the Navy Cross at Iwo Jima, where he was killed. He had eschewed a hero's retirement after his bravery at Guadalcanal made him a national celebrity in order to return to the fighting. He is considered one of the Marine Corps' greatest heroes, but Italian-Americans of that era made sharper distinctions, which revealed their dilemma. Paul Pisicano, a New York Sicilian, stated that John Basilone "was our hero. He did the right things, but he did them in the Pacific. He was shooting gooks, so that's okay. It would be very painful to see the same act of courage demonstrated against Italians."[19] Pisicano's opinion indicated the self-perception of his own whiteness in contrast to the Japanese, but a still-conflicted allegiance regarding the war in Italy.

The military returned Basilone to the United States mainland to utilize his heroism to promote a war-bond drive. At a New York press conference, Mayor La Guardia asked where Basilone's father came from, and the marine answered "Naples." The mayor indicated that his father came from Foggia, "but we are Americans."[20] Ultimately, Basilone renounced the safety of the homeland to continue the fight in the Pacific, which cost him his life.

Other Italian-American servicemen survived, but endured years of hardship as prisoners of war. Augie Donatelli played baseball or softball at the prisoners' camp in Germany and officiated games, a career that he resumed as a National League umpire after the war. Mickey Grasso also made it to the National League as a catcher with the New York Giants after two years in a prisoner-of-war camp. Mario "Motts" Tonelli was not so lucky. In Chicago he had been a superstar in four sports. "His Italian-immigrant parents, Celi and Lavania, didn't quite understand the big deal about sports in this country, but they understood the respect their son earned in a culture where slurs against recent arrivals were common."[21] Both the University of Southern California and Notre Dame vied for his football talents, but the issue was decided when a priest intervened with his mother on behalf of a Catholic education. Tonelli starred on the 1938 Notre Dame team before joining the professional Chicago Cardinals team at a salary of four thousand dollars. He enlisted in the US Army before the formal declaration of war and was sent to the Philippines as an artillery sergeant. When the Philippines fell to the Japanese in the aftermath of the Pearl Harbor attack, Tonelli and ten to twelve thousand other Americans, as well as more than sixty thousand Filipinos, became prisoners of war and were subjected to the notorious Bataan Death March, in which seven to ten thousand died. "Those who collapsed were either run through with a bayonet, shot or beheaded. Sometimes, they were run over by Japanese trucks. Mile upon mile, they were taunted and tortured, forced to walk in the searing heat and humidity without any food or water."[22] If a prisoner managed to escape, nine others were executed in retribution. Tonelli suffered from malaria, and lost nearly one hundred pounds during his forty-two-month ordeal in Japanese prison camps. Upon Tonelli's release, Charles Bidwill, owner of the Cardinals, employed him for one more game despite his frail condition so that he might gain an NFL pension. He played one more year with the Chicago Rockets of the All-American Football League. Years later a reporter described the ever-lasting legacy of what he had endured. "There is pain and horror in those eyes. Loss and outrage. Suffering beyond understanding." Despite his grief he continued to serve the United States as a successful politician who launched the first environmental protection agency in Chicago.[23]

Lou Zamperini suffered a fate similar to Tonelli. The son of Italian immigrants, he could not speak English as a youth. Taunted and bullied in school, he fought back fiercely, a quality that would later save his life. He embarked on a life of petty crime until an older brother, a distinguished athlete, taught him to use his physical abilities for more positive results. His father, a former boxer, constructed weight-lifting equipment for him. Zamperini set a national high school record for the mile run and made the 1936 US Olympic team. His athletic prowess earned an athletic scholarship to the University of Southern California, but World War II interrupted his quest for an Olympic medal in 1940 and he joined the US Army Air Corps as a bombardier. He barely survived a 1943 plane crash, only to drift at sea on a life raft for forty-seven days, when he was captured by the Japanese. He endured two harsh years of torture and slave labor as a prisoner of war, followed by years of nightmares. Still, he eventually forgave his tormentors and displayed his American patriotism as an Olympic torch bearer in five Olympiads.[24] Despite their ancestral ties to Italy, the Italian-Americans of the second generation had clearly favored an American identity.

World War II provided greater evidence of the transitional nature of Italian identity. Even the most incorrigible of the Italians demonstrated gratitude for their opportunities. Salvatore Lucania arrived in the United States as a young boy and soon found his way into petty criminal activities. He assumed an alias as Charles "Lucky" Luciano. Unable or unwilling to reform, he soon graduated to more substantial illegal activities, eventually becoming a New York crime boss. He had learned the lessons of capitalism well and restructured organized crime along corporate lines, making it more efficient and more profitable. Luciano dressed in the finest clothes, exemplifying the culture of consumption in America and the status that he had attained. Yet he never became an American citizen. His racketeering practices eventually got him arrested and sentenced to prison, but his clandestine efforts to aid the US government in uncovering Nazi spies on the New York docks worked in his favor. He used his contacts in Sicily to aid Allied forces in their invasion of the island that resulted in a deportation to Italy in lieu of prison. It is a story little known, as widespread media accounts focused on his criminal activities that reinforced a negative stereotype.[25]

Luciano's service was not an isolated incident. While Italian-Americans in the US Army died fighting in their ancestral homeland, others had concocted a scheme to liberate their birthplace. Army private Biagio "Max" Corvo, born in Sicily and the son of an antifascist newspaper editor in Middletown, Connecticut, began recruiting other Sicilian-dialect speakers, including Anthony Scariano (later a member of the Illinois legislature) and Frank Tarallo, a star athlete in Middletown and football player at the University of Alabama, for secret operations on the island. Tarallo infiltrated Sicily to report on German operations there and greatly aided the American invasion. Born in Italy in 1908, former football star and professional wrestler Joe Savoldi agreed to serve as a secret agent with the Office of Strategic Services (forerunner of the Central Intelligence Agency) in Italy. The Savoldi family did not immigrate to the United States until 1920. Savoldi's facility with local dialects in Italy proved invaluable, as it allowed him to operate as a local resident without suspicion. He took part in the 1943 landing at Salerno, and his covert operations helped to reveal the existence of German and Italian secret weapons.[26]

A much more substantial contribution to the Allied war effort came from Enrico Fermi, an Italian physicist with a Jewish wife. He had won the Nobel Prize in 1938 for his work on nuclear physics. An antifascist, he left Italy for the United States in 1939, where he worked on the Manhattan Project at the University of Chicago, achieving the first nuclear reaction that led to the development of the atomic bomb that finally ended the war in 1945. In such ways, both public and clandestine, did Italians demonstrate their allegiance to the United States.[27]

Sport and Working-Class Habitus

Despite the achievements of Fermi, second-generation Italians reserved their greatest admiration for athletes. Psychologist Irvin Child published his study of Italians in the midst of World War II and found continued resentment over the lack of full acceptance but vicarious pleasure in the symbolic recognition awarded to athletes. "He [the Italian] learns of the outfielder who, by developing skill in an American game and displaying a personality that appeals to American lovers of sport, has won a salary in five figures, a beautiful wife, and the adulation of thousands."[28] One of Child's respondents admitted that "I admire . . . lots of Italian baseball players. I admire all the Italians in any kind of sport, like Sarazen. . . . I admire any ex-champion. Or any Italian ballplayer like Di Maggio. I'm always especially interested in Italian players."[29] Author Patrick Gallo confessed to mixed loyalties when he stated, "The closest I came to being a Yankee was my passion for the New York Yankees and Joe DiMaggio."[30] Even Michael Musmano, previously an attorney for Sacco and Vanzetti and a judge who presided over the Nuremberg trials in postwar Germany, celebrated his return from a five-year sojourn with an Italian meal and a trip to Yankee Stadium to see Joe DiMaggio, Vic Raschi, Phil Rizzuto, and Yogi Berra. He explained, "Here my yearning to see Americans of Italian lineage recognized for demonstrated merit obtained thrilling realization."[31] The public demeanor of athletes like DiMaggio, featured in newspapers, newsreels, and magazines, taught young Italian-American males the proper behavioral practices necessary to gain acceptance.

Even local athletes became influential role models for neighborhood youth. Anthony Fornelli parlayed his football skills into an athletic scholarship and became a very influential lawyer and publisher of *Fra Noi*, the Italian newspaper in Chicago. Despite Fornelli's many accolades, years later a stranger informed him, "You don't know me but I went to St. Ignatius [high school] because of you. I saw you at the football games and the way you played made me want to go there."[32] In New Orleans Catholic high schools increasingly drew Italian athletes to their athletic teams, taking pride in the development of state champions over the course of the twentieth century.[33]

Such sentiments were shared secretly and sometimes openly by young women. One who eventually married a hometown hero explained, "He had a great physique. I couldn't help myself, I loved athletes."[34] Such expressions among the second generation marked their departure from their parents' ancestral culture and their accommodation within the mainstream American sporting culture. They were no longer Italians, but Italian-Americans. Italian-American identity superseded their ancestral roots by the World War II era, but it did not mean that they adhered to the entirety of the white middle-class Protestant value system. Italian food, languages, family loyalty, and physicality remained mainstays for the second generation. Sixty-three percent of that cohort remained in blue-collar work in 1950.[35]

Joe Garagiola's family maintained a bocce-ball court in their St. Louis backyard. Boxers Jake La Motta and Rocky Graziano retained their love for Italian cooking throughout their lives. La Motta favored sausage and peppers as "a great Italian meal" and cooked his own eggplant parmesan and pasta.[36] Graziano declared that "my idea of a good time is getting away from those skyscrapers to some Little Italy neighborhood, with a bunch of Italian guys in a bar like downtown Puglio's on Hester Street or the Leading Tavern in the Bronx, and laugh it up over old stories, while we load our stomachs with things like cheese, prosciutto, salami, pasta e fahzool, sausage and peppers, tripe, capozelle, everything flavored with garlic, big Italian salad, Italian bread, and strong wine."[37]

Phil Rizzuto, the New York Yankees' shortstop, recalled his joyful youth in his hometown. "It was one of the greatest times of my life because they [relatives] all played musical instruments; they'd sing, they'd tell stories in Italian, they'd make wine. As long as there was food on the table, everyone was happy."[38] The importance of food and language and their relationship to identity proved equally strong for Tito Francona among the next generation of pro ballplayers. When asked if he identified with his Italian ethnicity as a child, he responded, "Very much so. My dad had two brothers and two sisters and they all spoke Italian, and we ate Italian food."[39]

Most Italians and Italian-Americans remained mired in working-class occupations and retained their aspirations for greater economic progress by physical labor rather than by education. Yogi Berra admitted that "I had never been able to see any sense in me going to school," so he quit after the eighth grade to work in a coal yard for about twenty-five dollars per week. He signed a contract with the New York Yankees for only ninety dollars a month. Berra stated that "I'd rather be the Yankees catcher than the President." His neighbor Joe Garagiola signed a pro contract with the hometown Cardinals for five hundred dollars that allowed him to pay off the mortgage on the family home. Despite initial parental objections, the Hill neighborhood produced four Major League players and six Minor Leaguers, as well as six professional soccer players.[40] For many young males, sport still seemed a quicker and more lucrative avenue than schooling to American riches and recognition.

Joe DiMaggio provided some insight into the Italian mind-set when he stated, "A ball player's got to be kept hungry to become a big-leaguer. That's why no boy from a rich family ever made the big leagues."[41] DiMaggio expressed a clear working-class consciousness, made public in his disputes with the Yankee ownership over his salary. DiMaggio expected to be compensated according to his production in the capitalist system, yet he retained a distinct sense of his early poverty in his lifelong frugality, despite the millions of dollars he accumulated. His postbaseball lifestyle supported Bourdieu's notion of habitus, an entrenched predilection and outlook based on one's social class.[42]

Joyce Carol Oates expressed the concept of habitus and its adaptation to sport more eloquently. "Boxing is . . . the very soul of war in microcosm. . . . Boxing belongs to that species of mysterious masculine activity for which anthropologists use terms such as 'deep play.' . . . [I]t is a highly organized ritual that violates taboo. . . . It celebrates, not meekness, but flamboyant aggression. . . . Boxing is a stylized mimicry of a fight to the death. . . . '[B]oxing' is the art, but 'fighting' is the passion."[43] Boxing encompassed the Italian experience, a fight for survival, a fight for acceptance, and a fight for respect.

That sense of fury, desire, and physicality is apparent in the Italian boxers across generations. Battling Battalino, the featherweight champion from 1929 to 1932, quit school after the fifth grade, stating, "I never cared to go to school . . . I loved to fight, that's all."[44] Among the next generation of Italian fighters, Carmen Basilio fought on his school boxing team, stating, "That is the only reason I went to high school."[45] When the school discontinued the sport, Basilio joined the Marines at the age of seventeen, stating, "I wasn't interested in school after that."[46]

Jake La Motta, the son of an immigrant fruit and vegetable peddler, had an unhappy childhood. Accosted by schoolmates, La Motta came home crying, whereupon his father presented him with an ice pick and told him to use it on his assailants. "Here, you son of a bitch, you don't run away from nobody no more! I don't give a goddamn how many there are. Use that—dig a few of them! Hit 'em with it, hit 'em first, and hit 'em hard. You come home crying anymore, I'll beat the shit outta you more than you ever get from any of them! Ya understand?"[47] His father forced him to fight other kids for the amusement of adults and the coins the spectators offered for his performances. At the age of sixteen he went to juvenile prison for robbery. There a Catholic priest taught him the boxing craft. As an amateur boxer he pawned his awards to support the family during the Depression. La Motta began fighting professionally in 1941 and won the middleweight title by the end of the decade, but he is best known for his sense of rage, depicted in the movie *Raging Bull*. La Motta explained the poverty that filled his early life. "What I remember about the tenement as much as anything else is the smell. . . . [T]he smell gets a chance to sink into your soul. . . . [B]oiling diapers on the back of the stove. . . . And the food you eat when you're poor. All it does is keep you alive . . . food that's cooked in heavy grease. . . . And there was the heat in the summer . . . and the cold in the winter. . . . And the rats! . . . as big as goddamned alley cats. . . . You could hear them at night, too, in the walls, squealing and slamming around, afraid of nothing."[48]

Film critic Theresa Carilli contended that *Raging Bull* exemplified more than just La Motta's sense of rage. It represented the struggle for assimilation among the Italian-American working class, mired in poverty, a historical mistrust of outsiders, a fatalistic attitude, and an incomplete understanding of how to succeed in America.[49] La Motta fought not only his ring opponents, but the gangsters who controlled the sport. He resisted the machinations of the gangsters, but despite an outstanding record as a middleweight, he could not get the respect that he thought he deserved. La Motta, who had never been knocked out, had to agree to take a dive in a 1947 bout with Billy Fox in order to get a title fight. Such injustices only exacerbated the rage that consumed him.[50]

Still, Jake La Motta adhered to the honor code of the Italian streets. "Besides coming from the neighborhood I came from, I could never be a screw. You know, a stool pigeon or a rat. You could never do that in my business. Because of your ego, your manhood, your pride, whatever, you could never do anything like that. Even if you were being hurt and it was all wrong. You had to fight your own battle. The mob was on the other side, and I was on my own, so I had to take it on the chin."[51]

The distrust of others outside the community and a sense of fatalism continued to prevail. "As a bona fide street kid, La Motta never trusted the establishment; in fact, he never trusted anyone."[52] La Motta's distrust of his wife, aptly portrayed in *Raging Bull*, ended in divorce and six additional marriages.

Many poor Italian boys expended that rage in the boxing ring. Rocky Graziano (Thomas Rocco Barbella) exemplified the angst felt by Italian youth of the white underclasss. Like La Motta, he led a wayward life on the streets of New York. He obtained only a fifth grade education and spent six years in reform school for thievery. A policeman predicted his future. "Well, there goes another little guinea on his way. Good looking kid. But I can tell his kind. Look in his eyes, you see the devil himself. Ten years from now, the Death House at Sing Sing."[53] Graziano was drafted into the US Army, but after he knocked out a captain in an altercation he spent ten months in the prison at Leavenworth and was given a dishonorable discharge. His fists saved him from further incarceration.[54]

He claimed that "to be a fighter you can't be a smart guy. . . . [M]ostly all the fighters are guys with no education, with nothing."[55] Graziano reveled in the physicality and camaraderie of street life, and he adhered to an Italian sense of communalism, care, and self-help for the less able. Upon making a profit as a professional boxer, he bought a secondhand Cadillac, filled it with fifteen hundred dollars' worth of Christmas toys, and played Santa Claus for the poor children of his old neighborhood in New York. He then dispensed another fifty-five hundred dollars to their impoverished parents.[56]

His fighting prowess earned him the world middleweight championship in 1947, after which his New York neighborhood arranged a motorcade with banners flowing on the decorated street and horns blaring in his honor. He joyously reported that "they make me feel like some kind of king."[57] His three bouts with Tony Zale are considered to be among the fiercest in boxing history, and Graziano relished his opportunities for social mobility. Like all Italians, he was particularly proud of his ability to buy a home, stating, "[I]t ain't every jerk who can own a house in Brooklyn."[58] Such proud pronouncements also indicated a limited field of aspiration, contrary to WASP middle-class visions of the future.

Both La Motta and Graziano despaired at the prospect of a life outside the ring. La Motta grieved, "Here I was an uneducated kid and the better part of a million bucks had gone through my hands and I was only a little better than thirty years old, and now what? What was I going to do? Where was I going?" Graziano concurred. "What does Rocky Bob do when he don't fight? Learn a trade? Go on relief? Go back to robbing candy stores and Chinese laundries?"[59]

Both were more fortunate than most ex-fighters. La Motta turned to comedy to assuage his tortured soul, and his film biography, *Raging Bull*, became a national hit. Graziano's postboxing career led to a popular biography, television shows, and public speaking appearances, where he promoted Americanization and the opportunity afforded to him. He told a crowd at Fordham University, "I'm so glad my father took the boat, because this is the best country in the world."[60] By the 1960s Graziano lamented the dearth, in his opinion, of good fighters, because "we got no poor kids in the whole United States no more."[61] Despite his success he retained his working-class speech and demeanor. Gerald Early opined that "he found a way to make those beyond the pale of the ethnic, white slum tribe comfortable with what he was, comfortable with his tribalness, largely by making his audiences feel superior to it without really being threatened by it."[62]

Boxers with any semblance of education were an anomaly and held as suspect. Trainers and managers had a distinct aversion to educated boxers.

> They say that too much education softens a man and that is why the college graduates are not good fighters. They fight emotionally on the gridiron and they fight bravely and well in our wars, but their contribution in our rings has been insignificant. The ring has been described as the refuge of the under-privileged. Out of the down-trodden has come our greatest fighters. . . . An education is an escape, and that is what they are saying when they shake their heads—those who know the fight game—as you mention the name of a college fighter. Once the bell rings, they want their fighters to have no retreat, and a fighter with an education is a fighter who does not have to fight to live and he knows it. . . . Only for the hungry fighter is it a decent gamble.[63]

In a 1952 welterweight fight Carmen Basilio seemingly defeated Chuck Davey, only to have the boxing commission overrule the verdict and declare the match a draw. Basilio reasoned that "Davey was a college man with a master's degree, and we were nothing. We were from the wrong side of town."[64]

Roland La Starza, a heavyweight challenger in the post–World War II era, drew criticism for his education. Sportswriter Lewis Burton asked, "Can La Starza, contaminated by two years of college education, become heavyweight title holder, succeed to the throne held by Sullivan, Corbett, Jeffries, Dempsey, Tunney, and Louis but never by a college man?" Burton further criticized La Starza's caution in the ring. "He, like many another college man, can't see the need for taking punches or needless risks." A 1949 bout that took place in the Bronx between La Starza, the son of an immigrant, and Gino Buonvino, a boxer from Italy, split the allegiance of the crowd. The first generation backed Buonvino, while the Americanized offspring of immigrants cheered for La Starza.[65]

A study of boxing among Italians in Connecticut during and after World War II is indicative of how thoroughly the sport permeated the Italian community. The matches took place year-round, indoors from October to April and outdoors from May to September. Semipro fighters got five dollars for a three-round fight. Willie Pep (Guglielmo Papaleo), who would later gain the world featherweight championship, fought twenty-two times in 1941, but still complained that he was not getting enough work. (Pep fought until 1966.)[66]

Bouts against blacks or Hispanics carried racial ramifications by establishing the whiteness of Italian fighters. During the 1941 season 62 percent of the New Haven bouts and 73 percent of the Hartford matches were considered to be interracial. Italians composed 53 percent of the boxers that year, while blacks numbered 47 percent. The demographics changed to 31 percent Italian and 69 percent black in 1945, with 65 percent of the New Haven bouts and 28 percent of the fights in Hartford being interracial matches. The figures reflect the departure of many Italian fighters to military service during the war. By 1949 half of the New Haven fights and a third of those in Hartford were fought by Italians against non-Italians, even though the number of Italian boxers had dwindled to about 25 percent in both locations. Hispanic and African American boxers assumed much greater proportions after 1950, but Italians represented 50 percent of the local managers and promoters by that time, indicating that Italians perceived boxing as a vehicle for mobility. Sociologist Herbert Gans, however, drew a clear distinction between economic mobility and social mobility. Although the former provided greater income, it did not guarantee greater acceptance in social circles.[67]

Rocky Marciano and the Zenith of Italian-Americans

After a failed attempt at professional baseball, Rocky Marciano (Marchegiano) took up boxing. The son of Italian immigrants and a high school dropout, he had few future prospects until he discovered his talent in the US Army. He stated that "a guy who's got a chance to be a champion, is a dope to let it go. You can get rich. You can make friends, you can be something even if you're nobody starting out like me."[68] The parade of Italian fighters and their continued success only reinforced similar quests by young Italian-American men. Marciano would garner immense celebrity and a measure of wealth as the undefeated heavyweight champion of the world in the 1950s.[69]

Joey Maxim (Giuseppe Berardinelli) was not as fortunate. Maxim won the Cleveland Golden Gloves title and turned pro at the age of eighteen. Although he became the world light-heavyweight champ in 1950 and enjoyed a Hall of Fame career, it did not equate to socioeconomic mobility. He returned to working-class occupations as a Florida cab driver and a Las Vegas greeter in his postboxing career.[70]

Tony Pellone explained the family dynamics and the acquiescence of some Italian parents to the American sport forms:

> Whatever money I make I take home to my old man, and he would give me five dollars out of it. . . . Then the time I fought Bob Montgomery in the Garden I got $8,513 for my end. So I took it home and gave it to my old man and he said to me in Italian, "How you fixed?" I said that I'm broke. "All right," he said. He gave me thirteen dollars. I said "Hey, thirteen is unlucky. Give me fourteen dollars instead." Then my old man said, "No, give me one dollar back. That makes twelve."[71]

Second-generation boxers continued to adhere to the family hierarchy, loyalty, and responsibility despite the American emphasis on individuality and independence. Athletes like Graziano expressed their gratitude and loyalty to the United States, and the allegiance of the Italian-American servicemen who made the ultimate sacrifice for their country could no longer be doubted, but the second generation still lived within two cultures, no longer fully Italian, but not yet completely American.

Italians clung to the distinct sense of honor imbued over centuries in their ancestral homeland. Rocky Graziano feigned an injury to avoid a bout rather than accept a bribe of one hundred thousand dollars. Likewise, Joey Giardello turned down an offer of twelve thousand dollars, but failed to report it. He claimed that "the code of ethics he learned in the streets of Brooklyn prohibited any form of squealing, about fixes or anything else."[72] Rocky Marciano, too, placed little trust in bankers, accountants, and lawyers. He used aliases for his accounts and kept money in sacks, hidden away from prying eyes. His entourage and closest advisers were Italian friends.[73]

His biographer stated that "Marciano's ethnicity was a key part of his identity. The press saw him as Italian. Fans saw him as Italian. And, significantly, Marciano saw himself as Italian."[74] Lou Duva, a boxing trainer, said "he was a real Italian. . . . Italian food was his thing. We'd rather go into a little Italian restaurant, him and I, and grab a good Italian meal, rather than go to a fancy place where you had to put on a tux or be catered to."[75] Upon achieving success in the ring, Marciano announced that "the one thing I want to do is make a tour of Europe, especially Italy . . . and get acquainted with relatives. . . . The biggest thrill I can think of would be an audience with the pope."[76]

Marciano's Italian identity resonated with his ethnic fans. Angelo Dundee asserted that "he meant a lot to the Italian Americans, naturally. . . . He was loved and respected." Marciano carried the torch for Italians and "came to symbolize ethnicity at its midcentury crossroads."[77] The unbeaten Marciano stood atop the heavyweight ranks, a position symbolic of the toughest man in the world, and had to be acknowledged as the best to the gratification of all Italian-Americans. As the political Cold War between the United States and the communist countries set in, Marciano's symbolic status provided reassurance of power for all Americans.

Race and Racism

Boxing continued to allow Italians to draw comparisons between themselves and "others," as one means of measuring their individual and collective worth. Herbert Gans, in his study of the Italian community in Boston, found that "when an Italian boxer lost a fight to his Negro opponent, I was told scornfully about a West Ender who had mourned this as a loss of Italian pride."[78] The media attention on boxers focused on their ethnic identity. Italians assumed the role of "white hopes" in their bouts against black fighters. The Rocky

Marciano–Joe Louis bout assumed such connotations because Louis had knocked out a string of Italian challengers, including Al Ettore, Nathan Mann (Manchetti), Tony Galento, Gus Dorazio, Tony Musto, and Tami Muriello. Marciano's success, however, did not change the plight and only reinforced the habitus of working-class Italians.[79]

During World War II African Americans engaged in race riots in a number of cities when "the war for democracy" did not include equality for all American citizens. Schools and the armed forces were still segregated. Blacks lived in rural poverty in the South and in isolated ghettos in the North. Both black and white sportswriters decried the fact that African American baseball players could not play in the white Major Leagues. Professional football and professional basketball began to employ small numbers of black players in the postwar years, but neither carried the status of the "national game" of baseball at that time. Boxing stood as seemingly the only sport that adhered to the American belief in a true meritocracy, where one's ability counted more than the color of one's skin.

Race and racism became primary issues in American society after World War II, as racial consciousness among blacks assumed more strident activism. The pioneering entry of Jackie Robinson into Major League Baseball in 1947 opened the way for a legion of black athletes thereafter. President Harry Truman desegregated the armed forces a year later. The *Brown v. Board of Education* Supreme Court case in 1954 overturned such blatant discrimination and opened all public schools, institutions, and public facilities to every American. Many whites, however, did not easily acquiesce to such dictates, resulting in protests, confrontations, and violence over the ensuing decades.

Not only African Americans, but the growing number of Mexican and Puerto Rican migrants resurrected the debates over whiteness. Although Italians had seemingly gained the rights and privileges accorded that status, questions of loyalty during the war had jeopardized such gains. After the war stereotypes continued to prevail, as Italians clung to the lower rungs of the whiteness ladder. Although Willie Pep had been featherweight champion of the world since 1942, seven years later he was still described as "a swarthy lad with an ample nose."[80] After his retirement from baseball Dom DiMaggio attempted to join the Kittansett Country Club in Marion, Massachusetts, but was initially denied membership. He rationalized that "I was a jock, an Italian, and a Catholic."[81] Yogi Berra, too, was denied enrollment in a New Jersey country club. He reasoned that "they didn't like Italians then. I went to an Italian club; I got in there real quick."[82] As late as 1956 Jerry Casale, who had been an all-star pitcher in the Minor Leagues, charged bias when the Irish American hierarchy of the Boston Red Sox demoted him, Frank Malzone (who later won three Gold Gloves and made eight all-star appearances in MLB), and Ken Aspromonte to its San Francisco Minor League team with the feeble excuse that there was a big Italian population there.[83] Regardless of the truth of such assertions, the perceptions based on a long history of prejudicial acts fueled resentment. Italians' hold on whiteness still seemed tenuous.

Within such an environment the boxing matches of Rocky Marciano assumed greater symbolic importance. As the heavyweight champion, he carried the hopes of whites against a plethora of black challengers, yet sportswriters denigrated his body as "crude," with "inverted tree trunks for legs," and stated that he had "no Grecian graces, big calves, forearms, wrists and fingers, thick neck." In effect, he was still a "caveman," the same designation applied to Luis Angel Firpo in 1923.[84] *Life* offered slight praise couched in a derogatory image: "The swarthy slugger . . . is a real live edition of the comic strip champion, Joe Palooka: unassuming, clean-living, not too bright, a humble guy with a heart of gold." It went on to characterize his frugality as being cheap, but admitted that "when one of his victims, Carmine Vingo, was hanging between life and death after the knockout, Marciano paid $2,000 on his hospital bill."[85] *Time* described Marciano in dualistic terms as "a simple, good natured fellow. . . . He was as brilliant in sports as he was dull in books, and sports mean more to most boys. . . . [T]he rippling muscularity of his workouts bespeak an unclouded mind in a body sound as a brick. . . . To hero-hungry fans from Brockton and across the nation, Rocky is far more than a winner. . . . [H]e is Hercules, Ivanhoe, Paul Bunyan."[86]

After Marciano defeated Jersey Joe Walcott for the title in 1952, the *Boston Globe* tempered its commentary to bestow a marginal whiteness, explaining that "he did have the volatile temperament that is characteristic of his race, but he always was able to control it."[87]

With the retirement of Joe DiMaggio from the baseball field in 1951, Marciano largely represented the public image of Italian-Americans. The chronicle of his exploits wavered between ethnic stereotypes and the representation of the American dream that reinforced belief in the ideology of democracy and meritocracy. Many years after his death, his mother recounted that "as a little boy, he always wanted to be somebody and he became somebody, a real somebody—one of the greatest boxing champions, an international celebrity, and a good, respected, patriotic American."[88] The Marciano saga portrayed the heroic assimilationist paradigm of pulling oneself up by the bootstraps to make good and become a true American. Marciano's father had demonstrated his loyalty to his adopted country by enlisting in the Marines in World War I and fighting in France, where he was gassed and wounded. As an American, his son's childhood friends were an African American and a Jew, each allied with an Italian on the lowest levels of the whiteness scale. As a further mark of his assimilation, he married an Irish American woman.[89]

He learned toughness on the football and baseball fields of Brockton, Massachusetts, where he broke his nose, fingers, and teeth. He demonstrated his sense of masculinity early, refusing to wear a watch his mother had bought him because "only sissies wear this stuff."[90] He reportedly "gazed enviously at pictures of Charles Atlas in physical culture books and worked secretly before a mirror with a 'chest expander.'"[91] Boxing eventually proved to be a more tangible and public means of demonstrating his physicality.

Despite his Americanization, Marciano adhered to Italian cultural values. He allowed his manager to alter his family name, but insisted that it sound Italian. As an adult he frequently visited his parents for spaghetti and meatballs. He provided money for his siblings and friends. As the oldest son, he felt a familial responsibility. He used his winnings to purchase a home for his parents and sent them back to

Italy for the honeymoon they never had. His mother was elated. "Just five years before, we didn't have two nickels to rub together, and now our Rocky—the champion of the world—was sending us home." Her sense of identity still rested in the homeland.[92]

Rocky Marciano's transition to the all-American image was offset by the negative perceptions of boxing's hierarchy. The International Boxing Club, formed by Jim Norris and Arthur Wirtz in 1949, assumed control of the best fighters, arranged the championship matches in their selected arenas, and held the television rights to the prominent bouts over the next decade. The veiled power behind the IBC lay with Frankie Carbo, an Italian mobster and convicted murderer, and his chief lieutenant, Frank "Blinky" Palermo, who demanded kickbacks, fees, and a percentage of the profits in order to schedule fights, and he even determined the winners beforehand. The notoriety of the IBC and its Italian kingpins reached national proportions when Congress launched an investigation, and the US Justice Department charged the organization with violating the Sherman Anti-Trust Act by its monopolization of the sport. The case reached the Supreme Court, which affirmed the decision and resulted in the dissolution of the IBC, but Italians had once again been besmirched by criminal activities.[93] The media attention cast upon gangsters continued to reinforce stereotypes and question the fitness of Italians for American citizenship.

Italians fought with a particular fury both inside and outside the ring to safeguard their circumscribed status within the mainstream white society. While Italian boxers competed with black and Hispanic fighters for laurels, Italians joined other ethnics in urban battles against those individuals viewed as transgressors on their neighborhoods. In some northern cities friction between African Americans and Italians emerged in the 1930s, but with the migration of many southern blacks to the North in search of better jobs during the war, such confrontations only escalated thereafter. During World War II some Italian-American youths in New York went to Harlem to "beat up niggers. . . . [I]t was wonderful. It was new. The Italo-American stopped being Italo and started becoming American."[94] A sociologist reasoned that "it may also be said with certainty that the Negroes are the only group that the Italians are able to look down on quite consistently as of lower status than themselves."[95] In Chicago African American Catholics were confined to one parish, and in the liminal areas of convergence, such as adjoining neighborhoods, public parks, and beaches, confrontations erupted over usage. More serious riots, beatings, fire bombings, and even murders occurred when African American, Puerto Rican, or Mexican families attempted to rent or buy homes in previously all-white locations. The previously nonwhite ethnics, such as Poles, Slavs, and Italians, feared the loss of value in their cherished homes and the dilution of their attained whiteness. Among such working-class groups the use of force to protect their property and territory seemed a normal reaction.[96]

When violence broke out between Italians and Puerto Ricans in East Harlem, an Italian explained that "Puerto Ricans are not like us. We're American. We eat meat at least three times a week. What do they eat? Beans! So they work for beans. That's why we have trouble here."[97] The respondent had obviously not experienced the starvation that had forced his own family to seek the same progress sought by the Puerto Ricans. The Americanization of the Italian youth had hardened the sense of inclusion previously displayed by their parents in their acceptance of others also considered to be nonwhite.

The symbolic animosity was apparent in the boxing arenas, where some of the most brutal displays of aggression occurred in bouts between Italians and blacks. Russell Sullivan, the biographer of Rocky Marciano, attributes his ascendance and popularity at least partly to racial connotations because his fights were staged and interpreted as racial encounters. Marciano represented the next Great White Hope after a long succession of black heavyweight champions. Joe Louis had knocked out five Italian-American heavyweights, and Italians bet heavily when Marciano restored Italian pride in a 1951 knockout of his former hero. The wagers escalated when Marciano met Jersey Joe Walcott for the heavyweight title in 1952. An elderly Italian couple in Marciano's hometown of Brockton, Massachusetts, even mortgaged their home for gambling money. Sam Lacy, an African American sportswriter, reported that "hundreds of Marciano well-wishers, plus countless others who obviously had waited fifteen years for this to happen" rushed the ring. "The demonstration was one surpassing even the wildest expectations in the discovery of the long-missing 'white hope.'" Brockton feted Marciano with a parade after each of his knockout victories over Louis and Walcott.[98]

The racial overtones were not limited to the heavyweight ranks. A series of encounters between African American Sugar Ray Robinson and Italians Jake La Motta, Rocky Graziano, and Carmen Basilio for the middleweight title thrilled fight fans during the 1940s and 1950s. La Motta fought Robinson six times, ending the latter's long winning streak in 1943, before losing the next five encounters. The last, fought in 1951, became known as the St. Valentine's Day Massacre, a correlation to the famous Chicago gangland slaying in 1929. Tony De Marco's (Leonard Liotta) welterweight championship match with Johnny Saxton, an African American, in 1955 further established a racial dynamic to the key boxing matches of the decade. When Carmen Basilio lost the welterweight crown to Saxton in 1956, the Chicago crowd booed the decision for more than ten minutes. Basilio won the rematch by a technical knockout six months later and knocked out Saxton in two rounds in their final encounter in 1957. After Basilio defeated Sugar Ray Robinson in 1957, *Ring* magazine named him the "fighter of the year." Robinson, however, regained the championship in a brutal return match the next year. Boxing had seemingly been left to those persons on the lowest rungs of the economic ladder—blacks, Hispanics, and Italians. In later life, Rocky Graziano recognized the correlation between race, poverty, and boxing in the changing social dynamics of the civil rights era. "It's like the Puerto Ricans and the Blacks who come out of these same poor, tough neighborhoods today. Everybody dreams of becoming a rackie [racketeer], a fighter, or gettin [*sic*] into show biz. Any guy on the street could tell you there was no other way to bust out."[99]

American cities underwent rapid and symbiotic demographic change in the postwar era, as nonwhites increasingly moved to urban areas and suburbanization greatly expanded. In Chicago the black population numbered 277,731, only 8 percent of the total in 1940. By 1970 that figure had reached 1,102,620, one-third of the city's residents. Amid the tensions of dislocation and social change, boxing served as racial drama between those groups competing for similar spaces and employment opportunities.[100]

Overcoming Stereotypes

In 1952 the McCarran-Walter Act reinforced the previous immigration quotas, limiting the number of Italian immigrants to 5,654 per year. By contrast, northern and western Europeans continued to receive 85 percent of the entry visas. Such prohibitions continued to affirm the perception of Italians as undesirable within American society. Italians, however, continued to gain public notice, recognition, and acceptance in sports.

By the 1950s Eddie Arcaro had established himself as one of the greatest jockeys of all time, with five Kentucky Derby wins and two triple-crown victories. He won election to the horse-racing Hall of Fame in 1958. Gene Melchiorre, an All-American guard, led the Bradley University basketball team to the finals of both the National Invitational Tournament and the NCAA championship in the 1949–50 season and was the first pick in the National Basketball Association draft in 1951, but even that distinction was denigrated by the revelation of his participation in a national point-shaving scandal.[101] Al Cervi started his pro basketball career as a player with the Buffalo Bisons in 1938 and coached the Syracuse Nationals of the NBA from 1948 to 1953. In college football three Italian-Americans captured the highest honor, the Heisman Trophy: Angelo Bertelli of Notre Dame in 1943, Alan Ameche of Wisconsin in 1954, and Joe Bellino of Navy in 1960. Hank Lauricella, an All-American running back at Tennessee in 1951, was runner-up for the Heisman that year, and Ralph Guglielmi, a Notre Dame quarterback, won All-American honors in 1954 and later entry into the College Football Hall of Fame.[102] The successes of Italians on the college level indicated a growing awareness of the WASP middle-class value of education.

Johnny Berardino initially gained some recognition as a professional baseball player starting in 1939. He served three years in the American military during World War II and returned to the Major Leagues to win the 1948 World Series as an infielder with the Cleveland Indians. He retired in 1953 to seek an acting career, and his success resulted in a starring role as a doctor on the long-running soap opera *General Hospital* until his death in 1996.[103]

A larger number of Italians, however, continued to distinguish themselves on the athletic stage, particularly in the professional football ranks after World War II. Dante Lavelli of the Cleveland Browns, Gino Marchetti of the Baltimore Colts, Charley Trippi of the Chicago Cardinals, Andy Robustelli of the New York Giants, and Leo Nomellini of the San Francisco '49ers all served in World War II before Hall of Fame careers in the NFL. The 1940s and 1950s were a pivotal era, as the large number of Italian-American boxers, baseball, and football players visibly reinforced the acclaim won by Joe DiMaggio and sustained by Rocky Marciano.

One Italian-American, however, became an American icon as a coach. Vince Lombardi, one of Fordham's "Seven Blocks of Granite" as a lineman in the 1930s, won greater fame as the charismatic and authoritarian leader who resurrected the Green Bay Packers franchise in the 1960s.

At a time when the American media and congressional hearings focused on Italian criminals, Lombardi countered the negative perceptions as a staunch supporter of traditional American and Italian values. Lombardi, like DiMaggio and Marciano, was esteemed for toughness and physical prowess. He preached discipline, order, organization, religious devotion, and the sanctity of family life. For him, football presented a challenge to the body, mind, and spirit.[104]

Despite early coaching success, Lombardi felt the sting of racism as a dark-skinned Italian. After his inability to secure several head coaching positions, he lamented, "Here I am, an Italian, forty-two years old, and nobody wants me. Nobody will take me." In 1959 Green Bay took a chance that he could revive their storied franchise, and he responded with nine winning seasons, five NFL championships, and two Super Bowl wins. Lombardi died of cancer in 1970. The following year he was elected to the Pro Football Hall of Fame, and the NFL named the Super Bowl trophy in his honor.[105]

Lombardi left a lasting impression because he endeared himself to conservative Americans during the 1960s, an era of immense cultural revolution fostered by rebellious youth. Sportswriter Jerry Izenberg even claimed that Richard Nixon considered Lombardi as a vice presidential running mate in 1968, only to learn that Lombardi was a Democrat. Young Americans, particularly blacks and women, clamored for change and greater equality. Although Lombardi adhered to strict discipline, the work ethic, and a conservative ideology, he also worked diligently for racial progress. Having felt the sting of inferiority, he admonished his players and the Green Bay community regarding equality for all. When preseason exhibition games were played in the South he insisted that black players not be subjected to segregation practices.[106] Lombardi ruled his team as a dominant Italian father presiding over his family. He required discipline and adherence to rules and regulations, with an occasional stroke of benevolence for wayward children.

The increasing popularity of pro football, and its marriage with television, allowed it to surpass baseball as the American national game by the 1960s. Baseball, however, still held great appeal for the general population. Although no Italian players reached the glorified status of Joe DiMaggio, their sheer numbers greatly expanded their value and perception as Americans. In 1940 only fifteen Italian-American players appeared on MLB rosters, but 26 Italians among 409 players made it to the Major Leagues by 1952. Almost all of the players in 1940 came from the San Francisco area, but by 1952 they came mostly from the Northeast. Although baseball rosters reflected the dominant culture, with 77 percent of the 1940 players of Anglo and western European ancestry, the demographics began to change. Among the southern and eastern European ethnics, only Poles outnumbered Italians by 1952. The emphasis on physical prowess rather than education as a means to social mobility remained strong, as none of the Italian players in 1952 had graduated from college.[107]

More than 100 Italian-Americans appeared on MLB rosters in the 1940s and 1950s, indicating the extent of Americanization in the second generation. Baseball further enhanced the perception of a meritocracy when Lou Perini bought the Boston Braves in 1944 and Buzzy Bavasi assumed the general manager's role for the Dodgers in 1951. Perini even provided money and equipment for the expansion of baseball in Italy.[108]

Phil Rizzuto, a shortstop, second baseman Billy Martin (the son of an Italian mother), catcher Yogi Berra, and pitcher Vic Raschi were New York Yankee teammates, producing numerous World Series triumphs during the 1950s. Rizzuto won the 1950 Most Valuable Player Award, and Berra garnered the award on three occasions, as both made their way to the Hall of Fame. Despite such honors, Berra proclaimed that when he and his wife traveled to Italy to see his parents' hometown and meet relatives after the 1959 season, "I felt as though I had done one of the best things of my life."[109]

The Yankees often faced the Brooklyn Dodgers in the World Series, a team that featured all-star Italians in pitcher Ralph Branca and the strong-armed outfielder Carl Furillo. Roy Campanella, a three-time MVP as the Dodgers' catcher and a Hall of Fame inductee, was the product of a Sicilian father and an African American mother. Such players were particularly esteemed by the large Italian neighborhoods in Brooklyn.[110]

The Dodgers' rivals, the New York Giants, counted on pitchers Sal Maglie and Johnny Antonelli. Italian players brought new fans to the game and helped an older generation assimilate. When the Giants signed Joe Amalfitano to a contract in 1954, his immigrant father drank wine with the team scouts, then asked his son how much money he was offered. When the son told him it was thirty-five thousand dollars, the father remarked in Italian, "Isn't this a great country?"[111]

The Boston Red Sox had Frank Malzone, an eight-time all-star at third base, and Cleveland fans adored Rocky Colavito, a slugging outfielder. Colavito acknowledged his debt to earlier Italian players and even tried to copy Joe DiMaggio's batting stance. He explained that "there was always something special about Italian ballplayers. My favorite was always Joe DiMaggio. It was just his demeanor. A lot of the Italians in the neighborhood loved him." Colavito became a hero to Italians in Cleveland, and when the team traded him to Detroit in 1960 the fans erupted in protest, hanging the general manager in effigy. An editorial described him as "the most popular of the Indians, exemplifying young manhood at its best." In 1976 the Cleveland fans named him the "most memorable personality in Indians' history."[112]

Frank Malzone was a favorite until the 1960s, when hard-hitting infielder Rico Petrocelli became the darling of the Boston fans, while Tony and Billy Conigliaro patrolled the outfield. Petrocelli, the son of immigrants from Abruzzi, initially faced taunts and ethnic slurs in Boston, but "in the North End [Boston's Italian district] the Italians really made me feel welcome. They were great. . . . We [he and Tony Conigliaro] knew that the Italian Americans who had struggled in other fields were proud of us, and we wanted to go out there and do a good job." He also became an inspiration within his own family. "The only thing my father knew about baseball was DiMaggio, Rizzuto, Berra because he could relate to them. When you're struggling like my father was, then somebody makes it big, that gives others the confidence to go out and try to be successful."[113]

Ron Santo proved a favorite in Chicago as the Cubs third baseman and then enjoyed a long career as the team's radio broadcaster. He spent his whole fifteen-year career in the city with both the Cubs and the White Sox, winning five Gold Glove awards and appearing on nine all-star teams. Santo, too, extolled his Italian roots. He claimed that "I'm half Italian, half Swedish, and all Italian. . . . My mother, even though she was Swedish, could speak Italian with my dad. Tuesday, Thursday, Sunday, it was spaghetti. We were definitely an Italian family."[114]

Jim Fregosi played eighteen years in MLB with four different teams. His father owned a deli in San Francisco that doubled as an Italian clubhouse. Fregosi related that "every time I hit a home run in the big leagues, when the store opened in the morning, all the old Italians would come in and have a shot of whiskey with my dad."[115] Such local heroes helped to maintain a sense of community and an ethnic identity, as they concurrently drew ethnic fans into the mainstream.

Italians were drawn into the larger community of baseball fans who adopted a civic team and its players as their own. The Brooklyn Dodgers, with its bevy of Italian-American stars, proved a case in point. Because of the reserve clause in players' contracts that gave owners the right to their labor unless the team management decided to trade or release them, players often spent their entire career in one city. Players questioned such servitude as exploitation that held down their salaries and negated their ability to deliberate contractual terms. Individual stars, such as Joe DiMaggio, publicly negotiated his contracts in the media, but Danny Gardella, of the New York Giants, was the first to challenge the reserve clause. In 1946 Gardella, pitcher Sal Maglie, and others opted to play in the Mexican League for more money than their MLB owners were willing to offer them. Commissioner Happy Chandler banned the rebellious players from MLB for five years. Gardella sued MLB as a monopoly in 1947, but the league enjoyed an exemption from such charges because of a 1922 Supreme Court ruling. It would take more than twenty-five years before baseball players managed to gain free agency and sell their talents to the highest bidder.

Italian Influences on Mainstream Popular Culture

The Americanization of Italian youth became most evident within the popular culture that included both sport and music. Concurrently with the proliferation of Italian athletes, others assumed a major role in the music industry. The rise of Frank Sinatra as a singer and movie star only enhanced the status of Italian-Americans won by DiMaggio. Italian-American youth continued that ascendance in the rock-and-roll movement of the 1950s. As the second generation had rebelled against parental restrictions, the postwar Italian-Americans questioned WASP authority. Whereas Frank Sinatra, Perry Como, Tony Bennett (Benedetto), and Vic Damone (Vito Farinola) still appealed to a broad spectrum of Americans, young Italian musical groups and singers drew substantial followings that crossed ethnic and racial lines. The New York area produced Connie Francis (Franconero) as well as the Neons, the Regents, the Mystics, the Elegants, the Capris, Reparata (Mary Aiese) and the Delrons, Dion (Di Mucci) and the Belmonts, the Crests, Joey Dee (Di Nicola) and the Starliters, Frankie Valli (Castelluccio) and the Four Seasons, the Young Rascals, and Bobby Darin (Cassotto). Philadelphia produced Bobby Rydell (Ridarelli), Fabian (Forte), and Frankie Avalon (Avallone), and Bobby Vee (Velline) hailed from South Dakota, all of whom became teen idols as singers and actors in the 1950s and 1960s. Avalon paired with Annette Funicello in a series of beach movies that capitalized on the California surf culture of that era, symbolically tying Italians to the wholesome mainstream. Funicello, since her 1955 appearance on the Walt Disney Company's *Mickey Mouse Club* television show, capitalized on the family values favored by her ancestral culture and promoted by Disney.[116] Italians seemed to be in the forefront of youth culture in conflicting roles as both harbingers of change and supporters of the status quo.

Some groups, however, merged Italians with African Americans and Puerto Ricans and borrowed from the musical genres of other cultures in effecting a new sound known as doo-wop that capitalized on vocal harmony.[117] The groups drew large crowds for concerts and dances, whose sensual nature challenged WASP norms relative to expression and sexuality. Italian-Americans figured prominently in the musical revolution, as non-Italians adopted the "greaser" clothing, hairstyles, and urban street-corner culture, not unlike the co-optation of African American rap and hip-hop music by white suburban youth a generation later. Both cases represented a reversal of the cultural flow, and the rock-and-roll genre would eventually evolve into a politically oriented youth movement that challenged authority generally and the Vietnam War more specifically.

Although some Italian youths joined, and even helped to spur, the youthful rebellion, sporting practices and most athletes still upheld the mainstream social values. The athletic participation of

Italian-Americans signaled their long-sought inclusion within the confines of white society. Unlike their black counterparts, athletes generally represented a more conservative element and did little to jeopardize that tenuous status. The greater evidence of Italian athletes and entertainers signaled more widespread acceptance of and a level of comfort for Italians within the mainstream culture.

The Effects of Americanization

The post–World War II era brought significant changes to the American society. The war sparked a greater impetus on Americanization, as 1.75 million foreign-born residents became citizens. Nearly 80 percent of foreign-born Italians became naturalized by 1950. Italian-American men and women began to attend college in greater numbers. More Italian-American athletes appeared on college campuses, and education fostered greater social mobility, aspirations, and accumulation, qualities inconsistent with their parents' value systems and behavior patterns. Americans sought greater privacy and property, which they found in the growing middle-class movement toward suburbanization. From 1950 to 1960 suburbanites increased from 41 million to 60 million. By 1970 that figure reached 76 million, or 37 percent of the population. The new lifestyles, including sport and recreational practices, created broader social networks and increased the intermarriage rates of Italians with other ethnic groups. Fewer Italians adhered to the custom of arranged marriages. For those born in the 1930s, 62.9 percent of men and 61 percent of women married non-Italians. Marriages produced fewer children, and Italians had the second-lowest birthrate among the various ethnic groups by 1970. Unlike their parents' and grandparents' generations, large families were no longer essential to the family economy.[118]

Changing social, economic, and residential patterns affected the urban ethnic enclaves of the past. The Italian immigrant population of Philadelphia decreased from 48,721 in 1950 to only 25,629 by 1970. Such disbursement, however, did not necessarily indicate a wholesale departure from the culture constructed by immigrant parents.

Transplanted children returned to the old neighborhoods regularly, even weekly, for church services and to purchase Italian foods. Others returned regularly for recreation in the community social clubs and socialization with family members. In a study of one small town in Pennsylvania in 1964, life remained much like as it was in an ancestral village in Italy. Only sport and recreational activities drew the second generation out of the communal boundaries. For many Italian-Americans, sport provided a key means of social contact with non-Italians.[119]

Other studies showed that Italian culture remained relatively intact in the remaining enclaves in St. Louis, Boston, and New York. In such locations sports had drawn the second generation out of their insularity by 1940, and the transition to English showed that the third generation was unable to converse in their ancestral tongue. The Italian neighborhood of St. Louis, however, was still referred to as "Dago Hill" in the 1960s. In Boston's West End Italians were the majority in 1942. By 1957 they still numbered 42 percent of the residents, 61 percent of whom still labored in unskilled or semiskilled occupations. Children and youth still congregated in noisy streets, and girls still held responsibility for domestic chores. Only 26 percent of the females had completed high school, and only 2 percent had attended college courses. Although parents desired a better life for their children, they had not set goals for such achievement. Such a lack of strategy is consistent with Antonio Gramsci's dictum that the "working class feels, but it does not understand." Italians felt the pain of an industrial economy as the subordinate players in the capitalist system, but a lack of complete understanding of how the system functioned relegated them to traditional support networks of family and kin rather than pursuing the benefits of education. Only a select few athletes managed to bridge the gulf and capitalize on their physical abilities.[120]

Italians still adhered to working-class lifestyles and ethnic influences. Middle-class aspirations and individualism met with disdain, while being one's own boss, as an owner of a small business that serviced the community, gained acceptance. Although wine and olive oil were no longer made at home, Italian food retained a central role in the lives of the second and third generations. Family dinners continued to foster a sense of cohesion among families, and independent adult children still visited parents for Sunday meals and the banquets that accompanied religious festivals. Such meals were characterized by an abundance of inexpensive food, prepared by the women and eaten in an informal manner, as suggested by Bourdieu's concept of working-class habitus. Such occasions contrasted with the social ceremonies of the middle class, who espoused quality over quantity in the selection and preparation of food and the adherence to a more formal etiquette and hierarchical seating arrangements. In both cases patriarchy continued to dominate, as males were the recipients of female labor and attention. Residual elements of the Italian immigrant culture clearly persisted and indicated the still-ongoing process of cultural transition.[121] Athletes had played a great role in winning greater positive recognition for Italians in the United States. A federal committee that designated racial classifications in 1965 recognized the Americanization of Italians by assigning them within the white category. Still, the predominant working-class lifestyle among Italians and stereotyped physical characteristics did not ensure full inclusion into American society. The rebelliousness of youth during the 1950s and 1960s led them to assume divergent lifestyles, clothing, hairstyles, and mannerisms, as well as new forms of music. Although the youthful revolution crossed ethnic, racial, and even class lines, the pejorative sobriquet of "greasers" was usually directed at Italians, Greeks, Mexicans, and Filipinos. Furthermore, the distinctive sleeveless undershirts that marked urban males became known as "dago tees." The factionalization of the youth movement along racial lines in the 1960s exacerbated social and communal boundary lines that led to reactionary racial confrontations and violence. Although such aggression enacted and solidified Italian claims to whiteness, it also reified a subordinate working-class ideology among Italian youth at odds with the WASP middle-class mainstream. Too often a resort to physicality supplanted verbal negotiation.[122]

By the 1950s social class had superseded ethnicity. The neighborhood gangs of the previous generation not only persisted but grew, despite the efforts of social workers, police, and religious agencies.

Some labeled their organizations as "social-athletic clubs," but the physical confrontations of regulated athletic contests did not preclude more violent confrontations with perceived foes. The Little Sicily neighborhood of Chicago contained at least twenty clubs with 966 members in a six-by-nine-block area. Little Italy, on the city's West Side had at least seventy-five gangs with 2,000 participants. In both areas the youths assumed the self-appointed roles of community guardians against encroachments by blacks, Hispanics, or anyone else deemed to be an interloper or a threat. The Italian-American gangs had subverted the traditional Italian concepts of honor, family, and communalism to enhance their own power, something unavailable to them within the confines of the industrial labor force.[123] The lack of a full merger and complete integration within the American mainstream exemplified the maintenance of unequal power relations and the marginality of some groups. The vast majority who could not reach elite levels of athletic performance or were not gifted with musical talent found limited prospects without an education.

The negative perceptions of Italians thus continued with reverberations throughout the economy. Sociologists identified the conditions as an "hourglass economy," with fewer middle-level jobs, but an expansion of upper- and lower-level positions. A 1974 study in Chicago found that less than 2 percent of the 106 largest corporations had an Italian director, and less than 3 percent had Italians in executive positions. Seventy-five of the companies had no Italian officers at all. A year later a Detroit study uncovered similar egregious data. Eighty of the top 100 corporations had no Italian directors, and 78 had no Italian officers in their companies. A New York investigation determined that "City University . . . has historically practiced de facto discrimination against the Italian-American."[124] Both Joe Garagiola and Phil Rizzuto served on the joint committee of the Columbian Coalition and Anti-Defamation League of the B'nai B'rith that opposed prejudice against Italians and Jews in the medical schools' admission processes. Even the esteemed bioethicist Edmund Pellegrino had initially been denied entry to all the medical schools to which he had applied, even though he had graduated from St. John's University summa cum laude. One admissions director replied that he "might be happier with his own kind."[125] His father relied upon the traditional network of friends and associates to gain his son's acceptance, and Pellegrino became a leading physician and presidential adviser. Still, "Americans of Italian descent—especially those who have managed to achieve a fair amount of success—are concerned with the constant innuendo that credits their success to 'connections'" (that is, organized crime).[126]

In 1980 Italian scholars admitted that "education is a means to obtaining a job rather than as the basis for a career."[127] In contrast, Jews in particular took advantage of the educational resources in the United States to outdistance all other immigrant ethnic groups in terms of social mobility. Several social studies over the latter half of the twentieth century ranked Italians and Mexicans lowest relative to socioeconomic gains. New Yorkers, led by Joseph Colombo, formed an Italian-American anti-defamation league, and the city sponsored an Italian Culture Week in 1976 in an attempt to assuage the sense of prejudice. Despite at least three generations of Italians living in the United States, and the celebrity of athletes and entertainers, a sense of marginality still existed.[128]

Athletes and entertainers had achieved enough recognition, distinction, and respect to earn a level of acceptance within mainstream American society. Like other immigrant groups, the second generation had adopted and adapted to some of the dominant WASP norms, values, and standards and earned the designation of hyphenated Americans, an acknowledgment of partial inclusion in the mainstream society. The Americanization process continued throughout the middle decades of the twentieth century, but elements of the residual ancestral culture remained. Despite the obvious gains in social and economic capital of notable Americans of Italian descent, many others continued to seek refuge in the family and traditional values that have always provided a sense of comfort in an alien world. The first generation remained rooted in urban ethnic enclaves. Second- or third-generation offspring adhered to a sense of family and kin loyalty. High school attendance increased, but few attended college, with the notable exception of some athletes. Boxing and baseball, along with the entertainment industry, provided the most visible examples of Italian assimilation by the 1950s. Within a decade Italian football players gained national prominence as that sport surpassed baseball as the national game. The era of Joe DiMaggio, Rocky Marciano, and Vince Lombardi (as well as Frank Sinatra) arguably marked the zenith of the Italian-American impact on American popular culture, but it did so through the medium of physical performance, a continuing feature of the working-class habitus. Although Italian-Americans gained entry into the mainstream culture, their adherence to communalism rather than WASP individualism, and physical rather than academic prowess, still set them apart as incomplete sojourners on the path to full Americanization.

6

The Resurgence of Ethnicity

In February 1980 many Americans despaired at the seeming reversal of American global might as the United States stood helpless when Iranians seized the American Embassy and held its staff hostage and the Soviet army invaded Afghanistan. The force of sport as a political tool and psychological inspiration became apparent on the night of February 22 when

> a brash, young United States' hockey team struck a blow for American pride in the nation's cold war with Russia Friday at the Winter Olympics and left the powerful Soviet Union "Red-faced" by scoring one of the biggest upsets in sports history. Spurred on by thousands of screaming fans—many of them waving American flags,—the youngest-ever U.S. team upset the Soviets 4–3 to move into contention for the gold medal. The victory brought a telephone call from President Carter, touched off choruses of "God Bless America" in the U.S. team's locker room and ignited a celebration normally reserved for the Fourth of July. . . . [T]housands more hooted and hollered in the streets, many ringing cowbells, blowing horns and setting off fireworks long after the game ended.[1]

The winning goal had been scored by Mike Eruzione, the college-educated team captain and an American Italian who exemplified the cultural transition that had occurred over the past century. "We came together as a team six months ago from all parts of the United States, all different kinds of backgrounds and all kinds of ethnic beliefs."[2] As an American hero, Eruzione had melded into the mainstream, won acceptance and recognition, and achieved the American dream through sport. By the late twentieth century it might seem commonplace for a third- and even a fourth-generation of Italian-Americans to be thoroughly assimilated with little trace of their ancestral characteristics, becoming more American and less Italian in the process.

Yet two years later, when Italy won the soccer World Cup in 1982, residents of the Italian Federal Hill section of Providence, Rhode Island, exploded in an outburst of ethnic pride. In the Bronx "Monte Carmelesi poured into Main Street to celebrate. Cars decorated with Italian flags moved through the streets . . . , their horns blowing and their occupants cheering wildly. A particularly large crowd formed in Bishop Pernicone Square. It was one of the most impressive expressions of community solidarity that I have ever seen," reported an anthropologist doing field research in the neighborhood. Similar celebrations erupted in Italian neighborhoods in Brooklyn, Boston, Newark, and Baltimore.[3]

Such diverse experiences and practices of Italians in America preclude any universal generalization. They included the "birds of passage," who sought only a temporary residence, as well as those individuals who resided in ethnic urban enclaves, remote mining towns, Louisiana plantations, the canneries and wineries of California, as well as myriad other places. Many worked as laborers to build America. Some performed as athletes or entertainers, while others became bankers, corporate executives, and politicians. Italians such as Joe DiMaggio, Frank Sinatra, Lee Iacocca, Bart Giamatti, and Nancy Pelosi reached the pinnacles of success in the United States, while many others struggled. Higher education became more common among Italian-Americans, which provided more opportunities and greater recognition within mainstream society. Most Italians have been thoroughly acculturated, but not entirely assimilated. As late as the 1980s in the Monte Carmelo neighborhood of New York, many Italians still spoke the language of their ancestral land, adhered to traditional family practices and codes of honor, sheltered their daughters, married within their own ethnic group, and celebrated the saints' days in community religious festivals that marked a distinct Italian identity. One who had resided in the area for fifty-eight years proclaimed, "I'm a prisoner of the community and I say it joyously."⁴ Few such Little Italies remain, although some approximations have been transferred to suburban locations. Intermarriages produced mixed identities, and few retained the ability to speak their ancestral language by the third generation. Despite the hardships, setbacks, and integration within the American society, the grandchildren of the immigrants developed a distinct sense of pride in their Italian identity. Yet for many the sting of prejudice and a degree of marginality persist.

The Recognition of a Multicultural American Society

Assimilation differed between and within the various ethnic immigrant groups over the course of the twentieth century. Men, often owing to their greater exposure to the mainstream culture in the workplace and public life, assimilated faster than women. Children, exposed to American cultural values in the schools, parks, playgrounds, and popular culture, adapted their lives to one of conformity and acceptance. The middle class, invested in the educational opportunities and engaged in the capitalist economy, gained a greater level of inclusion within American society. As early as 1963, however, sociologists recognized that the full assimilation envisioned by the progressive reformers had not occurred. "The notion that the intense and unprecedented mixture of ethnic and religious groups in American life was soon to blend into a homogeneous end product has outlived its usefulness, and also its credibility. . . . The point about the melting pot . . . is that it did not happen."⁵

By the latter twentieth century Italian-Americans had formed an amalgamated culture that both adopted and adapted American values and merged them with residual elements of *Italianita*. Intermarriage with other groups and dispersal within the diverse American community became widespread among Italians. Italians who had achieved middle-class status mixed more readily with the mainstream. Some assumed leadership roles. In New Orleans a succession of Italian mayors ran the city. In New York Mario Cuomo, and later his son Andrew, governed the state, and Rudy Giuliani directed its largest city, while Alfonse D'Amato served as a senator in Washington, DC. Ethnic rivalries decreased, and Italians combined their St. Joseph Day parade with the Irish St. Patrick Day festival in a joint celebration in New Orleans, but Italian *festas* elsewhere continued to mark their religious differences from mainstream Catholicism. Ethnic enclaves still persisted, as urban neighborhoods relocated to largely ethnic suburbs, and Italian identity remained strong. A daughter of an Italian immigrant explained that despite her mother's twenty years of residence in Monte Carmelo in the Bronx, "she came from one Italy to another, so I have to speak Italian to her."[6] As late as 2004 the southeastern United States still numbered twenty-nine societies dedicated to preserving the Italian language and culture, and a more recent study found an increasing claim among Americans to Italian ethnicity and counted more than three million speakers of the Italian language. But the confusing mixture of identities affected Italian-Americans throughout the United States. Maria Reggio, a California resident, explained the gradual familial transition in identity. "Because I was raised in Monterey, we were a community of Italians, so I got that feeling of being Italian-American. But now we are more American Italian. But probably with my children it will just be American with a background of Italian."[7]

The third generation had not experienced the same traumas and troubles of their grandparents and parents. Most no longer spoke Italian, but they adhered to Italian food, family values, and, for the working class, a sense of fatalism. Scholar Michael Novak surmised that "working class families have no bright or altered future to look forward to. Day after day is the same."[8] Secure in their whiteness, but still tenuous in their sense of social acceptance owing to continued stereotypes reinforced by media, television, and movies, many Italians still operated on the fringes of the mainstream culture. Tom Scotto, a Sicilian working for the phone company, finally opened his own business after repeated denials for promotion because of his ethnicity. Joanne Detore, a third-generation Italian, still faced outright bigotry. Despite being an outstanding student, her high school romance with an Irish American boyfriend ended when his Ivy League–educated father confronted her with an unexpected rant.

> I know about you people. I was over there, in Italy, during the war. All of your men are hoodlums, mobsters, and all of your women are whores. You are nothing but an Italian whore! You'll amount to nothing, nothing I tell you. You'll end up pregnant and quitting school, one of those teenaged mothers on welfare, and I can't let my son go down with you, my dear. I have a duty to save my son. I never want to see you again in this house or near my son. Do you understand me?[9]

Another Irish American recounted his courtship of his Irish Italian wife: "Her maiden name is Fitzpatrick. That's the only reason I asked her out because she had an Irish last name. If her last name had been Italian, I probably never would have asked her out."[10] Sociologists identified intermarriage as the last step in the assimilation process, but even that rite did not guarantee inclusion. Such lack of full acceptance and underlying prejudice left residual doubts in the minds of Italian Americans."[11]

Italian-Americans proliferated in the popular culture that allowed for and even encouraged innovation and experimentation. Frank Sinatra exemplified such qualities in both his music and his values. In the post–World War II era, as tensions between Italians and blacks mounted, Sinatra preached tolerance and unity. His father had been a local boxer, but he commanded a national audience to wage his battles. As early as 1945 he took a stand against racism in a Harlem high school and then made thirty appearances throughout the country to denounce prejudice. In his life and in his music, "he never forgot what it was like to be unwanted."[12] After World War II Sinatra joined other actors and actresses in a free-speech crusade against McCarthyism, a stand that resulted in surveillance by the FBI. His campaign for social justice impaired his career. Still, Sinatra continued to cross racial lines and even befriended Sugar Ray Robinson, an African American boxer, in his 1958 rematch with Carmen Basilio, but maintained his Italian cultural values and Italian friendships. "Among young adults, he [Sinatra] was almost worshipped."[13] "Not since Valentino, wrote *Time* in July 1943, had 'American womanhood made such unabashed public love to an entertainer.' The *New Republic* noted one girl who wore a bandage for three weeks on her arm at the spot where 'Frankie touched me.' Another went to 56 consecutive performances in a theater where he was playing [this means five or six performances a day]."[14] Sinatra's adulation only grew as he aged. His melancholy renditions spoke not just to Italian conditions, but to the travails of all Americans in a manner that encompassed ethnic, racial, and class differences. Pete Hamill, an acquaintance and biographer of Sinatra, stated "Through the power of his art and his personality, he became one of a very small group that would permanently shift the image of Italian Americans."[15] Author Gay Talese maintained that "Sinatra allowed Italian-Americans like me to take pride in ourselves."[16] Baseball manager Tommy Lasorda concurred that "Sinatra made all us Italians proud."[17]

Sinatra retained a sense of the underdog throughout his life and, despite his triumphs, continued to face bigotry. At a young age he learned the meaning of "dago," "guinea," and "wop." In 1966 he and Dean Martin got into a fight with a patron at the Polo Lounge in Hollywood when the latter evoked an ethnic slur. Later in life he explained his contributions to the NAACP to an inquiring reporter by stating, "Because we've [Italians] been there too, man. It wasn't just black people hanging from those fucking ropes."[18]

Sinatra's Italian identity presented a vital part of his image and his consciousness. As a youth he hated the *Life with Luigi* radio show that caricatured Italians. He refused to Anglicize his surname when he got his big chance with the Harry James Orchestra, and he reasoned that "half the troubles I've had were because my name ended in a vowel."[19]

Sinatra's latter life reflected the transition in the Italian-American experience. Despite success negative images persisted. He continued to support civil rights, but perhaps too smug in his own attainment of whiteness, he regularly employed racial and ethnic jokes. Both Sinatra and Dean Martin were caricatured as unhealthy smokers and heavy drinkers. Performances with his famous "rat pack" of friends were characterized as "a glorification of the American alcoholic." Sinatra's self-indulgent womanizing, rudeness, and crude behavior overshadowed his generosity and loyalty. His close affiliation with gangsters and his bullying of transgressors continually called his character into question. In the 1970s he turned politically conservative and supported the Republican Party, like many other Italians.[20]

Other Italian movie stars emerged by the 1970s, along with a bevy of athletes, but contradictory images prevailed. Although athletes such as baseball all-stars Ron Santo, Joe Pepitone, and Sal Bando became household names, and football stars John Cappelletti, the 1973 Heisman Trophy winner, and the ill-fated Brian Piccolo espoused heroic Americanization, the actors' portrayals often retarded the Italian image. Sylvester Stallone is famous for his depictions of maladjusted Vietnam vet John Rambo in a series of films or his representation of the stalwart but demeaned and directionless boxer Rocky Balboa in the *Rocky* movies. Stallone's character, known as the Italian Stallion, portrayed stereotypical characteristics. The uneducated Rocky relied on his brawn and his strong work ethic, yet maintained a sense of honor and respect for women. The Rambo character was introduced in the movie *First Blood* in 1982 (derived from a 1972 novel by David Morrell) and serves as an allegory of the Italian-American experience. The product of a mixed marriage (Navajo father and Italian-American mother), and a disaffected Green Beret who had served and suffered for his country, the proud loner embarked on a vendetta of honor and vengeance when the oppressive local police force bloodied him and forced his hand. Mistreated, unaccepted, and disrespected in a foreign place, accused of polluting the town by his very presence, Rambo is portrayed as a rebellious outlaw, not unlike the gangster. His trusty hunting knife serves the same purpose as the feared stiletto of yesteryear. Like World War II, deemed to be disloyal, he confronts the full weight of the government response. Despite the odds, he triumphs by virtue of his resilience, toughness, and physical prowess.[21]

John Travolta became a national celebrity in his television portrayal of the underachieving Vinnie Barbarino during the 1970s. His macho and misogynistic Tony Manero character in *Saturday Night Fever* (1977), whose only talent is dancing, popularized the disco movement (and later spawned guido culture) as a disillusioned working-class youth seeking fulfillment within an overwhelming existence. Actors Al Pacino and Robert De Niro emerged during the same decade, often portraying the gritty side of life, but also reinforcing the negative stereotypes of Italian gangsters in such films as the *Godfather* series (1972, 1974, 1990), *Scarface* (1983), and *Goodfellas* (1990). Their superb acting ability, however, led film critic Leonard Maltin to claim that "they made urban ethnicity fashionable, and they did it through the sheer force of their talent."[22] Another Italian actor, James Gandolfini, starred in the long-running (1999–2007) *Sopranos* television series that pondered the continuing conflicts in Italian-American lives. The series explored family values, character, and ethics, albeit through the eyes of a violent gangster figure.[23] Historian Anthony Rotundo claimed that "the Sopranos gives us values such as loyalty, rootedness, and interdependence—values that have provided a foundation for Italian American manhood. . . . America . . . is hostile to those values."[24] Rather than portraying success via mainstream values, the series continued the stereotype of ill-gotten wealth via criminal activity.

Actor Tony Danza (Iadanza), the son of an Italian immigrant mother, achieved a more wholesome image. He initially embarked on an athletic career, winning a college scholarship to the University of Dubuque based on his talent as a wrestler. He pursued boxing in the Golden Gloves competition and then turned pro from 1976 to 1979 as he dabbled in theatrical work. His role as an ex-boxer in the long-running *Taxi* series on television convinced him to change his career path, which led to more television and movie roles as an actor, director, and producer.[25]

Meanwhile, actor Mark Giordano has been refused roles depicting Italian-Americans, despite his own ethnic background. Casting directors have told him that "he's not blue-collar enough and too intelligent to play an Italian American."[26] Sports, however, offer greater meritocracy, where physical abilities trump appearance or ancestry.

Current television portrayals of guido culture, the distinctive hedonistic, working-class lifestyle of youthful Italian-Americans in the Northeast, has unleashed a firestorm of resentment and debate among the Italian upper classes. The depiction of the youthful subculture remains mired in physicality, tempered by American materialism and consumption patterns that emphasize body image and appearance for both males and females. Similar to athletes, it is very much a performance culture of "stylized presentation of self and around symbolic meanings those performances have." Young men wear tight clothes and T-shirts to show off their muscularity and tattoos and are adorned with gold chains or gold crosses, as well as body piercings and gelled hairstyles, which are exhibited in public performances, often at dance clubs. Moreover, males engage in an aggressive form of masculine physicality that revolves around dancing, drinking, and fighting, the latter often an expression of the traditional value of protecting one's honor or turf. Such youth have refashioned themselves into an imagined community that excludes non-Italians and reinforces their own ethnic identity in a reversal of the past inferiority complex suffered by their immigrant ancestors.[27] In such a culture youths continue to contend with other ethnic or racial groups for a limited social space (Bourdieu's notion of the field) in American society. In New York such youth subcultures can be distinguished by the dance clubs that they frequent or are excluded from and by the musical styles that they prefer. Radio station WKTU caters specifically to the guido and guidette culture.[28]

Other Italian-American females carved out a sizable niche in popular culture in the music industry, where they have exerted considerably more power than Italian female athletes. Connie Francis (Concetta Franconero) emerged as a top pop singer in the 1950s, followed by Liza Minnelli, who earned accolades as both a singer and an actress. Louise Ciccone, better known as Madonna, has become a global icon as an entertainer who has continually reinvented her image over the past three decades. Stefani Germanotta, otherwise known as Lady Gaga, has similarly used her physicality to portray a pseudoidentity that is a product of her American experience. She felt that she did not fit in at a Catholic girls' school and then dropped out of New York University. She was able to leave her insecurities behind in the persona of Lady Gaga. Her music "speaks to people who are disconnected from society." It is a condition with which her Italian immigrant ancestors would have been familiar.[29]

Time has listed Lady Gaga among the world's one hundred most influential people, and she now refuses to use her given name. A music critic who observed a 2010 Chicago performance stated, "She's an incredible talent, but she's buried it in all this showy nonsense that she seems to think has grand, transcendent meaning. . . . She tried to out-sacrilege Madonna (a profane prayer, a bleeding angel statue, comparing herself to Jesus) and added, in possibly her truest statement (despite also explaining that, next to money, she really 'hates the truth'): I don't care who you are or what you believe, all I care is what you think of me."[30] Lady Gaga admitted that she lives "halfway between reality and fantasy all the time." Yet she claims that she is "an Italian New Yorker at heart."[31] Like the immigrants of a century ago, she still searches for recognition and acceptance but holds on to her ancestral roots. Her lyrics encompass the joy and misery of *Italianita*. She stated that "something that carries through all my songwriting is this undertone of grit and darkness and melancholy." In the process of transforming their identities, both Madonna and Lady Gaga have engaged elements of their Italian ancestral culture while also distancing themselves from the European experiences of their predecessors.[32]

A Convergence of Values in Sport

Italian athletes, however, maintained a more consistently positive image within American society. Sports required skills congruent with the Italian working-class value of physicality. One professional athlete remarked that "being a physical man in the modern world is becoming obsolete. The machines have taken the place of that."[33] Italians continued to be fixtures in a variety of sporting endeavors, but, despite gains in socioeconomic status, boxing retained a particular attraction. Ray "Boom Boom" Mancini initiated his professional career in 1979 and fought until 1992, winning the lightweight championship in 1981. Mancini is too often remembered for his 1982 match with Duk Koo Kim, a South Korean challenger who died five days after the fight owing to severe brain injury, a tragedy symbolic of the competing underclass aspirants in a now globalized sporting culture. ESPN, the global sports media conglomerate, characterized Mancini's quest for a championship, however, as a tribute to his Italian heritage and family values. His father had been a top contender before military service in World War II nullified his chance for a championship. Ray resurrected that dream to honor his father. When he was only thirteen years old he wrote a poem entitled "I Walk in Your Shadow." His nonstop brawling style endeared him to his Youngstown, Ohio, fans during a depressed economy. An unemployed steelworker stated that "I can tell you honestly, he's about all we've got that's good here. There's not much else to go on." Despite reaching the pinnacle of the sport, Mancini lost his endorsements after the nationally televised Kim bout, and the heroic underdog status no longer applied.[34]

Vinny Pazienza, a flamboyant lightweight, captured the world title in 1987 with a similar attitude and a chip on his shoulder. Pazienza gloried in his Italian identity and his toughness, continuing to fight until his 2004 retirement. Bobby Czyz, the son of a Polish father and an Italian mother, made his professional debut in 1980 and boxed until 1998, winning the light heavyweight and cruiserweight championships along the way. Paul Malignaggi, born in Brooklyn, but a Sicilian resident until age six, resembled the "birds of passage" of a century ago. He returned to the United States and embarked on a boxing career, winning the 2001 national amateur championship and the International Boxing Federation junior welterweight title in 2007. Malignaggi's ethnic Brooklyn following recalled the communal solidarity of the pre–World War II era, an element of the residual culture still present in contemporary times. The persistence of Italians as boxers also suggests an adherence to working-class habitus and the perception of the limited nature of social mobility in the mainstream economy.[35]

Such boxers carried a still distinct ethnicity into the ring, marked by their differences with their opponents. Middleweight contender Peter Manfredo Jr. wore the colors of the Italian flag on his trunks and declared himself the "Italian Warrior" and the pride of Providence, Rhode Island. Such boxers' fan base continued to represent a distinct communal consciousness. For both the fighters and their followers, boxing brought greater contact with an outside world, but maintained an assertion of ethnic and working-class values representative of earlier generations. For them the bourgeois life seemed irrelevant. Life remained hard and often short. Their bodies represented a means of pleasure and performance, dictating the choice of occupation and leisure that reinforced class differences. Despite generations of change they replicated a preexisting working-class culture that enhanced personal stature, local pride, and communal recognition via physical prowess that affirmed their ethnicity as well as class-specific beliefs and principles that transcended class lines. As the world modernized they found comfort in a more traditional existence.[36]

Throughout the past century Italians have been prominent not only as boxers, but as trainers within the sport. Cus D'Amato led Floyd Patterson to the heavyweight championship in 1956, making Patterson the youngest to ever win the title at the age of twenty-one. D'Amato served as not only a trainer, but surrogate father to Mike Tyson when he eclipsed Patterson's record by winning the heavyweight crown at the age of twenty in 1986, shortly after D'Amato's death in 1985. Lou Duva served as trainer, manager, and promoter for numerous champions, including Italians Joey Giardello (Carmine Tilelli), Bobby Czyz, and Vinnie Pazienza. Angelo Dundee handled Carmen Basilio, light-heavyweight champ Willie Pastrano, Muhammad Ali, George Foreman, and Sugar Ray Leonard, as well as ten other world champions.[37]

In another physically demanding sport, football, Italian-Americans have added to their collective laurels during recent decades. They have been most noticeable in the leadership roles of quarterback and linebacker. Among the Heisman Trophy winners were running back John Cappelletti (1973) and quarterbacks Vinny Testaverde (1986) and Gino Torretta (1992), while Dan Pastorini, Daryl Lamonica, Vince Ferragamo, Joe Montana, and Dan Marino enjoyed stellar NFL careers. The latter two are enshrined in the NFL Hall of Fame. Among the linebackers Doug Buffone, Joe Fortunato, Nick Buoniconti, Ted Hendricks, Phil Villapiano, and Mike Lucci stood out, with Buoniconti and Hendricks elected to the Hall of Fame. Italian leadership has been evident in the roles of coaches Carmen Cozza, Joe Paterno, Dick Vermeil, Lee Corso, and Bill Parcells (Italian mother), as well as owners Tony Morabito and Ed De Bartolo and Commissioner Paul Tagliabue. Paterno, in particular, exemplified the promise of sport for Italian-Americans. Born in Brooklyn in 1926, Paterno excelled in school and sports "because of the image in the back of my head of my mother expecting me to defend my honor, our family honor. I probably absorbed my shame of losing from my mother." His father imparted a love of opera, a strong work ethic, perseverance, and aspiration. His Catholic high school instilled a deep patriotism during World War II. Paterno attended Brown University through the beneficence of a football booster and played a dual role as quarterback and defensive back on its football team, yet he endured ethnic slurs. At a fraternity party, he overheard the question, "How did that dago get invited?" Initially rejected by other fraternities because of his ethnicity, he persevered to become the vice president of another and advocated membership for all ethnic groups. He relished debates because "I just wasn't about to let a Protestant think he was smarter than I was." Upon his graduation in 1950 he accompanied his coach to his new position at Penn State University, assuming the head coaching role in 1966 and becoming the winningest coach in collegiate history and a member of the College Football Hall of Fame. Paterno's faith and family values, vestiges of his Italian upbringing, characterized his coaching career. He made decisions "based on my feelings that I have a responsibility not only to myself and my family but to my church and my faith. . . . Some days I feel like I've got a hundred sons to worry about. If any squad member gets into a jam, it's like my own kid getting into a jam." Paterno's success earned him millions of dollars, and he contributed like sums to the university.[38] Such accolades in the sporting world gave evidence of Italian inclusion and accommodation within the mainstream popular culture and provide images contrary to the continuing criminal stereotypes.

Similar tributes can be accorded to the plethora of baseball luminaries. Billy Martin, Tommy Lasorda, Terry Francona, Tony La Russa, and Joe Torre managed their teams to numerous championships throughout the latter twentieth century. Lasorda exemplified the new Italian of the post–World War II era as a fiercely loyal and patriotic American who still loves Italy and retains Italian values and traits. Lasorda grew up as the son of an Italian immigrant truck driver, the second of five sons. As a youth he earned money in boxing matches arranged by his uncle. He said, "I fought all the time for any reason."[39] He turned down a professional boxing career to pursue baseball, but such combativeness marked his habitus and followed him throughout his career. Lasorda admired toughness in his long tenure as manager of the Los Angeles Dodgers, and he adhered to the value systems learned in his Italian home. He extolled hard work as an antidote to education in his appeals to young baseball players. "If you enroll in Lasorda University, your tuition will be perspiration, determination, and inspiration. And if you are lucky enough to graduate, you'll make more money than a professor at Harvard or Yale."[40] His office walls were covered with photos of religious figures, and he maintained a frugal lifestyle in a small stucco house despite his wealth. Lasorda craved food and companionship. He valued loyalty and honor, which he had learned from his father, who had waited eight long years to achieve revenge against an antagonist who had once pulled a gun on him. Lasorda's loyalty to the Dodgers' organization, which he viewed as his family, became legendary, yet he felt insecure and unappreciated. As the manager of the 2000 Olympic baseball team he felt the need to prove himself, despite his long and successful career. He did so by guiding the team to the gold medal, the first American team to defeat the Cubans in Olympic baseball competition. In the process he had to defeat the Italian team and define his own identity. He admitted that he loved Italy, the land of his father, but he was an American and he stated his allegiance to the United States. "You're not winning for one city or team, you're winning for an entire nation."[41]

Sport and the Fulfillment of American Dreams

Italians came to the United States in search of a better life, more opportunities, and a measure of respect. By the third generation a select few had fulfilled those expectations beyond their wildest dreams, and sports provided the means for some of them.

Nick Mileti, the son of Sicilian immigrants, found great opportunity in the United States. He initially embarked on a career as a lawyer, became an entrepreneur, and then became owner of the Cleveland Barons of the American Hockey League in 1968. In 1970 he acquired the Cleveland Cavaliers NBA franchise and bought the Cleveland Indians baseball team two years later. That same year he brought the Crusaders of the World Hockey Association to Cleveland. In 1974 he opened the Richfield Coliseum with a Frank Sinatra concert as a fund-raiser for the education of Italian-American children. In addition to his sports franchises Mileti owned radio stations, but despite his immense success in the United States he embarked on a three-year sojourn to Rome in 1989, which resulted in the authorship of three books on Italian personalities, society, and art and a new role as a film producer. He explained his new avocation and his adherence to his ethnicity as "I am Italian, of course I love beautiful things."[42]

Ed De Bartolo Jr. inherited his father's real estate fortune, but enhanced his own as a team owner. The De Bartolo family bought the San Francisco '49ers in 1977 and purchased the Pittsburgh Penguins National Hockey League (NHL) franchise a year later. His sister, Denise De Bartolo York, served as Penguins president until 1991 and acquired the '49ers in 2000. The family has been generous donors to the University of Notre Dame.

Jerry Colangelo made a similar journey toward great wealth and celebrity as a sports mogul. Colangelo parlayed his athletic skills into a college education and eventual ownership of the Arizona

Diamondbacks baseball team (Joe Garagiola served as the general manager), but he had even more extensive holdings outside of that sport. He had owned both the Phoenix Suns basketball team, as well as the Phoenix Mercury in the Women's National Basketball Association and the Arizona Rattlers in the Arena Football League. Colangelo was instrumental in bringing the NHL franchise to Phoenix. As the national director of USA Basketball, he guided the efforts of the US Olympic team to a gold medal in 2008. His dedication to the game won him election to the Basketball Hall of Fame.[43] His extensive entrepreneurial ventures in sport are indicative of the opportunities afforded to assimilated Italian-Americans, a far cry from the initial efforts of Cesare Orsini in 1877 New York.

Yet Colangelo never lost sight of his ethnicity. When he gained notice as a high school athlete, it was suggested that he Anglicize his name, but he refused, stating, "'I'll never do that. I'm too proud of my heritage." Years later his Arizona office featured a photo of his boyhood home in Chicago Heights, a largely Italian suburb, as well as the accordion on which he played Italian melodies for his grandfather and a statue of Christopher Columbus. Colangelo reasoned that "being born here, we're Americans. But we shouldn't lose sight of the fact that we're of Italian heritage, and we should be proud of that." He substantiated that sentiment by raising nearly two million dollars to build the Italian American Sports Hall of Fame in Chicago.[44]

Larry Lucchino's ascendance and his adherence to ethnicity resembled that of Colangelo as he assumed the roles of president and chief executive officer of the Baltimore Orioles (1988–93), San Diego Padres (1995–2001), and Boston Red Sox (2002). "There was definitely a sense of Italian food, culture, and family values that permeated our home." Although a basketball player at Princeton, he felt a sense of loss until he attended Yale Law School. "I liked New Haven because it had a very strong Italian culture and community." He returned to Calabria to meet his relatives. "I stayed in a farmhouse built in the sixteenth or seventeenth century, with frescoes on the wall. . . . I was welcomed with open arms. I sent a card to my parents letting them know I was going to find an Italian girl to marry."

Despite his thorough Americanization, he stated that "the older and wiser I get, the more I recover a sense of ethnic identity. I have a keen sense of pride in my heritage."[45]

A number of other American Italian entrepreneurs followed in the wake of their predecessors. Vince Naimoli owned the Tampa Bay Devil Rays from 1998 to 2005. Mark Attanasio bought the Milwaukee Brewers in 2005, but still finds time to take his parents and family to Italy each summer. Robert Castellini acquired the Cincinnati Reds in 2006.[46]

The rise of the sports moguls coincided with the ascendance of a host of very successful Italian-American basketball coaches: Lou Carnesecca, Rollie Massimino, Jim Valvano, P. J. Carlesimo, Mike Fratello, Rick Pitino, John Calipari, and Geno Auriemma. In 2004 St. John's University honored its longtime mentor by renaming and upgrading its basketball facility as the Carnesecca Arena. Such a litany of dignitaries is not limited to sporting circles, for Italian-Americans have reached the pinnacles of power as politicians (Mario and Andrew Cuomo, Geraldine Ferraro, Rudy Giuliani, Nancy Pelosi, and others), corporate executives (Lee Iacocca), and even as Supreme Court justices (Antonin Scalia and Samuel Alito). The short list provides ample evidence that Italians are no longer considered the "other." They have, to a great degree, assimilated within the mainstream and negated many of the persistent stereotypes. Still, Geraldine Ferraro contended that in her vice presidential campaign, she often had to deal with the assertions of Italian criminal stereotypes.[47]

Donna Lopiano, however, rose to prominence and power, without ethnic bias but within her family's ethnic influences. She built upon the experiences of Maud Nelson, Margaret Gisolo, and the Savona sisters to exemplify the possibilities for Italian-American women. Considered to be one of the most important figures in American sport, she excelled first as an athlete supported by a very "modern" mother, who was unlike her more traditional Italian siblings. Her parents, owners of an Italian restaurant, followed Italian customs, foods, and holidays. Lopiano remains committed to family and bought an Italian deli for her sister. As women's athletic director of the University of Texas, and then chief executive officer of the Women's Sports Foundation, she no longer faced a nativist backlash, but the entrenched patriarchy of the American sports bureaucracy. The tenacity she displayed as an athlete carried over to the corporate world, where she became a successful advocate for Title IX and women's athletic rights.

When Italy asked her to coach its national softball team she accepted, but refused to play and insisted that the country develop its own players rather than import Americans of Italian ancestry. Like Lasorda, she has maintained her Italian roots.[48]

Bart Giamatti, the grandson of an immigrant laborer, became president of Yale University and then the commissioner of baseball. He had developed his love for the game at an early age, and his explanation of that love served as a metaphor for the Italian-American identity. "Baseball is about going home and how hard it is to get there. Its wisdom says you can go home again but that you cannot stay. The journey must always start once more, the bat an oar over the shoulder, until there is an end to all this journeying."[49] Giamatti represented a clear indication of Italian amalgamation within the mainstream culture. Like Giammati's odyssey, Italians became Americans, but for many there remained a deep longing for the past and an incomplete journey.

Limited Assimilation

Assimilation, however, did not mean the inevitable, nonreversible linear progression suggested by modernization theorists. Although Italians moved from exclusion to marginality and finally to incorporation within the larger society, that assimilation process has not been complete for all Italian-Americans. A study of fourth-generation Italians in Dallas during the 1980s found that only 12 percent could identify Italian-language terms, yet 60 percent took pride in the achievements of Italians. Eighty percent retained Italian foods, while 84 percent adhered to the Catholic religion. Italian social clubs still played bocce, but they had also become Dallas Cowboys fans. In Minnesota bocce waned in Duluth, but persisted in the more isolated mining towns.

Bocce was so popular in Louisiana that the players held a statewide tournament. Wherever bocce was played, it remained a marker of Italian identity. In Philadelphia, New York, Boston, and Chicago, Italian suburbanites still maintained their ties to their old urban neighborhoods with regular, even weekly, visits. The Order of the Sons of Italy in Philadelphia still counted 90,000 members in the 1980s, and the Italian-American population actually increased from 132,630 in 1980 to 178,315 a decade later. By the 1990s Italians had joined the Irish in socialization, and former ethnic rivalries between the two groups were transferred to an annual softball game. In New Orleans the number of St. Joseph Day celebrations had increased by two thousand, and throughout America Italians continued to dance the tarantella at weddings into the twenty-first century.[50]

The new, amalgamated culture of the Americans of Italian origin might be characterized as American Italian by the third or fourth generation, yet another transitional stage in the assimilation process. I chose this term to indicate that this cohort differed distinctly from the culture of the first and second generation in a number of ways. By the midtwentieth century the grandchildren of Italian immigrants had more education than their forebears, but teachers too often belittled their parents and their ancestral culture. The second generation was taught to disdain their parents as un-American foreigners who did not speak English or embrace mainstream values. The children of the immigrants learned to live in, and largely accept, the working-class American culture. Their limited education trained them only for roles in the industrialized economy, although some who engaged in the building trades or produce markets became entrepreneurs with their own businesses. Many of their life lessons took place on the streets, in settlement houses, parks, and playgrounds, where site supervisors assumed the roles of surrogate parents as they instructed Italian children to play in the American way. Sport provided a means to escape their ancestral past, both psychologically and, to some degree, economically. The Italians of the Hill District in St. Louis produced an inordinate number of professional athletes, attributing much of their development to "Uncle" Joe Causino, a social worker.[51]

Yogi Berra, the Yankees' Hall of Fame catcher from the Hill District, still suffered years of caricature as a buffoon despite his physical prowess and his business acumen. Even sportswriter Robert Lipsyte, usually laudatory in his treatment, described Berra as "a cuddly savage who lusts after comic books, innocently scratches himself in public, loves children and dogs, exudes natural humor, and swings down from his tree house to excel in a game he would play for nothing."[52]

Despite such negativity sport assumed a primary role in the lives of Italian-American youth, unlike the grinding existence of their parents and grandparents. Sport continued to attract young Italians throughout the century. The disparate generations could agree on the value of physicality, something that the immigrants had brought from Italy, but in the New World it was expressed in different forms. Whereas the older generation labored, the younger one played, and found the means to turn their leisure pursuits into income as semipro and professional athletes and as a vehicle toward greater socioeconomic status and social capital. Even neighborhood stars earned a greater measure of respect, acceptance, and self-esteem. Individual sports, like boxing, accommodated Italian values of expression, toughness, and a strong work ethic, while team sports replicated the homosocial world of Italian communal life, where men and women did not mix.

Sport and Female Liberation

One of the ways in which Italians Americans clearly departed from the ancestral culture involved the liberation of women from the traditional domesticity of the past. Sport and the economy figured prominently in that process. As women and girls increasingly joined the workforce in the United States they greatly expanded their social worlds. Young women were increasingly drawn to the popular culture of music, dances, and sport. Industrial recreation programs offered opportunities for females in baseball, softball, basketball, track and field, and bowling. Schoolgirls were exposed to an even wider array of physical activities in the parks, playgrounds, and settlement houses. Italian females of the second and third generations clearly departed from the habits and lifestyles of their mothers in their pursuit of sport. Maud Nelson and Margaret Gisolo (as discussed in chapter 3) had intruded upon masculine space in their pursuit of baseball. They served as pioneers for following generations, and such nondomestic activities broadened the scope of girls' and women's lives immeasurably. Italian-American women would never again be solely Italians in their worldview or their practices. Yet the socially constructed Italian-American culture, no longer simply Italian, was not yet completely American.

By the latter half of the twentieth century American Italian women had built on the pioneering ventures of early female athletes. The recreational athletes of the 1930s spawned professional players by the next generation. Mildred Martorella Ignizio captured a number of bowling titles on the women's pro tour during the early 1970s, and Robin Romeo enjoyed a twenty-year span on the pro bowlers' tour, winning seventeen national titles and Bowler of the Year honors in 1989. Both Ignizio and Romeo are members of the Bowling Hall of Fame. Donna Caponi also had a long career on the women's professional golf tour, winning the US Open in 1969 and 1970 and induction into the Ladies Professional Golf Association Hall of Fame. Linda Fratianne held the US figure-skating championship from 1977 to 1980 and the world championship in 1977 and 1979, and she won an Olympic silver medal in 1980. Susan Notorangelo set a transcontinental record as a cyclist in 1989. Italians have produced their share of tennis stars as well. Mary Carillo, the product of an Italian-Irish marriage, won the French Open mixed-doubles title in 1977, and Jennifer Capriati was among the premier players, winning three Grand Slam events during her career and a gold medal at the 1992 Olympic Games. Mary Lou Retton (Rotundo) became America's darling as a gymnast at the 1984 Olympics, winning five medals and being named *Sports Illustrated*'s Sportswoman of the Year and the Amateur Athletic Union Athlete of the Year. Like the early female baseball players, women continue to expand their interests by encroaching on previously male domains. Cammi Granato added to the Olympic laurels as captain of the American women's ice hockey team. Her four goals in the 1998 competition helped the team to the gold medal. Her teammate Angela Ruggiero appeared on three Olympic teams.[53] For such American Italian women, American identity has superseded their ancestral roots.

The transition in the lives of American Italian women has been most evident in politics. Whereas their grandmothers lived largely apolitical existences within a constraining domestic sphere, women such as Ella Grasso, congresswomen (1970–74) and governor of Connecticut (1975–80), Geraldine Ferraro, congresswomen (1979–85) and vice presidential candidate (1984), and Nancy Pelosi, congresswoman (1987–) and Speaker of the House of Representatives (2007–11), became public figures. Pelosi's acceptance speech as Speaker of the House provided distinct evidence of the transition in women's lives over the course of the century, but also exhibited a sense of history and a reliance on Italian values as she invoked family, loyalty, and religion. She pointed to the continuing transition for all women. "For our daughters and granddaughters, today, we have broken the marble ceiling. For our daughters and our granddaughters, the sky is the limit, anything is possible for them."[54]

Sport as a Measure of American Italian Identity

The modern Olympic Games have spawned an intense nationalistic spirit since their inception in 1896. Originally intended as a fraternal exercise in sport and brotherhood to promote peace, they quickly degenerated into a comparison of cultural superiority, as national teams came to represent different political ideologies and social practices. Such assumptions took on particular significance during the Cold War period that followed World War II, and Italian-American athletes have held a particular prominence in the portrayal of a multicultural American identity and democratic values. Lindy Remigino proved a surprise as the upset winner of the 100-meter race in 1952 and ran a leg on the gold-medal relay team as well. Charlie Capozzoli, his Olympic teammate, ran the 5,000-meter race that same year. Marty Liquori was the best US miler at the 1968 Games and a three-time NCAA champion.

Mike Eruzione captained the ice hockey team in its stunning upset of the Soviet Union en route to its gold-medal performance against Finland in 1980. Eight years later Brian Boitano followed with an Olympic championship in figure skating. Donna de Varona made her first Olympic team as a thirteen-year-old swimmer in 1960. She won two gold medals at the 1964 Games and set eighteen world records in her career. Both the Associated Press and United Press International named her the athlete of the year in 1965, but her first love had been baseball. Unable to play because of the Little League prohibitions against girls, de Varona became an activist for Title IX and girls' sports after her Hall of Fame swimming career. Matt Biondi swam on three Olympic teams (1984, 1988, 1992), winning eleven medals (eight gold medals).[55] The variety of sports in which American Italians had reached such prominence provided ample evidence of their integration and gains in social capital by the late twentieth century. Their participation on the US Olympic team clearly marked the transition from an Italian identity to an American one.

Despite the nationalistic glory that Italians contributed to the American efforts in the Olympics, other Italians had not foregone their interest in the traditional Italian sports of bocce and soccer. Italians had formed their own soccer teams early in the twentieth century, supplementing their rosters with the flow of men from Italy. Unione Sportiva Italiana Virtus fielded a team in San Francisco as early as 1926. Umberto Magnaini, born in Brazil, owed his job to his soccer abilities as a player on a company team in Chicago. He later joined the Italo Maroons soccer club, formed in 1929 for competition in the Chicago International Soccer League. The Italian Hill neighborhood in St. Louis supplied players to the American national team throughout the middecades of the twentieth century, and Italian soccer clubs continue to operate today. Interest has not been limited to local teams, as many retain an interest in the professional soccer teams in Italy.[56]

Bocce, too, retained its hold in many of the Italian enclaves in the cities, as well as those individuals transplanted to the suburbs. Bocce continued to be played in New York, Chicago, Connecticut, Rhode Island, Arkansas, and California, and in other locations where sizable numbers of Italian-Americans or American Italians gathered. In 1985 the small community of Martinez, California, boasted of one thousand players in its bocce league, and the sport grew exponentially throughout the United States thereafter. In Los Gatos, California, three generations of Italians met at the bocce grounds to celebrate their heritage in food and recreation. Michael Nicosia, a Sicilian immigrant living in California, was selected for the US national team to compete in an international match in Canada in 1993. He noted his pride in the selection by stating, "It is quite a bit of honor for me to reach best in the U.S. at my age [*sic*]; but it's more an honor to represent the U.S. in another country." Bocce courts remain a fixture in the now gentrified Little Italy neighborhood of Chicago, and the sport continues to grow throughout the United States. A national championship has been held since 1980, and the 2011 affair featured television and Internet broadcasts. In 1996 Homewood, Illinois, a Chicago suburb, hosted the Bocce World Cup, the first time the event had been conducted in the United States. Orion, Michigan, hosted the World Championship in 2005. Although immigrants, such as Nicosia, have provided some impetus, bocce in the United States is largely a means for American Italians to celebrate the food, culture, and sport of their ancestral heritage.[57]

The ongoing ties of Italian-Americans and even American Italians to their ancestral homeland became evident with the inclusion of American sport forms in the Olympic Games. In 1984 Mike Mastrullo, an American Italian, chose to play for the Italian national ice hockey team. Since then, other Americans such as Gaspare Pizzo, Anthony Tuzzolino, and Robert Nardella, have opted to play for Italy. The temporary inclusion of baseball to the Olympic program (1992–2005) resulted in similar opportunities. During that time a bevy of American Italians joined the Italian national team by virtue of their heritage (one Italian ancestor). Nine of the twenty players on the 1984 Olympic team were born in America. John Franco assumed duties as the pitching coach for Team Italy in the 2006 World Baseball Classic competition that purportedly aimed to produce an international champion. At least thirteen players and four coaches of the

2009 Italian baseball team were American citizens who reside in the United States. Both Mike Piazza, a twelve-time all-star as a catcher in the Major Leagues, and pitcher Jason Grilli played for Italy in the World Baseball Classic. Piazza then became the hitting coach for the Italian team. He stated, "I wouldn't have missed this for the world. It's important to reconnect with your roots." The cultural flow of the early twentieth century has, in that sense, been reversed. American players retain their primary allegiance to the country of their birth, but have not forgotten their ancestral roots.[58]

Mike Scioscia, Dodgers catcher and later two-time manager of the year, conducted baseball clinics for the Italian Baseball Federation after the 1997 season. He acknowledged his ethnic pride in doing so. "I do have pride in being Italian. It's a great culture, and going to Italy really revitalized that feeling."[59] Piazza began offering baseball clinics for Italian players in 2002. He stated that "I went to Rome for a few days, and that whetted my appetite to go back. I've been back several times since. I've always looked for a bridge between the Italians who stayed and the people who migrated here. We grew up in the United States and we love this country, but we're very proud of our ancestry, the fact that Italy is a country of historical tradition. That's what I find fascinating."[60]

Numerous other American Italian baseball players have also retained or developed closer ties with the ancestral homeland. Dave Righetti, a pitcher for the Yankees, had a father who played for the San Francisco Seals of the Pacific Coast League. Righetti was traded in 1978 to the Yankees, where his ethnicity became a factor. "I was lucky to be traded to the Yankees. Being Italian there, you felt some pressure, but it was great. It was something to live up to. I remember, after my first or second year, they put me in the Columbus Day parade, and that was pretty cool. I got invited to marriages, weddings, just about everything." His ethnic pride endured throughout his career. "I'm very proud of my heritage. All my dad's best friends were Italians, including ex-ballplayers from the Seals. My kids are taking Italian, and we're definitely going to Italy to see my grandfather's town when I retire."[61]

Ken Caminiti, a star with the Houston Astros from 1989 to 1995, became closely involved with the Italian community in that city. "I'm part of the Italian American Foundation in Houston. In fact the year I got traded to San Diego, they gave me the Gold Glove Award. I hadn't won it, but they thought I deserved it, so they gave me a replica of the Gold Glove. I had tears in my eyes. It was such a great thing. I got three official Gold Gloves, but the one the Italian Americans gave me was probably more special."[62]

David Dellucci, an outfielder with Sicilian ancestry, played for several teams from 1997 to 2009. He described his appreciation and an historical sense of ethnicity and the role of sport across generations. "I take great pride in being an Italian American, and to be an Italian-American athlete is really something special. To follow in the footsteps of Joe DiMaggio and some of the legends, I feel privileged, and I hope the same for my son when he comes along."[63]

In 2002 Jason and Jeremy Giambi made history when they combined to hit sixty home runs, breaking the record for home runs by brothers in a season previously held by Joe and Vince DiMaggio. Jason commented upon the tribute with a sense of family and team honor as well as ethnic awareness. "It's nice to have, especially for my mom and dad. It keeps it in pinstripes and keeps it in the Italian family, too."[64]

Sal Fasano, a catcher with several teams from 1996 to 2008, is the son of Italian immigrants who adheres to a strong sense of family loyalty. In a 2006 interview he expressed his allegiance by noting, "It's a proud tradition, being Italian. I grew up speaking Italian, or actually Calabrese. It was a big deal when I moved away [to play with the Royals]. I have two boys now, Enzo and Angelo. The main reason I moved back to Chicago was to be near the family; my parents and grandparents still live there."[65]

Mark De Rosa started his MLB career in 1998 and acknowledged the centrality of family and the persistence of food in a 2007 interview. "Sundays were big pasta days, and all holidays were big Italian get-togethers. I think that's the key to an Italian family; everything revolves around a big meal."[66]

Mark Loretta, another Major Leaguer (1995–2009) with roots in Calabria, suggested a strong Italian influence. "I've got more English-Irish blood than Italian, but Italy's my favorite country to visit, and Florence is probably my favorite city in the world."[67]

Italy still held great allure for Barry Zito, a pitcher for the San Francisco Giants. During a 2007 interview he stated that "I take a lot of pride in being Italian. The Italians have probably contributed more to the world than anyone else, in literature, art, food, architecture, music. I'm going to Europe for the first time in November, and I'll spend eight days in Rome."[68]

Some third- and fourth-generation American Italians indicate an awareness of ethnicity but a greater identification with the United States. Terry Francona, in contrast to his father, Tito, stated, "My name is Italian, but I'm really not more Italian than anything else.... I'm proud of my name and my grandparents, but it doesn't really matter." Dustin Pedroia, the Rookie of the Year in 2007 and Most Valuable Player the following year as the second baseman for Francona's Boston Red Sox, favored the melting-pot view of ethnicity. "I know I'm Italian, Portuguese, and Spanish, but I just consider myself American."[69]

Identity and opportunity for some, however, remain contested. Much to the dismay of American soccer fans, New Jersey–born Giuseppe Rossi, the son of Italian immigrants, chose to return to Italy at age twelve to pursue a place on the Italian national team. At that time there was no guarantee of fame, fortune, or even selection for play at the elite level. In 2008, however, he led all scorers at the Beijing Olympic Games. In 2009 Rossi scored two goals against the US team in the Confederation Cup tournament, as his adopted country defeated the team from his American birthplace 3–1.[70] The United States and wealthy European countries have been importing foreign talent for their professional teams for years, and the increasingly globalized nature of sport and the search for top performers in the athletic labor force will likely result in similar decisions. Athletes will continue to seek opportunities that allow greater recognition and remuneration. The case of Rossi is somewhat different, however. He sought a greater challenge to his skills and assumed a different national identity in the process.

Both ethnic and racial identity continued to be problematic for some Italians as the end of the twentieth century neared. Life in the United States had brought new meanings to what it meant to be Italian or American. *Paesani* from Italy eventually dispersed in America. Their children intermarried with other ethnic and racial groups, producing hybrid Italian-Americans, which sometimes forced decisions regarding the predominant celebration of one or another culture within the larger American identity.

Transition in Race Relations

By the latter twentieth century the American Italians, particularly the ones of the urban working class, no longer felt an affinity with African Americans, whom they came to perceive as rivals in the quest for employment. In Philadelphia Mayor Frank Rizzo declared open warfare on the Black Panther Party during his tenure (1972–80). Blacks assumed the criminal and rebellious stereotypes that had been foisted upon Italians of the previous generation. Ironically, Rizzo lost a reelection bid to a black candidate, Wilson Goode. In the Italian Bensonhurst neighborhood of Brooklyn, African Americans were treated as transgressors with a beating in 1982 and a shooting in 1989 that both resulted in deaths. In 1991 Spike Lee produced *Jungle Fever*, a movie that portrayed the tension between blacks and Italians in the working-class neighborhood that offered only "entrapment, surrender, despair, and silence as a response to all feelings." Friends and families discouraged, and even ostracized, those individuals who looked to education as a means of social mobility. Despite four generations of Italians living in America, some had still not learned how to assimilate.[71] Similar altercations occurred in the Bronx when blacks and Puerto Ricans moved into Monte Carmelo.[72] An Italian male who wanted to safeguard his sense of whiteness replied to a question about intermarriage by stating that he accepted intermarriage between different ethnicities, but drew a racial line. "My children should marry a Caucasian. . . . They have nothing in common with the people from other races. A Chinese or a Japanese or a black person should not marry a Caucasian. . . . I would object very strongly if my child wanted to do something like that."[73]

As Italians moved to the suburbs in the latter twentieth century, many settled in communities that replicated their inner-city ethnic experience. Blacks were largely excluded or segregated within their own suburban locations. For example, as late as 2000, the historically Italian suburb of Melrose Park, west of Chicago, had a black population of only 3 percent. The adjacent suburb of Stone Park became a hub of organized criminal activity, but still encompasses the Italian Cultural Center.[74]

The growing conservatism of Italians was evident in their political transition as well. Whereas 77 percent of Italian-Americans supported the more liberal Democratic Party in 1964, only 39 percent did so twenty years later, as working-class ethnic groups, in general, failed to equate blacks' struggles for equality with the past hardships of their own parents and grandparents.[75]

Sport as Amelioration

Italians in Pittsburgh, however, failed to draw such boundaries in respect to their athletic heroes. As the Black Power movement of the 1960s and 1970s fostered a reactionary resurgence in ethnic pride, Pittsburgh reveled in the feats of Steelers' running back Franco Harris, the offspring of a black father and an Italian mother. The Pittsburgh Italians created a Harris fan club in 1972, known as Franco's Italian Army, including a local priest as the chaplain. They celebrated at the football stadium with Italian flags, signs, food, and wine. One member brought the *corno*, the Italian horns to ward off the evil eye of folklore, while others placed curses on opponents. "One army member compared the atmosphere of food and fun to the Italian American family life of his youth." They inducted Frank Sinatra into the army as an honorary general, and the group drew national attention during televised games. During the December 31, 1972, game against Miami, a season in which the Dolphins went undefeated, Franco's army had a plane drop leaflets on the Miami players that called for their surrender to an "ethnically superior force," a playful reversal of past perceptions of Italian inferiority. The next year Franco's Italian Army commandeered thirty-seven buses for the trip to Cleveland. The camaraderie and membership united the urban East Liberty neighborhood of first-generation Italians to those individuals who had fled to the suburbs in a common cause, as an expression of ethnic pride after years of suppression.[76]

The joy of the Italian celebrants, however, was not to last. African Americans, dismayed and disturbed by the Italian co-optation of Harris's identity, confronted the fan club, and the player became alienated from the black community in Pittsburgh. Racial tension heightened until the club was disbanded in 1977.[77] Race had superseded ethnicity, but the phenomenon had brought the Italian quest for racial inclusion to an inverse cycle in which Italians who had been considered black became white and a black became an Italian, as they adopted a presumably African American athlete in a city that had ardently resisted integration. The quest for a hero provided the impetus for Italians to identify with Franco Harris, and his athletic achievements allowed for the temporary amelioration of racial differences.

Amalgamated Culture

The merger of transatlantic cultures portrayed a particular irony in 1994 when a concert by the world's most famous opera tenors, the Italian Luciano Pavarotti and Spaniards Placido Domingo and Jose Carreras, took place in Los Angeles's Dodgers Stadium. Italian high art mixed with American popular culture as the announcer extolled the performance with sports analogies for the 1.3 billion television viewers, indicating that the singers were "covering all their bases" and "scoring goals right and left."[78] The analogy seemed fitting, given the Italian contributions to American sporting culture.

Despite Italians' myriad contributions to American culture, and perhaps partly because of the southern Italians' adherence to their ancestral culture, a persistent prejudice toward them remains evident in media images and in popular culture that serve as a litmus test for full acceptance and inclusion. Sociologists Tomatsu Shibutani and Kian Kwan have argued that the acceptance (social distance) and treatment of persons within a society depend not on what he or she is, but on how that person is defined. Despite the accumulation of wealth and social mobility, Italians may still experience a social distancing from others. John Segalla, a wealthy builder, was denied membership in a Connecticut golf club with the rebuke, "Too bad you have an Italian name." He retaliated by constructing his own golf course in 1993.[79] A 1996 survey found that 75 percent of respondents still believed that "most Italian Americans are associated in some way with organized crime."[80] Another assessment of the third generation showed that more than 25 percent sensed that they were discriminated against even if they did not experience it. The feeling was most prevalent in higher-level occupations.[81] Such bias is not universal, however. Nick Zagotta, president of the private Flossmoor Country Club outside Chicago, stated, "Fifty years ago, an Italian or Catholic could not get into Flossmoor, and now I'm president."[82]

Within the Italian-American community factionalism still simmers. A 1990 interview with a third-generation Italian revealed, "There's Italians, and there's Wops. And the Wops—they're from Palermo in Sicily and . . . from Castagna in Calabria." Northern Italians claim the invasion and influence of fashion mavens Armani, Versace, Dolce and Gabbana, Prada, and Zegna as well as the sleek and luxurious Lamborghini, Maserati, and Ferrari automobiles that serve as status symbols in the United States, while the southerners provided laborers and athletes. Still, the bifurcation of Italian-Americans is evident in the consistent media characterization of and public sanction to negative portrayals of southern Italians as gangsters in television, movie, and marketing campaigns. In 1999 Dom DiMaggio, still smarting over the treatment of his parents during World War II, called for a congressional investigation of civil rights abuses aimed at Italians.[83]

More recent scholarly analysis seems to bear out DiMaggio's contentions. Despite socioeconomic and educational gains, Italians seem to lack the respect their forefathers so earnestly sought. Sociologists Richard Alba and Dalia Abdel-Hady have determined that although Italians represent 5.6 percent of the population, the American born represent only 4 percent of college professors and less than 2 percent of the membership in the prestigious American Academy of Arts and Sciences. The City University of New York has recognized Italian-Americans as a "protected class," similar to the federally mandated affirmative action groups (black, Hispanic, Asian, Pacific Islander, American Indian, Alaskan natives, and women) since 1976. Despite such a designation, the ongoing survey of hiring practices at CUNY has indicated that Italian-Americans have fared poorly in comparison to other minority groups at all levels (faculty, higher education officers, executives, deans, and full-time staff) from 1978 to 2006 (see appendix B).[84] Italian-Americans represent only 3 percent of students at the Ivy League universities and less than 1 percent of its faculties.[85] The lack of inclusion in such powerful institutions suggests a lack of respect, limited recognition, and exclusion from leadership roles, if not discrimination. Historically, sport more so than education provided the image of meritocracy in the Italians' adopted land, but it proved to be both a blessing and a curse. It afforded recognition, respect, and pride, but the concerted focus on physicality rather than education limited opportunities.[86]

More recently, the physicality and performance aspects of the guido youth culture have elicited bigoted and nativist responses redolent of the 1920s. A 2003 website on the New York nightclub scene remarked that "the women were incredible, lots of races, Spanish, Italian, black, white, all the mixes were there and friendly." Such comments continue to characterize Italians as racialized "others" and nonwhite.[87] Web message boards continue to disparage the guido culture with racist and ethnic slurs. One claimed that "all Italians from Sicily are part Black. Since the island was invaded and there [sic] women were raped by Africans that's why they are so dark. Get it?" A commentator on a WAXQ-FM morning radio show allegedly stated that "Italians are niggers that have lost their memories."[88]

Conclusion

That continued lack of full inclusion is evident in Italians' self-perceptions and the ways in which they commemorate their identity. Stuart Hall has claimed that "identification is constructed on the backs of a recognition of some common origin or shared characteristics with another person or group, or with an ideal, and with the natural closure of solidarity and allegiance established upon this foundation."[89] Italian immigrants, particularly the ones from southern Italy and Sicily, had no sense of common origin or shared characteristics. Italian newspaper editors in the United States, mostly northern Italians, attempted to construct an Italian identity rooted in the Columbus myth and via the construction of memorial monuments to northern Italian heroes, matters of irrelevance for the vast majority of the immigrants. Their image of themselves was shaped and reshaped in the United States over the course of generations.[90]

The first generation of immigrants held primary allegiance to family and *paesani* rather than to any national state. Racialized as nonwhites, exploited, and oppressed, they had to overcome negative stereotypes and nativist attitudes. They had to contend with a new language, divergent values, and labor within an industrial economy. Their children, greatly influenced by Americanization processes and with no memories of an ancestral homeland, adopted and adapted new lifestyles and new identities of a liminal existence, living within two cultures as Italian-Americans. Their leisure lives and their sporting practices moved them toward a new ideology as well as different concepts of masculinity and femininity.

That identity, rooted in a working-class existence for most Italians, included acceptance of some precepts of the American creed, but differed with the dominant white Anglo-Saxon Protestant middle-class vision of citizenry. Such differences became evident in sporting practices. Male athletes, especially working-class boxers, "imbued sport with a masculine value system of their own which differed markedly from the manly Christian ideal."[91] The economically disadvantaged groups admired both strength and toughness, a necessity in their everyday lives. Denied access to material success and social status, sport proved an essential means to the retention of masculinity. Athletic Italian girls and women, as well, departed stridently from the domestic expectations of the past in the expression and delight of their physical abilities. Team sports reinforced the communal nature of southern Italian lives, as neighborhood fans banned together in support of the local representatives of their new identity as Italian-Americans. Teams that emanated from local church parishes or social clubs allowed residents to selectively participate in American society as they symbolized the retention of traditional religious and cultural values. Such community teams reinforced ethnic solidarity among Italian immigrants and their offspring as they also gradually incorporated practitioners and fans into the mainstream. Sport remained a contested field where Italians crossed cultural boundaries and competed with other ethnic groups for recognition, respect, and acceptance within a multicultural American society.[92]

The second generation of Italian-Americans answered the question of their loyalty to their adopted country by their service in World War II. The emergence of athletes, such as Joe DiMaggio and Rocky Marciano as "American" heroes, enabled Italians to solidify their status within the society, while entertainers like Frank Sinatra, though a cultural icon, presented continuing questions regarding Italians' criminal associations.

While the second generation worked hard to establish its claim to citizenship, the Americanization of the third and fourth generations remained incomplete. The third generation fully accepted their American identity, more comfortable in their achievement of whiteness. Class and racial consciousness gained greater prominence in the tumultuous civil rights era, but Italian-American pride asserted itself in a resurgence of ethnicity in the latter decades of the twentieth century. Italian values continued to coincide with class habitus in the admiration of toughness and physical prowess. Sport, music, and crime remained as viable means to social mobility.

The fortunes of the Wizard Arrow athletic club in Chicago served as representative of similar processes under way in other areas of Italian settlement. Founded in the World War I era of the first generation of immigrants, the club included many Italians in a multicultural membership by World War II and fully engaged in American sport forms that fostered greater assimilation. The third generation, children of the former members, resurrected the club within the same neighborhood that they still inhabited. Italian members still lived in close proximity to their parents, siblings, and extended family. An adherence to Italian food remained a mainstay for the third generation.

When one Italian family moved to the suburbs, the son returned nightly to the old neighborhood to retain his social and athletic ties. When he and other members of the club died prematurely, they were buried in their team football jerseys, emblematic of the physical prowess esteemed by their working-class acquaintances. When one of the Italian members was murdered within the tavern that served as club headquarters by a recently paroled convict whom he befriended, the city closed the site permanently, effectively ending the organization.[93] A sense of communalism, fatalism, family, and group loyalty had survived over three generations.

The fourth generation retained an American identity, but like the third displayed ethnic pride in its continued participation in religious and neighborhood festivals, choice of foods, and a celebration of the Italian lifestyle as they perceived it. Although many assimilated successfully within the mainstream culture, the guido culture personified by the *Jersey Shore* television series portrayed young Italians as hedonistic, proud, and with a perceived cultural superiority. Such Italian youths altered and remade the American Italian identity to fit their own psychic needs. They adhere to Italian family values as they interpret them. "A Guido's family is very important to him, and the same goes for a Guidette. A Guido is always protective of his family members. They always respect and stick up for their mothers and grandmothers. . . . A Guido always watches over their sisters and never lets a guy go near them. Guidos usually live at home until they get married. . . . A Guidette looks for protection and financial support from their family. Guidettes are very close with their fathers."[94]

As the thug image took hold of the youth culture, American Italian youths of the fourth generation sported Al Capone T-shirts, while others displayed Italian or Sicilian flags or colors in their attire at local festivals. An Italian identity has become more cherished than an American one among those individuals involved in the guido culture. In Ital Chat, an online chat room, those participants born in Italy are granted higher status than American-born youth, and FBIs (full-blooded Italians) have greater social capital than persons of mixed ancestry.[95]

Italians in New York displayed both Italian and American flags at the neighborhood recreational facilities, and festival bands played the national anthems of both countries. In Chicago the entertainers at Italian neighborhood festivals continue to sing in the Italian vernacular and comprehension by the audience is assumed. In 2009 the Order of the Sons of Italy, an advocacy group supporting Italian language and culture as well as closer ties to Italy, still claimed more than six hundred thousand members in more than seven hundred chapters across the United States. In the Hill District of St. Louis, still largely Italian, both Italian and American flags adorned houses, fire hydrants were painted in the Italian tricolor, and statues of the Virgin Mary still occupied the yards of the neighborhood. The continued celebration of distinct religious values in the saints' days festivals (more than 250 celebrations in 2009), the ongoing conflict between American individualism and loyalty to the Italian family, and an adherence to Italian foods are indicators that American Italians still need to embrace the past. Historian Michael Kammen maintained that "we arouse and arrange our memories to suit our psychic needs."[96] If that is so, then how do American Italians of later generations commemorate their American past?

Despite Italian gains in social, economic, and political capital, the most visible Italian-American monuments are no longer dedicated to Christopher Columbus, or even to national leaders, statesmen or

-women, or military heroes, but to athletic heroes in the popular culture. Fans still revel in the physicality of numerous Italian boxers and entertainers, such as Madonna or Lady Gaga. The latter even compares herself to the athletes that preceded her. "I'm always in the boxing ring. But I have a one-two punch: ambition and drive."[97] Historians have claimed that "public monuments reflect and shape the communities that erect and preserve them, making them keys to understanding both the past and how it is used in the present."[98]

Sociologist Joseph Healey has determined that sport memories are social reconstructions that link a person to a larger group. Such shared memories can provide a sense of identity and signal emotional transitions.[99] Sport can also serve a ritual function in the transformation of identity. Hilmi Ibrahim stated that "it provides the psychological foundation for the gradual shift from one status to another."[100] The transition from a local identity to an Italian one took place largely in America, and the transfer of identity and loyalty from Italy to the United States proved to be an emotionally wrenching one for Italian families. Perhaps such reconstructions of identity are characteristic of the transient American culture where cars, houses, and even spouses get recycled on a regular basis and celebrities continually reinvent their images in order to sustain their popularity.

The recycling of history occurs with each generation and is perhaps a necessity for nostalgia in a nation of immigrants, for one cannot recall what he or she has not experienced. In that sense nostalgia can create intergenerational bonds that "structure, maintain, and reconstruct identities," as grandparents, parents, and children fulfill the roles of spectators across time. Constructed collective memories serve as bridges to the past and serve the needs of the future. For American Italians visible and public memorials serve as a nostalgic link to past generations, provide ties to *Italianita* that was and is both joy and sorrow, a continued longing for acceptance, and the overcoming of doubts and slanders.[101]

Memorials to Joe DiMaggio, erected decades after his storied baseball career, are still venerated. DiMaggio is memorialized in an eponymous children's hospital in Florida, a playground in San

Francisco, a highway in New York City, a memorial plaque and headstone in Yankee Stadium, and a grandiose statue in a plaza across from the National Italian American Sports Hall of Fame in what had been the Little Italy neighborhood of Chicago. "Monuments dedicated to sportspeople celebrate moments, events, or deeds that are purported to have exemplary cultural significance. In celebrating such deeds monuments tailor the past to satiate the psychic needs of the community."[102] The memorial, dedicated in 1991 to mark the fiftieth anniversary of DiMaggio's fifty-six-game hitting streak, serves as a cultural marker for Italians. It represents the man and the feat that earned them a sense of identity as Americans. It represents style, grace, achievement, and excellence, the attributes that American Italians want to present to the public. But it also masks the insularity, the hardship, and the physical, emotional, and psychic pain encompassed by DiMaggio's (and the collective Italian) journey to acceptance. The statue represents physical prowess rather than the education or high culture esteemed by the upper classes, perhaps more fitting for the millions of working-class Italians who labored to build and find the American dream. It rests in a historically Italian neighborhood, rather than a more public site or thoroughfare dedicated and visible to all Americans. For some, like Frank Sinatra, who did it "my way," others still echo the lyrics of Paul Simon's song. "Where have you gone, Joe DiMaggio? A nation [or at least a segment of it] turns its lonely eyes to you." The continuing evocation of DiMaggio indicates a psychic need, a nostalgic turn to a more glorious era, and an ongoing quest for respect. It also marks an era of conflicted identity that is still apparent among many American Italians.[103]

 A multitude of athletes of Italian ancestry represent themselves as Americans on the Olympic team, while others, raised in the United States, choose to play for the Italian national teams. Al Dinon, born in South Philadelphia to Italian immigrants, attained the American dream. He played football, baseball, and roller hockey as a child and soccer in college. He learned the American value system well and prospered as a middle-class businessman. He spent his money traveling back to Italy, fifteen to twenty times by his own estimation. As late as

2009 he declared that "Italy's the best place in the world."[104] Joseph Tusiani, a university professor and award-winning poet, who had resided in the United States for more than a half century, still wondered where he belonged. He made annual pilgrimages back to Italy and wondered, "Two languages, two lands, perhaps two souls . . . Am I a man or two halfs of one?" Fourth-generation youths attending annual neighborhood festivals still cavort in a variety of T-shirts that declare them to be Italians, while guidos treasure their ancestry and still contend with other racial and ethnic groups for recognition and respect, suggesting that the process of Americanization and the full shaping of identity is still under way.[105] Scholars at the 2011 Calandra Institute colloquium confirmed such a determination when they continued to question "What is Italian-American culture(s) . . . How is Italian-American identity reproduced?" and concluded, "We may think we have created Italian America, but we have yet to create Italian Americans."[106]

Appendixes

Notes

Bibliography

Index

APPENDIX A

Italian-American Boxers, *Ring* Magazine Rankings, 1924–39

	Champions	*Contenders (top 10)*
1924	1	17
1925	1	11
1926	1	8
1927	2	9
1928	3	9
1929	3	9
1930	2	11
1931	2	14
1932	1	11
1933	0	14
1934	0	14
1935	1	12
1936	1	13
1937	2	9
1938	0	11
1939	1	13

Note: Italian nationals (that is, Primo Carnera and others) are not included; only those boxers who were identified as American are included. The number is likely higher owing to the use of aliases or incomplete biographical information.

APPENDIX B

Average Annual Employment Rates at CUNY by Race and Ethnicity

Faculty	*Higher Ed.* 1978	2006	*Officers* 1978	2006	*Executives/Deans* 1978	2006
Non-Italian Whites	76%	60%	69%	40%	78%	57%
Non-Italian minorities	19%	35%	26%	52%	17%	37%
Italian-Americans	5%	5%	6%	8%	5%	6%

Full-Time Staff	1993	2006
Blacks	37%	36%
Hispanics	18%	24%
Asian/Pacific Islander	3%	7%
Italian American	8%	5%

Note: Percentages are rounded off.

Notes

Introduction

1. Jacob Burckhardt, *The Civilization of the Renaissance in Italy*; Hans Baron, *The Crisis of the Early Italian Renaissance*; Ernst Cassirer, Paul Oskar Kristeller, and John Herman Randall Jr., *The Renaissance Philosophy of Man*; Chuck Wills, *Destination America: The People and Cultures That Created a Nation*, 23.

2. Similar to African Americans of mixed blood who are racially categorized as black, I include those of mixed parentage as Italian Americans in my analysis. Jim Rattray, "New Evidence Found of New York's 1st Italian," *Brooklyn Sunday Mirror*, Oct. 23, 1955, 24B, Box 1st Italian-American History, Italian-Americans Pre–Civil War folder, Giovanni Schiavo Papers; Cosmo F. Ferrara, *Profiles of Italian Americans: Achieving the Dream and Giving Back*; Wills, *Destination America*, 166–67; Nancy Watkins, "Minds over Matter."

3. Stuart Hall, "Who Needs Identity?," 2.

4. Benedict Anderson, *Imagined Communities: Reflections on the Origin and Spread of Nationalism*, 5–7.

5. Barbara Misztal, *Theories of Social Memory*, 132–39; Paul Connerton, *How Societies Remember*.

6. Anthony Cardoza, "'Making Italians'? Cycling and National Identity in Italy, 1900–1950," maintains that, except for the imposed nationalism of the fascist regime, such divisiveness continued into the 1990s.

7. Michael Walzer, "What Does It Mean to Be an American?"

8. Rudolph J. Vecoli, "European Americans: From Immigrants to Ethnics."

9. Pierre Bourdieu, *Distinction: A Social Critique of the Judgment of Taste*.

10. Andrew J. Diamond, *Mean Streets: Chicago Youths and the Everyday Struggle for Empowerment in the Multiracial City, 1908–1969*, 57.

11. Robert E. Washington and David Karen, *Sport, Power, and Society: Institutions and Practices*, 343.

12. Graziella Parati and Ben Lawton, eds., *Italian Cultural Studies*.

13. Quintin Hoare and Geoffrey N. Smith, eds., *Selections from the Prison Notebooks of Antonio Gramsci*. Hegemony theory assumes a continual power struggle between dominant and subordinate groups to establish the norms, values, and standards in a society, in which subordinate groups might accept, reject, adopt, or adapt the dictates of the dominant group. Parati and Lawton, *Italian Cultural Studies*; Ewa Morawska, "The Sociology and History of Immigration"; Donna R. Gabaccia, "Is Everywhere Nowhere? Nomads, Nations, and the Immigrant Paradigm of United States History"; Joseph Sciorra, "Points South and West II"; Sebastian Fichera, *Italy on the Pacific: San Francisco's Italian Americans*.

14. Craig Calhoun et al., *Contemporary Social Theory*, 261.

15. Nadia Urbinati, "The South of Antonio Gramsci and the Concept of Hegemony," in *Italy's "Southern Question": Orientalism in One Country*, edited by Jane Schneider, 147.

16. Schneider, *Italy's "Southern Question,"* 1–12; John Dickie, *Darkest Italy: The Nation and Stereotypes of the Mezzogiorno, 1860–1900*.

17. Susan K. Brown and Frank D. Bean, "New Immigrants, New Models of Assimilation"; Richard D. Alba and Victor Nee, *Remaking the American Mainstream: Assimilation and Contemporary Immigration*.

1. The Lack of Identity

1. *New York Times*, May 28, 1877, 2 (quote); June 25, 1877, 8; June 27, 1877, 8.

2. *New York Times*, June 29, 1877, 8.

3. *New York Times*, June 29, 1877, 8; July 15, 1877, 8; July 22, 1877, 12; July 24, 1877, 3; Mar. 1, 1878, 2.

4. Andrei S. Markovits and Steven L. Hellerman, *Offsides: Soccer and American Exceptionalism*.

5. http://www.baseball-reference.com/bullpen/Buttercup_Dickerson; "Buttercup" Dickerson, born in Maryland in 1858, is generally acknowledged as the first Italian professional baseball player, but Lawrence Baldassaro, *Beyond DiMaggio: Italian Americans in Baseball*, 424n3, claims that Pessano was a middle name adopted from the delivering physician, which was a family custom. Joseph Dorinson, "'Poosh 'Em Up, Tony!': Italian Americans and Baseball," in *Horsehide, Pigskins, Oval Tracks, and Apple Pie: Essays on Sport and American Culture*, edited by James Vlasich, 41, cites a study by Richard Renoff and Joseph A. Vacarelli, "Italian Americans and Baseball," 107, which claims Vincent "Sandy" Nava, who played for Providence and Baltimore between 1882 and 1886, as the first Italian player in the Major Leagues.

6. *Webster's New World Dictionary*, s.v. "nation."

7. Annette R. Hofmann, "From Jahn to Lincoln: Transformation of Turner Symbols in a New Cultural Setting," 1946–47.

8. Gertrud Pfister, "Lieux de Memoire: Sites of Memories and the Olympic Games."

9. Venice joined the Italian state as a result of a treaty in 1866, and the Papal States, with the exception of Vatican City, were annexed by 1870. Spencer M. Di Scala, *Italy: From Revolution to Republic, 1700 to the Present*, 94–124; Gay Talese, *Unto the Sons*, 461; Dickie, *Darkest Italy*, 44 (quote). David A. J. Richards, *Italian American: The Racializing of an Ethnic Identity*, 99–100, indicates 120,000 troops in southern Italy by 1865. See Cardoza, "Making Italians?"; and Gigliola Gori, "Care, Cure, and Training of the Body according to Italian Medicine of the Nineteenth Century," on continuing political, religious, and social class divisions thereafter.

10. Frances M. Malpezzi and William M. Clements, *Italian-American Folklore*, 27, 33 (quote).

11. Gary Ross Mormino, *Immigrants on the Hill: Italian-Americans in St. Louis, 1882–1982*, 74 (quote); Regina Barreca, ed., *Don't Tell Mama*, 90, 209, 319, 367; James A. Crispino, *The Assimilation of Ethnic Groups: The Italian Case*, 17, 24; Herbert J. Gans, *The Urban Villagers: Group and Class in the Life of Italian-Americans*, 199; Patrick J. Gallo, *Old Bread, New Wine: A Portrait of the Italian-Americans*, 27–31; Jerre Mangione and Ben Morreale, *La Storia: Five Centuries of the Italian American Experience*, 34, 44, 326–29.

12. Norbert Elias, *The Civilizing Process: The History of Manners*; Bourdieu, *Distinction*; Peter Burke, *Popular Culture in Early Modern Europe*; John McClelland and Brian Merrilees, eds., *Sport and Culture in Early Modern Europe*.

13. Robert C. Davis, *The War of the Fists: Popular Culture and Public Violence in Late Renaissance Venice*; Gertrud Pfister and Liu Yueye, eds. *Sports—the East and the West*, 12–19.

14. Gertrud Pfister, "Research on Traditional Games: The Scientific Perspective."

15. Elizabeth Robbins Pennell, "Sports at the Home of the Carnival," 587. Thanks to Gertrud Pfister for calling this citation and those of the *New York Times* on pallone to my attention.

16. Pennell, "Sports at the Home of the Carnival"; David Chapman and Gigliola Gori, "Strong, Athletic, and Beautiful: Edmondo De Amicis and the Ideal Italian Woman." Carmelo Bazzano, "The Italian-American Sporting Experience," dates the establishment of the soccer association to 1885. Simon Martin, "Italian Sport and the Challenges of Its Recent Historiography," cites a Turin Gymnastic Society as early as 1844, but generally laments the dearth of scholarship on sport in Italy and a particular lack of interest in southern Italy.

17. Di Scala, *Italy*, 148; Bazzano, "Italian-American Sporting Experience," 106–7; Pennell, "Sports at the Home of the Carnival."

18. Gigliola Gori, *Italian Fascism and the Female Body: Sport, Submissive Women, and Strong Mothers*, 38, 44–45, 213n4.

19. Malpezzi and Clements, *Italian-American Folklore*, 151–97; Adria Bernardi, *Houses without Names: The Italian Immigrants of Highwood, Illinois*, 57–58, 207–8; Richard Gambino, *Blood of My Blood: The Dilemma of the Italian-Americans*, 149–55; Angelo Mazzoleni, *La Famiglia nei rapporti coll' individuo e colla societa*, Box 168, Folder 4, 5, Ernest W. Burgess Papers.

20. Malpezzi and Clements, *Italian-American Folklore*, 26 (quote); Andrew F. Rolle, *The Italian Americans: Troubled Roots*, 3. A. V. Margavio and Jerome J. Salomone, *Bread and Respect: The Italians of Louisiana*, 28, indicates that plant lice destroyed Italian vineyards in the 1870s.

21. Richards, *Italian American*, 104–12. Humbert S. Nelli, *From Immigrant to Ethnics: The Italian Americans*, 19, 41, estimates 80 percent of immigrants were from the Mezzogiorno, 75 percent of them men, and the vast majority between fourteen and forty-five years of age. George A. Dorsey, "Stream of Emigration Pours from Campania," *Chicago Tribune*, July 20, 1910, 8, estimated five stowaways per ship on each voyage from Naples to New York. Others avoided the Italian passport requirements by embarking from French or Greek ports. He estimated 1,225 stowaways per year from Naples. Mangione and Morreale, *La Storia*, 79–85; George A. Dorsey, "Sicilian Immigrant Brings Ideas Strange to America," *Chicago Tribune*, June 2, 1910, 10 (quote); Dorsey, "Sicilian Guides," 8, on maximum wage.

22. Antonio Mangano, "The Effect of Immigration upon Italy," in *Charities and the Commons* (Feb. 1908), 1475–78, 1484–86, in Stanley Feldstein and Lawrence Costello, *The Ordeal of Assimilation: A Documentary History of the White Working Class, 1830–1970s*, 17–24; Patrick J. Gallo, ed., *The Urban Experience of Italian-Americans*, 14; Donna R. Gabaccia, *From Sicily to Elizabeth Street: Housing and Social Change among Italian Immigrants, 1880–1930*, 24–49.

23. Marx cited in Raymond A. Belliotti, *Seeking Identity: Individualism versus Community in an Ethnic Context*, 30.

24. Ibid., 30 (quote); Rolle, *Italian Americans*, 7.

25. Gambino, *Blood of My Blood*, 26 (quote); Malpezzi and Clements, *Italian-American Folklore*, 224–45.

26. See Franco La Cecla, *Pasta and Pizza*, on the role of food in the construction of cultural, ethnic, and national identity.

27. Gambino, *Blood of My Blood*, 3, 8, 26–27, 146; Rudolph M. Bell, "Emigration from Four Italian Villages: Strategy and Decision," in Gallo, *Urban Experience*, 9–35; Malpezzi and Clements, *Italian-American Folklore*, 69; Michael Cimino cited

in Fred L. Gardaphe, *From Wise Guys to Wise Men: The Gangster and Italian American Masculinities*, 84 (quote); Belliotti, *Seeking Identity*, 38–44.

28. Belliotti, *Seeking Identity*, 2–3; Rolle, *Italian Americans*, 111–15; Malpezzi and Clements, *Italian-American Folklore*, 37–38, 48, 69; Maria Laurino, *Were You Always an Italian? Ancestors and Other Icons of Italian America*.

29. Alexander De Conde, *Half Bitter, Half Sweet: An Excursion into Italian-American History*, 4–16, 71, 75, 86; Salvatore J. La Gumina, *Wop! A Documentary History of Anti-Italian Discrimination*, 23.

30. De Conde, *Half Bitter, Half Sweet*, 81.

31. Wills, *Destination America*, 164.

32. Richard D. Alba, "The Twilight of Ethnicity among Americans of European Ancestry: The Case of the Italians," in *Ethnicity and Race in the U.S.A.: Toward the Twenty-First Century*, edited by Richard D. Alba, 136.

33. Wilson cited in Vincent J. Cannato, *American Passage: The History of Ellis Island*, 230–31. See *La Paroli dei Socialisti*, Mar. 23, 1912, Foreign Language Press Survey, for a belated protest by Italians to Wilson's book.

34. *L'Italia*, Dec. 1, 1906; Apr. 10, 1909.

35. Arthur Sweeney, "Mental Tests for Immigrants," *North American Review* 215 (May 1922), 600–612, cited in La Gumina, *Wop!*, 193, 196.

36. The nativist movement grew out of the anti-Catholic sentiments of white, Anglo-Saxon Protestants in the 1830s, who considered Catholicism to be alien to democratic principles in its allegiance to the pope. Nativists considered the benefits of the American democracy to be their own birthright and saw the immigrants as interlopers. It expanded in reaction to the Irish and German immigrants of the 1840s and evolved into the Know-Nothing political party. The nativist sentiments of the Ku Klux Klan after the Civil War extended to Jews and blacks. Nativism took refuge in the ideology of social Darwinism and, in the extreme, among white supremacist groups thereafter.

37. Harvey Zorbaugh, *The Gold Coast and the Slum*, 160–61.

38. Among such studies, see Robert E. Park and Herbert A. Miller, *Old World Traits Transplanted*; Louis Wirth, *The Ghetto*; Zorbaugh, *Gold Coast and the Slum*; Paul F. Cressey, "The Succession of Cultural Groups in the City of Chicago"; Oscar Handlin, *The Uprooted: The Epic Story of the Great Migrations That Made the American People*; Rudolph J. Vecoli, "Contadini in Chicago: A Critique of the Uprooted"; Sam Bass Warner and Colin Burke, "Cultural Change and the Ghetto"; Humbert S. Nelli, *Italians in Chicago, 1880–1930*; Thomas Lee Philpott, *The Slum and the Ghetto: Neighborhood Deterioration and Middle-Class Reform, Chicago, 1880–1930*.

39. Virginia Yans-McLaughlin, "Patterns of Work and Family Organization: Buffalo's Italians."

40. George E. Pozzetta, "The Mulberry District of New York City," in *Little Italies in North America*, edited by Robert F. Harney and Vincent J. Scarpacci, 7–40.

41. William M. De Marco, *Ethnics and Enclaves: Boston's Italian North End*, 107.

42. Stefano Luconi, *From Paesani to White Ethnics: The Italian American Experience in Philadelphia*, 30.

43. Gary Ross Mormino, "The Hill upon a City: The Evolution of an Italian-American Community in St. Louis, 1882–1950," in *Little Italies in North America*, edited by Harney and Scarpacci.

44. David R. Roediger, *Working toward Whiteness: How America's Immigrants Became White; The Strange Journey from Ellis Island to the Suburbs*, 35.

45. Chad Heap, *Slumming: Sexual and Racial Encounters in American Nightlife, 1885–1940*, 122; Gabaccia, *From Sicily to Elizabeth Street*, 71–97; Gallo, *Old Bread, New Wine*, 44, 46, 48, 52; Luconi, *From Paesani to White Ethnics*, 26; John Bodnar, Roger Simon, and Michael P. Weber, *Lives of Their Own: Blacks, Italians, and Poles in Pittsburgh, 1900–1960*, 103; Gallo, *Old Bread, New Wine*, 48; Marco, *Ethnics and Enclaves*, 76–80; Joseph Maselli and Domenic Candeloro, *Italians in New Orleans*, 43–45.

46. Allan McLaughlin, "Italian and Other Latin Immigrants," *Popular Science Monthly*, Aug. 1904, 341–47, in La Gumina, *Wop!*, 152–53 (quote).

47. "A New Weapon against the Enemy," *New York Times*, June 28, 1908, 6. A 1901 New York law required tenements to provide windows and a fire escape, but not baths. Tenants shared a central sink, toilet, and laundry tub. See Emelise Aleandri, *Little Italy*, 24; and Jacob A. Riis, *The Children of the Poor*, 15–17, 94, on residential and death rates.

48. Luconi, *From Paesani to White Ethnics*, 26; Gallo, *Old Bread, New Wine*, 48, 52; Bodnar, Simon, and Weber, *Lives of Their Own*, 102–6.

49. Gaetano De Fillippis, "Social Life in an Immigrant Community," 31–39, Box 130, Folder 2, Burgess Papers; John T. McGreevy, *Parish Boundaries: The Catholic Encounter with Race in the Twentieth Century*; Bruce P. Zummo, *Little Sicily: Reminiscences and Reflections of Chicago's Near North Side*, 55–56; Malpezzi and Clements, *Italian-American Folklore*, 116–32; Lizabeth Cohen, *Making a New Deal: Industrial Workers in Chicago, 1919–1939*, 88–90.

50. De Marco, *Ethnics and Enclaves*, 46, 64–65 (quote).

51. Ibid., 64–65 (quote). See Bass Warner and Burke, "Cultural Change and the Ghetto," on the literature and nature of urban ghettoes.

52. Phylis Cancilla Martinelli, "Pioneer Paesani in Globe, Arizona," 153–69; Rudolph J. Vecoli, "Italians in Minnesota's Iron Range," in *Italian Immigrants in Rural and Small Town America*, edited by Rudolph J. Vecoli, 179–89; Phylis Cancilla Martinelli, "Examining the Relationships of Italians and Mexicans in a

'Mexican Camp' and a 'White Man's Camp': Mexicans and Euro Latinos in the Arizona Copper Industry, 1900–1930," 55–65; Linda Pacini Pitelka, "Indians and Italians: The Boundaries of Race and Ethnicity in Rural Northern California, 1890–1920," in *Italian Immigrants Go West: The Impact of Locale on Ethnicity*, edited by Janet E. Worrall, Carol Bonomo Albright, and Elvira G. Di Fabio, 66–78.

53. Elizabeth Fussell, "Constructing New Orleans, Constructing Race: A Population History of New Orleans," 850; Margavio and Salomone, *Bread and Respect*, 55, 182. See Gerald R. Gems, *Windy City Wars: Labor, Leisure, and Sport in the Making of Chicago*, 112–14, on the Chicago Hebrew Institute; and Gerald R. Gems, "Sport and the Forging of a Jewish-American Culture: The Chicago Hebrew Institute."

54. Philip V. Cannistraro and Gerald Meyer, "Italian American Radicalism: An Interpretive History," in *The Lost World of Italian American Radicalism*, edited by Cannistraro and Meyer, 12.

55. Worrall, Albright, and Di Fabio, *Italian Immigrants Go West*; *Petaluma Argus*, June 12, 1887, 3, cited in Paola A. Sensi-Isolani, "Tradition and Transition in a California Paese," in *Italian Immigrants*, edited by Vecoli, 88–109.

56. Carol Lynn McKibben, *Beyond Cannery Row: Sicilian Women, Immigration, and Community in Monterey, California, 1915–99*, 1–2.

57. Ibid., 2–3, 5, 17–18, 58–60, 68–79.

58. *Bolletino dell Emigrazione*, 1912, no. 4, 20–43, Italian Societies folder, Schiavo Papers, indicates 1,116 such societies in the United States by 1910. Gambino, *Blood of My Blood*, 31–33; De Conde, *Half Bitter, Half Sweet*, 103–4; Luconi, *From Paesani to White Ethnics*, 31, 50–51; Gallo, *Old Bread, New Wine*, 51; John W. Briggs, *An Italian Passage: Immigrants to Three American Cities*, 152; Cohen, *Making a New Deal*, 69 (quote).

59. Benjamin Rader, "The Quest for Subcommunities and the Rise of American Sport."

60. Gabaccia, *From Sicily to Elizabeth Street*, xv–xvii; Mina Carson, *Settlement Folk: Social Thought and the American Settlement Movement, 1885–1930*, 103–5; Jane Addams, *The Second Twenty Years at Hull House*, 366–67 (quote).

61. De Amicis cited in Chapman and Gori, "Strong, Athletic, and Beautiful," 1979.

62. Carson, *Settlement Folk*, 103–5, 108, 232, 103 (quote). Among the voluminous literature on settlement houses, see Jane Addams, *Twenty Years at Hull House*; Addams, *Second Twenty Years at Hull House*; Graham Taylor, *Chicago Commons through Forty Years*; and Allen F. Davis, *Spearheads for Reform: The Social Settlements and the Progressive Movement, 1890–1914*.

63. Italian American Directory Company, *Gli Italiani negli Stati Uniti d'America*.

64. See Jane Addams, "Public Recreation and Social Morality"; and Gems, *Windy City Wars*, 102–14. There is a significant amount of literature on the playground movement. For example, see Cary Goodman, *Choosing Sides: Playground and Street Life on the Lower East Side*; Dominick Cavallo, *Muscles and Morals: Organized Playgrounds and Urban Reform, 1880–1920*; Elizabeth Halsey, *The Development of Public Recreation in Metropolitan Chicago*; Roy Rosenzweig, *Eight Hours for What We Will: Workers and Leisure in an Industrial City, 1870–1920*; Stephen Hardy, *How Boston Played: Sport, Recreation, and Community, 1865–1915*; and Steven Riess, *City Games: The Evolution of American Urban Society and the Rise of Sports*.

2. Constructing an Italian Identity

1. "John Dundee One of the Best Boxers from Sunny Italy's Shores," *Trenton (NJ) Evening Times*, Nov. 22, 1915, 8.

2. John A. Garaty, *The American Nation: A History of the United States*, 473.

3. Pierre Bourdieu, *Outline of a Theory of Practice*.

4. Wills, *Destination America*, 165; Nelli, *From Immigrant to Ethnics*, 76; Mormino, *Immigrants on the Hill*, 20–22; Bernardi, *Houses without Names*, 79, 82 (quotes).

5. In 1864 the US government enacted a contract labor law to attract immigrant labor in the midst of the Civil War. By the 1880s, nativists and labor unions perceived the immigrants as a threat. Marie Hall Ets, *Rosa: The Life of an Italian Immigrant*, 168, 171–72; De Conde, *Half Bitter, Half Sweet*, 86, 87.

6. Stephen Steinberg, *The Ethnic Myth: Race, Ethnicity, and Class in America*, 98, 141–44; Karen Brodkin, *How Jews Became White Folks: And What That Says about Race in America*, 63–65; Cannistraro and Meyer, *Lost World of Italian American Radicalism*, 6; Bodnar, Simon, and Weber, *Lives of Their Own*, 17; Margavio and Salomone, *Bread and Respect*, 100; Roediger, *Working toward Whiteness*, 77.

7. Gallo, *Old Bread, New Wine*, 118.

8. Margavio and Salomone, *Bread and Respect*, 111.

9. Bodnar, Simon, and Weber, *Lives of Their Own*, 99; McKibben, *Beyond Cannery Row*; Jennifer Guglielmo, *Living the Revolution: Italian Women's Resistance and Radicalism in New York City, 1880–1945*, 69; Diane C. Vecchio, *Merchants, Midwives, and Laboring Women: Italian Migrants in Urban America*, 3, 15, 32, 67–68, 83 (quote).

10. J. Guglielmo, *Living the Revolution*, 183–209 (183, 184, respectively, on the quotes).

11. Gems, *Windy City Wars*, 44–47, 58–59; Wilma J. Pesavento, "Sport and Recreation in the Pullman Experiment, 1880–1900"; Stanley Buder, *Pullman: An Experiment in Industrial Order and Community Planning, 1880–1930*, viii (quote).

12. http://hoopedia.nba.com/index.php?title=Forrest_%22Red%22_DeBernardi; http://hoopedia.nba.com/index.php?title=Golden_Cyclones; http://www.niashf.org/index2.cfm?ContentID=58&InducteeID=106.

13. http://eh.net/encyclopedia/article/whaples.work.hours.us; David Nasaw, *Children of the City: At Work and at Play*, 113; Zummo, *Little Sicily*, 51; De Filippis, "Social Life in an Immigrant Community," 8; David Nasaw, *Going Out: The Rise and Fall of Public Amusements*; Briggs, *Italian Passage*, 144–50; Baldassaro, *Beyond DiMaggio*, 56.

14. See Perry Duis, *The Saloon: Public Drinking in Chicago and Boston, 1880–1920*; Kathy Piess, *Cheap Amusements: Working Women and Leisure in Turn-of-the-Century New York*; Lewis A. Erenberg, *Steppin' Out: New York Nightlife and the Transformation of American Culture, 1890–1930*; Nasaw, *Going Out*; Madelon Powers, *Faces along the Bar: Lore and Order in the Workingman's Saloon, 1870–1920*, on commercialized leisure; Judith Butler, *Undoing Gender*, on performative gender.

15. Nasaw, *Going Out*, 80–95.

16. See Duis, *Saloon*; Piess, *Cheap Amusements*; Erenberg, *Steppin' Out*; Nasaw, *Going Out*; Powers, *Faces along the Bar*.

17. See *L'Italia*, Mar. 2–3, 9–11, 16–17, 1895 (all in FLPS), on Romulus's appearance in Chicago. Other data on Romulus come from Edmond Desbonnet, *Les rois de la force* (1912), graciously supplied and translated by David Chapman. See David L. Chapman, *Sandow the Magnificent: Eugen Sandow and the Beginnings of Body Building*; and Robert Ernst, *Weakness Is a Crime: The Life of Bernarr Macfadden*, on the early physical culture movement.

18. Nancy C. Carnevale, *A New Language, a New World: Italian Immigrants in the United States, 1890–1945*, 97, 114–35; Giorgio Bertellini, "Duce/Divo: Masculinity, Racial Identity, and Politics among Italian Americans in 1920s New York City." See Diane Pecknold, review of *Blues Empress in Black Chattanooga: Bessie Smith and the Emerging Urban South*, in *Journal of American History* 96, no. 2 (2009): 572, on theater as social space; and J. Guglielmo, *Living the Revolution*, 174, on female performers.

19. Cohen, *Making a New Deal*, 104–5, 133–44, 327–31; Ferrara, *Profiles of Italian Americans*, 162–67. See Park and Miller, *Old World Traits Transplanted*, 51–52, on the transition in the musical tastes of ethnic youth.

20. Cohen, *Making a New Deal*, 104–5, 133–44, 327–31; Bruce A. Linton, "A History of Chicago Radio Station Programming, 1921–1931, with an Emphasis on Stations WMAQ and WGN"; J. Fred MacDonald, *Don't Touch that Dial! Radio Programming in American Life from 1920 to 1960*; Theodore C. Grame, *Ethnic Broadcasting in the United States*; Carnevale, *New Language, New World*, 158, 173–77. See Park and Miller, *Old World Traits Transplanted*, 51–52, on the transition in the musical tastes of ethnic youth.

21. The confusion over Valentino's birthplace could be owing to journalists' confusion over his birthplace in Apulia and Caltanissetta in Sicily or the growing tendency to lump Italians together as an ethnic group regardless of their regional and linguistic differences. Bertellini, "Duce/Divo," 689 (quote).

22. Lucy Moore, *Anything Goes: A Biography of the 1920s*; Joshua Zeitz, *Flapper: A Madcap Story of Sex, Style, Celebrity, and the Women Who Made America Modern*, 259, 262 (quote).

23. Roosevelt speech at Harvard, Feb. 23, 1907, Reel 15, Walter Camp Papers. On the diverse literature on masculinity, see Mark C. Carnes and Clyde Griffen, eds., *Meanings for Manhood: Constructions of Masculinity in Victorian America*; E. Anthony Rotundo, *American Manhood: Masculinity from the Revolution to the Modern Era*; and Clifford Putney, *Muscular Christianity: Manhood and Sports in Protestant America, 1880–1920*.

24. Hall, *World's Work*, cited in Kim Townsend, *Manhood at Harvard: William James and Others*, 207. On the feminization of culture, see Ann Douglas, *The Feminization of American Culture*; Patricia Marks, *Bicycles, Bangs, and Bloomers*; and Susan Cahn, *Coming on Strong: Gender and Sexuality in Twentieth-Century Women's Sport*.

25. J. F. A. Adams, "Neglect of Physical Training," *Educational Review* 11 (Mar. 1896): 273–76, cited in Putney, *Muscular Christianity*, 31.

26. Margavio and Salomone, *Bread and Respect*, 49.

27. "John Dundee One of the Best Boxers from Sunny Italy's Shores," *Trenton (NJ) Evening Times*, Nov. 22, 1915, 8.

28. http://newsandsociety.org/american-mobsters-paul-kelly-paolo-vaccarelli; http://query.nytimes.com/mem/archive-free/pdf?res=F20712F7385A12738DDD AF0894D0405B858CF1D3; http://www.herbertasbury.com/billthebutcher/eastman.asp; Steven A. Riess, "A Fighting Chance: The Jewish-American Boxing Experience, 1890–1940." See Timothy J. Gilfoyle, *A Pickpocket's Tale: the Underworld of Nineteenth Century New York*, for insight into the criminal world of the era; and *New York Times*, Apr. 6, 1905, for particulars on the Kelly Gang.

29. Thorstein Veblen, *Theory of the Leisure Class: An Economic Study of Institutions*; Greg King, *A Season of Splendor: The Court of Mrs. Astor in Gilded Age New York*.

30. http://www.boxrec.com/media/index.php?title=Fireman_Jim_Flynn&action =history; Thomas Hauser and Stephen Brunt, *The Italian Stallions: Heroes of Boxing's Glory Days*, 14.

31. See Eddie Smith, "Billy Papke Wins Fight for Second Meeting with Ketchel," *Oakland Tribune*, May 16, 1909, 23; and "Not Single Italian Fighter Has Been a Titleholder," *Washington Post*, Oct. 19, 1913, 53, for examples of Italian nationalities revealed despite the use of aliases.

32. "Not a Single Italian Fighter Has Been a Titleholder." See *Naugatuck (CT) Daily News*, Apr. 6, 1897, 2; Apr. 1, 1897, 5; and Oct. 1, 1898, 1; as well as *Trenton (NJ) Evening Times*, 8, for recognition of Leon as champion. He was generally recognized as champion at 105 pounds before the bantamweight limit was officially fixed at 112 pounds. Leon, however, lost several bouts to Jimmy Barry, now considered to be the champion of that era. Leon's officially recorded bouts ended in 1904, but he may have fought as late as 1909.

33. Riess, "Fighting Chance," 234, indicates that the dozen Italian champions of the 1920s equaled the Irish as the largest among ethnic groups. Riess, *City Games*, 111, cites two dozen Italian champs during the 1920s and 1930s, with Italians also supplying the most contenders in the latter decade. The transition in name change is apparent by 1915, as Tony Caponi and Frank Picato fought under their own names.

34. Matthew P. Llewellyn, "Viva Italia! Viva Italia! Dorando Pietri and the North American Professional Marathon Craze, 1908–10," suggests the Pietri tour as the awakening of Italian identity in the United States, but the efforts of the Italian newspaper editors preceded the running tour by decades. I contend that the process of identity formation was a more gradual one.

35. *New York Times*, Nov. 18, 1908, 7.

36. *Chicago Tribune*, Nov. 26, 1908, 14; *New York Times*, Nov. 26, 1908, 1 (quotes); Nov. 28, 1908, 6; Dec. 7, 1908, 7.

37. *New York Times*, Dec. 16, 1908, 1; Dec. 19, 1908, 10; Dec. 28, 1908, S1; Jan. 2, 1909; Jan. 14, 1909, 10; Jan. 20, 1909, 10.

38. Cianfarra cited in Bazzano, "Italian-American Sporting Experience," 108.

39. *New York Times*, Jan. 12, 1909, 7; *Chicago Tribune*, Feb. 26, 1909, 10. The occupations of Italians in Chicago was ascertained by comparing names and addresses of those mentioned in the *Chicago Tribune* account to the *Chicago City Directory*, which elicited matches for Oscar Durante, editor of the *L'Italia* newspaper, as well as saloon owners, a tailor, a printer, a bartender, and a liquor salesman.

40. *Chicago Tribune*, Feb. 26, 1909, 10; Mar. 16, 1909, 8; *New York Times*, Mar. 16, 1909, 7; Apr. 3, 1909, 7 (quote).

41. *New York Times*, May 9, 1909, S1; Apr. 21, 1909, 5.

42. David E. Martin and Roger W. H. Gynn, *The Olympic Marathon*, 94; http://www.jubileemarathon.se/start/context/cfm?Sec_ID=2067&Rac_ID=170&Lan_ID=3; http://www.flickr.com/photos/richard_arthur_norton?4151878237/; http://www.flickr.com/photos/richard_arthur_norton/3045747933/; http://www.sports-reference.com/olympics/athletes/st/gaston-strobino-1.html. Quotations are from accounts in the *Janesville (WI) Daily Gazette*, Aug. 8, 1912, 3; and the *Waterloo (IA) Times-Tribune*, July 30, 1912, 2.

43. *New York Times*, Dec. 4, 1908, 9; Dec. 7, 1908, 7; July 31, 1913; the *Chicago Tribune*, Jan. 4, 1909, 10, also carried the announcement of a wrestling

match between Leo Pardello and the Bulgarian Yussiff Mahmout. Frank A. Young, "Darker Races at the Olympiad," *Chicago Defender*, July 6, 1912, 5, referred to the popular interest in athletes from the "darker races," which included African Americans, American Indians, Hawaiians, Japanese, and Italians. See Cardoza, "Making Italians?," on the embryonic, but frenzied, nationalistic state of cycle racing in Italy at the time.

44. B. Anderson, *Imagined Communities*; Eric Hobsbawm and Terence Ranger, eds., *The Invention of Tradition*; Pierre Nora, ed., *Realms of Memory: The Construction of the French Past*.

45. Jeffrey E. Mirel, *Patriotic Pluralism: Americanization Education and European Immigrants*, 101–57; Briggs, *Italian Passage*, 177; Nelli, *From Immigrant to Ethnics*, 124. See Talese, *Unto the Sons*, 227, on Carlo Barsotti, founder of *Il Progresso*; and Luconi, *From Paesani to White Ethnics*, 36–37, on C. A. Baldi, editor of *L'Opinione*. Although most leaders were northern Italians, Baldi was born in Salerno.

46. Nelli, *From Immigrant to Ethnics*, 124; Briggs, *Italian Passage*, 129–33, 185, 298; Luconi, *From Paesani to White Ethnics*, 33–36, on Philadelphia; Orm Overland, *Immigrant Minds, American Identities: Making the United States Home, 1870–1930*, 69–70, on Columbus statues. Talese, *Unto the Sons*, 227; and Aleandri, *Little Italy*, 28–30, indicates Carlo Barsotti, a Pisan immigrant and editor of *Il Progresso*, as the spark behind the Italian memorials in New York. John Graf and Steve Skorpad, *Chicago's Monuments, Markers, and Memorials*, 43. *La Tribuna Italiana*, June 18, 1904; May 23, 1903, June 4, 1904; June 17, 1905; July 15, 1906, FLPS; *L'Italia*, Oct. 15, 1887; Oct. 12, 1893; Oct. 17, 1893; Oct. 12, 1913, FLPS, provide accounts of heroic celebrations.

47. Murray G. Phillips, Mark E. O'Neill, and Gary Osmond, "Broadening Horizons in Sport History: Films, Photographs, and Monuments," 283.

48. Hobsbawm and Ranger, *Invention of Tradition*.

49. *La Parola dei Socialisti*, July 10, 1910, FLPS; *L'Italia*, June 27, 1920, FLPS; Overland, *Immigrant Minds*, 9, 36, 66.

50. "The City Turns Out to Honor Columbus," *New York Times*, Oct. 13, 1911; Briggs, *Italian Passage*, 125; Malpezzi and Clements, *Italian-American Folklore*, 107–9; Belliotti, *Seeking Identity*, 162–63; Thomas A. Guglielmo, *White on Arrival: Italians, Race, Color, and Power in Chicago, 1890–1945*, 31; Overland, *Immigrant Minds*, 49 (quote). See the work of Nora, *Realms of Memory*; and B. Anderson, *Imagined Communities*, on collective memory and the social construction of national identities.

51. Courts often overturned such legislation, giving employers an upper hand in labor negotiations, but Kriste Lindenmeyer, *The Greatest Generation Grows Up:*

American Childhood in the 1930s, 49, 53, 111, indicates that all states had child labor laws and compulsory education laws by 1930. See John A. Garraty, *The American Nation: A History of the United States*, 486, 573; Blum et al., *The National Experience*, 486; Gems, *Windy City Wars*, 70–71; David Nasaw, *Schooled to Order: A Social History of Public Schooling in the United States*; David J. Hogan, *Class and Reform: School and Society in Chicago, 1880–1930*; William J. Reese, *Power and the Promise of School Reform: Grassroots Movements during the Progressive Era*; and David L. Angus, "Conflict, Class, and the Nineteenth Century Public High School in the Cities of the Midwest."

52. Mirel, *Patriotic Pluralism*, 19.

53. Gems, *Windy City Wars*, 66–74.

54. Chapman and Gori, "Strong, Athletic, and Beautiful," 1978.

55. Leonard Covello, *The Social Background of the Italo-American School Child*, 326.

56. Bazzano, "Italian-American Sporting Experience," 109.

57. Carroll D. Wright, *Ninth Special Report of the Commissioner of Labor, the Italians in Chicago: A Social and Economic Study*, 376, indicates average weekly wages as follows: coal miners at $7.15 for 60 hours, musicians at $5.79 for 35.5 hours, organ grinders at $3.81 for 67.5 hours, barbers at $7.26 for 83.8 hours, bootblacks at $3.33 for 76 hours, laborers at $7.27 for 60.7 hours, street sweepers at $8.19 for 58 hours, newsboys at $2.28 for 55.9 hours, fruit peddlers at $4.33 for 48 hours, rag pickers at $2.14 for 42.4 hours, railroad laborers at $7.06 for 60.1 hours, candy factory workers at $6.45 for 56.9 hours, hod carriers at $8.87 for 50.7 hours, seamstresses at $2.43 for 42 hours, and housewives who doubled as pants finishers earned $1.57 for 60.8 hours of work. Salvatore J. La Gumina, "American Education and the Italian Immigrant Response," in *American Education and the European Immigrant, 1840–1940*, edited by Bernard J. Weiss, 61–77; John Bodnar, "Schooling and the Slavic-American Family, 1900–1940," in *American Education and the European Immigrant*, edited by Weiss, 78–95.

58. See J. Guglielmo, *Living the Revolution*, 69–75, on work in the garment industry; Riis, *Children of the Poor*, 21, 92, 96, 106; Gambino, *Blood of My Blood*, 236–48; Lindenmeyer, *Greatest Generation Grows Up*, 67–68; and Gems, *Windy City Wars*, 69, 70 (quote).

59. Gambino, *Blood of My Blood*, 245–51.

60. John Andreozzi, "Italian Farmers in Cumberland," in *Italian Immigrants*, edited by Vecoli, 121. Box 1, Folder 1, 8, Anthony Sorrentino Papers, indicates similar experiences.

61. Edward R. Kantowicz, *Corporation Sole: Cardinal Mundelein and Chicago Catholicism*, 70.

62. Zummo, *Little Sicily*, 20, 27, 42; Maselli and Candeloro, *Italians in New Orleans*, 7, 80.

63. Zorbaugh, *Gold Coast and the Slum*, 160.

64. Di Liberto interview, 21–22, in Italians in Chicago, Oral History Project, Special Collections, University of Illinois at Chicago; Riha interview, Villa St. Ben, Oral History Project.

65. Brian McKenna and Mark L. Ford, "Professional Baseball and Football: A Close Relationship"; Abbaticchio file, Baseball Hall of Fame; http://www.the diamondangle.com/archive/aug01/abbaticchio.html; http://www.baseball-fever.com/showthread.php?77598-Ed-Abbaticchio.

66. Garoni file, Baseball Hall of Fame; http://www.baseball-almanac.com/players/player.php?p=garonwiol; Baldassaro, *Beyond DiMaggio*, 17; Robert Payton Wiggins, *The Federal League of Baseball Clubs: The History of an Outlaw League, 1914–1915*, 136; *Chicago Tribune*, Aug. 4, 1912, 16; Mar. 15, 1914, B2; Mangione and Morreale, *La Storia*, 373, 375.

67. Ping Bodie file, Baseball Hall of Fame; Ira Berkow, "The Extraordinary Life and Times of Ping Bodie," in *Reaching for the Stars: A Celebration of Italian Americans in Major League Baseball*, edited by Larry Freundlich, 49–64; Sam Weller, "Ping Bodie Hero of Sox Victory," *Chicago Tribune*, May 15, 1911, 12 (quote); *Chicago Tribune*, Feb. 8, 1912, C2.

68. Sam Weller, "Ping's Bat Scores Victory for Sox," *Chicago Tribune*, May 26, 1911, 11.

69. Sam Weller, "Ping Bodie Hero: Saves White Sox," *Chicago Tribune*, May 29, 1911, 11.

70. Ping Bodie, "Baserunning," *Chicago Daily Tribune*, June 4, 1913, 15; Handy Andy, "Bodie Slips Away: Stage Loses Him," *Chicago Daily Tribune*, Oct. 16, 1913, 13; *Chicago Tribune*, Apr. 18, 1914, 15; *Chicago Tribune*, May 14, 1914, 15.

71. *New York Times*, Mar. 8, 1918, 8. See *New York Times*, June 21, 1920, 22; and July 19, 1920, 17, for other references to Bodie's ethnicity.

72. *New York Times*, Mar. 28, 1918, 12.

73. *New York Times*, Apr. 22, 1920, 17. See Brad Kvederis, "Recalling the 1908 'Vallejos,' a State Amateur Runner-Up Squad," *Vallejo Times-Herald*, Apr. 10, 2005; and Dwight Chapin, "Link to a Glorious Past; From S. F. Sandlots to the Majors and Back," *San Francisco Chronicle*, Sept. 16, 2001, on the nexis of baseball leagues in the San Francisco area that produced nearly two dozen Italian MLB players, many from the North Beach area. Bodie played for the 1908 Vallejo team.

74. Josh Chetwynd, *Baseball in Europe*, 40. Both Albert Spalding, in 1889, and Charles Comiskey, in 1913, had made unsuccessful attempts to introduce baseball to Italy. Italy now supports a professional baseball league as well as an Olympic team. See http://italian.about.com/od/italianculture/a/aa030409a.htm.

75. Briggs, *Italian Passage*, 135; Roediger, *Working toward Whiteness*, 85; Moschella interview, Ellis Island Oral History Collection, EI 23.

76. Bazzano, "Italian-American Sporting Experience," 107, indicates an Italian soccer federation as early as 1885, but organization of the sport did not move beyond local competitions until the turn of the twentieth century. See Mormino, *Immigrants on the Hill*; and Derek Van Rheenen, "The Promise of Soccer in America: The Open Play of Ethnic Subcultures," for the viability of the game thereafter.

77. De Conde, *Half Bitter, Half Sweet*, 127.

78. Mark Choate, *Emigrant Nation: The Making of Italy Abroad*, 204, 206, 212–13 (quote); Luconi, *From Paesani to White Ethnics*, 39; Briggs, *Italian Passage*, 134; Ets, *Rosa*, 239; Lynne Ahnert, ed., *An American Journey: Our Italian Heritage*, 33, 166; Talese, *Unto the Sons*, 297; Mangione and Morreale, *La Storia*, 340, claim that Italians constituted only 4 percent of the American population but 12 percent of the US Army personnel. De Conde, *Half Bitter, Half Sweet*, 144, 156–57. Joseph Salituro, "Italian Americans and Nationalism: A Case of Mixed Loyalties, in *To See the Past More Clearly: The Enrichment of the Italian Heritage, 1890–1990*, edited by Harral E. Landry, 256–67, cites a 1916 study of sixty to seventy thousand returnees to Italy.

79. Mirel, *Patriotic Pluralism*, claims that nearly a half-million foreigners in the United States were drafted and composed 18 percent of the American military force. The National Italian American Foundation also cites the figure of three hundred thousand and claims another eighty-seven thousand Italian nationals in US service. See *L'Italia*, Mar. 18, 1917 (FLPS) on fund-raising efforts. See Edward G. Lengel, *To Conquer Hell: The Meuse-Argonne, 1918*, 30, 32, 36, 188, 207, 424–25, for Italian Americans serving in the US military.

80. Lengel, *To Conquer Hell*, 30, 32.

81. Peter Heller, *"In This Corner . . . !": 42 World Champions Tell Their Stories*, 53, on Herman; Everett M. Skehan, *Rocky Marciano: Biography of a First Son*, 6–7; Keith McClellan, *The Sunday Game: At the Dawn of Professional Football*, 141, 152–55, 159, 160, 208 (quote), 240, 338, 374; Maselli and Candeloro, *Italians in New Orleans*, 114.

82. Arthur Sweeney, MD, "Mental Tests for Immigrants," 608, 603; See Lengel, *To Conquer Hell*, for Italians who served in combat roles with distinction.

83. Briggs, *Italian Passage*, 159.

84. Richards, *Italian American*, 114.

85. Emory S. Bogardus, *Immigration and Race Attitudes*, 25, 48 (quote), 109.

86. Laurino, *Were You Always an Italian?*, 118; Margavio and Salomone, *Bread and Respect*, 190, 197. See *La Parola del Popolo*, a socialist newspaper, Apr. 14, 1923 (FLPS), on opposition to the rise of fascism.

87. Garraty, *American Nation*, 622–23.

3. Winning Whiteness

1. "Plucky Brignoli," *Boston Daily Globe*, Apr. 20, 1899; *Outing*, June 1897, 306; *Outing*, Oct. 1898, 92; *Outing*, June 1899, 316; *La Notizia*, Oct. 13, 1933, 6; http://www.familysearch.com/Eng/Search/Census/household_record.asp?HOUSEHOLD_CODE=1880US. Primary source documents and the 1880 census list the family name as Brignoli, while current accounts use Brignolia. The *Boston Globe* referred to him as such on May 6, 1899, 7; Sept. 5, 1899, 11; June 18, 1901, 7; and July 5, 1902, 3.

2. "Plucky Brignoli," *Boston Daily Globe*, Apr. 20, 1899, 1, 3; "Reception to Brignolia and Maguire," *Boston Daily Globe*, May 6, 1899, 7.

3. Eugene Buckley, "For the Marathon Race," *Boston Daily Globe*, Apr. 15, 1900, 9. Neither runner finished the 1900 race because of cramps.

4. *Boston Daily Globe*, July 31, 1916, 7; "Brignolia Recalls His Many Sports Feats," *Portland (ME) Press Herald*, July 20, 1950, 17.

5. "Fans Await Resumption of Boxing Bouts Here Tonight," *Lowell Sun*, Dec. 1, 1927, 40; *Oakland Tribune*, Jan. 25, 1933, 9; Feb. 27, 1933, 10. See Monika Stodolska and Konstantinos Alexandris, "The Role of Recreational Sport in the Adaptation of First Generation Immigrants in the United States," 403, on the continued adherence to athletic role models in contemporary immigrant populations.

6. See Cardoza, "Making Italians?," 357, on the promotion of cycling in Italy by bicycle manufacturers in the early twentieth century. Cycling and cycle racing had been well established in the United States by that time. http://www.ddavid.com/formula1/depalma.htm; http://motorsportshalloffame.com/main/03_halloffame.htm.

7. Lee D. Baker, *From Savage to Negro: Anthropology and the Construction of Race, 1896–1954*, 29–52, 99–126; Matthew Frye Jacobson, *Whiteness of a Different Color: European Immigrants and the Alchemy of Race*; Reginald Horsman, *Race and Manifest Destiny: The Origins of American Racial Anglo-Saxonism*.

8. Gilfoyle, *Pickpocket's Tale*, 289; Jacobson, *Whiteness of a Different Color*, 31–38; Schneider, *Italy's "Southern Question"*; Dickie, *Darkest Italy*; Richards, *Italian American*, 107; La Gumina, *Wop!*, 102 (quote).

9. Yehudi O. Webster, *The Racialization of America*, 33–63.

10. For examples of the Chicago School, see Park and Miller, *Old World Traits Transplanted*; Robert E. Park, Ernest Burgess, and Roderick D. McKenzie, *The City*; and Ernest W. Burgess, ed., *The Urban Community*. An overview is provided by Stow Persons, *Ethnic Studies at Chicago, 1905–1945*.

11. Victor W. Turner, *The Ritual Process: Structure and Anti-Structure*; Hoare and Smith, *Prison Notebooks of Gramsci*.

12. Whiteness studies and their debates can be followed in Horsman, *Race and Manifest Destiny*; David R. Roediger, *The Wages of Whiteness: Race and the Making of the American Working Class*; Theodore W. Allen, *The Invention of the White Race: Racial Oppression and Social Control*; Baker, *From Savage to Negro*; Jacobson, *Whiteness of a Different Color*; Matthew Frye Jacobson, *Barbarian Virtues: The United States Encounters Foreign Peoples at Home and Abroad, 1876–1917*; Roediger, *Working toward Whiteness*; Eric Arnesen, "Whiteness and the Historians' Imagination"; Peter Kolchin, "Whiteness Studies: The New History of Race in America"; C. Richard King, "Cautionary Notes on Whiteness and Sport Studies"; and Ian Haney Lopez, *White by Law: The Legal Construction of Race*, 4–5 (quote).

13. Richard W. Rees, *Shades of Difference: A History of Ethnicity in America*, 13.

14. Arnesen, "Whiteness and the Historians' Imagination," 57; Jacobson, *Whiteness of a Different Color*, 13, 22–31; Rees, *Shades of Difference*, 45–55.

15. As the title suggests, T. Guglielmo, *White on Arrival*, argues for instant recognition, whereas Richards, *Italian American*, disagrees, and Jacobson, *Whiteness of a Different Color*, opts for the achievement of whiteness in the interwar period, 1918–45.

16. T. Guglielmo, *White on Arrival*, 13.

17. Quotes are from La Gumina, *Wop!*, 24, as is the *New York Times* citation, Apr. 16, 1876, 31.

18. La Gumina, *Wop!*, 32–51, 62, 80, 87–113; Richard Gambino, *Vendetta: The True Story of the Largest Lynching in U.S. History*, 142–43 (quote); De Conde, *Half Bitter, Half Sweet*, 125; Gallo, *Old Bread, New Wine*, 114–17, 121–26; Margavio and Salomome, *Bread and Respect*, 200–212. See Peter Vellon, "Between White Men and Negroes: The Perception of Southern Italian Immigrants through the Lens of Italian Lynchings," in *Anti-Italianism: Essays on a Prejudice*, edited by William J. Connell and Fred Gardaphe, 23–32.

19. American Citizen, "Sicilian Immigrants," *New York Times*, May 25, 1909.

20 Robert M. Lombardo, *The Black Hand: Terror by Letter in Chicago*.

21. Caroline Waldron Merithew, "Making the Italian Other: Blacks, Whites, and the Inbetween in the 1895 Spring Valley, Illinois, Race Riot," in *Are Italians White? How Race Is Made in America*, edited by Jennifer Guglielmo and Salvatore Salerno, 79–97. The convicted included Italian, Polish, and French miners, but the majority of those indicted were Italians.

22. Baker, *From Savage to Negro*, 73–80, 88; Gambino, *Vendetta*, 64, 133; James R. Barrett and David Roediger, "Inbetween Peoples: Race, Nationality, and the 'New Immigrant' Working Class"; Roediger, *Working toward Whiteness*, 37–39.

23. Gambino, *Blood of My Blood*, 77; Donna R. Gabaccia, "Race, Nation, Hyphen: Italian-Americans and American Multiculturalism in Comparative Perspective," in *Are Italians White?*, edited by J. Guglielmo and Salerno, 44–59; De

Conde, *Half Bitter, Half Sweet*, 91; clipping, *Outlook*, Nov. 16, 1907, 556, Box Immigration Studies Articles, Report of Commissioner-General of Immigration, 1903 folder, Schiavo Papers; Gallo, *Old Bread, New Wine*, 118; Mangione and Morreale, *La Storia*, 212; Roediger, *Working toward Whiteness*, 47, 74, 76 (quote), 77. Roediger indicates that 11 percent of Hispanic miners and 43 percent of Anglo miners in Arizona got three dollars or more per day, while only 6 percent of Italians did so. Among the New York subway workers, Italians were also paid less than black and Irish laborers in 1896.

24. Dominic T. Ciolli, "The 'Wop' in the Track Gang," 61–63, Box IAC, Immigrants in America folder, Schiavo Papers.

25. Edward Alsworth Ross, *The Old World in the New: The Significance of Past and Present Immigration to the American People*, 101, 113.

26. Ibid., 104.

27. Ibid., 108.

28. Ibid., 118.

29. *Bolletino dell Emigrazione*, 1912, no. 4, 20–43, Italian Societies folder, Schiavo Papers.

30. Ross, *Old World in the New*, 114 (emphasis added), 117.

31. Ibid., 293.

32. Cubberley, *Changing Conceptions of Education*, 1909, cited in Roediger, *Working toward Whiteness*, 19.

33. Madison Grant, *The Passing of the Great Race; or, The Racial Basis of European History*, 26.

34. Ibid., 121 (quote), 198.

35. Ibid., 65, 140, 150, 197 (quote); Hall cited in De Conde, *Half Bitter, Half Sweet*, 119. On Hall, see Cannato, *American Passage*, 100–106.

36. Roberts cited in La Gumina, *Wop!*, 182.

37. Brodkin, *How Jews Became White Folks*, 95.

38. Noel Ignatiev, *How the Irish Became White*; Roediger, *Working toward Whiteness*, 127; Richard Havers, *Sinatra*, 19 (quote).

39. La Gumina, *Wop!*, 221, 328, 329–30 (quote).

40. Howard B. Woolston, "Rating the Nations: A Study in the Statistics of Opinion." The study rated native white Americans, Germans, English, Jews, Scandinavians, Irish, French Canadians, Slavs, Italians, and African Americans based on the opinions of only ten respondents, all of whom held middle-class social status.

41. Robert M. Fogelson, *Bourgeois Nightmares: Suburbia, 1870–1930*, 103.

42. Ibid., 126–31.

43. Park and Miller, *Old World Traits Transplanted*, 51.

44. Cannistraro and Meyer, *Lost World of Italian American Radicalism*, 1; Gallo, *Old Bread, New Wine*, 99–103.

45. Cannistraro and Meyer, *Lost World of Italian Radicalism*, 3, 5, 18; Gallo, *Old Bread, New Wine*, 95. See J. Guglielmo, *Living the Revolution*; and Dominic L. Candeloro, *Chicago's Italians: Immigrants, Ethnics, Americans*, 117–23, on Italian organizational efforts, especially its complete domination of the hod carriers' and laborers' union.

46. Gallo, *Old Bread, New Wine*, 88; Roediger, *Working toward Whiteness*, 76 (quote).

47. Dominic L. Candeloro, *Italians in Chicago*, 27; William Kornblum, *Blue Collar Community*, 197–99; Roediger, *Working toward Whiteness*, 39; Cannistraro and Meyer, *Lost World of Italian American Radicalism*, 43n108.

48. Vecchio, *Merchants, Midwives, and Laboring Women*, 3, 32, 49–57; Donna R. Gabaccia, *Immigration and American Diversity*, 148; Cannistraro and Meyer, *Lost World of Italian American Radicalism*, 5, 15, 16, 18, 43, 118, 121–22, 193.

49. La Gumina, *Wop!*, 198–200.

50. Alan Dawley, *Struggles for Justice: Social Responsibility and the Liberal State*, 83; http://www.lucyparsonsproject.org/iww/kornbluh_bread_roses.html; William Preston, *Aliens and Dissenters: Federal Suppression of Radicals, 1903–1933*; Robert K. Murray, *Red Scare: A Study in National Hysteria, 1919–1920*.

51. Barrett and Roediger, "Inbetween Peoples."

52. Alessandro Marchese Family Papers, Boxes 2–3.

53. Park and Miller, *Old World Traits Transplanted*, 103.

54. Cannistraro and Meyer, *Lost World of Italian American Radicalism*, 8; Paul Avrich, *Sacco and Vanzetti: The Anarchist Background*; Dawley, *Struggles for Justice*, 288–90; Lisa McGirr, "The Passion of Sacco and Vanzetti: A Global History," 1096. La Gumina, *Wop!*, 239–42, indicates that the testimonies of more than twenty Italian witnesses in the trial were dismissed, the jury foremen referred to Italians as "dagoes," an appeals judge referred to Italians as "a race of pickpockets," and the trial judge vowed to get the "anarchist bastards." Carnevale, *New Language, New World*, 87–91, states that the Italian interpreter, a friend of the judge and an extortionist in the Italian community, distorted the translations of the defendants. See *La Parola del Popolo*, Jan. 7 and Jan. 14, 1922 (FLPS), on fund-raising efforts. See Ron Briley, "The Legend of Sacco and Vanzetti: Keeping the Story Alive in Literature, Song, and Film," on the continuing influence of the affair.

55. http://www.ebrary.com/stanford/Dillingham1.html; Wills, *Destination America*, 158–59; T. Guglielmo, *White on Arrival*, 76–84, 78 (quote).

56. Gambino, *Blood of My Blood*, 278–86; Gallo, *Old Bread, New Wine*, 134. See Lombardo, *Black Hand*, on the media construction of Italian criminality.

57. Lombardo, *Black Hand*, 137–38.

58. Margavio and Salomone, *Bread and Respect*, 120 (quote), 188–242; Gambino, *Blood of My Blood*, 289–302.

59. Park, Burgess, and McKenzie, *The City*, 112 (quote). See Laurence Bergreen, *Capone: The Man and the Era*; and Elliott J. Gorn, *Dillinger's Wild Ride*, on public interest in criminals of the era. Rocky Graziano with Ralph Corsel, *Somebody Down Here Likes Me Too*, details Graziano's friendship with Capone and the hero worship of gangsters by neighborhood youth.

60. Raymond Sayler, "A Study of Behavioral Problems of Boys in Lower North Community," Box 135, Folder 4, Burgess Papers.

61. T. Guglielmo, *White on Arrival*, 83–84; Vincent Panella, *The Other Side: Growing Up Italian in America*, 29; Gardaphe, *From Wise Guys to Wise Men*, 10, 11 (quote).

62. Gardaphe, *From Wise Guys to Wise Men*, xvi.

63. Gorn, *Dillinger's Wild Ride*, xix.

64. Robert Leuci, "Hooks," in *Reaching for the Stars*, edited by Freundlich, 65–86; Frank Di Liberto interview, Italians in Chicago, Oral History Project, Special Collections, University of Illinois at Chicago; Frank Di Benedetto, personal communication, Feb. 7, 2009. See Graziano with Corsel, *Somebody Down Here Likes Me Too*; and Chris Anderson and Sharon McGehee, with Jake LaMotta, *Raging Bull II*, on support and control of boxers by crime figures.

65. J. Guglielmo and Salerno, *Are Italians White?*, 35, 73; Mormino, *Immigrants on the Hill*, 61–62; T. Guglielmo, *White on Arrival*, 66; Ahnert, *American Journey*, 194, 225; Margavio and Salomone, *Bread and Respect*, 212–14; Talese, *Unto the Sons*, 227–28; *Bulletin of Italian American National Union*, Apr. 1925, WPA Foreign Language Press Survey (FLPS), Reel IIB3; Alphonse Leone interview, Domenick Di Mucci interview, Antonio Faustini interview, all in Italians in Chicago, Oral History Project, Special Collections, University of Illinois at Chicago; Dominic Candeloro, "Suburban Italians: Chicago Heights, 1890–1975," in *Ethnic Chicago*, by Peter d'A. Jones and Melvin G. Holli, 180–209; Mangione and Morreale, *La Storia*, 162.

66. Bogardus, *Immigration and Race Attitudes*; Briggs, *Italian Passage*, 275, 331.

67. Michael Frontani, "From the Bottom to the Top: Frank Sinatra, the American Myth of Success, and the Italian-American Image," lists such films as *Bull Weed* (1927), *Little Caesar* (1930), *Scarface* (1932), and *Roaring Twenties* (1939).

68. Lopez, *White by Law*, 74–84; T. Guglielmo, *White on Arrival*.

69. Jacobson, *Whiteness of a Different Color*, 4.

70. Du Bois cited in Roediger, *Working toward Whiteness*, 133.

71. Cohen, *Making a New Deal*, 24.

72. Carnevale, *New Language, New World*, 60–61, 63 (quote); Jacobson, *Whiteness of a Different Color*, 83, 93; Garraty, *American Nation*, 622–23; De Conde, *Half Bitter, Half Sweet*, 179.

73. Sweeney quoted in Joann Detore-Nakamura, "'Good Enough': An Italian American Memoir," in *Anti-Italianism*, edited by Connell and Gardaphe, 118–19; Cannato, *American Passage*, 344.

74. Powers, *Faces along the Bar*, 83.

75. Nasaw, *Children of the City*, 121–31, 195–96; Cohen, *Making a New Deal*, 120–29, 123 (quote).

76. http://www.redhotjazz.com/jdurante.html.

77. For insights into the class, gender, and ethnic dimensions of early commercialized popular culture, see Erenberg, *Steppin' Out*; Nasaw, *Going Out*; and Paul G. Cressey, *The Taxi Dance Hall: A Sociological Study in Commercialized Recreation and City Life*. Cohen, *Making a New Deal*, 147; Maselli and Candeloro, *Italians in New Orleans*, 8, 71–74; Margavio and Salomone, *Bread and Respect*, 179–80; *Il Bolletino Sociale*, Apr. 15, 1929, FLPS; Rolle, *Italian Americans*, 169–71. See Marchese Family Papers, Folders 16, 18, 22, for the typical singing career of Lina Allesandro and Nick Palmisano.

78. See Heap, *Slumming*, 124–25, 185, 221, on the popularity of slumming. Cressey, "Succession of Cultural Groups in Chicago," 279–80 (quote). See Lawrence D. Hogan, *Shades of Glory: The Negro Leagues and the Story of African-American Baseball*, 182, on Alvalony and black semipro teams in New York. The New York Rens and the Harlem Globetrotters basketball teams emerged from their nightclub roots during the interwar era.

79. http://www.biography.com/people/lou-costello-162971; http://www.rottentomatoes.com/celebrity/lou_costello/biography.php.

80. Graziano and Corsel, *Somebody Down Here Likes Me Too*, 165.

81. *Bulletin Italo-American National Union* (Jan. 1928), FLPS; Don W. Riggs, *History of St. Donatus Parish*, indicates that the Chicago-area Italian parish produced at least eleven professional athletes after World War I. Gerald R. Gems, "Sport, Religion, and Americanization: Bishop Sheil and the Catholic Youth Organization"; http://en.wikipedia.org/wiki/Louis_Laurie. See Peter T. Alter, "Serbs, Sports, and Whiteness," in *Sports in Chicago*, edited by Elliott J. Gorn, 113–27, on public displays of whiteness; Harry Edwards, "Social Change and Popular Culture: Seminal Developments at the Interface of Race, Sport, and Society"; and Bryan Denham, "Correlates of Pride in the Performance Success of United States Athletes Competing on an International Stage."

82. Bourdieu, *Outline of a Theory of Practice*.

83. See John Bodnar, "Materialism and Morality: Slavic-American Immigrant and Education, 1890–1940"; and Alba, *Ethnicity and Race in the U.S.A.*, 140, on the school dropout rates. Heller, *"In This Corner . . . !,"* 141. Mirel, *Patriotic Pluralism*, 56, 111, indicates that only about one-third of all American youth ages fourteen to seventeen attended high school in 1920. Lindenmeyer, *Greatest Generation*

Grows Up, 224, 264, states that 54.9 percent the same cohort attended high school a decade later, but only 16.4 percent remained for four years. The figures for Italian youth were considerably lower.

84. Yogi Berra and Ed Fitzgerald, *Yogi: The Autobiography of a Professional Baseball Player*, 51.

85. Anthony L. La Ruffa, *Monte Carmelo: An Italian-American Community in the Bronx*, 53.

86. Bourdieu, *Outline of a Theory of Practice*.

87. http://www.exploratorium.edu/baseball/nelson.html; http://www.barbaragregorich.com/clem.htm; Sarah Bair, "American Sports, 1910–1919," 160–61.

88. Fred D. Cavinder, *More Amazing Tales from Indiana*, 124–25; Gail Ingham Berlage, "From Bloomer Girls' Baseball to Women's Softball: A Cultural Journey Resulting in Women's Exclusion from Baseball," in *The Cooperstown Symposium on Baseball and American Culture, 1999*, edited by Peter M. Rutkoff, 245–60; "Margaret Gisolo," photocopy adopted from Barbara Gregorich, *Women at Play*, 30–31, miscellaneous folder, Italian American Renaissance Foundation Library; http://www.niashf.org/index2.cfm?ContentID=58&InducteeID=100. See *Port Arthur (TX) News*, July 1, 1928, 10; *Mason City (IA) Globe-Gazette*, July 19, 1928, 17; and *Frederick (MD) News-Post*, Apr. 26, 1931, 3, on national celebrity and barnstorming. Angela Teja and Marco Impiglia, "Italy," in *European Cultures in Sport: Examining the Nations and Regions*, edited by James Riordan and Arnd Kruger, 145–46.

89. Berkow, "The Extraordinary Life and Times of Ping Bodie," 61; John J. Pinelli, "From San Francisco Sandlots to the Big Leagues: Babe Pinelli," in *Baseball and the American Dream: Race, Class, Gender, and the National Pastime*, edited by Robert Elias, 138.

90. "Curves and Bingles," *New York Times*, Apr. 22, 1920, 17.

91. Lawrence Baldassaro and Richard A. Johnson, eds., *The American Game: Baseball and Ethnicity*, 101; Baldassaro, *Beyond DiMaggio*, 35–39; Edward G. White, *Creating the National Pastime: Baseball Transforms Itself, 1903–1953*.

92. Sidney Fields, "Hat's Off," *New York Daily Mirror*, clipping in Pinelli file, Baseball Hall of Fame; http://www.sdabu.com/history_main.htm.

93. Samuel O. Regalado, *Viva Baseball: Latin Major Leaguers and Their Special Hunger*, 72.

94. Baldassaro, *Beyond DiMaggio*, 70 (quote), 74, 102 on Cuccinello.

95. *Corriere D'America*, Dec. 21, 1933, 7, and Baldassaro, *Beyond DiMaggio*, 86, on Melillo; *Corriere D'America*, Oct. 4, 1936, 11 (quote). Freundlich, *Reaching for the Stars*, 204–300, lists at least forty-seven Italians on Major League teams during the decade. Baldassaro, *Beyond DiMaggio*, 98, counts fifty-four Italian players.

96. Joseph A. Burger, "Baseball and Social Mobility for Italian Americans in the 1930s," 10–11.

97. Covello, *Social Background*, 300, cites the stereotypical quote from the *Report of the Causes of Crime, National Commission on Law Observance and Enforcement* (Washington, DC, 1931), 2:3, 4–5.

98. Russi interview AKRF-83 and Vacca interview EI-200, Ellis Island Oral History Collection; Sorrentino Papers, 8–9. Sorrentino later became a social worker and used sport to attract juvenile delinquents in Chicago.

99. Italian American Directory Company, *Gli Italiani negli Stati Uniti d'America*, 164; Ron Brocato, *The Golden Game: When Prep Football Was King in New Orleans*, 48, photocopy in miscellaneous folder, Italian American Renaissance Foundation Library; Paul Gallico, *Farewell to Sport*, 290; Keith McClellan, "Thomas J. Holleran, the Akron Pros' Signal Caller," *Coffin Corner*; McClellan, *Sunday Game*, 366 (quote).

100. http://www.hickoksports.com/biograph/littlelou.shtml.

101. Matti Goksoyr, "Nationalism."

102. Mitchell cited in Michael Oriard, *King Football: Sport and Spectacle in the Golden Age of Radio and Newsreels, Magazines, the Weekly and the Daily Press*, 256.

103. John Billi, "U.S. Sports Firmament Is Dotted with Many First Magnitude Stars of Italian Origin"; G. Billi, "Per l'All-Italian, 1937"; *Corriere D'America*, Nov. 1, 1932, 7; Nov. 3, 1932, 7; Nov. 4, 1932, 7; Nov. 5, 1932, 7; Nov. 8, 1932, 7; Nov. 10, 1932, 7; Nov. 11, 1932, 7; Nov. 13, 1932, 13; Nov. 17, 1932, 17; Nov. 22, 1932, 7; Nov. 26, 1932, 7; Nov. 27, 1932, 9; Nov. 29, 1932, 7. Billi did not include any southern schools in his survey. Jack Cavanaugh, *The Gipper: George Gipp, Knute Rockne, and the Dramatic Rise of Notre Dame Football*, 212, 251, 253. Cavanaugh claims that Carideo relayed signals to Savoldi in Italian until an Italian speaking player for Pitt managed to foil their strategies in one game. http://www.und.com/sports/m-footbl/mtt/carideo_frank00.html. Savoldi was expelled from Notre Dame for marrying before graduation and soon capitalized on his fame as a professional wrestler.

104. http://www.stanfordalumni.org/news/magazine/2003/marapr/departments/examinedlife.html. Louisiana American Italian Sports Hall of Fame, Seventh Annual Induction Banquet Program 1992, on Trombatore, at Italian American Sports Hall of Fame.

105. Raymond Sayler, "A Study of Behavioral Problems of Boys in Lower North Community," Box 135, Folder 4, 24–26, Burgess Papers. See *Bulletin of Italo-American National Union*, Apr. 1933, FLPS, the political organization of an athletic club with 225 members, 95 percent of whom were Italians.

106. *Bulletin Italo-American National Union*, Jan. 1937, FLPS.

107. William Simons, Samuel Patti, and George Hermann, "Bloomfield: An Italian Working Class Neighborhood," in *Italian Americana*, edited by Bruno A. Arcudi and Richard Gambino, 104, 112.

108. Frederic M. Thrasher, *The Gang: A Study of 1,313 Gangs in Chicago*, considered neighborhood social-athletic clubs to be gangs owing to their engagement in petty crimes, although some were involved in felonious activities. Gerald R. Gems, "The Neighborhood Athletic Club: An Ethnographic Study of a Working-Class Athletic Fraternity in Chicago, 1917–1984"; *Chicago American*, Nov. 14, 1936, 16; personal papers of Frank Di Benedetto, club officer. See Mario Avignone interview, Italians in Chicago, Oral History Project, Chicago History Museum, for similar developments with the Mystery Athletic Club that included Italians, Poles, and Lithuanians at Palmer Park on the south side of the city.

109. Frank Di Liberto interview, Italians in Chicago, Oral History Project, Special Collections, University of Illinois at Chicago; Nick Zaranti interviews, Box 2, 13; Mario Bruno interview, Box 3, 47–59.

110. Diamond, *Mean Streets*, 46, 319n12; Cohen, *Making a New Deal*, 145 (quote).

111. Isadore Seligs, "A Study of the Basement Social Clubs of Lawndale District, 11, Box 142, Folder 3; and Raymond Sayler, "A Study of Behavior Problems of Boys in Lower North Community," Box 135, Folder 4, Burgess Papers.

112. Hedonism is apparent in Gorn, *Dillinger's Wild Ride*; and Zeitz, *Flapper*; and in the lives of sport stars. On the latter, see Leigh Montville, *The Big Bam: The Life and Times of Babe Ruth*; and Robert W. Creamer, *Babe: The Legend Comes to Life*.

113. *Corriere D'America*, Nov. 8, 1932, 7; Dec. 8, 1933, 6; Dec. 12, 1933, 7; Dec. 25, 1933, 7; Oct. 11, 1933, 11; Nov. 22, 1936, 11; Bruno Muzzacavallo file, Chicago Oral History Project; Fred Ebetino interview EI 481, Ellis Island Oral History Collection; La Gumina, *Wop!*, 122; Joe McGuigan, "Vic Ghezzi Is Golf's Victor Mature," in Box Sol–Sz, Schiavo Papers; John Sayle Watterson, *The Games Presidents Play: Sports and the Presidency*, 110; George Kirsch, *Golf in America*, 88, 119–20; http://www.wgv.com/hof/member.php?member=1102.

114. John Sugden, *Boxing and Society: An International Analysis*, 5, 7, 54–88, 182–85, 194–96; Riess, "Fighting Chance," 234; and S. Kirson Weinberg and Henry Around, "The Occupational Culture of the Boxer," 460, on the succession of ethnic boxing champions. Dr. Juan Reilly quoted in "Frank Klaus Sees Firpo in Action," *New York Times*, Sept. 2, 1923, 18. See *Uniontown (PA) Morning Herald*, July 16, 1923, 6; and *Oakland Tribune*, Sept. 14, 1923, 34, for examples of other denigratory characterizations of Firpo.

115. "Firpo Had the Title within His Grasp," *New York Times*, Sept. 15, 1923, 1. See also Sid Sutherland, "Latin Lacks Ring Wit to Cope with Yank, the Experienced," *Chicago Tribune*, Sept. 15, 1923, 11.

116. Joseph S. Page, *Primo Carnera: The Life and Career of the Heavyweight Boxing Champion*, 31, 37.

117. Arne K. Lang, *Prizefighting: An American History*, 90–95; Page, *Primo Carnera*, 118–19; Sugden, *Boxing and Society*, 36 (quote).

118. Heller, *"In This Corner . . . !,"* 328.

119. Gallico, *Farewell to Sport*, 58, 66. See Jeffrey T. Sammons, *Beyond the Ring: The Role of Boxing in American Society*, 86–91, for a critical assessment of Carnera's boxing career.

120. Rob Ruck, Maggie Jones Patterson, and Michael P. Weber, *Rooney: A Sporting Life*, 99.

121. Gaze theory was popularized by French scholars Jacques Lacan and Michel Foucault. For applications to sport, see the Forum articles in the *Journal of Sport History* 29, no. 3 (2002); and Mike Huggins, "The Sporting Gaze: Towards a Visual Turn in Sport History—Documenting Art and Sport."

122. See *Bulletin Italo-American National Union*, July 1934, for an account of Balbo at the World's Fair. See Scott Ackman and Christopher Schwarz, "Dubious Legacy," and heated retorts to the piece in *Chicago Magazine*, Oct. 2008, 14, on the enduring legacy of the Balbo trip in Chicago.

123. Gugleilmo, *Living the Revolution*, 218 (quote); Luconi, *From Paesani to White Ethnics*, 84–94; Stefano Luconi, "Forging an Ethnic Identity: The Case of Italian Americans," 19, on monetary contributions; Fichera, *Italy on the Pacific*, 136, claims ten thousand gold rings and as much as fifty thousand dollars in cash and tons of scrap metal for the Ethiopian campaign delivered by San Franciscans; Candeloro, *Italians in Chicago*, 71–76; T. Guglielmo, *White on Arrival*, 118, 122, 125.

124. Gori, *Italian Fascism and the Female Body*, 18, 21–30; Thomas B. Morgan, *Italian Physical Culture Demonstration*; Chetwynd, *Baseball in Europe*, 40, on baseball; Talese, *Unto the Sons*, 460; Stewart Brown quoted in *Corriere D'America*, Dec. 27, 1936, 10. See *Corriere D'America*, Nov. 1, 1932, 7; Nov. 4, 1932, 7; Nov. 5, 1932, 7; Nov. 6, 1932, 9, pt. 3; Nov. 7, 1932, 7; Nov. 8, 1932, 7, for a small sample of cycling, auto racing, and soccer news. G. N. Longarini, "Italy Considered Most Dangerous Sports Rival of United States in 1936 Olympic Games in Berlin," *La Notizia*, Oct. 13, 1933, 6, Box Sol–Sz, Schiavo Papers; Mark Dyreson et al., "American Sports, 1930–1939," in *Encyclopedia of Sports in America*, edited by M. Nelson, 249. See *Bulletin Italo-American National Union*, Jan. 1936, on the promotion and funding of Italian-language schools in the United States.

125. Chapman, *Sandow the Magnificent*; Patricia Vertinsky, "'Weighs and Means': Examining the Surveillance of Fat Bodies through Physical Education Practices in North America in the Late Nineteenth and Early Twentieth Centuries," 449–68.

126. Kenneth R. Dutton, *The Perfectible Body: The Western Ideal of Male Physical Development*, 137.

127. Gardaphe, *From Wise Guys to Wise Men*, 27, 34; Rolle, *Italian Americans*, 171–72; Ellexis Boyle, "Measuring Up to American Manhood: Racism and the Development of 'Race' in the History of Competitive Bodybuilding"; John F. Kasson, *Houdini, Tarzan, and the Perfect Man: The White Male Body and the Challenge of Modernity in America*, 32; Charles Gaines, *Charles Atlas, Yours in Perfect Manhood*.

128. Dutton, *Perfectible Body*, 221.

129. David Coad, *The Metrosexual: Gender, Sexuality, and Sport*, 146; http://en.wikipedia.org/wiki/Tony_Sansone.

130. Gerald R. Gems and Gertrud Pfister, *Understanding American Sport*, 11; Bourdieu, "Program for a Sociology of Sport"; Kath Woodward, *Boxing, Masculinity, and Identity*, 64–70; Eric Jensen, "Body by Weimar: Athletes, Gender, and German Modernity."

131. Frederick, MD, Post, Oct. 12, 1936, 1; John D. Fair, *Muscletown: Bob Hoffman and the Manly Culture of York Barbell*, 44 (quote), 45, 64, 121, 189, 259. Other Italian team members included Tony Maniscalco, Phil Grippaldi, and Joe Puleo. The latter two were members of the 1968 Olympic team.

132. Harry Markson, "Life Story of Tony Galento," clipping, sports advertising scrapbooks box, Italian American Sports Hall of Fame; Silvio De Cristoforo, "'Two Ton Tony,'" 6 (quote).

133. Patricia Boscia-Mule, *Authentic Ethnicities: The Interaction of Ideology, Gender Power, and Class in the Italian-American Experience*; Rees, *Shades of Difference*, 5–31, 72–109; Belliotti, *Seeking Identity*, 110, 165 (quote).

134. *Bulletin Order of the Sons of Italy*, May 15, 1934, FLPS.

135. Richards, *Italian American*, 178–81; Harry Jebsen, "Assimilation in a Working Class Suburb: The Italians of Blue Island, Illinois," in *Urban Experience*, edited by Gallo, 64–84, shows only two intermarriages by 1928 but a 38.9 percent rate of home ownership. Nelli, *From Immigrant to Ethnic*, 124, counts more than thirty-eight thousand subscribers to an Italian newspaper in Chicago in 1921. Carnevale, *New Language, New World*, 40, counted seventy-three weekly Italian papers still existent in 1930. Florian Girometta, *St. Anthony of Padua Italian National Parish Diamond Jubilee Book, 1903–1978*, 16–17, indicates a gradual transition to English in parish meetings.

136. Anna Zaloha, "A Study of the Persistence of Italian Customs among 143 Families of Italian Descent Members of Social Clubs at Chicago Commons"; De Marco, *Ethnics and Enclaves*, 38; Carnevale, *New Language, New World*, 21–42, 72, 117, 136–56; Luconi, *From Paesani to White Ethnics*, 55; Gaetano De Filippis, "Social Life in an Immigrant Community," Box 130, Folder 2, Burgess Papers.

137. Kantowicz, *Corporation Sole*; Richard M. Swiderski, *Voices: An Anthropologist's Dialogue with an Italian-American Festival*; Weiss, *American Education and the European Immigrant*, xiv; Dominic Candeloro, "Italian-Americans," in

Multiculturalism in the United States: A Comparative Guide to Acculturation and Ethnicity, edited by John D. Buenker and Lorman A. Ratner, 173–92; Zummo, *Little Sicily*, 55–56; McKibben, *Beyond Cannery Row*, 98–114, 104 (quote).

138. Cohen, *Making a New Deal*, 92–93.

139. Robert A. Orsi, *The Madonna of 115th Street: Faith and Community in Italian Harlem* and "The Religious Boundaries of an In-between People: Street Feste and the Problem of the Dark-Skinned Other in Italian Harlem, 1920–1990," in *Gods of the City*, edited by Robert A. Orsi, 257–88; and Joseph Sciorra, "'We Go Where the Italians Live': Religious Processions as Ethnic and Territorial Markers in a Multi-ethnic Brooklyn Neighborhood," 311, both in Orsi, *Gods of the City*.

140. De Conde, *Half Bitter, Half Sweet*, 332. De Conde misstates the year of the riot as 1921.

141. Roediger, *Working toward Whiteness*, 111–17, 128 (quote), 191; Zorbaugh, *Gold Coast and the Slum*, 148, *Corriere D'America*, Dec. 3, 1933, 5S; T. Guglielmo, *White on Arrival*, 45–58, 113–25. On the Jersey City, Harlem, and Brooklyn race riots of 1935, see Theresa E. Runstedtler, "In Sport the Best Man Wins: How Joe Louis Whupped Jim Crow"; George Samuel Schuyler, *Ethiopian Stories*, 14; and Jay Maeder, "Smashup Ethiopia, 1935," *New York Daily News*, June 15, 2000 at http://articles.nydailynews.com/2000-06-15/news/18131296_1_addis-ababa-emperor-haile....

142. Roediger, *Working toward Whiteness*, 220 (quote), 223–34.

143. Matthew Frye Jacobson, *Roots Too: White Ethnic Revival in Post–Civil Rights America*, 33–34, cites Lloyd Warner and Leo Srole, *Social Systems of American Ethnic Groups*, on distinctions between Caucasian groups.

4. The Emergence of Sport as a Cultural Force

1. The composite description of the fight is gleaned from Henry L. Farrell, "Dempsey Retains Championship in Great Battle," *Wisconsin State Journal*, Sept. 15, 1923; "Dempsey Retains Title in Ferocious Ring Battle," *Cumberland (MD) Evening Times*, Sept. 15, 1923, 3; "Jack Dempsey Retains Title in Cave-Man Battle with Firpo," *Alton (IL) Evening Telegraph*, Sept. 15, 1923, 6.

2. Robert E. Park, *Cultural Conflict and the Marginal Man*, http://en.wikipedia.org/wiki/Robert_E._Park.

3. Roediger, *Working toward Whiteness*, 8; W. E. B. Du Bois, *The Souls of Black Folk*. See also Orsi, "Religious Boundaries," in *Gods of the City*.

4. Gems, *Windy City Wars*; Hartmut Keil and John B. Jentz, eds., *German Workers in Industrial Chicago, 1850–1910*; Annette R. Hofmann, ed., *Turnen and Sport: Transatlantic Transfers*.

5. John S. Brubacher and Willis Rudy, *Higher Education in Transition: A History of American Colleges and Universities*; Margavio and Salomone, *Bread and Respect*,

16; Rolle, *Italian Americans*, 17; Gambino, *Blood of My Blood*, 113, 140–41; Gallo, *Old Bread, New Wine*, 21, 28–32; Bodnar, Simon, and Weber, *Lives of Their Own*, 124–32. On the immigrant offspring, see Briggs, *Italian Passage*, 224–25, 296; Maria Parrino, ed., *Italian American Autobiographies*; Carlo Bianco, "Italian Folk Culture Transplanted: Methods of Documentation," in *Italian Immigrants*, edited by Vecoli, 75–87; Irvin L. Child, *Italian or American? The Second Generation in Conflict*.

6. Gregory Bateson, *Mind and Nature: A Necessary Unity*, 123–26, 134–35, 141–50.

7. Susan Cotts Watkins and Angela D. Danzi, "Women's Gossip and Social Change: Childbirth and Fertility Control among Italian and Jewish Women in the United States, 1920–1940"; Malpezzi and Clements, *Italian-American Folklore*, 241.

8. Graziano with Corsel, *Somebody Down Here Likes Me Too*, xii.

9. Luconi, *From Paesani to White Ethnics*, 78; De Conde, *Half Bitter, Half Sweet*, 169; Gallo, *Old Bread, New Wine*, 172–79, 199–216. Roediger, *Working toward Whiteness*, 193, gives figures of 91 percent for the fourteen- to fifteen-year-olds and 54.4 percent for sixteen- to seventeen-year-olds.

10. Mormino, *Immigrants on the Hill*, 116–17, provides home ownership rates of 69 percent in Philadelphia, 59 percent in St. Louis, 45 percent in Buffalo, 52 percent in Syracuse, 47 percent in San Francisco, 42 percent in Cleveland, 41 percent in Chicago, and 31 percent in Boston. Fichera, *Italy on the Pacific*, 73, concurs with the San Francisco figures. Zaloha, "Study of the Persistence of Italian Customs"; Malpezzi and Clements, *Italian-American Folklore*, 77; Talese, *Unto the Sons*, 449. See De Liberto interview, Italians in Chicago, Chicago History Museum, 17, on pasta as a daily ritual.

11. Jerre Mangione, *An Ethnic at Large: A Memoir of America in the Thirties and Forties*, 13–33. Di Liberto, *Italians in Chicago*, 41, offers similar language issues; and Panella, *Other Side*, express similar feelings of difference and conflicted identity. See Joanne Detore-Nakamura, "Good Enough," in *Anti-Italianism*, edited by Connell and Gardaphe, 117–29, for the continued alienation of the third generation.

12. Carnevale, *New Language, New World*, 142–43, 146; Gallo, *Old Bread, New Wine*, 255; Frank Di Benedetto, personal communication, Feb. 7, 2009; De Fillipis, "Social Life in an Immigrant Community," Burgess Papers. Ferrara, *Profiles of Italian Americans*, 59 (quote); see 76, 93, 164 for others whose names were Anglicized.

13. Talese, *Unto the Sons*, 4.

14. Hoare and Smith, *Prison Notebooks of Gramsci*, 418.

15. Bodnar, Simon, and Weber, *Lives of Their Own*, 245–53; McKibben, *Beyond Cannery Row*, 41, 53–64; Gary Ross Mormino, "The Playing Fields of St. Louis:

Italian Immigrants and Sports, 1925–1941," 8, 17. S. Watkins and Danzi, "Women's Gossip and Social Change," indicated that of 59 Italian women interviewed in New York, Philadelphia, and Providence, 74–84 percent of fathers held blue-collar jobs, while 86–88 percent of their husbands held blue-collar jobs, suggesting no social mobility.

16. Briggs, *Italian Passage*, 135–36. See Box 130, Folder 2, Burgess Papers, for intergenerational differences relative to popular culture. See Americo Moreschi, Lawrence Spallita, Frank Mariani, Valentino Lazzaeretti, Mario Avignone, Sarah Lagattuta, Nick Zaranti, Ernesto Dalle Molle, and Mario Bruno interviews, Italians in Chicago Oral History Project, Chicago History Museum.

17. Simone Cinotto, "Leonard Covello, the Covello Papers, and the History of Eating Habits among Italian Immigrants in New York," 515 (quote); Zeitz, *Flapper*. See Gaetano De Filippis, "Case Study-Mary," Box 130, Folder 2, Burgess Papers, for the story of an eighteen-year-old who married a fifty-year-old Anglo sports promoter, greatly increasing her social and economic capital.

18. Cavalieri, KM 019; Rucci, AKRF-83; and Pavan, EI 468 interviews in Ellis Island Oral History Collection.

19. Catalano interview, KM-79, Ellis Island Oral History Collection.

20. Gems, *Windy City Wars*; Benjamin G. Rader, *American Sports: From the Age of Folk Games to the Age of Spectators*; John M. Carroll, *Red Grange and the Rise of Modern Football*; Creamer, *Babe*; Mark Dyreson, "The Emergence of Consumer Culture and the Transformation of Physical Culture: American Sport in the 1920s."

21. http://www.cyberboxingzone.com/boxing/ross-t.htm; Jim Waltzer, *The Battle of the Century: Dempsey, Carpentier, and the Birth of Modern Promotion*, 31, 40–41. Flynn (Chiariglione) knocked out Jack Dempsey in 1917.

22. Steven A. Riess, *Sport in Industrial America, 1850–1920*, 147–49; Ross (Rosario) Scarantino interview, EI-160, Ellis Island Oral History Collection; Sorrentino Papers, 9; Mormino, *Immigrants on the Hill*, 199; Maselli and Candeloro, *Italians in New Orleans*, 93–94, 96; Hauser and Brunt, *Italian Stallions*, 15–16.

23. Hauser and Brunt, *Italian Stallions*, 15.

24. J. Billi, "U.S. Sports Firmament," 7.

25. Canzoneri, Dundee, Corbett, Ambers, Mandell, Wolgast, Genaro, and LaBarba files, Boxing Hall of Fame; Petrolle information from Jo Ann Stack (daughter), phone interview by the author, Feb. 2, 2010.

26. Willie Pep with Robert Sacchi, *Willie Pep Remembers . . . Friday's Heroes*, 4–8, 5 (quote).

27. http://www.vtboxhwr.org/buffbanq.htm; http://boxrec.com/media/index.php/Battling_Battalino; http://international.loc.gov/cgi-bin/query/S?/ammem/cdni@field(Sub4+@od1(Boxing+coaches-; http://boxrec.com/media/index.php/The_Ring_Magazine%27s_Annual_Ratings:_1924; *Chicago Daily Journal*, Jan.

10, 1925, 15; Gerard O'Neill and Dick Lehr, *The Underboss: The Rise and Fall of a Mafia Family*, 27; Arthur J. Todd, *Chicago Recreation Survey, 1937*, vol. 3, *Private Recreation*, 102; *Il Corriere Italico*, Jan. 20, 1937; Feb. 20, 1937, FLPS.

28. See Gems, *Windy City Wars*, 182–83, 191–92, on the offerings of the Catholic Youth Organization, the Knights of Columbus, and the newspapers in Chicago.

29. Maselli and Candeloro. *Italians in New Orleans*, 67; Gary B. Youmans, *The Onion Picker: Carmen Basilio and Boxing in the 1950s*, 143; M. Nelson, *Encyclopedia of American Sports*, 222; Todd, *Chicago Recreation Survey*, vol. 2 *Commercial Recreation*, 79 (quote).

30. Bishop Bernard J. Sheil, ed., *CYO Survey* 2, no. 6 (1953): 8.

31. Gems, "Sport, Religion, and Americanization"; Sheil Papers, Catholic Archdiocese of Chicago; Roger L. Treat, *Bishop Sheil and the CYO*, 120–21 (quote). A CYO survey of fifteen hundred boxers found only 5 percent aspired to ring careers, while others hoped to become doctors, lawyers, engineers, teachers, musicians, journalists, and businessmen. See Gerald R. Gems, "The Politics of Boxing: Resistance, Religion, and Working Class Assimilation," for a more complete analysis. The Sorrentino Papers at the Chicago History Museum indicate that the CYO strategy continued to be implemented by social workers in the ensuing decades.

32. *New World*, Nov. 1, 1935, 10; Nov. 29, 1935, 10; Dec. 13, 1935, 16; Thrasher, *Gang*, 81 (quote). The CYO program, which operated in all Chicago Catholic parishes, had the added benefit of incorporating ethnic national parishes within the archdiocesan hierarchy. They had previously resisted control by Irish American clergy.

33. Newspaper clipping, Ambers file, International Boxing Hall of Fame.

34. "How I will Take Another Title from Armstrong," magazine clipping, ibid.

35. Norman B. Hill, "Can Canzoneri Win Another Crown?," *The Arena*, July 10, 1929, 12–13, 35, Canzoneri file, International Boxing Hall of Fame; Nat Fleischer, ed., *Ring* 8, no. 8 (1934): 54, Chicago History Museum.

36. Panella, *Other Side*, 21; Loic Wacquant, "The Social Logic of Sparring: On the Body as a Practical Strategist," in *Physical Culture, Power, and the Body*, edited by Jennifer Hargreaves and Patricia Vertinsky, 146–47 (quote). The same case could be made for the numerous Jewish champions who preceded the Italians in the 1920s.

37. Frank X. Briante, "Lauds Italian Fighters," *Corriere D'America*, Dec. 16, 1933, 7. Fausto Batella, *Gridiron Gladiators: Italian-Americans in College, Semipro & Pro Football*, 7, states that Briante played football for New York University and for the Staten Island Stapletons (1929) and Newark Tornadoes (1930) as a professional. Riess, "Fighting Chance," 234; and Weinberg and Arond, "Occupational Culture of the Boxer," 460, indicate that Italians produced the most champions and contenders during the era.

38. Sports Advertising Scrapbooks, Schiavo Papers; see Heller, *"In This Corner . . . !,"* 223–24, on the Conn fight; Talese, *Unto the Sons*, 32, 549.

39. Gerald R. Gems, *For Pride, Profit, and Patriarchy: Football and the Incorporation of American Cultural Values*, 111–50.

40. Ruck, Patterson, and Weber, *Rooney: A Sporting Life*, 54–55.

41. Ronald H. Bayor, *Neighbors in Conflict: The Irish, Germans, Jews, and Italians of New York City, 1929–1941*; McGreevy, *Parish Boundaries*, 15–18; Murray Sperber, *Shake Down the Thunder: The Creation of Notre Dame Football*, 318 (quote), 338. The references to Marchy Schwartz, a Jewish player, and halfback Jack Elder, as well as the Irish "micks," denoted the polyglot composition of the team. Ben Kane, a Jewish player on the 1930 team, asserts that he was one of four or five Jews on the squad, http://www.wsbt.com/news/local/12312606.html. Outside of the historically black colleges, only a relative handful of African American players appeared on college teams during the era.

42. Brocato, "The Golden Game," miscellaneous folder, 90-10, Italian American Renaissance Library; Gerald R. Gems, "The Prep Bowl: Football and Religious Acculturation in Chicago, 1927–1963"; Edward R. Kantowicz, "Cardinal Mundelein of Chicago and the Shaping of Twentieth Century American Catholicism"; Charles Shanabruch, "The Catholic Church's Role in the Americanization of Chicago's Immigrants, 1833–1928"; Kantowicz, *Corporation Sole*.

43. Child, *Italian or American?*, 121.

44. Michael O'Brien, *Vince: A Personal Biography of Vince Lombardi*, 25, 30.

45. Avignone, Zaranti, and Magnaini interviews, Bruno interview (quotes on 47 and 57, respectively), Italians in Chicago, Chicago History Museum; Frank Di Benedetto Personal Papers. Murry Nelson, *The Originals: The New York Celtics Invent Modern Basketball*, 22, makes the point that mixed ethnic teams also drew a larger fan base and enhanced commercial opportunities.

46. N. Elias, *Civilizing Process*; Norbert Elias, *The History of Manners: Power and Civility*; Norbert Elias and Eric Dunning, *Quest for Excitement: Sport and Leisure in the Civilizing Process*.

47. Di Benedetto Personal Papers. Gems, *Windy City Wars*, 102–11, indicates suspensions from play and discontinuation of games when boys did not meet middle-class standards of play.

48. Mormino, "Playing Fields of St. Louis"; Mormino, *Immigrants on the Hill*, 203–6; Mormino, "Hill upon a City," 156.

49. Batella, *Gridiron Gladiators*, 5; John Kieran and Arthur Daley, *The Story of the Olympic Games*, 124–25; Allen Barra, *Yogi Berra: Eternal Yankee*, 10, on the World Cup.

50. Italian Maroons Soccer Club file, Italians in Chicago, Chicago History Museum. See *Bridgeport (CT) Telegram*, June 16, 1958, 7, on an interethnic soccer

league; and Van Rheenen, "Promise of Soccer in America," for ongoing soccer leagues in San Francisco. La Ruffa, *Monte Carmelo*, 67.

51. http://www.columbia.edu/cu/record/archives/vol20/vol20_iss1/record 2001.34.html.

52. Frank J. Cavaioli, "Ray Barbuti," in *The Italian American Experience: An Encyclopedia*, edited by Salvatore J. La Gumina et al., 54–55; http://findarticles.com /p/articles/mi_qa5518/is_200307/ai_n21340086/pg_3/?tag=content;col1,. See *Bismarck (ND) Tribune*, Apr. 4, 1928, 8; *Appleton (WI) Post-Crescent*, Apr. 3, 1928, 21; *Waterloo (IA) Evening Courier*, Apr. 6, 1928, 10; *Circleville (OH) Herald*, Apr. 4, 1928, 3; and *Salt Lake City Tribune*, Feb. 4, 1929, 13, as examples of recognition as a national hero.

53. Mormino, *Immigrants on the Hill*, 203–6; Mormino, "Hill upon a City"; Mugnaini interview, in Fair, *Muscletown*, 54; personal correspondence with Marino Mazzei, undated, Chicago Maroons Soccer Club; Bernardi, *Houses without Names*, 209; http://www.niashf.org/index2.cfm?ContentID=40&InducteeID=96.

54. http://www.ishof.org/honorees/92/92egsaville.html; http://www.hickok sports.com/history/usgymchamps.shtml; http://www.sports-reference.com/olympics /athletes/ca/connie-caruccio-lenz-1.html. Thanks to Gertrud Pfister for alerting me to the gymnasts.

55. Gems, *Windy City Wars*, 40–42, 191–92; Ned Polsky, *Hustlers, Beats, and Others*, 28.

56. Polsky, *Hustlers, Beats, and Others*, 28.

57. Willie Mosconi and Stanley Cohen, *Willie's Game: An Autobiography*, 22.

58. Mosconi and Cohen, *Willie's Game: An Autobiography*; *Corriere D'America*, Dec. 12, 1933, 7; Dec. 17, 1933, 11; Dec. 20, 1933, 7; Dec. 23, 1933, 7; *Chicago Tribune*, Dec. 18, 1954, B3; June 29, 1933, 24; June 30, 1933, 29; Dec. 20, 1934, 28; Feb. 10, 1937, 29.

59. Arch Ward, "In the Wake of the News," *Chicago Tribune*, Feb. 15, 1951, B1.

60. Mosconi and Cohen, *Willie's Game: An Autobiography*, 25. See Polsky, *Hustlers, Beats, and Others*, for the lifestyle of a hustler.

61. Mosconi and Cohen, *Willie's Game: An Autobiography*, 48 (quote); Polsky, *Hustlers, Beats, and Others*, 30.

62. Ernesto Dalle Molle interview, Italians in Chicago, Box 4; *Corriere D'America*, Dec. 21, 1933, 7; Dec. 6, 1936, 11; Victor Kalman, "Falcaro the Great"; "Andy Varippapa: Bowling's Greatest Showman," http://www.bowl.com/article View.aspx?i=11475&f=1. See http://www.niashf.org/Inductee_Search.php?f=1&iid =131 and http://bowlinghistory.wordpress.com/2009/06 on Marino. See Steven J. Overman, *Living Out of Bounds: The Male Athlete's Everyday Life*, 8, 72, on Salvino's work ethic; and http://www.pba.com.

63. William Foote Whyte, *Street Corner Society: The Social Structure of an Italian Slum*, 14–23; Mormino, "Playing Fields of St. Louis," 8.

64. Whyte, *Street Corner Society*, 140.

65. Todd, *Chicago Recreation Survey*, 2:53–54. Chicago counted 1,030 billiard halls in 1929. Gerald R. Gems, Linda J. Borish, and Gertrud Pfister, *Sports in American History: From Colonization to Globalization*, 239, 240 (quotes).

66. Rucci interview, AKRF-83, Ellis Island Oral History Collection.

67. Materia interview, EI 481, Ellis Island Oral History Collection.

68. Baldassaro, *Beyond DiMaggio*, 179.

69. Ibid., 132–35, 132–33 (quote).

70. Bruno interview, Italians in Chicago, Chicago History Museum, Box 3; *Chicago Sun-Times*, Feb. 8, 1988, 18 on Yacilla.

71. Thomas Barthel, *Baseball's Peerless Semipros: Bushwick*, 122, 130–31, 157, 165.

72. *Chicago Sun-Times*, Sept. 14, 1988, 15.

73. Leone interview, Italians in Chicago project, University of Illinois at Chicago, Special Collections.

74. Leuci, "Hooks," 74.

75. Ibid., 84.

76. Riggs, *History of St. Donatus Parish*, n.p.; Box CRCC, file 4/4, Chicago History Collection. Mormino, *Immigrants on the Hill*, 203, indicates fifty-one players were suspended for rough play and fighting in the community-regulated soccer league.

77. Baldassaro and Johnson, *The American Game*, 97; Baldassaro, *Beyond DiMaggio*, 47–48, recognized only twelve Italian players during the 1920s and claims a figure of 6.8 percent for 1941 (178, 431n34). Freundlich, *Reaching for the Stars*, 204–300; Burger, "Baseball and Social Mobility."

78. Baldassaro, *Beyond DiMaggio*, 65–74; Lazzeri cited in the *Sporting News*, Dec. 11, 1930, in Lawrence Baldassaro, "Go East Paesani: Early Italian Major Leaguers from the West Coast," in *Italian Immigrants Go West*, edited by Worrall, Albright, and Di Fabio, 100–108, 106 (quote).

79. Stephen Fox, *Big Leagues: Professional Baseball, Football, and Basketball in National Memory*, 106–7; Baldassaro, "Go East Paesani," 106 (quote); Gardaphe, *From Wise Guys to Wise Men*, 256–57.

80. For examples, see *Manitowoc (WI) Herald News*, June 22, 1927, 9; *San Antonio Light*, July 28, 1927, 14; *Burlington (NC) Daily Times*, Sept. 1, 1927, 4; *Port Arthur (TX) News*, Mar. 12, 1928, 18; *Newcastle (PA) News*, July 2, 1928, 18; *Bismarck (ND) Tribune*, Sept. 13, 1928, 12; *Ogden (UT) Standard Examiner*, Feb. 8, 1931; *Lima (OH) News*, June 11, 1931, 6; *Frederick (MD) News-Post*, Mar. 10,

1932, 3; *Jefferson City (MO) Post Tribune*, June 22, 1929, 8; *Altoona (PA) Mirror*, Apr. 29, 1937, 13; *Arizona Independent Republic*, Oct. 9, 1939, 8; *Lowell (MA) Sun*, June 10, 1947, 1; *Racine (WI) Journal Times*, July 13, 1948, 17.

81. Baldassaro, *Beyond DiMaggio*, 84.

82. Crosetti file, Baseball Hall of Fame; http://www.law.com/regionals/ca/opinions/dec/a091113.shtml#footnote. The players lost the case in 2001 when the judge declared the use of their images and baseball records to be judged as news items.

83. Gardaphe, *From Wise Guys to Wise Men*, 257, cites Harry T. Brundidge of the *Sporting News*, Feb. 4, 1932.

84. Lombardi file, Baseball Hall of Fame; Baldassaro, *Beyond DiMaggio*, 150–58.

85. Herb Graffis, "The Unstoppable Philibuck," *American Legion Magazine*, Nov. 1945, 29, 70–71, Cavarretta file, Baseball Hall of Fame.

86. Cavarretta file, Baseball Hall of Fame; Joe Goddard, "What's Up with Phil Cavarretta," *Chicago Sun-Times*, Sept. 29, 2002, A94; Donald Honig, "A Special Breed," in *Reaching for the Stars*, edited by Freundlich, 19–41; Chicago Park District, *Third Annual Report, 1937*, 146; *Bulletin Italo-American National Union*, Mar. 1935, 1439. New York and Chicago high school teams engaged in mythical national championship games as early as 1902 in football and 1920 in baseball.

87. Baldassaro, *Beyond DiMaggio*, 106–11, 109 (quote).

88. Italian-language weekly newspapers numbered seventy-three by 1930, in Carnevale, *New Language, New World*, 40; Montville, *Big Bam*, 159–71; Bruce J. Evensen, *When Dempsey Fought Tunney: Heroes, Hokum, and Storytelling in the Jazz Age*; Thomas B. Littlewood, *Arch: A Promoter, Not a Poet*, 77–86; http://www.lib.niu.edu/2007/iht07140124.html claims forty-five daily Chicago papers, including the ethnic and craft press.

89. Baldassaro, *Beyond DiMaggio*, xi–xii (quote).

90. http://www.baseball-reference.com/bullpen/Vince_DiMaggio; Dom DiMaggio file, Baseball Hall of Fame; Lawrence Baldassaro, "Lazzeri to DiMaggio to Giamatti: Italian-Americans in Baseball," in *The Cooperstown Symposium on Baseball and American Culture, 1998*, edited by Thomas L. Altherr, 109–18, 111 (quote).

91. Joe Di Maggio, *Lucky to Be a Yankee*, 152.

92. David Jones, *Joe DiMaggio*, 141.

93. Ibid., 26.

94. William M. Simons, "Comparative Ethnicity: Joe DiMaggio and Hank Greenberg," in *The Cooperstown Symposium on Baseball and American Culture, 2000*, edited by William M. Simons, 237–56; Noel F. Busch, "Joe DiMaggio: Baseball's Most Sensational Big League Star Starts What Should Be His Best Year So Far," 64.

95. Busch, "Joe DiMaggio," 66–67.

96. White, *Creating the National Pastime*, 269; Jonathan Eig, *Luckiest Man: The Life and Death of Lou Gehrig*, 207; Anthony A. Yoseloff, "From Ethnic Hero to National Icon: The Americanization of Joe DiMaggio"; Busch, "Joe DiMaggio," 68. Numerous other players reported being subjected to ethnic slurs and bigotry during the era. See Baldassaro, *Beyond DiMaggio*, 38, 111–12, 125–27, 134, 136, 183, 267.

97. Wilfrid Sheed, "Joe DiMaggio: The Making of a King," in *Reaching for the Stars*, edited by Freundlich, 87–103; D. Jones, *Joe DiMaggio*, 68, on voting; William Simons, "Joe DiMaggio and the Ideal of American Masculinity," in *Cooperstown Symposium*, edited by Rutkoff, 227–44; Augustus Loschi, "'Joe' DiMaggio: Ball Player and Gentleman," *Sons of Italy* 11, no. 5 (1938), Schiavo Papers, Box De Moro thru [*sic*] Duse (quote).

98. Baldassaro, *Beyond DiMaggio*, 226, 228.

99. *Red, White, and Green, Commemorative Issue II* 21, no. 2 (1999): 4, Italian American Renaissance Library. Professor John Soares, a Providence native, reiterated the large number of Yankee fans in Boston and Providence due to "the success of guys like Rizzuto, Berra, DiMaggio." Personal e-mail, July 29, 2009.

100. Cuomo cited in Simons, "Comparative Ethnicity," in *Cooperstown Symposium*, edited by Simons, 248.

101. *Pride and Passion: The Italians in America*, WYIN, Chicago (PBS), July 4, 2010.

102. Rick Talley, "DiMaggio's record captivated a nation," *Chicago Sun-Times* clipping, Apr. 1, 1978, sec. 4, 1–2, in Angelo Di Iacova file, Italians in Chicago, Chicago History Museum.

103. D. Jones, *Joe DiMaggio*, 103.

104. See Baldassaro, *Beyond DiMaggio*, 160, on Camilli; Richard Ben Cramer, *Joe DiMaggio: The Hero's Life*; Talese, *Unto the Sons*, 49–54; Gallo, *Old Bread, New Wine*, 255; Simons, "Comparative Ethnicity," in *Cooperstown Symposium*, edited by Simons, 248; Yoseloff, "From Ethnic Hero to National Icon," 10; Simons, "Joe DiMaggio and the Ideal of American Masculinity," in *Cooperstown Symposium*, edited by Rutkoff, 227–44 (quote); http://www.sfmuseum.org/hist8/joltinjoe.html on the DiMaggio song.

105. Ernest Hemingway, *The Old Man and the Sea*, 75, http://www.novelguide.com/oldmanandthesea/metaphoranalysis.html.

106. Robert Elias, *The Empire Strikes Out: How Baseball Sold U.S. Foreign Policy and Promoted the American Way Abroad*, 238.

107. Gems and Pfister, *Understanding American Sport*, 298.

108. Although Italian internment paled in comparison to Japanese Americans, the federal government acknowledged restrictions on and surveillance of more than six hundred thousand Italians, including forced removal from the West Coast in

H.R. 2442 in 1999 and Public Law 106-451 in 2000. See http://www.italian historical.org/hr2442106thcongress.pdf. Stephen Fox, *The Unknown Internment: An Oral History of the Relocation of Italian Americans during World War II*, 69; Luconi, "Forging an Ethnic Identity," 32; Mormino, *Immigrants on the Hill*, 218; *Prisoners in Our Own Home: The Italian American Experience as America's Enemy Aliens*; Luconi, "Forging an Ethnic Identity," 32; Richards, *Italian American*, 193.

109. DiMaggio's marriage to actress Dorothy Arnold in 1939 was in trouble, and he had a young son, born in 1941, but Cramer, *Joe DiMaggio*, 206–14, describes ulterior motives for DiMaggio's enlistment. La Gumina, *Wop!*, 265; Simons, "Comparative Ethnicity," in *Cooperstown Symposium*, edited by Simons, 248 (quote).

110. D. Jones, *Joe DiMaggio*, 68.

111. David Halberstam, *Everything They Had*, 98.

112. Richard C. Crepeau, SPORTHIST@pdomain.uwindsor.ca.

113. Dom DiMaggio file, Baseball Hall of Fame. Michael Eric Dyson, "Be Like Mike? Michael Jordan and the Pedagogy of Desire," 735, cites Terry Boers, "Getting Better All the Time," *Inside Sports* (May 1990), in *Signs of Life in the U.S.A.: Readings on Popular Culture for Writers*, edited by Sonia Maasik and Jack Solomon, 734–42.

114. Freundlich, *Reaching for the Stars*, 204–300.

115. Michael Oriard, "Football, Cultural History, and Democracy."

116. Maselli and Candeloro, *Italians in New Orleans*, 98; Mike Sandrolini, "Hitting for the Cycle," *Red, White & Green, Commemorative Issue VI* 21, no. 5 (2000): 7–8; http://www.aagpbl.org/players/index.cfm?do=player.details&playerid=221; http://thediamondangle.com/archive/sep05/mandella.html.

117. http://www.sportsmanagementresources.com/our-consultants/donna-lopiano; *Bridgeport (CT) Telegram*, Apr. 2, 1954–May 30, 1970; *Bridgeport (CT) Post*, May 26, 1963–May 27, 1970.

5. Hyphenated Americans

1. Gayle Talbot, "Best Heavy Fight in 21 Years: Talbot," *Dixon (IL) Evening Telegraph*, Sept. 25, 1952, 10 (quote); *Brainerd (MN) Daily Dispatch*, Sept. 25, 1952, 6.

2. See B. Anderson on imagined communities and Goksoyr, "Nationalism," on the role of television and the promotion of nationalism.

3. Nathan Glazer and Patrick Moynihan, *Beyond the Melting Pot*, xxxiii, cited in Steinberg, *Ethnic Myth*, 59.

4. Di Prima quoted in Roediger, *Working toward Whiteness*, 3.

5. Gambino, *Blood of My Blood*, 289, cites O. D. Duncan and S. Lieberson, *Journal of Sociology* (Jan. 1959), but does not indicate the other ethnic groups.

6. Girometta, *St. Anthony of Padua*, 16–17.

7. Joe Garagiola, *Baseball Is a Funny Game*, 13; Berra and Fitzgerald, *Yogi*, 18. Baldassaro, *Beyond DiMaggio*, 132, 164, 282, 314, 330, 336, indicates the use of Italian in ballplayers' homes well into the twentieth century.

8. Carnevale, *New Language, New World*, 139, 151–52.

9. Ibid., 164–68; La Gumina, *Wop!*, 266; Alba, *Ethnicity and Race in the U.S.A.*, 142–43. See *Corriere D'America*, Nov. 1, 1932, for an example of the trend toward bilingual publication; and Grame, *Ethnic Broadcasting*, on developments in radio.

10. Roseanne De Luca Braun, "Made in Hollywood: Italian Stereotypes in the Movies," http://www.osia.org/documents/Made-in-Hollywood.pdf.

11. La Gumina, *Wop!*, 249–64; Talese, *Unto the Sons*, 15, 41, 585; Diane Fittipaldi, "Restrictions on Italian Americans during World War II," University of St. Thomas, 2007, http://www.slideshare.net/FittipaldiD/restrictions-on-italian-americans-during-world-war-ii.

12. Cramer, *Joe DiMaggio*, 202.

13. McKibben, *Cannery Row*, 95.

14. Fox, *Unknown Internment*, 108.

15. C. Anderson and McGehee with LaMotta, *Raging Bull II*, 10.

16. Fox, *Unknown Internment*, 13–14, 20, 62, 81–86, 95–96, 98, 108–10, 154, 156; McKibben, *Beyond Cannery Row*, 87–90; Carnevale, *New Language, New World*, 162–63; Luconi, "Forging an Ethnic Identity," 29 (quote); Di Tomaso interview, EI 1067, Ellis Island archives.

17. *Prisoners in Our Own Home*; T. Guglielmo, *White on Arrival*, 173; Mormino, *Immigrants on the Hill*, 219–20; Berra and Fitzgerald, *Yogi*, 67–78; R. Elias, *Empire Strikes Out*, 338; Larry Smith, *Iwo Jima: World War II Veterans Remember the Greatest Battle of the Pacific*, 96–97; Paola A. Sensi-Isolani, "Tradition and Transition in a California Paese," in *Italian Immigration*, edited by Vecoli, 88–109; Mangione, *Ethnic at Large*, 345; Gambino, *Blood of My Blood*, 313–16, 321, estimates as many as 1.5 million Italian American men in US military services during the war. Official records are indeterminate.

18. L. Smith, *Iwo Jima*, 103–5, 105 (quote).

19. Gallo, *Old Bread, New Wine*, 232; Mangione and Morreale, *La Storia*, 341; Italian American Sports Hall of Fame, New Orleans; Pete Hamill, *Why Sinatra Matters*, 133, states thirteen Italian Americans were awarded the Medal of Honor, http://www.cimorelli.com/pie/heroes/basilone.htm; Jim Proser with Jerry Cutter, *I'm Staying with My Boys: The Heroic Life of Sgt. John Basilone, USMC*; Luconi, "Forging an Ethnic Identity," 30 (quote).

20. Proser, *I'm Staying with My Boys*, 261–62.

21. John E. Dreifort, "Anything but Ordinary: POW Sports in a Barbed Wire World"; Bryan Smith, "To Hell and Back," *Chicago Sun-Times*, Feb. 3, 2002, A24.

22. Edward Jablonski, *Pictorial History of the World War II Years*, 117–18; B. Smith, "To Hell and Back," A26.

23. B. Smith, "To Hell and Back," A23.

24. Laura Hillenbrand, *Unbroken: A World War II Story of Survival, Resilience, and Redemption*; http://www.usc.edu/dept/pubrel/trojan_family/summer03/F_Zamperini.html.

25. Talese, *Unto the Sons*, 609–11; http://www.time.com/time/time100/builder/profile/luciano3.html; http://www.redicecreations.com/article.php?id=3548.

26. See Salvatore J. La Gumina, *The Humble and the Heroic: Wartime Italian Americans*, 162–66, on Corvo's enterprise. http://www.nps.gov/history/history/online_books/oss/chap8.pdf; Savoldi's service detailed in OSS Records (RG 226), Entry 92A, COI/OSS Central Files, Box 42, Folder 687, National Archives II.

27. Gallo, *Old Bread, New Wine*, 231–32.

28. Barreca, *Don't Tell Mama*, 278; Child, *Italian or American?*, 127, 42 (quote).

29. Child, *Italian or American?*, 128.

30. Gallo, *Old Bread, New Wine*, 255.

31. Russell Sullivan, *Rocky Marciano: The Rock of His Times*, 243.

32. Ferrara, *Profiles of Italian Americans*, 148.

33. Ron Brocato, *The Golden Game: When Prep Football Was King in New Orleans*, Italian American Sports Hall of Fame. Jesuit High School won the state football championship in 1933, the first private school to do so.

34. Leuci, "Hooks," in *Reaching for the Stars*, edited by Freundlich, 66.

35. Michael B. Katz and Mark J. Stern, *One Nation Divisible: What America Was and What It Is Becoming*, 106.

36. Carlo De Vito, *Yogi: The Life and Times of an American Original*, 5; C. Anderson and McGehee with LaMotta, *Raging Bull II*, 145 (quote), 172, 239.

37. Graziano and Corsel, *Somebody Down Here Likes Me Too*, 206.

38. Baldassaro, *Beyond DiMaggio*, 234–35.

39. Ibid., 314.

40. Berra and Fitzgerald, *Yogi*, 51, 21, respectively (quotes), 52, 63; Mormino, *Immigrants on the Hill*, 118, 235.

41. Paul Dickson, *Baseball's Greatest Quotations*, 141.

42. Cramer, *Joe Di Maggio*; Buzz Bissinger, "For Love of Di Maggio."

43. Joyce Carol Oates, *Mike Tyson* (1986), http://www.usfca.edu/~southerr/boxing/Tyson.html. See Loic Wacquant, "The Social Logic of Boxing in Black America: Towards a Sociology of Pugilism," on the habitus of working-class boxers.

44. Heller, *"In This Corner...!,"* 141.

45. David Iamele, "Basilio," *Cigar Smoker*, 83, clipping in Basilio file, International Boxing Hall of Fame.

46. K. V. Stark, "The Champ Was a Marine," *Leatherneck* (Dec. 1992), 32–37, 33 (quote), in ibid.

47. Gerald Early, "The Romance of Toughness: La Motta and Graziano," 393.

48. Ibid., 394; Brunt, "The Exodus," 14–15; and Barney Nagler, "The Story of a Champion," both in *Italian Stallions*, by Hauser and Brunt, 115–35.

49. Theresa Carilli, "Still Crazy after All These Years: Italian Americans in Mainstream Films," in *Cultural Diversity and the U.S. Media*, edited by Yahya Kamalipour and Theresa Carilli, 111–24.

50. A *New York Times* account is offered at http://www.rarenewspapers.com/view/557479.

51. Joe Bruno, *Penthouse* clipping, La Motta file.

52. Clipping, La Motta file, International Boxing Hall of Fame.

53. Rex Lardner, "The Improbable Graziano," in *Italian Stallions*, by Hauser and Brunt, 79.

54. Lardner, "The Improbable Graziano."

55. Heller, *"In This Corner . . . !,"* 287.

56. W. C. Heinz, "Goodbye, Graziano."

57. Graziano and Corsel, *Somebody Down Here Likes Me Too*, 133.

58. Lardner, "The Improbable Graziano," 89.

59. James W. Pipkin, *Sporting Lives: Metaphor and Myth in American Sports Autobiographies*, 114–15.

60. W. C. Heinz, "Rocky Graziano Revisited," in *Italian Stallions*, by Hauser and Brunt, 93.

61. Ibid., 95.

62. Early, "Romance of Toughness," 403.

63. *Ring*, July 1950, 245, cited in Weinberg and Arond, "Occupational Culture of the Boxer," 461–62.

64. Ed Linn, "Carmen Basilio Reaches for the Jackpot," in *Italian Stallions*, edited by Hauser and Brunt, 182.

65. Lewis Burton, "A Heavyweight Named Roland," in *Italian Stallions*, by Hauser and Brunt, 195, 199.

66. Richard Renoff, "Italian Americans and Professional Boxing in Connecticut, 1941–1951," in *Italian Americans and Their Public and Private Life*, edited by Frank J. Cavaioli, Angela Danzi, and Salvatore J. La Gumina, 212–27.

67. Ibid.; Herbert J. Gans, "Acculturation, Assimilation, and Mobility."

68. Youmans, *Onion Picker*, 73.

69. Sullivan, *Rocky Marciano*, 155–56, 290–93.

70. Maxim obituary, sports box, Italian American Renaissance Library; http://www.ibhof.com/pages/about/inductees/modern/maxim.html.

71. Youmans, *Onion Picker*, 73–74.

72. W. C. Heinz, "Somebody Up There Likes Him," 90, on bribe, Graziano file; Mike Rathet, "A Said 'No' to the Mafia," *Boxing Scene*, clipping, 30–34, 30 (quote), Giardello file, both at the International Boxing Hall of Fame.

73. Michael Marley, "Rocky Marciano: Where Did All the Money Go?," 64–67, clipping in Marciano file, International Boxing Hall of Fame; Sullivan, *Rocky Marciano*, 242.

74. Sullivan, *Rocky Marciano*, 238.

75. Ibid., 242.

76. Arch Ward, "In the Wake of the News," *Chicago Tribune*, Sept. 25, 1953, pt. 4:2.

77. Sullivan, *Rocky Marciano*, 244, 4.

78. Gans, *Urban Villagers*, 34.

79. Lang, *Prizefighting: An American History*, 125.

80. Diamond, *Mean Streets*, 193–239; Barney Nagler, "The Return of Willie Pep," in *Italian Stallions*, edited by Hauser and Brunt, 53.

81. Baldassaro, *Beyond DiMaggio*, 221.

82. Ibid., 254.

83. Ibid., 315–16. MLB played two all-star games per year from 1959 to 1962, giving Malzone eight appearances during six different seasons.

84. Sullivan, *Rocky Marciano*, 68, 75–94, 174 (quotes), 228–53.

85. Marshall Smith, " . . . And New Champion?," 107, 109–10; Sullivan, *Rocky Marciano*, 44–45, gives a figure of twenty-five hundred dollars.

86. "Personality."

87. *Boston Globe*, Sept. 26, 1952, 1, 19, cited in Sullivan, *Rocky Marciano*, 244, 248, on *Washington Post*.

88. Lena Marciano and Michael Vaveris [sic], "I Never Wanted Him to Fight!," *Brockton (MA) Enterprise*, Feb. 11, 1980, 29.

89. Ibid., 30; Lena Marciano and Michael Varveris, "Rocky Was Mischievous," *Brockton (MA) Enterprise*, Feb. 13, 1980, 37, 40–41; Lena Marciano and Michael Varveris [sic], "Rocky's Very First Fight Was for His Life," *Brockton (MA) Enterprise*, Feb. 12, 1980, 21, 23; Lena Marciano and Michael Varveris, "Wedding Bells for Rocky," *Brockton (MA) Enterprise*, Feb. 17, 1980, 45, 48.

90. Marciano and Varveris, "Rocky Was Mischievous," 37, 40–41; Marciano and Varveris, "Rocky's Very First Fight Was for His Life," 21, 23 (quote).

91. M. Smith, " . . . And New Champion?," 112.

92. Sullivan, *Rocky Marciano*, 144–63, 246; Lena Marciano and Michael Varvaris [sic], "Rocky Heeded Joe Monte's Advice," *Brockton (MA) Enterprise*, Feb. 15, 1980, 58; Lena Marciano and Michael Varveris, "13 Proves Lucky for Rocky," *Brockton (MA) Enterprise*, Feb. 18, 1980, 37; Lena Marciano and Michael Varveris,

"Rocky Never Had Cause to Regret Hanging Up His Gloves," *Brockton (MA) Enterprise*, Feb. 19, 1980, 33 (quote), 36.

93. Sullivan, *Rocky Marciano*, 52–59, 87, 204–8; Youmans, *Onion Picker*, 68–70, 81, 95, 108; Sugden, *Boxing and Society*, 41–42, 49. See Sammons, *Beyond the Ring*, 136–40, 151–77, for a detailed account of the rise and fall of the IBC.

94. Diamond, *Mean Streets*, 100–101, 134–51, 156, 160–68, 199–219; T. Guglielmo, *White on Arrival*, 146, 155–72; Roediger, *Working toward Whiteness*, 137.

95. Child, *Italian or American?*, 35–36.

96. Diamond, *Mean Streets*, 206–19. See Gerald D. Suttles, *The Social Order of the Slum: Ethnicity and Territory in the Inner City*, 45–46, on Italian segregation by parish in Chicago.

97. Cinotto, "Leonard Covello," 519. See La Ruffa, *Monte Carmelo*, 19–20, for similar confrontations in that community.

98. Lang, *Prizefighting: An American History*, 124–27; Sullivan, *Rocky Marciano*, 86–95, 115–30, 128 (quote).

99. Youmans, *Onion Picker*, 21, 88–92, 119–22, 132–36, 153–56, 184; Graziano and Corsel, *Somebody Down Here Likes Me Too*, 58 (quote).

100. Michael H. Ebner, "Suburbs and Cities as Dual Metropolis," in *Chicago Neighborhoods and Suburbs: A Historical Guide*, edited by Ann Durkin Keating, 29–54.

101. The 1924 quota limited total immigration to 165,000. It allowed for 51,227 Germans and 34,007 from the United Kingdom but only 3,845 Italians. http://historymatters.gmu.edu/d/5078. The son of a gardener, Melchiorre's basketball skills won him a college scholarship and preeminent status as an All-American. Although he scored seventy-one points in one tournament game, he was implicated in the point-shaving scheme, which resulted in his banishment from the NBA. See Joe Goldstein, "Explosion: 1951 Scandals Threaten College Hoops," http://espn.go.com/classic/s/basketball_scandals_explosion.html.

102. http://www.state.gov/r/pa/ho/time/cwr/87719.htm; Luconi, *From Paesani to White Ethnics*, 121–22; Ron Onesti, "A Thoroughbred of a Guy," *Red, White, and Green, Commemorative Issue VII* (2003): 2–3, Italian Renaissance Foundation Library; Maselli and Candeloro, *Italians in New Orleans*, 99; Jim O'Donnell, "A Brave Spirit," *Chicago Sun-Times*, Mar. 25, 2001, 148A–152A. Melchiorre never played in the NBA due to implication in the famous point-shaving scandal of 1951. La Gumina et al., *Italian American Experience*, 610. Lauricella later had a distinguished political career in Louisiana. http://www.und.com/sports/m-footbl/mtt/guglielmi_ralph00.html.

103. http://www.baseballlibrary.com/ballplayers/player.php?name=Johnny_Berardino_1917; http://www.baseball-almanac.com/players/player.php?=berarjo0/.

104. La Gumina, *Wop!*, 280–98; De Conde, *Half Bitter, Half Sweet*, 382; David Maraniss, *When Pride Still Mattered: A Life of Vince Lombardi*, 21, 91, 107.

105. Maraniss, *When Pride Still Mattered*, 146–99, 165 (quote); http://www.vincelombardi.com/about/bio3.htm.

106. Jerry Izenberg, *Through My Eyes: A Sports Writer's 58 Year Journey*, 44; Maraniss, *When Pride Still Mattered*, 241–42.

107. http://www.hardballtimes.com/main/article/sociology-of-the-mlb-player-1952/ provides a comparative survey of ethnic groups on MLB rosters in 1940 and 1952. Baldassaro, *Beyond DiMaggio*, 178, 431n34, claims thirty-seven Italian Major Leaguers in 1941.

108. Freundlich, *Reaching for the Stars*, 204–300; Baldassaro, *Beyond DiMaggio*, 397, 402. See Chetwynd, *Baseball in Europe*, 47, on Perini's role in Italy.

109. Baldassaro, *Beyond DiMaggio*, 253.

110. Halberstam, *Everything They Had*, 115–18. George Vecsey, "The Barber and the Rifle," in *Reaching for the Stars*, edited by Freundlich, 105–29. See the reminiscences of Lorraine Sciulli, a female player of the era who dreamed of playing for the Dodgers, at http://www.junipercivic.com/juniperberryarticle.asp?nid=327.

111. Baldassaro, *Beyond DiMaggio*, 56; Anthony Valerio, "Sal Maglie in Paradise," in *Reaching for the Stars*, edited by Freundlich, 169–89.

112. Baldassaro, *Beyond DiMaggio*, 312–14.

113. Ibid., 324, 321–22.

114. Ibid., 329–30.

115. Ibid., 381.

116. "The East Coast, Italian Americans & Rock N Roll History," *Red, White, and Green, Commemorative Issue VII* 23, no. 8 (2003): 5; Italian Americans and Early Rock & Roll, exhibition brochure, Queens College, May 10, 2003; http://www.filmreference.com/film/58/Frankie-Avalon.html; http://www.spiritus-temporis.com/frankie-avalon/; http://www.bobbyvee.com/bio.html; http://www.imdb.com/name/nm003104/bio.

117. "East Coast, Italian Americans & Rock N Roll History," 5; Italian Americans and Early Rock & Roll, exhibition brochure, Queens College, May 10, 2003; Diamond, *Mean Streets*, 6–7, 45–46, 50–51.

118. Alba, *Ethnicity and Race in the U.S.A.*, 142–50; Mirel, *Patriotic Pluralism*, 138, on 1950 citizenship; Sensi-Isolani, "Traditions and Transition in a California Paese," 102–5; David L. Andrews, "Contextualizing Suburban Soccer: Consumer Culture, Lifestyle Differentiation, and Suburban America," 39, 45; William Egelman, William Gratzer, and Michael D'Angelo, "Italian Americans in Suburbia: Italian Americans in Westchester County, New York," in *Italian Immigrants Go West*, edited by Worrall, Albright, and Di Fabio, 91–99. Weiss, *American Education and the European Immigrant*, 164–65, contends that Irish Catholics, German Catholics,

and Scandinavian Protestants maintained the highest college attendance rates until the 1960s. Gambino, *Blood of My Blood*, 245–46, cites a 1969 survey that showed only 5.9 percent of Italian Americans over age thirty-five with a college education, lower than all other groups except Hispanics. Only 27.6 percent had completed high school. Of those aged twenty-five to thirty-four, only 11 percent had a college education, still second lowest, but 50.4 percent obtained a high school diploma, second highest among ethnic groups. Gans, *Urban Villagers*, 208; Gambino, *Blood of My Blood*, 77; Margavio and Salomone, *Bread and Respect*, 138. Gans, "Acculturation, Assimilation, and Mobility," 155–58, explains that the moves to suburbia and intermarriage did not necessarily mean greater social mobility.

119. Luconi, *From Paesani to White Ethnics*, 138–39; Carla Bianco, "Italian Folk Culture Transplanted: Methods of Documentation," in *Italian Immigrants*, edited by Vecoli, 75–87.

120. De Vito, *Yogi*, 4; De Conde, *Half Bitter, Half Sweet*, 330; Gallo, *Old Bread, New Wine*, 260–71; Gans, *Urban Villagers*, 7–8, 14, 22–25, 27–54, 59–60, 74–103; Hoare and Smith, *Prison Notebooks of Gramsci*, 418.

121. Gans, *Urban Villagers*, 33, 186, 200–253; Margavio and Salomone, *Bread and Respect*, 169; Cinotto, "Leonard Covello," 510–15; Bourdieu, *Distinction*, 169–75, 194–99. See Raymond Williams, *The Sociology of Culture*, 204–5, on residual elements.

122. Brodkin, *How Jews Became White Folks*, 73–74; Roediger, *Working toward Whiteness*, 42–43; Rees, *Shades of Difference*, 151–56; Diamond, *Mean Streets*.

123. Diamond, *Mean Streets*, 72, 161–71; Sorrentino Papers, Box 3, Folder 1; Suttles, *Social Order of the Slum*. See Stodolska and Alexandris, "Role of Recreational Sport," 382, on the role of social class and the adherence to ethnicity.

124. See Richard D. Alba and Victor Nee, "Rethinking Assimilation Theory for a New Era of Immigration," 847, on the "hourglass economy." Gallo, *Old Bread, New Wine*, 277–89, 286 (quote); Margavio and Salomone, *Bread and Respect*, 189–90, 197. Among the studies on ethnic social mobility, see David L. Featherman, "The Socioeconomic Achievement of White Religio-Ethnic Subgroups: Social and Psychological Explanations"; and Gans, "Acculturation, Assimilation, and Mobility."

125. Ferrara, *Profiles of Italian Americans*, 135 (quote).

126. Clipping, Feb. 11, 1972, in Joe Garagiola file, Baseball Hall of Fame.

127. La Gumina et al., *Italian American Experience*, 598.

128. Steinberg, *Ethnic Myth*, 135–50; Barry R. Chiswick, "The Skills and Economic Status of American Jewry: Trends over the Last Half-Century." Colombo, a crime syndicate boss, objected to the federal government's usage of the terms *Mafia* and *Cosa Nostra*, but ironically he was shot at an Italian Unity rally in 1971. Mayor Abe Beame endorsed the Italian Cultural Week, a program already undertaken by Italian American educators in the city.

6. The Resurgence of Ethnicity

1. "U.S. Hockey Team Stuns Russia," *Hutchison (KS) News*, Feb. 23, 1980, 41.
2. "U.S. Members to Split," *Logansport (IN) Pharos-Tribune*, Feb. 25, 1980, 8.
3. John Soares, Providence resident at the time, personal communication, Nov. 1, 2008; La Gumina et al., *Italian American Experience*, 595; La Ruffa, *Monte Carmelo*, 108 (quote).
4. La Ruffa, *Monte Carmelo*, 54.
5. Jacobson, *Roots Too*, 1, quotes Nathan Glazer and Daniel Patrick Moynihan, *Beyond the Melting Pot*, 1970, xcvii.
6. La Ruffa, *Monte Carmelo*, 55 (quote). The author identifies at least twenty-one such Italian clusters in and around New York City, 136–39.
7. Herbert J. Gans, "Symbolic Ethnicity and Symbolic Religiosity: Towards a Comparison of Ethnic and Religious Acculturation," 580, 582; Mary C. Waters, *Ethnic Options: Choosing Identities in America*, 55 (quote); Vincenzo Milione and Christine Gambino, *Si, Parliamo Italiano! Globalization of the Italian Culture in the United States*, 17, 29, 30; Maselli and Candeloro, *Italians in New Orleans*, 45, 56–63, 83–85; McKibben, *Beyond Cannery Row*, 105–22; "The Joy of Growing Up Italian."
8. Michael Novak, *The Rise of the Unmeltable Ethnics: Politics and Culture in the Seventies*, 20–23; 24 (quote), 45; Gallo, *Old Bread, New Wine*, 260–71; Waters, *Ethnic Options*, 116–20, 135–36.
9. Detore-Nakamura, "Good Enough," 122–23.
10. Waters, *Ethnic Options*, 69 (quote), 96, 142–44.
11. Gans, "Acculturation, Assimilation, and Mobility," 156. Michael Barone, *The New Americans: How the Melting Pot Can Work Again*, 146, indicates that a majority of Italian Americans had married non-Italians by 1979.
12. Dennis McCafferty, "Remembering Sinatra," *USA Weekend*, May 2–4, 2008, 8–10, 8 (quote).
13. Gerald Meyer, "When Frank Sinatra Came to Italian Harlem: The 1945 'Race Riot' at Benjamin Franklin High School," in *Are Italians White?*, edited by Guglielmo and Salerno, 161–76; http://21stcenturymanifesto.wordpress.com/2010/02/21/frank-sinatra-just-as-communist-as-the-pope/; Youmans, *Onion Picker*, 186; Gans, *Urban Villagers*, 192 (quote).
14. Frontani, "From the Bottom to the Top," 223.
15. Hamill, *Why Sinatra Matters*, 37.
16. McCafferty, "Remembering Sinatra," 10.
17. *Pride and Passion*, WYIN (PBS), July 4, 2010.
18. Hamill, *Why Sinatra Matters*, 31, 38, 45 (quote); Graziano with Corsel, *Somebody Down Here Likes Me Too*, 166.

19. Hamill, *Why Sinatra Matters*, 38, 44 (quote), 48–49, 71.

20. http://21stcenturymanifesto.wordpress.com/2010/02/21/frank-sinatra-just-as-communist-as-the-pope/; Anthony Summers and Robbyn Swan, *Sinatra: The Life*, 246 (quote).

21. Ted Kotcheff, dir., *Rambo: First Blood* (Orion Pictures, 1982).

22. See Carilli, "Still Crazy after All These Years," for a review of *Saturday Night Fever*; and Donald Tricarico, "Guido on MTV: Tangled Up in the Feedback Loop," in *Guido: Italian/American Youth and Identity Politics*, edited by Letizia Airos and Ottorino Cappelli, 106–14, on the birth of guido culture. Leonard Maltin, "Pacino De Niro Together," *USA Weekend* (Sept. 5–7, 2008), 6–8, 6 (quote).

23. Martha Bayles, "We Are All Sopranos."

24. Rotundo cited in Jacobson, *Roots Too*, 26.

25. http://www.biography.com/people/tony-danza-9542599.

26. Ferrara, *Profiles of Italian Americans*, 153.

27. The *Jersey Shore* program features the guido and guidette lifestyles in a purported reality television series. For the ire raised by such depictions and the heated debate, see Airos and Cappelli, *Guido*; Donald Tricarico, "Youth Culture, Ethnic Choice, and the Identity Politics of Guido"; http://www.i-italy.org/; http://www.i-italy.org/sections/specials/society/guido-italian-american-youth-style; and Donald Tricarico, "Narrating Guido: Contested Meanings of an Italian American Youth Subculture," in *Anti-Italianism*, edited by Connell and Gardaphé, 163–200, 165 (quote).

28. Tricarico, "Narrating Guido," in *Anti-Italianism*, edited by Connell and Gardaphé, 170–82, 198.

29. Anderson Cooper, "Lady Gaga," *60 Minutes*, June 5, 2011.

30. Thomas Conner, "Before the Fame," *Chicago Sun-Times*, Apr. 1, 2010, 6D–7D; Thomas Conner, "Soooul-Shattering Lady Gaga," *Chicago Sun-Times*, Apr. 8, 2010, 4A–5A (quote 4A).

31. Jon Pareles, "Lady Gaga's Roaring Retort," *International Herald Tribune*, May 21–22, 2011, 17.

32. Ibid., 21.

33. Hockey player Eric Nesterenko, quoted in Studs Terkel, *Working*, 385.

34. E. M. Swift, "Boom Boom Time Again"; ESPN, "Triumph and Tragedy: The Ray Mancini Story," Dec. 16, 2007. Quote from "A Sketch of Ray 'Boom Boom' Mancini, clipping in Ray Mancini file, International Boxing Hall of Fame.

35. http://www.boxrec.com/list_bouts.php?human_id=582&cat=boxer;http://en.wikipedia.org/wiki/Paul_Malignaggi. See Alba and Nee, "Rethinking Assimilation Theory," 836, 847, on economic social mobility.

36. See Gems, "Neighborhood Athletic Club," for analysis of a multiethnic community sport organization that included Italians.

37. http://en.wikipedia.org/wiki/Lou_Duva; John Kass, "Memories of Joey G."; http://www.usatoday.com/sports/boxing/2008-02-16-424287464_x.htm.

38. Michael O'Brien, *No Ordinary Joe: The Biography of Joe Paterno*, 6, 38, 37, 225, 260; George Paterno, *Joe Paterno: The Coach from Byzantium*; http://en.wikipedia.org/wiki/Joe_Paterno. Paterno's reputation was besmirched and his victory total reduced by the NCAA due to a child sex abuse scandal perpetrated by a former assistant coach, Jerry Sandusky.

39. Tommy Lasorda and David Fisher, *The Artful Dodger*, 7.

40. Bill Plaschke with Tommy Lasorda, *I Live for This! Baseball's Last True Believer*, 57.

41. Ibid., xiii–xiv, 112, 191–93, 204–16, 215 (quote).

42. Baldassaro, *Beyond DiMaggio*, 405; Debbie Hanson, "Nick J. Mileti," http://www.clevelandseniors.com/people/mileti.htm.

43. http://nbc5streetteam.wordpress.com/2009/05/11/distinguished-chicagoan-jerry-colangelo-interview/; http://www.nba.com/suns/news/jerry_colangelo_bio.html.

44. Baldassaro, *Beyond DiMaggio*, 406–9 (quotes on 406, 408).

45. Ibid., 413–14.

46. Ibid., 409–12.

47. http://www.stjohns.edu/campuses/enhancements/carnesecca; *Pride and Passion: The Italians in America*, July 4, 2010, WYIN (PBS), Chicago.

48. Donna Lopiano, e-mail to the author, July 30, 2010.

49. Halberstam, *Everything They Had*, 112–13; Dorinson, "'Poosh 'Em Up, Tony!,'" in *Horsehide, Pigskin, Oval Tracks, and Apple Pie*, edited by Vlasich, 49; Margavio and Salomone, *Bread and Respect*, 262–63, reports 10 percent Italian-language proficiency and a 70 percent intermarriage rate among the fourth generation in New Orleans.

50. Marcelo M. Saurez-Orozco, "Everything You Ever Wanted to Know about Assimilation but Were Afraid to Ask," in *Life in America: Identity and Everyday Experience*, edited by Lee D. Baker, 45–62; Valentine J. Belfiglio, "Cultural Traits of Italian Americans Which Transcend Generational Differences," in *The Italian Americans through the Generations*, edited by Rocco Caporale, 126–42; Vecoli, *Italian Immigrants*, 132, 188; Mary Elaine Lora, "The Roman Bowl"; La Ruffa, *Monte Carmelo*, 72, 83, 108; Luconi, *From Paesani to White Ethnics*, 138–39, 149; Margavio and Salomone, *Bread and Respect*, 242.

51. Mormino, *Immigrants on the Hill*, 200–206, 235; Lawrence A. Wenner and Steven J. Jackson, "Sport, Beer, and Gender in Promotional Culture: On the Dynamics of a Holy Trinity," in *Sport, Beer, and Gender: Promotional Culture and Contemporary Social Life*, edited by Lawrence A. Wenner and Steven J. Jackson, 1–32. Barone, *New Americans*, 146, indicates that Italians reached educational parity with the

national average by the 1970s, but La Gumina et al., *Italian American Experience*, 598–99, claim that despite Italians having higher college enrollment than all other ethnic groups in the 1990s, they still suffered the highest high school dropout rates.

52. De Vito, *Yogi*, 73, 74 (quote).

53. http://www.wibchistoryhub.com/display.asp?ID=2340110062003111313548242; http://www.niashf.org/index2.cfm?ContentID=40&InducteeID=202; http://hockey.teamusa.org/athlete/athlete/1343.

54. http://www.lifeinitaly.com/culture/Italian-american-politicians.

55. Kieran and Daley, *Story of the Olympic Games*, 237–38, 259; http://www.usatf.org/halloffame/TF/showBio.asp?HOFIDs=97; http://www.gale.cengage.com/free_resources/chh/bio/devarona_d.htm; http://www.olympic.org/uk/athletes/profiles/bio_uk.asp?PAR_I_ID=37496.

56. See Van Rheenen, "Promise of Soccer in America," for Italian teams in San Francisco; Magnaini interview, Italians in Chicago; Marino Mazzei, Maroons Soccer Club, personal communication, Oct. 1987; La Ruffa, *Monte Carmelo*, 23, 72–75.

57. La Ruffa, *Monte Carmelo*, 72, 83; Salvatore J. La Gumina, *The Italian American Experience: An Encyclopedia*, 110; "An Italian Sports Legacy Catches on in California," *Philadelphia Inquirer*, July 14, 1985, A2; "Courts in Session during Any Season Bocce, Pasta Play Well Together in Los Gatos," *San Jose Mercury News*, Mar. 16, 1998, 47; Jodie Jacobs, "On a Roll with Bocce This Week, an International Sport Gets a Local Spin," *Chicago Tribune*, Oct. 20, 1996, Tempo Northwest sec. 1; "From Bocce to Verdi, That's an Italian Festival," *San Jose Mercury News*, Sept. 29, 1993, 1 (quote), http://nl.newsbank.com/nl-search/we/Archives?p_product=SJ&s_site=mercurynews&p_multi=SJ&p_theme=realcities&p_action=search&p_maxdocs=200&p_topdoc=1&p_text_direct-0=0EB71BD33057F4E3&p_field_direct-0=document_id&p_perpage=10&p_sort=YMD_date:D&s_trackval=GooglePM; Barra, *Yogi Berra: Eternal Yankee*, 10. See http://www.campodibocce.com/Livermore/PDF/Marketing%20&%20Sponsorship%20Opportunity.pdf on the organization and growth of bocce in the United States.

58. John Soares, personal communication, July 29, 2009; http://mlb.mlb.com/news/article.jsp?ymd=20081123&content_id=3689880&vkey=news_mlb&fext=.jsp&c_id=mlb; Chetwynd, *Baseball in Europe*, 54, 56; Baldassaro, *Beyond DiMaggio*, 355, 363 (quote).

59. Baldassaro, *Beyond DiMaggio*, 388.

60. Ibid., 364–65.

61. Ibid., 353.

62. Ibid., 344.

63. Ibid., 336.

64. Ibid., 346.

65. Ibid., 336.

66. Ibid., 336.

67. Ibid., 337.

68. Ibid., 350.

69. Ibid., 315, 337.

70. Jere Longman, "Young Soccer Star Is Close to Completing His Italian Dream, NYTimes.com, June 9, 2009. For reactions to Rossi's perceived defection, see http://www.soccerbyives.net/soccer_by_ives/2009/06/hating-rossi.html.

71. Carilli, "Still Crazy after All These Years," 119–20.

72. Gambino, *Blood of My Blood*, 329–46; http://www.nytimes.com/1991/07/17/obituaries/frank-rizzo-of-philadelphia-dies-at-70-a-hero-and-villain.html; Laurino, *Were You Always Italian?*, 122–31; La Ruffa, *Monte Carmelo*, 20.

73. Waters, *Ethnic Options*, 109.

74. See John R. Logan, Richard D, Alba, and Shi-yun Leung, "Minority Access to White Suburbs: A Multiregional Comparison," a study of the eleven largest metropolitan areas in the United States; and James R. Grossman, Ann Durkin Keating, and Janice L. Rieff, eds., *The Encyclopedia of Chicago*, 520–21, 784–85. Both Melrose Park and Stone Park had a majority Hispanic population by 2004.

75. Jacobson, *Roots Too*, 180–87, 202–3.

76. Rees, *Shades of Difference*, 152; Ruck, Patterson, and Weber, *Rooney: A Sporting Life*, 404–5, 428; Nicholas P. Ciotola, "Spignesi, Sinatra, and the Pittsburgh Steelers: Franco's Italian Army as an Expression of Ethnic Identity, 1972–1977," 276, 277.

77. Ciotola, "Spigneri, Sinatra, and the Pittsburgh Steelers," 283. See Robert Trumpbour, "Civil Rights and Sports Landmarks: Jobs and Activism in the Construction of Pittsburgh's Three Rivers Stadium," for racial conflict in the city that was somewhat assuaged by its interracial sports teams.

78. Norma Bouchard, "The Phenomenon Bocelli: Rethinking Italian Cultural Identity," in *The Italians of New York*, edited by Philip V. Cannistraro, 162.

79. Salvatore J. La Gumina, "Prejudice and Discrimination: The Italian American Experience Yesterday and Today," in *Anti-Italianism*, edited by Connell and Gardaphe, 111.

80. Shibutani and Kwan cited in Alba and Nee, "Rethinking Assimilation Theory," 538; Richard D. Alba and Dalia Abdel-Hady, "Galileo's Children: Italian Americans' Difficult Entry into the Intellectual Elite," 7.

81. Martin N. Marger, *Race & Ethnic Relations: American and Global Perspectives*, 210.

82. Teddy Greenstein, "Change Runs Its Course," *Chicago Tribune*, Apr. 19, 2009, sec. 3:8.

83. La Gumina, *Wop!*, 2; Laurino, *Were You Always Italian?*, 54–76, 82; Malpezzi and Clements, *Italian American Folklore*, 34 (quote); Vincent Morris, "Joe D's

Bro Tells of Bias vs. U.S. Italians," *New York Post*, Oct. 27, 1999, clipping in Dom DiMaggio file, Baseball Hall of Fame.

84. http://hr.hunter.cuny.edu/policies/nd/html; http://qcpages.qc.cuny.edu/calandra/socio/affirm07.html. The number of applicants and their ethnicity is not included in the survey. See Joseph v. Scelsa, "Affirmative Action for Italian Americans: The City University of New York Story," in *Anti-Italianism*, edited by Connell and Gardaphe, 87–93; and Donna Chirico, "The Role of the Italian American Faculty Staff Advisory Council," for particulars.

85. http://www.italian-american.com/italaffm.htm.

86. Alba and Abdel-Hady, "Galileo's Children."

87. Tricarico, "Narrating Guido," in *Anti-Italianism*, edited by Connell and Gardaphe, 179.

88. Ibid., 185, 186.

89. Hall, "Who Needs Identity?," 2.

90. Karen A. Cerulo, "Identity Construction: New Issues, New Directions."

91. Ibid., 387; R. L. Jones, "A Deviant Sports Career: Toward a Sociology of Unlicensed Boxing," 49, citing Holt, *Sport and the British*, 173.

92. Gems, *Windy City Wars*, 226.

93. For a complete history of the club, see Gems, "Neighborhood Athletic Club."

94. Tricarico, "Narrating Guido," in *Anti-Italianism*, edited by Connell and Gardaphe, 182.

95. Ibid., 183.

96. La Ruffa, *Monte Carmelo*, xviii, 116, 144; Barra, *Yogi Berra: Eternal Yankee*, 3, 10; Michael Kammen, *Mystic Chords of Memory: The Transformation of Tradition in American Culture*, 9 (quote); http://www.osia.org/ on religious celebrations and Order of Sons of Italy membership. Gans, "Symbolic Ethnicity and Symbolic Religiosity," points to such ethnic distinctions that can last over several generations, while Alba and Nee, "Rethinking Assimilation Theory," 834, asserts that the focus on family solidarity has been co-opted as part of the American middle-class value system.

97. Pareles, "Lady Gaga's Roaring Retort," 21.

98. David Paul Nord, "The Uses of Memory: An Introduction"; Phillips, O'Neill, and Osmond, "Broadening Horizons in Sport History," 283.

99. Joseph F. Healey, "An Exploration of the Relationship between Memory and Sport."

100. Hilmi Ibrahim, "The Nature of Ritual."

101. Fred Davis, *Yearning for Yesterday: A Sociology of Nostalgia*, 11, 31 (quote); Gerald R. Gems, "Monuments to Memory."

102. Phillips, O'Neill, and Osmond, "Broadening Horizons in Sport History," 285.

103. http://lyricstrue.net/bandsongtext/Paul_Simon_&_Art_Garfunkel/Mrs._Robinson.html. The Order of the Sons of Italy offers a set of baseball cards featuring Italian American baseball heroes with its membership; see http://www.osia.org/.

104. Al Dinon interview, May 5, 2009, Villa St. Ben, Oral History Project.

105. Maria Perrino, ed., *Italian American Autobiographies*, vi.

106. Joseph Sciorra, "Real Italians," 41; and Fred L. Gardaphe, "Organized Culture," 72, both in *Guido*, edited by Airos and Cappelli.

Bibliography

Archival Sources

Burgess, Ernest W. Papers. Univ. of Chicago, Special Collections.
Camp, Walter. Papers. Yale Univ. Archives, New Haven, CT.
Catholic Archdiocese of Chicago Archives. Chicago.
Center for Migration Studies. Staten Island, NY.
Chicago City Directory. Chicago: Chicago Directory, 1909.
Chicago History Collection. Washington Library, Chicago.
Ellis Island Oral History Collection. New York.
Florence Roselli Library at Casa Italia. Stone Park, IL.
Foreign Language Press Survey. Chicago History Museum.
Frank Di Benedetto Personal Papers. Chicago.
International Boxing Hall of Fame. Canastota, NY
International Swimming Hall of Fame. Fort Lauderdale, FL.
Italian American Renaissance Foundation Library. New Orleans.
Italian American Sports Hall of Fame. New Orleans.
Italians in Chicago, Oral History Project. Chicago History Museum.
———. Special Collections, Univ. of Illinois at Chicago.
Marchese, Alessandro. Family Papers. Williams Research Center, New Orleans.
National Baseball Hall of Fame. Cooperstown, NY.
Prisoners in Our Own Home: The Italian American Experience as America's Enemy Aliens. Brooklyn College exhibit, Oct. 2005.
Schiavo, Giovanni. Papers. Italian American Renaissance Foundation Library. New Orleans.
Sorrentino, Anthony. Papers. Chicago History Museum.
Villa St. Ben, Oral History Project. North Central College Archives, Naperville, IL.

Works Progress Administration. Foreign Language Press Survey, 1942. Chicago.

Other Sources

Ackman, Scott, and Christopher Schwarz. "Dubious Legacy." *Chicago Magazine* (Aug. 2008): 60–64.
Addams, Jane. "Public Recreation and Social Morality." In *Charities and the Commons*, edited by Edward T. Devine, 18, no. 18 (1907): 492–94.
———. *The Second Twenty Years at Hull House.* New York: Macmillan, 1930.
———. *Twenty Years at Hull House.* New York: Macmillan, 1910.
Ahnert, Lynne, ed. *An American Journey: Our Italian Heritage.* Canastota, NY: Canastota, 1998.
Airos, Letizia, and Ottorino Cappelli, eds. *Guido: Italian/American Youth and Identity Politics.* New York: Bordighera Press, 2011.
Alba, Richard D., ed. *Ethnicity and Race in the U.S.A.: Toward the Twenty-First Century.* 1988. Reprint, New York: Routledge, 1989.
Alba, Richard D., and Dalia Abdel-Hady. "Galileo's Children: Italian Americans' Difficult Entry into the Intellectual Elite." *Sociological Quarterly* 46, no. 1 (2005): 3–18.
Alba, Richard D., and Victor Nee. *Remaking the American Mainstream: Assimilation and Contemporary Immigration.* Cambridge, MA: Harvard Univ. Press, 2003.
———. "Rethinking Assimilation Theory for a New Era of Immigration." *International Migration Review* 31, no. 4 (1997): 826–74.
Aleandri, Emelise. *Little Italy.* Chicago: Arcadia, 2002.
Allen, Theodore W. *The Invention of the White Race: Racial Oppression and Social Control.* London: Verso, 1998.
Altherr, Thomas L., ed. *The Cooperstown Symposium on Baseball and American Culture, 1998.* Jefferson, NC: McFarland, 1998.
Anderson, Benedict. *Imagined Communities: Reflections on the Origin and Spread of Nationalism.* 1983. Reprint, New York: Verso, 1991.
Anderson, Chris, and Sharon McGehee with Jake La Motta. *Raging Bull II.* Secaucus, NJ: Lyle Stuart, 1986.
Andrews, David L. "Contextualizing Suburban Soccer: Consumer Culture, Lifestyle Differentiation, and Suburban America." *Sport in Society* 2, no. 3 (1999): 31–53.

Angus, David L. "Conflict, Class, and the Nineteenth Century Public High School in the Cities of the Midwest." *Curriculum Inquiry* 18, no. 1 (1988): 7–31.

Arcudi, Bruno A., and Richard Gambino, eds. *Italian Americana* 7, no. 1 (1981).

Arnesen, Eric. "Whiteness and the Historians' Imagination." *International Labor and Working Class History* 60 (Fall 2001): 3–32.

Avrich, Paul. *The Haymarket Tragedy*. Princeton, NJ: Princeton Univ. Press, 1984.

———. *Sacco and Vanzetti: The Anarchist Background*. Princeton, NJ: Princeton Univ. Press, 1991.

Bair, Sarah. "American Sports, 1910–1919." In *Encyclopedia of Sports in America: A History from Foot Races to Extreme Sports*, edited by Murry Nelson. Westport, CT: Greenwood Press, 2009.

Baker, Lee D. *From Savage to Negro: Anthropology and the Construction of Race, 1896–1954*. Berkeley: Univ. of California Press, 1998.

———, ed. *Life in America: Identity and Everyday Experience*. Malden, MA: Blackwell, 2004.

Baldassaro, Lawrence. *Beyond DiMaggio: Italian Americans in Baseball*. Lincoln: Univ. of Nebraska Press, 2011.

Baldassaro, Lawrence, and Richard A. Johnson, eds. *The American Game: Baseball and Ethnicity*. Carbondale: Univ. of Southern Illinois Press, 2002.

Baron, Hans. *The Crisis of the Early Italian Renaissance*. Princeton, NJ: Princeton Univ. Press, 1966.

Barone, Michael. *The New Americans: How the Melting Pot Can Work Again*. Washington, DC: Regnery, 2001.

Barra, Allan. *Yogi Berra: Eternal Yankee*. New York: W. W. Norton, 2009.

Barreca, Regina, ed. *Don't Tell Mama*. New York: Penguin Books, 2002.

Barrett, James R., and David Roediger. "Inbetween Peoples: Race, Nationality, and the 'New Immigrant' Working Class." *Journal of American Ethnic History* 16, no. 3 (1997): 3–44.

Barthel, Thomas. *Baseball's Peerless Semipros: Bushwick*. Haworth, NJ: St. Johann Press, 2009.

Bass Warner, Sam, and Colin Burke. "Cultural Change and the Ghetto." *Journal of Contemporary History* 4, no. 4 (1969): 173–87.

Batella, Fausto. *Gridiron Gladiators: Italian-Americans in College, Semipro & Pro Football*. New York: iUniverse, 2007.

Bateson, Gregory. *Mind and Nature: A Necessary Unity.* 1979. Reprint, New York: Bantam Books, 1988.

Bayles, Martha. "We Are All Sopranos." *Chronicle of Higher Education,* Dec. 6, 2002, B14–15.

Bayor, Ronald H. *Neighbors in Conflict: The Irish, Germans, Jews, and Italians of New York City, 1929–1941.* Baltimore: Johns Hopkins Univ. Press, 1978.

Bazzano, Carmelo. "The Italian-American Sporting Experience." In *Ethnicity and Sport in North American History and Culture,* edited by George Eisen and David K. Wiggins, 103–16. Westport, CT: Praeger, 1994.

Bederman, Gail. *Manliness and Civilization: A Cultural History of Gender and Race in the United States, 1880–1917.* Chicago: Univ. of Chicago Press, 1995.

Belliotti, Raymond A. *Seeking Identity: Individualism versus Community in an Ethnic Context.* Lawrence: Univ. Press of Kansas, 1995.

Bergreen, Laurence. *Capone: The Man and the Era.* New York: Simon & Schuster, 1994.

Bernardi, Adria. *Houses without Names: The Italian Immigrants of Highwood, Illinois.* Urbana: Univ. of Illinois Press, 1990.

Berra, Yogi, and Ed Fitzgerald. *Yogi: The Autobiography of a Professional Baseball Player.* Garden City, NY: Doubleday, 1961.

Bertellini, Giorgio. "Duce/Divo: Masculinity, Racial Identity, and Politics among Italian Americans in 1920s New York City." *Journal of Urban History* 31, no. 5 (2005): 685–726.

Billi, G. "Per l'All-Italian, 1937." *Il Progresso Italo-Americano,* Nov. 26, 1937.

Billi, John. "U.S. Sports Firmament Is Dotted with Many First Magnitude Stars of Italian Origin." *Il Progresso Italo-Americano,* Nov. 9, 1930.

Bissinger, Buzz. "For Love of Di Maggio." *Vanity Fair,* Sept. 2000, 360–76.

Blok, Anton. *The Mafia of a Sicilian Village, 1860–1960: A Study of Violent Peasant Entrepreneurs.* 1974. Reprint, Prospect Heights, IL: Waveland Press, 1988.

Bodnar, John. "Materialism and Morality: Slavic-American Immigrant and Education, 1890–1940." *Journal of Ethnic Studies* 3–4 (Winter 1976): 1–20.

Bodnar, John, Roger Simon, and Michael P. Weber. *Lives of Their Own: Blacks, Italians, and Poles in Pittsburgh, 1900–1960.* Urbana: Univ. of Illinois Press, 1983.

Bogardus, Emory S. *Immigration and Race Attitudes*. Boston: D. C. Heath, 1928.

Bogue, Allan G. *Frederick Jackson Turner: Strange Roads Going Down*. Norman: Univ. of Oklahoma Press, 1998.

Boscia-Mule, Patricia. *Authentic Ethnicities: The Interaction of Ideology, Gender Power, and Class in the Italian-American Experience*. Westport, CT: Greenwood Press, 1999.

Bourdieu, Pierre. *Distinction: A Social Critique of the Judgment of Taste*. Translated by Richard Nice. Cambridge, MA: Harvard Univ. Press, 1984.

———. *Outline of a Theory of Practice*. Cambridge: Cambridge Univ. Press, 1977.

———. "Program for a Sociology of Sport." *Sociology of Sport Journal* 5 (1988): 153–61.

Boyle, Ellexis. "Measuring Up to American Manhood: Racism and the Development of 'Race' in the History of Competitive Bodybuilding." *Stadion* 31, no. 1 (2005): 71–85.

Briggs, John W. *An Italian Passage: Immigrants to Three American Cities*. New Haven, CT: Yale Univ. Press, 1978.

Briley, Ron. "The Legend of Sacco and Vanzetti: Keeping the Story Alive in Literature, Song, and Film." *Studies in Popular Culture* 31, no. 2 (2009): 101–21.

Brodkin, Karen. *How Jews Became White Folks: And What That Says about Race in America*. New Brunswick, NJ: Rutgers Univ. Press, 1998.

Brown, Susan K., and Frank D. Bean. "New Immigrants, New Models of Assimilation." Migration Policy Institute, 2006. http://www.migrationinformation.org/feature/display.cfm?.id=442.

Brubacher, John S., and Willis Rudy. *Higher Education in Transition: A History of American Colleges and Universities*. New Brunswick, NJ: Transaction, 1997.

Buder, Stanley. *Pullman: An Experiment in Industrial Order and Community Planning, 1880–1930*. New York: Oxford Univ. Press, 1968.

Buenker, John D., and Lorman A. Ratner, eds. *Multiculturalism in the United States: A Comparative Guide to Acculturation and Ethnicity*. Westport, CT: Greenwood Press, 1992.

Burckhardt, Jacob. *The Civilization of the Renaissance in Italy*. New York: Harper Colophon, 1958.

Burger, Joseph A. "Baseball and Social Mobility for Italian-Americans in the 1930s." Unpublished ms., Center for Migration Studies.

Burgess, Ernest W., ed. *The Urban Community*. Chicago: Univ. of Chicago Press, 1926.

Burke, Peter. *Popular Culture in Early Modern Europe*. New York: Harper & Row, 1978.

Busch, Noel F. "Joe Di Maggio: Baseball's Most Sensational Big League Star Starts What Should Be His Best Year So Far." *Life*, May 1, 1939, 62–69.

Butler, Judith. *Undoing Gender*. New York: Routledge, 2004.

Cahn, Susan. *Coming on Strong: Gender and Sexuality in Twentieth-Century Women's Sport*. New York: Free Press, 1994.

Calhoun, Craig, Joseph Gerteis, James Moody, Steven Pfaff, and Indermohan Virk. *Contemporary Social Theory*. Oxford: Blackwell, 2002.

Candeloro, Dominic L. *Chicago's Italians: Immigrants, Ethnics, Americans*. Chicago: Arcadia, 2003.

———. *Italians in Chicago*. Chicago: Arcadia, 1999.

———, ed. *The Italians of New York*. New York: New-York Historical Society, 1999.

Cannato, Vincent J. *American Passage: The History of Ellis Island*. New York: Harper, 2009.

Cannistraro, Philip V., and Gerald Meyer, eds. *The Lost World of Italian American Radicalism*. Westport, CT: Praeger, 2003.

Caporale, Rocco, ed. *The Italian Americans through the Generations*. New York: American Italian Historical Association, 1986.

Cardoza, Anthony "'Making Italians'? Cycling and National Identity in Italy, 1900–1950." *Journal of Modern Italian Studies* 15, no. 3 (2010): 354–77.

Carnes, Mark C., and Clyde Griffen, eds. *Meanings for Manhood: Constructions of Masculinity in Victorian America*. Chicago: Univ. of Chicago Press, 1990.

Carnevale, Nancy C. *A New Language, a New World: Italian Immigrants in the United States, 1890–1945*. Urbana: Univ. of Illinois Press, 2009.

Carroll, John M. *Red Grange and the Rise of Modern Football*. Urbana: Univ. of Illinois Press, 2004.

Carson, Mina Carson. *Settlement Folk: Social Thought and the American Settlement Movement, 1885–1930*. Chicago: Univ. of Chicago Press, 1990.

Cassirer, Ernest, Paul Oskar Kristeller, and John Herman Randall Jr. *The Renaissance Philosophy of Man*. Chicago: Univ. of Chicago Press, 1948.

Cavaioli, Frank J., Angela Danzi, and Salvatore J. La Gumina, eds. *Italian Americans and Their Public and Private Life*. New York: American Italian Historical Association, 1993.

Cavallo, Dominick. *Muscles and Morals: Organized Playgrounds and Urban Reform, 1880–1920*. Philadelphia: Univ. of Pennsylvania Press, 1981.

Cavanaugh, Jack. *The Gipper: George Gipp, Knute Rockne, and the Dramatic Rise of Notre Dame Football*. New York: Skyhorse, 2010.

Cavinder, Fred D. *More Amazing Tales from Indiana*. Bloomington: Indiana Univ. Press, 2003.

Cerulo, Karen A. "Identity Construction: New Issues, New Directions." *Annual Review of Sociology* 23 (1997): 385–409.

Chapman, David L. *Sandow the Magnificent: Eugen Sandow and the Beginnings of Bodybuilding*. Urbana: Univ. of Illinois Press, 1994.

Chapman, David, and Gigliola Gori. "Strong, Athletic, and Beautiful: Edmondo De Amicis and the Ideal Italian Woman." *International Journal of the History of Sport* 27, no. 11 (2010): 1968–87.

Chetwynd, Josh. *Baseball in Europe*. Jefferson, NC: McFarland, 2008.

Chicago Park District. *Third Annual Report, 1937*. Chicago: Chicago Park District, 1938.

Child, Irvin L. *Italian or American? The Second Generation in Conflict*. New Haven, CT: Yale Univ. Press, 1943.

Chirico, Donna. "The Role of the Italian American Faculty Staff Advisory Council." *Il Bolletino* (Winter 2011): 6.

Chiswick, Barry R. "The Skills and Economic Status of American Jewry: Trends over the Last Half-Century." *Journal of Labor Economics* 11, no. 1, pt. 1 (1993): 229–42.

Choate, Mark I. *Emigrant Nation: The Making of Italy Abroad*. Cambridge, MA: Harvard Univ. Press, 2008.

Cinotto, Simone. "Leonard Covello, the Covello Papers, and the History of Eating Habits among Italian Immigrants in New York." *Journal of American History* 91, no. 2 (2004): 497–521.

Ciotola, Nicholas P. "Spignesi, Sinatra, and the Pittsburgh Steelers: Franco's Italian Army as an Expression of Ethnic Identity, 1972–1977." *Journal of Sport History* 27, no. 2 (2000): 271–89.

Coad, David. *The Metrosexual: Gender, Sexuality, and Sport.* Albany: State Univ. of New York Press, 2008.

Cohen, Lizabeth. *Making a New Deal: Industrial Workers in Chicago, 1919–1939.* New York: Cambridge Univ. Press, 1990.

Connell, William J., and Fred Gardaphe, eds. *Anti-Italianism: Essays on a Prejudice.* New York: Palgrave Macmillan, 2010.

Connerton, Paul. *How Societies Remember.* Cambridge: Cambridge Univ. Press, 1991.

Covello, Leonard. *The Social Background of the Italo-American School Child.* Totowa, NJ: Rowman & Littlefield, 1972.

Cramer, Richard Ben. *Joe Di Maggio: The Hero's Life.* New York: Simon & Schuster, 2000.

Creamer, Robert W. *Babe: The Legend Comes to Life.* New York: Simon & Schuster, 1974.

Cressey, Paul G. "The Succession of Cultural Groups in the City of Chicago." PhD diss., Univ. of Chicago, 1930.

———. *The Taxi Dance Hall: A Sociological Study in Commercialized Recreation and City Life.* Chicago: Univ. of Chicago Press, 1932.

Crispino, James A. *The Assimilation of Ethnic Groups: The Italian Case.* Staten Island, NY: Center for Migration Studies, 1980.

Davis, Allen F. *Spearheads for Reform: The Social Settlements and the Progressive Movement, 1890–1914.* New York: Oxford Univ. Press, 1967.

Davis, Fred. *Yearning for Yesterday: A Sociology of Nostalgia.* New York: Free Press, 1979.

Davis, Robert C. *The War of the Fists: Popular Culture and Public Violence in Late Renaissance Venice.* New York: Oxford, 1994.

Dawley, Alan. *Struggles for Justice: Social Responsibility and the Liberal State.* Cambridge, MA: Belknap Press, 1991.

De Conde, Alexander. *Half Bitter, Half Sweet: An Excursion into Italian-American History.* New York: Charles Scribner's Sons, 1971.

De Cristoforo, Silvio. "'Two Ton Tony.'" *Red, White, and Green Sports* (Oct. 1985): 6–7, 37.

De Marco, William M. *Ethnics and Enclaves: Boston's Italian North End.* Ann Arbor, MI: UMI Research Press, 1981.

Denham, Bryan E. "Correlates of Pride in the Performance Success of United States Athletes Competing on an International Stage." *International Review for the Sociology of Sport* 45, no. 4 (2010): 457–73.

De Sanctis, Donna. "Take Off the Apron." *Adweek*, Nov. 13, 2006, 19.

De Vito, Carlo. *Yogi: The Life and Times of an American Original.* Chicago: Triumph Books, 2008.

Diamond, Andrew J. *Mean Streets: Chicago Youths and the Everyday Struggle for Empowerment in the Multiracial City, 1908–1969.* Berkeley: Univ. of California Press, 2009.

Dickie, John. *Darkest Italy: The Nation and Stereotypes of the Mezzogiorno, 1860–1890.* New York: St. Martin's Press, 1999.

Dickson, Paul. *Baseball's Greatest Quotations.* New York: Collins, 2008.

Di Maggio, Joe. *Lucky to Be a Yankee.* 1947. Reprint, New York: Grosset & Dunlap, 1951.

Di Scala, Spencer M. *Italy: From Revolution to Republic, 1700 to the Present.* Boulder, CO: Westview Press, 1995.

Douglas, Ann. *The Feminization of American Culture.* New York: Anchor Press, 1977.

Dreifort, John E. "Anything but Ordinary: POW Sports in a Barbed Wire World." *Journal of Sport History* 34, no. 3 (2007): 415–37.

Du Bois, W. E. B. *The Souls of Black Folk.* New York: Vintage Books, 1990.

Duffy, Matt. "Giuseppe Garibaldi: A Blue Shirt?." http://www.militaryhistoryonline.com/19thcentury/articles/giuseppegaribaldi.aspx.

Duis, Perry. *The Saloon: Public Drinking in Chicago and Boston, 1880–1920.* Urbana: Univ. of Illinois Press, 1983.

Dutton, Kenneth R. *The Perfectible Body: The Western Ideal of Male Physical Development.* New York: Continuum, 1995.

Dyreson, Mark. "The Emergence of Consumer Culture and the Transformation of Physical Culture: American Sport in the 1920s." *Journal of Sport History* 16, no. 3 (1989): 261–81.

Early, Gerald. "The Romance of Toughness: La Motta and Graziano." *Antioch Review* 45, no. 4 (1987): 385–408.

Edwards, Harry. "Social Change and Popular Culture: Seminal Developments at the Interface of Race, Sport, and Society." *Sport in Society* 13, no. 1 (2010): 59–71.

Eig, Jonathan. *Luckiest Man: The Life and Death of Lou Gehrig.* New York: Simon & Schuster, 2005.

Elias, Norbert. *The Civilizing Process: The History of Manners.* New York: Urizen Books, 1978.

———. *The History of Manners: Power and Civility.* New York: Pantheon Books, 1982.

Elias, Norbert, and Eric Dunning. *Quest for Excitement: Sport and Leisure in the Civilizing Process.* Oxford: Blackwell, 1986.

Elias, Robert, ed. *Baseball and the American Dream: Race, Class, Gender, and the National Pastime.* Armonk, NY: M. E. Sharpe, 2001.

———. *The Empire Strikes Out: How Baseball Sold U.S. Foreign Policy and Promoted the American Way Abroad.* New York: New Press, 2010.

Erenberg, Lewis A. *Steppin' Out: New York Nightlife and the Transformation of American Culture, 1890–1930.* Chicago: Univ. of Chicago Press, 1984.

Ernst, Robert. *Weakness Is a Crime: The Life of Bernarr Macfadden.* Syracuse, NY: Syracuse Univ. Press, 1991.

Ets, Marie Hall. *Rosa: The Life of an Italian Immigrant.* Madison: Univ. of Wisconsin Press, 1970.

Evensen, Bruce J. *When Dempsey Fought Tunney: Heroes, Hokum, and Storytelling in the Jazz Age.* Knoxville: Univ. of Tennessee Press, 1996.

Fair, John D. *Muscletown: Bob Hoffman and the Manly Culture of York Barbell.* University Park: Pennsylvania State Univ. Press, 1999.

Featherman, David L. "The Socioeconomic Achievement of White Religio-Ethnic Subgroups: Social and Psychological Explanations." *American Sociological Review* 36 (Apr. 1971): 207–22.

Feldstein, Stanley, and Lawrence Costello. *The Ordeal of Assimilation: A Documentary History of the White Working Class, 1830–1970s.* Garden City, NY: Anchor Books, 1974.

Ferrara, Cosmo F. *Profiles of Italian Americans: Achieving the Dream and Giving Back.* New York: Bordighera Press, 2010.

Fichera, Sebastian. *Italy on the Pacific: San Francisco's Italian Americans.* New York: Palgrave Macmillan, 2011.

Finley, M. I., Denis Mack Smith, and Christopher Duggan. *A History of Sicily.* New York: Penguin Books, 1987.

Fogelson, Robert M. *Bourgeois Nightmares: Suburbia, 1870–1930.* New Haven, CT: Yale Univ. Press, 2005.

Fox, Stephen. *Big Leagues: Professional Baseball, Football, and Basketball in National Memory.* New York: William Morrow, 1994.

———. *The Unknown Internment: An Oral History of the Relocation of Italian Americans during World War II.* Boston: Twayne, 1990.

Freundlich, Larry, ed. *Reaching for the Stars: A Celebration of Italian Americans in Major League Baseball*. New York: Ballantine Books, 2003.

Friedman, Nick. *Mike Piazza*. New York: Chelsea House, 2007.

Frontani, Michael. "From the Bottom to the Top: Frank Sinatra, the American Myth of Success, and the Italian-American Image." *Journal of American Culture* 28, no. 2 (2005): 216–30.

Fussell, Elizabeth. "Constructing New Orleans, Constructing Race: A Population History of New Orleans." *Journal of American History* 94, no. 3 (2007): 846–55.

Gabaccia, Donna R. *From Sicily to Elizabeth Street: Housing and Social Change among Italian Immigrants, 1880–1930*. Albany: State Univ. of New York Press, 1984.

———. *Immigration and American Diversity*. Cornwall: Blackwell, 2002.

———. "Is Everywhere Nowhere? Nomads, Nations, and the Immigrant Paradigm of United States History." *Journal of American History* 86, no. 3 (1999): 1115–34.

Gaines, Charles. *Charles Atlas: Yours in Perfect Manhood*. New York: Simon and Schuster, 1982.

Gallico, Paul. *Farewell to Sport*. New York: Alfred A. Knopf, 1950.

Gallo, Patrick J. *Ethnic Alienation: The Italian-Americans*. Cranbury, NJ: Fairleigh Dickinson Univ. Press, 1974.

———. *Old Bread, New Wine: A Portrait of the Italian-Americans*. Chicago: Nelson-Hall, 1981.

———, ed. *The Urban Experience of Italian-Americans*. Staten Island, NY: American Italian Historical Association, 1977.

Gambino, Richard. *Blood of My Blood: The Dilemma of the Italian-Americans*. 1974. Reprint, Garden City, NY: Anchor Books, 1975.

———. *Vendetta: The True Story of the Largest Lynching in U.S. History*. 1977. Reprint, Toronto: Guernica, 1998.

Gans, Herbert J. "Acculturation, Assimilation, and Mobility." *Ethnic and Racial Studies* 30, no. 1 (2007): 152–64.

———. "Symbolic Ethnicity and Symbolic Religiosity: Towards a Comparison of Ethnic and Religious Acculturation." *Ethnic and Racial Studies* 17, no. 4 (1994): 577–92.

———. *The Urban Villagers: Group and Class in the Life of Italian-Americans*. New York: Free Press, 1962.

Garagiola, Joe. *Baseball Is a Funny Game.* Philadelphia: J. B. Lippincott, 1960.

Garaty, John A. *The American Nation: A History of the United States.* New York: Harper & Row, 1983.

Garb, Margaret. "Regulating Urban Living." *Chicago History* 35, no. 3 (2008): 5–29.

Gardaphe, Fred L. *From Wise Guys to Wise Men: The Gangster and Italian American Masculinities.* New York: Routledge, 2006.

Garraty, John A. *The American Nation: A History of the United States.* New York: Harper & Row, 1983.

Gems, Gerald R. *For Pride, Profit, and Patriarchy: Football and the Incorporation of American Cultural Values.* Lanham, MD: Scarecrow Press, 2000): 111–50.

———. "Monuments to Memory." *Chicago History* 36, no. 1 (2008): 5–25.

———. "The Neighborhood Athletic Club: An Ethnographic Study of a Working-Class Athletic Fraternity in Chicago, 1917–1984." *Colby Quarterly* 32, no. 1 (1996): 36–44.

———. "The Politics of Boxing: Resistance, Religion, and Working Class Assimilation." *International Sports Journal* 8, no. 1 (2004): 89–103.

———. "The Prep Bowl: Football and Religious Acculturation in Chicago, 1927–1963." *Journal of Sport History* 2, no. 3 (1996): 284–302.

———. "Sport, Religion, and Americanization: Bishop Sheil and the Catholic Youth Organization." *International Journal of the History of Sport* (Aug. 1993): 233–41.

———. "Sport and the Forging of a Jewish-American Culture: The Chicago Hebrew Institute." *Journal of American Jewish History* 83 (Mar. 1995): 15–26.

———. *Windy City Wars: Labor, Leisure, and Sport in the Making of Chicago.* Lanham, MD: Scarecrow Press, 1997.

Gems, Gerald R., Linda J. Borish, and Gertrud Pfister. *Sports in American History: From Colonization to Globalization.* Champaign, IL: Human Kinetics, 2008.

Gems, Gerald R., and Gertrud Pfister. *Understanding American Sport.* London: Routledge, 2009.

Gilfoyle, Timothy J. *A Pickpocket's Tale: The Underworld of Nineteenth Century New York.* New York: W. W. Norton, 2006.

Girometta, Florian. *St. Anthony of Padua Italian National Parish Diamond Jubilee Book, 1903–1978.* Chicago: St. Anthony, 1978.

Goksoyr, Matti. "Nationalism." In *Routledge Companion to Sports History*, edited by S. W. Pope and John Nauright, 268–94. London: Routledge, 2010.

Goodman, Cary. *Choosing Sides: Playground and Street Life on the Lower East Side*. New York: Schocken Books, 1979.

Gori, Gigliola. "Care, Cure, and Training of the Body According to Italian Medicine of the Nineteenth Century." *International Journal of the History of Sport* 26, no. 9 (2009): 1218–38.

———. *Italian Fascism and the Female Body: Sport, Submissive Women, and Strong Mothers*. London: Routledge, 2004.

Gorn, Elliott J. *Dillinger's Wild Ride*. New York: Oxford Univ. Press, 2009.

———, ed. *Sports in Chicago*. Urbana: Univ. of Illinois Press, 2008.

Graf, John, and Steve Skorpad. *Chicago's Monuments, Markers, and Memorials*. Chicago: Arcadia, 2002.

Grame, Theodore C. *Ethnic Broadcasting in the United States*. Washington, DC: American Folklife Center, 1980.

Grant, Madison. *The Passing of the Great Race; or, The Racial Basis of European History*. New York: Charles Scribner's Sons, 1916.

Graziano, Rocky, with Ralph Corsel. *Somebody Down Here Likes Me Too*. New York: Stein & Day, 1981.

Grossman, James R., Ann Durkin Keating, and Janice L. Rieff, eds. *The Encyclopedia of Chicago*. Chicago: Univ. of Chicago Press, 2004.

Guglielmo, Jennifer. *Living the Revolution: Italian Women's Resistance and Radicalism in New York City, 1880–1945*. Chapel Hill: Univ. of North Carolina Press, 2010.

Guglielmo, Jennifer, and Salvatore Salerno, eds. *Are Italians White? How Race Is Made in America*. New York: Routledge, 2003.

Guglielmo, Thomas A. *White on Arrival: Italians, Race, Color, and Power in Chicago, 1890–1945*. New York: Oxford Univ. Press, 2003.

Halberstam, David. *Everything They Had*. New York: Hyperion, 2008.

Hall, Stuart. "Who Needs Identity?" In *Questions of Cultural Identity*, edited by Stuart Hall and Paul Du Gay, 1–17. London: Sage, 1996.

Halsey, Elizabeth. *The Development of Public Recreation in Metropolitan Chicago*. Chicago: Chicago Recreation Commission, 1940.

Hamill, Pete. *Why Sinatra Matters*. Boston: Little, Brown, 1998.

Handlin, Oscar. *The Uprooted: The Epic Story of the Great Migrations That Made the American People*. New York: Grosset & Dunlap, 1951.

Hardy, Stephen. *How Boston Played: Sport, Recreation, and Community, 1865–1915.* Boston: Northeastern Univ. Press, 1982.

Hargreaves, Jennifer, and Patricia Vertinsky, eds. *Physical Culture, Power, and the Body.* Milton Park, Abingdon, UK: Routledge, 2007.

Harney, Robert F., and Vincent J. Scarpacci, eds. *Little Italies in North America.* Toronto: Multicultural History Society of Ontario, 1981.

Hauser, Thomas, and Stephen Brunt. *The Italian Stallions: Heroes of Boxing's Glory Days.* Toronto: Sport Media, 2003.

Havers, Richard. *Sinatra.* New York: DK, 2004.

Healey, Joseph F. "An Exploration of the Relationship between Memory and Sport." *Sociology of Sport Journal* 8, no. 3 (1991): 213–27.

Heap, Chad. *Slumming: Sexual and Racial Encounters in American Nightlife, 1885–1940.* Chicago: Univ. of Chicago Press, 2009.

Heinz, W. C. "Goodbye, Graziano." In *Best from Sport*, by Al Silverman, 88–95. New York: Bartholomew House, 1961.

———. "Somebody Up There Likes Him." *Ring*, Oct. 1981, 88–99.

Heller, Peter. *"In This Corner . . . !": 42 World Champions Tell Their Stories.* 1973. Reprint, New York: Da Capo Press, 1974.

Hemingway, Ernest. *The Old Man and the Sea.* New York: Charles Scribner's Sons, 1952.

Hillenbrand, Laura. *Unbroken: A World War II Story of Survival, Resilience, and Redemption.* New York: Random House, 2010.

Hirschman, Charles, Josh De Wind, and Philip Kasinitz, eds. *The Handbook of International Migration: The American Experience.* New York: Russell Sage Foundation, 1999.

Hoare, Quintin, and Geoffrey N. Smith, eds. *Selections from the Prison Notebooks of Antonio Gramsci.* New York: International, 1971.

Hobsbawm, Eric, and Terence Ranger, eds. *The Invention of Tradition.* Cambridge: Cambridge Univ. Press, 1983.

Hofmann, Annette R. "From Jahn to Lincoln: Transformation of Turner Symbols in a New Cultural Setting." *International Journal of the History of Sport* 26, no. 13 (2009): 1946–62.

———, ed. *Turnen and Sport: Transatlantic Transfers.* Munich: Waxmann, 2004.

Hogan, David J. *Class and Reform: School and Society in Chicago, 1880–1930.* Philadelphia: Univ. of Pennsylvania Press, 1985.

Hogan, Lawrence D. *Shades of Glory: The Negro Leagues and the Story of African-American Baseball.* Washington, DC: National Geographic, 2006.

Horsman, Reginald. *Race and Manifest Destiny: The Origins of American Racial Anglo-Saxonism.* Cambridge, MA: Harvard Univ. Press, 1981.

Huggins, Mike. "The Sporting Gaze: Towards a Visual Turn in Sport History—Documenting Art and Sport." *Journal of Sport History* 35, no. 2 (2008): 311–29.

Ibrahim, Hilmi. "The Nature of Ritual." *Journal of Physical Education, Recreation, and Dance* (Nov.–Dec. 1988): 26.

Ignatiev, Noel. *How the Irish Became White.* New York: Routledge, 1995.

Italian American Directory Company. *Gli Italiani negli Stati Uniti d'America.* New York: Andrew H. Kellogg, 1906.

Izenberg, Jerry. *Through My Eyes: A Sports Writer's 58 Year Journey.* Haworth, NJ: St. Johann Press, 2009.

Jablonski, Edward. *Pictorial History of the World War II Years.* Garden City, NY: Doubleday, 1977.

Jacobson, Matthew Frye. *Barbarian Virtues: The United States Encounters Foreign Peoples at Home and Abroad, 1876–1917.* New York: Hill and Wang, 2000.

———. *Roots Too: White Ethnic Revival in Post–Civil Rights America.* Cambridge, MA: Harvard Univ. Press, 2006.

———. *Whiteness of a Different Color: European Immigrants and the Alchemy of Race.* Cambridge, MA: Harvard Univ. Press, 1998.

Jensen, Eric. "Body by Weimar: Athletes, Gender, and German Modernity." Newberry Seminar on Sport and Culture, Chicago, Apr. 3, 2009.

Jones, David. *Joe DiMaggio.* Westport, CT: Greenwood Press, 2004.

Jones, Peter d'A., and Melvin G. Holli. *Ethnic Chicago.* Grand Rapids, MI: William B. Eerdmans, 1981.

Jones, R. L. "A Deviant Sports Career: Toward a Sociology of Unlicensed Boxing." *Journal of Sport and Social Issues* 21, no. 1 (1997): 37–52.

"The Joy of Growing Up Italian." Commemorative Issue 5, *Red, White, and Green Sports* 22, no. 6 (2001): 19.

Juliani, Richard N., and Philip Cannistraro, eds. *Italian Americans: The Search for a Usable Past.* Staten Island, NY: American Italian Historical Association, 1989.

Kalman, Victor. "Falcaro the Great." *Sports Illustrated*, Sept. 13, 1954. http://vault.sportsillustrated.cnn.com/vault/article/magazine/MAG 1129052/2/index.htm.

Kamalipour, Yahya, and Theresa Carilli, eds. *Cultural Diversity and the U.S. Media*. Albany: State Univ. of New York Press, 1998.

Kammen, Michael. *Mystic Chords of Memory: The Transformation of Tradition in American Culture*. New York: Alfred A. Knopf, 1991.

Kantowicz, Edward R. "Cardinal Mundelein of Chicago and the Shaping of Twentieth Century American Catholicism." *Journal of American History* 68, no. 1 (1981): 52–68.

———. *Corporation Sole: Cardinal Mundelein and Chicago Catholicism*. Notre Dame, IN: Univ. of Notre Dame Press, 1983.

Kass, John. "Memories of Joey G." *Red, White, and Green Sports* 3, no. 8 (1982): 6, 8, 22.

Kasson, John F. *Houdini, Tarzan, and the Perfect Man: The White Male Body and the Challenge of Modernity in America*. New York: Hill and Wang, 2001.

Katz, Michael B., and Mark J. Stern. *One Nation Divisible: What America Was and What It Is Becoming*. New York: Russell Sage Foundation, 2006.

Keating, Ann Durkin, ed. *Chicago Neighborhoods and Suburbs: A Historical Guide*. Chicago: Univ. of Chicago Press, 2008.

Keil, Hartmut, and John B. Jentz, eds. *German Workers in Industrial Chicago, 1850–1910*. De Kalb: Northern Illinois Univ. Press, 1983.

Kieran, John, and Arthur Daley. *The Story of the Olympic Games*. Philadelphia: J. B. Lippincott, 1961.

Kimmel, Michael. *Manhood in America: A Cultural History*. New York: Free Press, 1996.

King, C. Richard. "Cautionary Notes on Whiteness and Sport Studies." *Sociology of Sport Journal* 22, no. 3 (2005): 397–408.

King, Greg. *A Season of Splendor: The Court of Mrs. Astor in Gilded Age New York*. Hoboken, NJ: John Wiley & Sons, 2009.

Kirsch, George B. *Golf in America*. Urbana: Univ. of Illinois Press, 2009.

Kolchin, Peter. "Whiteness Studies: The New History of Race in America." *Journal of American History* 89, no. 1 (2002): 154–73.

Kornblum, William. *Blue Collar Community*. Chicago: Univ. of Chicago Press, 1974.

La Cecla, Franco. *Pasta and Pizza.* Chicago: Prickly Paradigm Press, 2007.
La Gumina, Salvatore J. *The Humble and the Heroic: Wartime Italian Americans.* Youngstown, NY: Cambria Press, 2006.
———. *The Italian American Experience: An Encyclopedia.* New York: Garland, 1999.
———. *Wop! A Documentary History of Anti-Italian Discrimination.* 1973. Reprint, Toronto: Guernica, 1999.
La Gumina, Salvatore, Frank Cavaioli, Salvatore Primeggia, and Joseph Varacalli, eds. *The Italian American Experience: An Encyclopedia.* New York: Garland, 2000.
Landry, Harral E., ed. *To See the Past More Clearly: The Enrichment of the Italian Heritage, 1890–1990.* Staten Island, NY: American Italian Historical Association, 1994.
Lang, Arne K. *Prizefighting: An American History.* Jefferson, NC: McFarland, 2008.
La Ruffa, Anthony L. *Monte Carmelo: An Italian-American Community in the Bronx.* New York: Gordon and Breach, 1988.
Lasorda, Tommy, and David Fisher. *The Artful Dodger.* New York: Arbor House, 1985.
Laurino, Maria. *Were You Always an Italian?: Ancestors and Other Icons of Italian America.* New York: W. W. Norton, 2000.
Lengel, Edward G. *To Conquer Hell: The Meuse-Argonne, 1918.* New York: Henry Holt, 2008.
Libby, Bill. *Andretti.* New York: Grosset & Dunlap, 1970.
Lindenmeyer, Kriste. *The Greatest Generation Grows Up: American Childhood in the 1930s.* Chicago: Ivan R. Dee, 2005.
Linton, Bruce A. "A History of Chicago Radio Station Programming, 1921–1931, with an Emphasis on Stations WMAQ and WGN." PhD diss., Northwestern Univ., 1953.
Littlewood, Thomas B. *Arch: A Promoter, Not a Poet.* Ames: Iowa State Univ. Press, 1990.
Llewellyn, Matthew P. "Viva Italia! Viva Italia! Dorando Pietri and the North American Professional Marathon Craze, 1908–1910." *International Journal of the History of Sport* 25, no. 6 (2008): 710–36.
Logan, John R., Richard D. Alba, and Shi-yun Leung. "Minority Access to White Suburbs: A Multiregional Comparison." *Social Forces* 74, no. 3 (1996): 851–81.

Lombardo, Robert M. *The Black Hand: Terror by Letter in Chicago.* Urbana: Univ. of Illinois Press, 2010.

Lopez, Ian Haney. *White by Law: The Legal Construction of Race.* New York: New York Univ. Press, 2006.

Lora, Mary Elaine. "The Roman Bowl." *Dixie*, Aug. 30, 1978, 24, 33, 36.

Luconi, Stefano. "Forging an Ethnic Identity: The Case of Italian Americans." *Revue Français d'Études Americaines*, no. 96 (2003): 1–33.

———. *From Paesani to White Ethnics: The Italian Experience in Philadelphia.* Albany: State Univ. of New York Press, 2001.

Maasik, Sonia, and Jack Solomon, eds. *Signs of Life in the U.S.A.: Readings on Popular Culture for Writers.* New York: Bedford / St. Martin's, 2006.

MacDonald, J. Fred. *Don't Touch That Dial! Radio Programming in American Life from 1920 to 1960.* Chicago: Nelson-Hall, 1979.

Malpezzi, Frances M., and William M. Clements. *Italian-American Folklore.* Little Rock, AK: August House, 1992.

Mangione, Jerre. *An Ethnic at Large: A Memoir of America in the Thirties and Forties.* Syracuse, NY: Syracuse Univ. Press, 1978.

Mangione, Jerre, and Ben Morreale. *La Storia: Five Centuries of the Italian American Experience.* New York: HarperCollins, 1992.

Maraniss, David. *When Pride Still Mattered: A Life of Vince Lombardi.* New York: Simon & Schuster, 1999.

Margavio, A. V., and Jerome J. Salomone. *Bread and Respect: The Italians of Louisiana.* Gretna, LA: Pelican, 2002.

Marger, Martin N. *Race & Ethnic Relations: American and Global Perspectives.* Belmont, CA: Thomson Learning, 2005.

Marino, Dan. *Dan Marino: My Life in Football.* Chicago: Triumph Books, 2005.

Markovits, Andrei S., and Steven L. Hellerman. *Offsides: Soccer and American Exceptionalism.* Princeton, NJ: Princeton Univ. Press, 2001.

Marks, Patricia. *Bicycles, Bangs, and Bloomers.* Lexington: Univ. Press of Kentucky, 1990.

Martin, David E., and Roger W. H. Gynn. *The Olympic Marathon.* Champaign, IL: Human Kinetics, 2000.

Martin, Simon. "Italian Sport and the Challenges of Its Recent Historiography." *Journal of Sport History* 38, no. 2 (2011): 199–209.

Maselli, Joseph, and Domenic Candeloro. *Italians in New Orleans.* Chicago: Arcadia, 2004.

McClellan, Keith. *The Sunday Game: At the Dawn of Professional Football.* Akron, OH: Univ. of Akron Press, 1998.

———. "Thomas J. Holleran, the Akron Pros' Signal Caller." *Coffin Corner* 30, no. 6 (2008): 14.

McClelland, John, and Brian Merrilees, eds. *Sport and Culture in Early Modern Europe.* Toronto: Univ. of Toronto Press, 2009.

McGirr, Lisa. "The Passion of Sacco and Vanzetti: A Global History." *Journal of American History* 93, no. 4 (2007): 1085–1115.

McGreevy, John T. *Parish Boundaries: The Catholic Encounter with Race in the Twentieth Century.* Chicago: Univ. of Chicago Press, 1996.

McKenna, Brian, and Mark L. Ford. "Professional Baseball and Football: A Close Relationship." *Coffin Corner* 29, no. 6 (2007): 12–16.

McKibben, Carol Lynn. *Beyond Cannery Row: Sicilian Women, Immigration, and Community in Monterey, California, 1915–99.* Urbana: Univ. of Illinois Press, 2006.

Milione, Vincenzo, and Christine Gambino. *Si, parliamo Italiano! Globalization of the Italian Culture in the United States.* New York: John D. Calandra Italian American Institute, 2009.

Mirel, Jeffrey E. *Patriotic Pluralism: Americanization Education and European Immigrants.* Cambridge, MA: Harvard Univ. Press, 2010.

Misztal, Barbara. *Theories of Social Memory.* Maidenhead, UK: Open Univ., 2003.

Montcreiff, Robert P. *Bart Giamatti: A Profile.* New Haven, CT: Yale Univ. Press, 2007.

Montville, Leigh. *The Big Bam: The Life and Times of Babe Ruth.* New York: Doubleday, 2006.

Moore, Lucy. *Anything Goes: A Biography of the 1920s.* New York: Overlook Press, 2010.

Morawska, Ewa. "The Sociology and History of Immigration." In *Immigration Reconsidered: History, Sociology, and Politics,* by Virginia Yans-McLaughlin, 187–238. New York: Oxford Univ. Press, 1990.

Morgan, Thomas B. *Italian Physical Culture Demonstration.* New York: Macfadden Books, 1932.

Mormino, Gary Ross. *Immigrants on the Hill: Italian-Americans in St. Louis, 1882–1982.* Columbia: Univ. of Missouri Press, 2002.

———. "The Playing Fields of St. Louis: Italian Immigrants and Sports, 1925–1941." *Journal of Sport History* 9, no. 2 (1982): 5–19.

Mosconi, Willie, and Stanley Cohen. *Willie's Game: An Autobiography*. New York: Macmillan, 1993.
Murray, Robert K. *Red Scare: A Study in National Hysteria, 1919–1920*. Westport, CT: Greenwood Press, 1980.
Nasaw, David. *Children of the City: At Work and at Play*. Garden City, NY: Anchor Press, 1985.
———. *Going Out: The Rise and Fall of Public Amusements*. New York: Basic Books, 1993.
———. *Schooled to Order: A Social History of Public Schooling in the United States*. New York: Oxford Univ. Press, 1979.
Nelli, Humbert S. *From Immigrant to Ethnics: The Italian Americans*. New York: Oxford Univ. Press, 1983.
———. *Italians in Chicago, 1880–1930*. New York: Oxford Univ. Press, 1970.
Nelson, Bruce C. *Beyond the Martyrs: A Social History of Chicago Anarchism, 1870–1900*. New Brunswick, NJ: Rutgers Univ. Press, 1988.
Nelson, Murry, ed. *Encyclopedia of Sports in America: A History from Foot Races to Extreme Sports*. Westport, CT: Greenwood Press, 2009.
———. *The Originals: The New York Celtics Invent Modern Basketball*. Bowling Green, OH: Bowling Green Univ. Popular Press, 1999.
Nora, Pierre. *Realms of Memory: The Construction of the French Past*. New York: Columbia Univ. Press, 1997.
Nord, David Paul. "The Uses of Memory: An Introduction." *Journal of American History* 85, no. 2 (1998): 409–10.
Novak, Michael. *The Rise of the Unmeltable Ethnics: Politics and Culture in the Seventies*. 1971. Reprint, New York: Macmillan, 1972.
O'Brien, Michael. *No Ordinary Joe: The Biography of Joe Paterno*. 1998. Reprint, Nashville: Rutledge Hill Press, 1999.
———. *Vince: A Personal Biography of Vince Lombardi*. New York: William Morrow, 1987.
O'Neill, Gerard, and Dick Lehr. *The Underboss: The Rise and Fall of a Mafia Family*. New York: Public Affairs, 1989.
Oriard, Michael. "Football, Cultural History, and Democracy." *Journal of Sport History* 29, no. 2 (2002): 241–49.
———. *King Football: Sport and Spectacle in the Golden Age of Radio and Newsreels, Magazines, the Weekly, and the Daily Press*. Chapel Hill: Univ. of North Carolina Press. 2001.

Orsi, Robert A., ed. *Gods of the City*. Bloomington: Indiana Univ. Press, 1999.

———. *The Madonna of 115th Street: Faith and Community in Italian Harlem*. New Haven, CT: Yale Univ. Press, 1985.

Overland, Orm. *Immigrant Minds, American Identities: Making the United States Home, 1870–1930*. Urbana: Univ. of Illinois Press, 2000.

Overman, Steven J. *Living Out of Bounds: The Male Athlete's Everyday Life*. Lincoln: Univ. of Nebraska Press, 2010.

Page, Joseph S. *Primo Carnera: The Life and Career of the Heavyweight Boxing Champion*. Jefferson, NC: McFarland, 2011.

Panella, Vincent. *The Other Side: Growing Up Italian in America*. Garden City, NY: Doubleday, 1979.

Parati, Graziella, and Ben Lawton, eds. *Italian Cultural Studies*. Boca Raton, FL: Bordighera Press, 2001.

Park, Robert E. *Cultural Conflict and Marginal Man*. New York: Scribner's, 1937.

Park, Robert E., Ernest Burgess, and Roderick D. McKenzie. *The City*. Chicago: Univ. of Chicago Press, 1925.

Park, Robert E., and Herbert A. Miller. *Old World Traits Transplanted*. New York: Harper & Brothers, 1921.

Parrino, Maria, ed. *Italian American Autobiographies*. St. Paul: Univ. of Minnesota Immigration History Research Center, 1993.

Paterno, George. *Joe Paterno: The Coach from Byzantium*. N.p.: Sports Publishing, 2001.

Paxson, Frederic L. "The Rise of Sport." *Mississippi Valley Historical Review* 4 (1917): 143–68.

Pennell, Elizabeth Robbins. "Sports at the Home of the Carnival." *Outing*, Mar. 1887.

Pep, Willie, with Robert Sacchi. *Willie Pep Remembers . . . Friday's Heroes*. New York: Friday's Heroes, 1973.

Perrino, Marai, ed. *Italian American Autobiographies*. St. Paul: Univ. of Minnesota Immigration History Research Center, 1993.

"Personality." *Time*, Sept. 22, 1952, 50.

Persons, Stow. *Ethnic Studies at Chicago, 1905–1945*. Urbana: Univ. of Illinois Press, 1987.

Pesavento, Wilma J. "Sport and Recreation in the Pullman Experiment, 1880–1900." *Journal of Sport History* 9, no. 12 (1982): 38–62.

Pfister, Gertrud. "Lieux de Memoire: Sites of Memories and the Olympic Games." *Sport in Society* 14, no. 4 (2011): 412–29.

———. "Research on Traditional Games: The Scientific Perspective." *Journal of Comparative Physical Education and Sport* 19, no. 2 (1997): 53–65.

Pfister, Gertrud, and Liu Yueye, eds. *Sports—the East and the West*. St. Augustin, Germany: Academia Verlag, 1999.

Phillips, Murray G., Mark E. O'Neill, and Gary Osmond. "Broadening Horizons in Sport History: Films, Photographs, and Monuments." *Journal of Sport History* 34, no. 2 (2007): 271–93.

Philpott, Thomas Lee. *The Slum and the Ghetto: Neighborhood Deterioration and Middle-Class Reform, Chicago, 1880–1930*. New York: Oxford Univ. Press, 1978.

Piess, Kathy. *Cheap Amusements: Working Women and Leisure in Turn-of-the-Century New York*. Philadelphia: Temple Univ. Press, 1986.

Pipkin, James W. *Sporting Lives: Metaphor and Myth in American Sports Autobiographies*. Columbia: Univ. of Missouri Press, 2008.

Plaschke, Bill, with Tommy Lasorda. *I Live for This! Baseball's Last True Believer*. New York: Houghton Mifflin, 2007.

Polsky, Ned. *Hustlers, Beats, and Others*. Chicago: Aldine, 1967.

Powers, Madelon. *Faces along the Bar: Lore and Order in the Workingman's Saloon, 1870–1920*. Chicago: Univ. of Chicago Press, 1998.

Preston, William. *Aliens and Dissenters: Federal Suppression of Radicals, 1903–1933*. New York: Harper & Row, 1963.

Proser, Jim, with Jerry Cutter. *I'm Staying with My Boys: The Heroic Life of Sgt. John Basilone, USMC*. New York: St. Martin's Griffin, 2010.

Putney, Clifford. *Muscular Christianity: Manhood and Sports in Protestant America, 1880–1920*. Cambridge, MA: Harvard Univ. Press, 2001.

Rader, Benjamin G. *American Sports: From the Age of Folk Games to the Age of Spectators*. Englewood Cliffs, NJ: Prentice Hall, 1983.

———. "The Quest for Subcommunities and the Rise of American Sport." *American Quarterly* 29 (1977): 355–69.

Rasenberger, Jim. *America, 1908*. New York: Scribner, 2007.

Rees, Richard W. *Shades of Difference: A History of Ethnicity in America*. Lanham, MD: Rowman & Littlefield, 2007.

Reese, William J. *Power and the Promise of School Reform: Grassroots Movements during the Progressive Era*. Boston: Routledge and Kegan Paul, 1986.

Regalado, Samuel O. *Viva Baseball: Latin Major Leaguers and Their Special Hunger.* Urbana: Univ. of Illinois Press, 1998.

Renoff, Richard, and Joseph A. Vacarelli. "Italian Americans and Baseball." *Nassau Review* 6, no. 1 (1990).

Richards, David A. J. *Italian American: The Racializing of an Ethnic Identity.* New York: New York Univ. Press, 1999.

Riess, Steven. *City Games: The Evolution of American Urban Society and the Rise of Sports.* Urbana: Univ. of Illinois Press, 1989.

———. "A Fighting Chance: The Jewish-American Boxing Experience, 1890–1940." *American Jewish History* 74, no. 3 (1985): 223–54.

———. *Sport in Industrial America, 1850–1920.* Wheeling, IL: Harlan Davidson, 1995.

Riggs, Don W. *History of St. Donatus Parish.* N.p., 1981.

Riis, Jacob A. *The Children of the Poor.* 1892. Reprint, New York: Arno Press, 1971.

Riordan, James, and Arnd Kruger, eds. *European Cultures in Sport: Examining the Nations and Regions.* Bristol, UK: Intellect Books, 2003.

Roediger, David R. *The Wages of Whiteness: Race and the Making of the American Working Class.* 1991. Reprint, London: Verso, 1999.

———. *Working toward Whiteness: How America's Immigrants Became White; The Strange Journey from Ellis Island to the Suburbs.* New York: Basic Books, 2005.

Rolle, Andrew F. *The Italian Americans: Troubled Roots.* Norman: Univ. of Oklahoma Press, 1980.

Rosenzweig, Roy. *Eight Hours for What We Will: Workers and Leisure in an Industrial City, 1870–1920.* New York: Cambridge Univ. Press, 1983.

Ross, Edward Alsworth. *The Old World in the New: The Significance of Past and Present Immigration to the American People.* New York: Century, 1914.

Rotundo, E. Anthony. *American Manhood: Masculinity from the Revolution to the Modern Era.* New York: Basic Books, 1993.

Ruck, Rob, Maggie Jones Patterson, and Michael P. Weber. *Rooney: A Sporting Life.* Lincoln: Univ. of Nebraska Press, 2010.

Runstedtler, Theresa E. "In Sport the Best Man Wins: How Joe Louis Whupped Jim Crow." In *In the Game: Race, Identity, and Sports in the Twentieth Century,* edited by Amy Bass, 47–91. New York: Palgrave Macmillan, 2005.

Rutkoff, Peter M., ed. *The Cooperstown Symposium on Baseball and American Culture, 1999.* Jefferson, NC: McFarland, 2000.

Sammons, Jeffrey T. *Beyond the Ring: The Role of Boxing in American Society.* Urbana: Univ. of Illinois Press, 1988.

Schneider, Jane, ed. *Italy's "Southern Question": Orientalism in One Country.* New York: Oxford Univ. Press, 1998.

Schoor, Gene. *Roy Campanella: Man of Courage.* New York: G. P. Putnam's Sons, 1959.

Schuyler, George Samuel. *Ethiopian Stories.* Boston: Northeastern Univ. Press, 1994.

Sciorra, Joseph. "Points South and West II." Terre Promesse: Excursions towards Italian Topographies Conference, Calandria Institute, New York, Apr. 22–24, 2010.

Shanabruch, Charles. "The Catholic Church's Role in the Americanization of Chicago's Immigrants, 1833–1928." PhD diss., Univ. of Chicago, 1975.

Simons, William M. *The Cooperstown Symposium on Baseball and American Culture, 2000.* Jefferson, NC: McFarland, 2001.

Skehan, Everett M. *Rocky Marciano: Biography of a First Son.* Boston: Houghton Mifflin, 1977.

Smith, Larry. *Iwo Jima: World War II Veterans Remember the Greatest Battle of the Pacific.* New York: W. W. Norton, 2008.

Smith, Marshall. " . . . And New Champion?" *Life*, Sept. 22, 1952, 107–18.

Sperber, Murray. *Shake Down the Thunder: The Creation of Notre Dame Football.* New York: Henry Holt, 1993.

Steinberg, Stephen. *The Ethnic Myth: Race, Ethnicity, and Class in America.* Boston: Beacon Press, 1989.

Stodolska, Monika, and Konstantinos Alexandris. "The Role of Recreational Sport in the Adaptation of First Generation Immigrants in the United States." *Journal of Leisure Research* 36, no. 3 (2004): 379–413.

Sugden, John. *Boxing and Society: An International Analysis.* Manchester: Manchester Univ. Press, 1996.

Sullivan, Russell. *Rocky Marciano: The Rock of His Times.* Urbana: Univ. of Illinois Press, 2002.

Summers, Anthony, and Robbyn Swan. *Sinatra: The Life.* New York: Alfred A. Knopf, 2005.

Suttles, Gerald D. *The Social Order of the Slum: Ethnicity and Territory in the Inner City.* Chicago: Univ. of Chicago Press, 1968.

Sweeney, Arthur, MD. "Mental Tests for Immigrants." *North American Review* 115 (1922): 600–612.

Swiderski, Richard M. *Voices: An Anthropologist's Dialogue with an Italian-American Festival.* Bowling Green, OH: Bowling Green Univ. Popular Press, 1987.

Swift, E. M. "Boom Boom Time Again." *Sports Illustrated*, July 13, 1981, 45–52.

Talese, Gay. *Unto the Sons.* New York: Alfred A. Knopf, 1992.

Taylor, Graham. *Chicago Commons through Forty Years.* Chicago: John F. Cuneo, 1936.

Terkel, Studs. *Working.* New York: Pantheon Books, 1972.

Thernstrom, Stephan. *The Other Bostonians: Poverty and Progress in the American Metropolis.* Cambridge, MA: Harvard Univ. Press, 1973.

Thrasher, Frederic M. *The Gang: A Study of 1,313 Gangs in Chicago.* 1927. Reprint, Chicago: Univ. of Chicago Press, 1963.

Todd, Arthur J. *Chicago Recreation Survey, 1937.* Chicago: Chicago Recreation Commission and Northwestern Univ., 1938.

Townsend, Kim. *Manhood at Harvard: William James and Others.* New York: W. W. Norton, 1996.

Treat, Roger L. *Bishop Sheil and the CYO.* New York: Julian Messner, 1951.

Tricarico, Donald. "Youth Culture, Ethnic Choice, and the Identity Politics of Guido." *Voices in Italian Americana* 18, no. 1 (2007): 34–86.

Trumpbour, Robert. "Civil Rights and Sports Landmarks: Jobs and Activism in the Construction of Pittsburgh's Three Rivers Stadium." *International Journal of the History of Sport* 25, no. 11 (2008): 1565–82.

Turner, Victor W. *The Ritual Process: Structure and Anti-Structure.* Chicago: Aldine, 1969.

Valerio, Anthony. *Bart: A Life of A. Bartlett Giamatti by Him and about Him.* New York: Harcourt, Brace, Jovanovich, 1991.

Van Rheenen, Derek. "The Promise of Soccer in America: The Open Play of Ethnic Subcultures." *Soccer & Society* 10, no. 6 (2009): 781–94.

Veblen, Thorstein. *Theory of the Leisure Class: An Economic Study of Institutions.* 1899. Reprint, New York: Penguin, 1994.

Vecchio, Diane C. *Merchants, Midwives, and Laboring Women: Italian Migrants in Urban America.* Urbana: Univ. of Illinois Press, 2006.

Vecoli, Rudolph J. "Contadini in Chicago: A Critique of the Uprooted." *Journal of American History* 51, no. 3 (1964): 407–17.

———. "European Americans: From Immigrants to Ethnics." In *The Reinterpretation of American History and Culture*, edited by William H. Cartwright and Richard L. Watson Jr., 81–112. Washington, DC: National Council for the Social Studies.

———, ed. *Italian Immigrants in Rural and Small Town America*. New York: Italian Historical Association, 1987.

Vertinsky, Patricia. "'Weighs and Means': Examining the Surveillance of Fat Bodies through Physical Education Practices in North America in the Late Nineteenth and Early Twentieth Centuries." *Journal of Sport History* 35, no. 3 (2008): 449–68.

Vlasich, James A., ed. *Horsehide, Pigskin, Oval Tracks, and Apple Pie: Essays on Sport and American Culture*. Jefferson, NC: McFarland, 2006.

Wacquant, Loic. "The Social Logic of Boxing in Black America: Towards a Sociology of Pugilism." *Sociology of Sport Journal* 9 (1992): 221–54.

Waltzer, Jim. *The Battle of the Century: Dempsey, Carpentier, and the Birth of Modern Promotion*. Santa Barbara, CA: Praeger, 2011.

Walzer, Michael. "What Does It Mean to Be an American?" *Social Research* 57, no. 3 (1990): 591–614.

Warner, Lloyd, and Leo Srole. *Social Systems of American Ethnic Groups*. New Haven, CT: Yale Univ. Press, 1945.

Washington, Robert E., and David Karen. *Sport, Power, and Society: Institutions and Practices*. Boulder, CO: Westview Press, 2010.

Waters, Mary C. *Ethnic Options: Choosing Identities in America*. Berkeley: Univ. of California Press, 1990.

Watkins, Nancy. "Minds over Matter." *Chicago Tribune Magazine*, Nov. 30, 2008, 31.

Watkins, Susan Cotts, and Angela D. Danzi. "Women's Gossip and Social Change: Childbirth and Fertility Control among Italian and Jewish Women in the United States, 1920–1940." *Gender & Society* 9, no. 4 (1995): 469–90.

Watterson, John Sayle. *The Games Presidents Play: Sports and the Presidency*. Baltimore: Johns Hopkins Univ. Press, 2006.

Webster, Yehudi O. *The Racialization of America*. New York: St. Martin's Press, 1992.

Weinberg, S. Kirson, and Henry Arond. "The Occupational Culture of the Boxer." *American Journal of Sociology* 57, no. 5 (1952): 460–69.

Weiss, Bernard J., ed. *American Education and the European Immigrant, 1840–1940*. Urbana: Univ. of Illinois Press, 1982.

Wenner, Lawrence A., and Steven J. Jackson, eds. *Sport, Beer, and Gender: Promotional Culture and Contemporary Social Life*. New York: Peter Lang, 2009.

White, G. Edward. *Creating the National Pastime: Baseball Transforms Itself, 1903–1953*. Princeton, NJ: Princeton Univ. Press, 1996.

Whyte, William Foote. *Street Corner Society: The Social Structure of an Italian Slum*. Chicago: Univ. of Chicago Press, 1943.

Wiggins, Robert Payton. *The Federal League of Baseball Clubs: The History of an Outlaw League, 1914–1915*. Jefferson, NC: McFarland, 2009.

Williams, Raymond. *The Sociology of Culture*. New York: Schocken Books, 1981.

Wills, Chuck. *Destination America: The People and Cultures That Created a Nation*. New York: DK, 2005.

Wirth, Louis. *The Ghetto*. 1956. Reprint, Chicago: Univ. of Chicago Press, 1928.

Woodward, C. Vann. *The Comparative Approach to American History*. New York: Basic Books, 1968.

Woodward, Kath. *Boxing, Masculinity, and Identity*. London: Routledge, 2007.

Woolston, Howard B. "Rating the Nations: A Study in the Statistics of Opinion." *American Journal of Sociology* 22, no. 3 (1916): 381–90.

Worrall, Janet E., Carol Bonomo Albright, and Elvira G. Di Fabio, eds. *Italian Immigrants Go West: The Impact of Locale on Ethnicity*. Cambridge, MA: Italian American Historical Association, 2003.

Wright, Carroll D. *Ninth Special Report of the Commissioner of Labor: The Italians in Chicago, a Social and Economic Study*. Washington, DC: Government Printing Office, 1897.

Yans-McLaughlin, Virginia. "Patterns of Work and Family Organization: Buffalo's Italians." *Journal of Interdisciplinary History* 2, no. 2 (1971): 299–314.

Yoseloff, Anthony A. "From Ethnic Hero to National Icon: The Americanization of Joe DiMaggio." *International Journal of the History of Sport* 16, no. 3 (1999): 1–20.

Youmans, Gary B. *The Onion Picker: Carmen Basilio and Boxing in the 1950s*. Syracuse, NY: Campbell Road Press, 2007.

Young, Dick. *Roy Campanella*. New York: Grosset & Dunlap, 1952.

Zaloha, Anna. "A Study of the Persistence of Italian Customs among 143 Families of Italian Descent Members of Social Clubs at Chicago Commons." Master's thesis, Northwestern Univ., 1937.

Zeitz, Joshua. *Flapper: A Madcap Story of Sex, Style, Celebrity, and the Women Who Made America Modern*. New York: Crown, 2006.

Zorbaugh, Harvey. *The Gold Coast and the Slum*. Chicago: Univ. of Chicago Press, 1929.

Zummo, Bruce P. *Little Sicily: Reminiscences and Reflections of Chicago's Near North Side*. Chicago: Near North, 2001.

Index

Abbaticchio, Ed, 46, 75
acculturation, xv, 12–13, 19, 34–35, 40–41, 101, 180
African Americans, 8, 13, 14, 24, 45, 52, 61–62, 64, 66–67, 74–75, 77, 82, 85, 88, 89, 99–100, 103, 107, 109, 117, 128, 132, 157, 159–66, 168, 169, 172–73, 176, 183–84, 190, 206–8, 210–11
Alito, Samuel, 195
All American Girls Professional Baseball League, 138
Ambers (D'Ambrosio), Lou, 33, 114
Americanization, xiii–xiv, 12–13, 19–21, 29, 34–35, 41–46, 83, 91, 102–217
amusement parks, 27–28
Angott (Engotti), Sammy, 33
Antonelli, Johnny, 169
Apostoli, Fred, 115
Arcaro, Eddie, 166
Arizona, 17, 24, 63, 193–94
Aspromonte, Ken, 161
assimilation, xiii–xvi, 3, 12, 29–30, 41–46, 54, 58, 71, 74, 82, 97–101, 103, 105–7, 118–20, 162, 178, 180–217
Atlas, Charles (Angelo Siciliano), 93–95, 162
Auriemma, Geno, 195

auto racing, 56, 92
Avalon (Avallone), Frankie, 172

Balbo, Italo, 91
Bambace sisters, 25
Bando, Sal, 185
Barbuti, Ray, 121
Barsotti, Carlo, 36
baseball, 1–3, 6, 19, 26, 27, 42–43, 46–49, 51, 55–56, 77, 79, 80–83, 87, 92, 100, 102, 107, 108, 123, 125, 126–39, 140, 145–46, 149–52, 157, 160, 167, 168–71, 178, 184, 185, 192–94, 199, 201, 202–4, 216; in Italy, 49, 169, 202–3, 238
Basilio, Carmen, 90, 152, 156, 165, 184, 190
Basilone, John, 146
basketball, 20, 26, 77, 79, 85–86, 100, 107, 160, 193–95, 199
Bateson, Gregory, 104
Battaglia, Murray, 84
Battalino (Battaglia), Christopher "Battling," 79–80, 111, 112, 152
Bavasi, Buzzy, 169
Bellino, Joe, 166
Bennett (Benedetto), Tony, 78, 171
Berardino, Johnny, 167

Berra, Lawrence "Yogi," 80, 143, 145, 150–51, 161, 169, 170, 198
Bertelli, Angelo, 145–46, 166
Billi, John, 85
billiards, 15, 26, 73, 87, 107, 122–26
Biondi, Matt, 201
birds of passage, 11, 39, 70–71, 180, 189
Black Hand, 61, 72, 143
Boas, Franz, 96
bocce, 6–7, 27, 49, 107, 125, 127, 151, 196–97, 201–2
Bodie, Ping (Francesco Pizzolo), 47–49, 75
body culture, 93–96, 108, 187, 190
Bogardus, Emory, 53
Boitano, Brian, 201
Bonura, Henry "Zeke," 130–31
Boston, 14, 15, 16–17, 20, 42, 46, 54, 68, 69, 80, 97, 112, 159, 169–70, 174, 180, 195, 197
Bourdieu, Pierre, xiii, 13, 23, 59, 79, 116, 152, 175, 187
bowling, 6, 22, 26, 27, 103, 124–26, 199
boxing, 6, 19, 22–23, 32–34, 47, 56–57, 67, 73, 77, 79–80, 86, 87, 89–92, 95, 100, 102, 109–16, 123, 125, 131, 140, 148, 152–67, 178, 183–84, 186, 189–90, 192, 198, 215
Branca, Ralph, 169
Brida, Clementine. *See* Maud Nelson
Brignoli(a), Lawrence, 55–56, 75
British (English), 2, 7, 35, 37, 88, 100–101, 119, 205
Brooklyn, 2, 41, 76, 98, 99, 111, 125, 128, 134, 138, 139, 155, 158, 169, 171, 180, 189, 191, 206

Bruno, Mario, 87, 118–19, 127, 129
Bushwicks, 127

Cabrini, Mother Frances, 16
California, xv, 10, 17–18, 24, 62, 98, 107, 111–12, 113, 136, 138, 144, 172, 180, 202, 208
Calipari, John, 195
Camilli, Dolph, 129, 134
Caminiti, Ken, 203
Canzoneri, Tony, 110–11, 114–15
Cappelletti, John, 185, 191
Capone, Al, 32, 73, 214
Caponi, Donna, 199
Carideo, Frank, 85, 117, 247
Carlesimo, P. J., 195
Carnera, Primo, 90–92, 99, 146
Carnesecca, Lou, 195
Caruccio, Consetta "Connie," 95, 122
Caruso, Enrico, 28–29, 80
Catholic Youth Organization, 79, 113–14, 118, 122, 254
Cavaretta, Phil, 129–31
Chicago, xv, 13, 14, 15, 19, 20, 26, 34, 36–37, 38, 39, 42, 45, 47–48, 56, 61, 69, 72, 74, 75, 76–77, 79, 80, 82, 83–84, 86–87, 91, 93, 97, 99, 100, 106, 112–13, 115, 118, 120, 124, 126–31, 142–43, 147, 149, 150, 165–67, 170, 176, 194, 197, 201–2, 204, 207, 213, 214, 216
Chicago School of Sociology, 13, 20, 58, 61, 73, 87, 96, 102
citizenship, 20, 16, 103, 135–37, 142, 144, 148, 163, 173, 211–12
class consciousness, 70–72, 128, 152, 212

clubs, 18–19, 27, 32, 38, 39, 46, 55, 74, 77, 83–84, 86–87, 95, 107, 112, 118, 120, 174, 176, 187, 196, 201, 213
Colangelo, Jerry, 193–94
Colavito, Rocky, 169–70
Columbus, Christopher, xi, 39–41, 105, 194, 203, 211, 214
Como, Perry, 78, 171
Corso, Lee, 191
Costello, Harry, 51–52
Costello (Cristillo), Lou, 77–78
Covello, Leonard, 105–6
crime (criminals), 32–33, 57, 60–61, 69, 72–73, 102, 113, 140, 143, 148, 153, 163, 166, 167, 177, 182, 186, 191, 195, 206, 209, 212–13, 267
Crosetti, Frank, 82, 129
Cuccinello, Al, 127–28
Cuomo, Andrew, 181, 195
Cuomo, Mario, 181, 195
cycling, 6, 29, 38, 92, 199
Czechs (Bohemians), 14, 64, 78
Czyz, Bobby, 189, 190

D'Amato, Alfonse, 182
D'Amato, Cus, 190
Damone, Vic (Vito Farinola), 171–72
Danza (Iadanza), Tony, 186
Da Prato, Jerry (Nero), 51–52
De Amicis, Edmondo, 20
De Bartolo family, 191, 193
De Bernardi, Forrest "Red," 26
Dellucci, David, 204
De Niro, Robert, 186
De Palma, Ralph, 56, 75
De Pietro, Joe, 95

De Rosa, Mark, 204
de Varona, Donna, 201
Di Benedetto, Frank, 106, 119
Dickerson, Lewis Pessano "Buttercup," 2, 226
Di Liberto, Frank, 45
DiMaggio, Dominic, 131, 137, 161, 209–10
DiMaggio, Joe, 82–83, 131–39, 144, 150, 152, 162, 167, 168, 169–70, 171, 178, 180, 204, 212, 215–16
DiMaggio, Vince, 131, 204
Di Melio, Albert "Luby," 116–17
Dinon, Al, 216–17
Donatelli, Augie, 146
Donatucci, Martin "Hooks," 86
Donelli, Aldo "Buff," 121
Du Bois, W. E. B., 75, 103
Dundee, Angelo, 159, 190
Dundee, Johnny (Giuseppe Carrora), 22, 111
Durante, Jimmy, 76
Duva, Lou, 159, 190

education, xiii, 6, 8, 12, 13, 20–21, 23, 40, 41–45, 50, 52–53, 65, 76, 79–80, 81, 103, 106, 107, 108, 126, 146, 151–52, 154–56, 166, 168, 173, 174, 176–78, 180–81, 184, 186–87, 192, 193, 197, 206, 210, 216
Eruzione, Mike, 179–80, 201
ethnicity, xvi, 6, 17, 27, 28–32, 34, 38, 45, 67–101, 107, 115–16, 120, 142–43, 159, 168–71, 173–75, 179–217
eugenics, 66, 75

Fabian (Forte), 172
Falcaro, Joe, 125
Farfariello, "Little Butterfly." *See* Eduardo Migliaccio
Fasano, Sal, 204
Fazio, Buzz, 125
fencing, 5, 6, 27, 92
Fermi, Enrico, xii, 149
Ferraro, Geraldine, 195, 200
Firpo, Angel Luis, 89–90, 102, 161
Flynn, Fireman Jim (Andrew Chiariglione), 33, 109
folk games, 5
food, 8, 9, 14, 50, 105–7, 142, 151, 153, 159, 162, 164, 170, 174–75, 182, 192, 194, 195, 196, 202, 204–5, 207, 213, 214
football, 5, 6, 19, 20, 46, 51–52, 79, 83–84, 87, 88, 107, 108–9, 116, 121, 127, 149, 150, 160, 162, 167, 178, 185, 190–91, 216
Francis (Franconero), Connie, 172, 187
Francona, Terry, 192, 205
Francona, Tito, 51, 205
Fratello, Mike, 195
fraternal organizations, 18–19, 39, 41, 62, 64–65, 78–79, 86, 96–97, 112–23, 130, 133, 143, 197, 214
Fratianne, Linda, 199
Fregosi, Jim, 170–71
Funicello, Annette, 172
Furillo, Carl, 169

Galento, Tony, 95–96, 160
Gallico, Paul, 84, 90, 113
gambling, 23, 27, 28, 32, 73, 87–88, 110, 126, 128, 164, 166
Gandolfini, James, 186
gangs (gangsters), 20, 32–33, 72–74, 75, 79, 86, 87, 90–91, 100, 107, 112, 113, 120, 125–26, 130, 136, 143, 148, 153–54, 163, 165, 175–76, 183, 185–86, 209
Garagiola, Joe, 145, 151–52, 176
Garatti-Saville, Eleanor, 122
Garibaldi, Giuseppe, 3, 40–41
Garoni, Willie, 46
Gasperano, Mary, 25
Genaro (Di Genaro), Frankie, 111–12
gender, 8, 9, 14, 20, 25, 28–29, 43, 80–81, 95, 138–39, 150, 154, 162, 185, 198–200, 211
Germany (Germans), 7, 11, 13, 16, 50, 64, 66, 67, 73, 78, 82, 87, 92, 93, 94, 98, 103, 120, 135, 144, 146, 149, 150
Ghezzi, Vic, 88
Giamatti, Bart, 180, 196
Giambi, Jason, 204
Giardello, Joey (Carmine Tilelli), 158–59, 190
Gionfriddo, Al, 129
Gisello, Margaret, 81, 95, 199
Giuliani, Rudy, 181–82, 195
Golden Gloves, 113, 115, 145, 158, 186
golf, 88, 109, 121, 146, 161, 199, 209
Golzio, Carrie, 25
Gramsci, Antonio, xiv, 58, 107, 174
Grant, Madison, 65–66, 75
Grasso, Ella, 200
Graziano, Rocky (Thomas Rocco Barbella), 78, 105, 151, 154–55, 158, 165
guido culture, 186–87, 210–11, 213–14, 217
gymnastics, 6, 20, 36, 42, 92, 103, 122, 199

habitus, xiii, 31–32, 47, 59, 82, 104, 110, 119, 129, 140, 142, 152, 160, 175, 178, 192, 212–13
Hall, G. Stanley, 31
Harris, Franco, 207–8
hegemony theory, xiv, 28, 43, 101, 107, 226
Hemingway, Ernest, 134–35
Herman (Gulotta), Pete, 32, 33, 51, 110–11
Hispanics, 24, 44, 49, 67, 89, 107, 120, 157, 160, 163–65, 172, 175–76, 177, 206, 210
horse racing, 5–6, 55–56, 87–88, 166

Iacocca, Lee, 180, 195
ice hockey, 180–81, 193–94, 199–200, 202
identity, xv, 3, 19, 21, 22–54, 96, 100–217; American, xv, 3, 11, 19, 31–32, 96, 113, 121, 127, 139, 162, 182–217; Italian, xv, 12–14, 19, 21, 22–54, 79, 91, 110, 122, 135, 162–63, 184, 188, 189–90, 195, 216–17; Italian-American, xv, 19, 29, 34–35, 76–78, 102–200
ideology, 31, 33–34, 40–43, 162, 168, 175, 200, 211
Ignizio, Mildred Martorella, 199
immigration, xi–xiii, 9–15, 53–54, 72, 108–9, 142, 228; quotas, 13, 53–54, 75–76, 91, 139, 166, 265
Iori, Agnes, 26–27
Irish, 11, 13, 14, 16, 19, 24, 32, 33–34, 37, 45, 59–60, 67, 72, 73, 74, 79, 82, 87, 89, 100–101, 115, 116, 117, 120, 161, 162, 182–83, 199, 205

Italian newspapers, 35, 36, 38–41, 51, 81–85, 92, 99, 115, 121, 143, 150, 235, 250
Italy, xii–xiii, xv–xvi, 3–12, 21, 31, 40, 43, 44, 46–47, 49, 71, 81, 90–93, 97, 99–104, 108, 125, 137, 141–42, 182, 202, 207; culture, xiii–xvi, 4–10, 18, 31, 37, 44, 47, 72–73, 80, 97, 102–4, 106, 108, 124, 131, 137–38, 151, 158, 162, 174–75, 177–78, 180–81, 191, 194, 202, 207; education, xiii, 6, 8, 12–13, 43, 79, 97, 106; geography, xiii, xvi, 4, 7; history, xii, xv, 3–12, 21, 40, 90–92, 97, 99–100; regional groups, xii–xiii, xv–xvi, 4, 14, 23, 209; sports, xiv, 1–2, 4–7, 11, 22, 34, 46, 49, 78, 81, 90, 92, 120, 125, 239

jazz, 29, 76, 107
Jews, 11, 19, 32, 34, 45, 50, 57, 72, 75, 79, 87, 89, 97, 98, 100–101, 105, 116, 117, 120, 149, 162, 176–77

Kelly, Hugo (Ugo Micheli), 22, 32–33
Kelly, Paul (Paolo Vaccarelli), 32–33
Ku Klux Klan, 16, 74, 82, 117

LaBarba, Fidel, 112
labor, 7–8, 15, 17–18, 23–26, 33, 41, 43, 61–63, 68–71, 107, 128, 171, 174, 176, 232; child, 24, 25, 41–44, 60, 88; in Italy, 7–8; padrones, 10, 15, 23–24, 60;

labor (*cont.*)
   strikes, 10, 25, 27, 64, 68, 69, 105; in United States, 14–15, 17–18, 23–24, 61–63, 68–71, 107, 128, 174, 176, 232; wages, 8, 24, 43, 44, 62, 64, 83, 151–52, 157, 158, 237, 242
Lady Gaga (Stefani Germanotta), xii, 187–88, 215
La Guardia, Fiorello, xii, 105, 135, 146
Lambroso, Cesare, 57
La Motta, Jake, 145, 151, 153–55, 165
language, 12, 14, 20, 22–23, 24, 29, 36, 39, 42, 47, 51–53, 58, 65, 76, 78, 79, 97, 101, 102, 104, 105–6, 131, 140–43, 147, 151, 174, 180–82, 196, 197, 203, 204, 214, 247
La Porte, Frank, 47
La Rocca, Nick, 77
La Russa, Tony, 192
Lasorda, Tommy, 134, 184, 192–93, 196
Lazzeri, Tony, 82, 129
Leon, Casper (Gaspare Leoni), 22, 32, 34, 235
Little, Lou (Luigi Piccolo), 84
Little Italy, 13–15, 20, 23, 33, 50, 61, 72–73, 86–87, 98, 99, 105, 113, 151, 176, 180–81, 202, 216
Lombardi, Ernie, 129–30
Lombardi, Vince, 118, 167–68, 178
Lodigiani, Dario, 127
Lopiano, Donna, ix–x, 139, 195–96
Loretta, Mark, 205
Louisiana, xv, 17, 24, 60–62, 74, 110, 180, 197
Lucchino, Larry, 194–95

Luciano (Lucania), Charles "Lucky," 32, 148
Luisetti, Angelo Enrico "Hank," 85–86
Lunardoni Cumiskey, Ada, 122
lynching, 60–61, 72, 74

Macfadden, Bernarr, 28, 92–93
Madonna (Louise Ciccone), xii, 187–88, 215
Mafia, 72, 78
Maglie, Sal, 169, 171
Malignaggi, Paul, 189
Malzone, Frank, 161, 169–70
Mancini, Ray "Boom Boom," 189
Mandell (Mandella), Sammy, 33, 111
Manfredo, Peter, 190
marathons, 35–38, 55
Marcantonio, Vito, 105
Marchegiano, Piero, 51
Marchese, Anthony, 70
Marciano, Rocky, 51, 141, 157–62, 164–65, 167, 178, 212
Marino, Dan, 191
Marino, Hank, 125
Martin, Dean (Dino Crocetti), 78, 184–85
masculinity, 30–32, 76, 91–92, 94, 95, 97, 115, 124, 125–26, 134, 150, 154, 162, 170, 186–89, 211–12
Massimino, Rollie, 195
Maxim, Joey (Giuseppe Berardinelli), 158
Melillo, Oscar, 129
memory, 3, 38–41, 141, 211, 214–15
Menchetti, Lew, 128
Merullo, Len, 127
Mezzogiorno, 7–11, 228

Migliaccio, Eduardo, Farfariello (Little Butterfly), 29
migration, 10–12, 21, 23
Mileti, Nick, 193
Minnelli, Liza, 78, 187
Mitchell, Elmer, 84–85
Monroe, Marilyn, 136–37
Montana, Joe, 191
Monterey, California, 18, 24, 98, 107, 182
Morabito, Tony, 191
Morra, 7
Mosconi, Willie, 123–24
movies, 29–30, 76, 182, 185–86, 209
music, 29–30, 35–37, 76, 103, 107, 142, 151, 171–73, 175, 176, 184, 187–88, 194, 199, 208–9, 213, 215
Musmano, Michael, 150
Mussolini, Benito, 53, 90–94, 99–100, 120, 135–36, 143–45

Naples, 5, 6, 34, 146
National Football League, 84, 121, 124, 167–68, 191
National League, 2, 81, 146
Nelson, Maud (Clementine Brida), 80–81, 195, 199
New Orleans, 17, 45, 60–61, 72, 76–77, 83–84, 110–11, 118, 130, 138, 150, 181–82, 197
newspapers, 1–2, 48, 60–61, 81, 113, 131
New York, xv, 1–2, 14–15, 19, 20, 22, 24–27, 32–38, 42, 46–48, 52, 60, 64, 67, 69, 73, 77, 82, 90–91, 97, 105, 110, 111, 113, 114–15, 118, 127, 135, 143, 146, 148, 151, 155, 163, 169, 172, 174, 176–77, 180, 181–83, 187–88, 197, 202, 203, 210, 214, 216, 230
Notre Dame, 85, 117–18, 145, 146, 166

Oliva brothers, 124
Oliva, Nick, 76–77
Olympics, 35, 38, 79, 92, 95, 100, 111–12, 113, 121–22, 130, 148, 179, 192, 194, 199–202, 205, 216, 250
Orsini, Cesare, 1, 194
Ottino, Mario (Max Ott), 49

Pacino, Al, 186
padrones. *See* labor
Palio, 5–6
Pallone, 1–2
Papal states, 4, 227
parks, 20–21, 31, 42, 45, 78, 108, 110, 119, 130, 181, 197, 199
Passatella, 6
Pastrano, Willie, 190
Paterno, Joe, 191–92
Paterson, New Jersey, 25, 38
Pavarotti, Luciano, 208
Pazienza, Vinnie, 189, 190
peasants, 6–10, 11, 31, 47, 50, 59, 66, 75, 78, 104
Pedroia, Dustin, 205
Pellegrino, Edmund, 176–77
Pelosi, Nancy, 180, 195, 200
Pep (Papaleo), Willie, 112, 157, 160–61
Pepitone, Joe, 185
Perini, Lou, 169
Petraglia, Johnny, 125

Petrillo, Jimmy, 77
Petrolle, Billy, 111
Philadelphia, 14, 15, 16, 18, 34, 48, 69, 91, 111, 123, 127, 173–74, 197, 216
physical education, 42, 92, 103, 108, 138
Piazza, Mike, 203
Piccolo, Brian, 185
Pietri, Dorando, 35–37
Pinelli, Babe (Rinaldo Paolinelli), 81–82
Pitino, Rick, 195
Pittsburgh, 28, 46, 86, 90, 107, 121, 128, 193, 207–8
playgrounds, 19–21, 31, 42, 45, 69, 78, 108, 110, 181, 197, 199
Poles (Polish), 13, 14, 16, 52, 67, 73, 77, 78, 87, 100, 107, 111, 164, 168, 189
politicians, 12, 20, 28, 32, 86, 87, 102, 105, 117, 118–19, 133, 147, 149, 168, 180–82, 195, 200, 265
Ponselle (Ponzillo), Rosa, 29
popular culture, xiii–xiv, 27–30, 54, 62, 76, 93, 107–8, 142, 171–73, 183, 199, 208–9
Prima, Louis, 29, 77
public monuments, 40, 211, 214–16
Pullman, George, 26

race (racialization), xvi, 6, 12–13, 21, 24, 27, 31, 34, 37, 41, 52, 55, 57–66, 68–76, 89–90, 94, 96–101, 102, 109, 143, 159–65, 167–68, 175, 183–84, 197, 206–8, 210–12, 235–36
Raschi, Vic, 150, 169
Red Scare, 70–72, 74

religion, 16–17, 45, 67, 74, 85, 86, 97–98, 104, 110, 113–14, 116–18, 120, 143, 146, 150, 159, 161, 164, 180, 182, 188, 191, 192, 196–97, 200, 209, 212, 214; Catholicism, 16–17, 45, 50, 67, 74, 85, 110, 113–14, 143, 146, 150, 159, 161, 164, 188, 191, 196, 209; festivals, 7, 16, 19, 98, 104, 175, 180, 182, 197, 214; folk, 16, 17, 98, 104; Protestantism, xvi, 12, 16, 17, 19, 23, 28, 67, 73, 74, 97, 191, 212
Remus (Giacomo Zaffarana), 28
Retton (Rotundo), Mary Lou, 199
Revolya, Johnny, 88
Righetti, Dave, 203
Riha, Ruth, 45
Risorgimento, 21
Rizzo, Frank, 206
Rizzuto, Phil, 150–51, 169, 170, 176
Robinson, Jackie, 160
Robinson, Sugar Ray, 165, 183–84
Romeo, Robin, 199
Romolo (Cosimo Molino), 28
Roosevelt, Theodore, 30–31
Ross, Edward Alsworth, 63–65
Rossi, Giuseppe, 205–6
rowing, 6, 54, 57
Rydell (Ridarelli), Bobby, 172

Sacco, Nicola, 71–72, 136, 150, 243
saloons (taverns), 15, 26, 76, 95, 103, 114, 123, 125
Salvino, Carmen, 125
Sandow, Eugen, 28, 93
San Francisco, 17–18, 27, 47, 85, 91, 115, 127, 129, 134, 136, 144, 161, 167, 168, 170, 193, 201, 203, 205, 215–16

Sansone, Tony, 94–95
Santo, Ron, 170, 185
Sarazen, Gene (Eugenio Saraceni), 88–89, 150
Savona sisters, 138, 195
Savoldi, Joe, 85, 117, 149, 247
Savoy, House of, 3–4
Scalabrini priests, 16
schools, 31, 40, 42–45, 52–53, 62–63, 76, 78, 80, 83–84, 106, 108–9, 115, 118, 121, 143–44, 146, 150, 152, 160, 176, 181, 188
scientists, 56–60, 63–66, 101
Sciorra, Joseph, ix, 98–99
Scioscia, Mike, 203
settlement houses, 19–20, 31, 42, 45, 113, 126, 197, 199
Sheil, Bishop Bernard J., 113
Siciliano, Angelo. *See* Charles Atlas
Sicily (Sicilians), xii, xv–xvi, 4, 7–8, 13, 14, 18, 21, 28, 32, 34, 40, 45, 49, 57, 61–64, 69–70, 80, 91, 95, 98, 100–101, 104–8, 131–37, 144–46, 148–49, 169, 182, 189, 193, 202, 204, 209, 210–11, 214
Siena, 5
Sinatra, Frank, xii, 67, 78, 134, 171, 178, 180, 183–85, 193, 207, 212, 216
soccer, 5, 6, 26, 49, 92, 120–22, 152, 180, 201, 205–6, 216
social class, xvi, 3–6, 19, 27, 32, 35, 39, 50, 68, 70, 75, 77, 83, 87–89, 95–96, 106, 110, 112–13, 115–16, 119, 122–26, 129, 142, 151–55, 160, 174–75, 181–84, 186–90, 197, 206, 211–13, 216
social Darwinism, 31, 34, 35–38, 57–66, 94

softball, 86, 87, 127, 138–39, 146, 196, 199
Stallone, Sylvester, 185–86
St. Angelo, George, 45
St. Ives, Henri, 37
St. Louis, 34, 36, 47, 82, 107, 120, 126, 129, 143, 145, 151, 174, 197–98, 201, 214
Strobino, Gaston, 37–38
Swedes, 13, 37, 38, 45
swimming, 6, 20, 122, 131, 201

Tagliabue, Paul, 191
Tamburello, 1–2
Tarantella, 7, 197
Tasinari, Alfredo, 16–17
tennis, 1, 5, 6, 26, 199
Terlazzo, Tony, 95, 122
Testaverde, Vinny, 191
theater, 5, 12, 27, 28–29, 48, 62, 77–78, 93, 165, 167, 184, 186
Tonelli, Mario "Motts," 146–47
Torre, Joe, 192
track and field, 6, 26, 35–38, 55, 57, 83, 94, 100, 108–9, 121, 127, 148, 199, 200
Travolta, John, 186
Turner, Victor, 58
Tusiani, Joseph, 217

Valenti, Anna, 25
Valentino, Rudolph (Rodolfo Guglielmi), 29–30, 143, 184, 234
Valli (Castelluccio), Frankie, 172
Valvano, Jim, 195
Vanzetti, Bartolomeo, 71–72, 136, 150, 243
Varipappa, Andy, 125

Vee (Velline), Booby, 172
Venice, 5, 15, 227
Victor Emmanuel II, King, 3–4, 40
Vinci, Chuck, 95

welfare capitalism, 25–26, 69, 199
weightlifting, 20, 28, 95, 122, 148, 250
whiteness, 45, 54–101, 136, 142, 146, 157, 160–62, 164, 175, 184, 206–7, 210–12
Wizard Arrows, 86–87, 118–19, 124, 213
Wolgast, Midget (Joseph Loscalzo), 33, 111
women (girls), 7–9, 14, 20, 24–26, 29, 43, 45, 68, 69, 75, 77, 80–81, 104–5, 107–8, 122, 125, 138–39, 142, 150, 168, 174, 175, 182–84, 187–88, 194–96, 198–99, 210–12
World War I, 32, 50–53, 62, 69, 70, 74, 84, 110, 162, 213
World War II, 73, 81, 86, 121, 136–37, 140, 142–49, 152, 154, 157, 158, 160, 163, 167, 173, 189, 191, 209–10, 212, 213
wrestling, 5, 6, 20, 27, 95–96, 186, 235–36

Yacilla, Rocco "Lewa," 127, 129
Young Corbett III (Raffaele Capabianca Giordano), 33, 111

Zamperini, Lou, 147–48
Zarenti, Nick, 87
Zito, Barry, 205